D1569886

Education and Psychology of the Gifted Series
JAMES H. BORLAND, EDITOR

The Nature and Nurture of Giftedness:
A New Framework for Understanding Gifted Education
DAVID YUN DAI

Nuturing Talent in High School:
Life in the Fast Lane
LAURENCE COLEMAN

Rethinking Gifted Education
JAMES H. BORLAND, Editor

Multicultural Gifted Education
DONNA Y. FORD and J. JOHN HARRIS III

Reversing Underachievement Among Gifted Black Students:
Promising Practices and Programs
DONNA Y. FORD

Out of Our Minds:
Anti-Intellectualism and Talent Development in American Schooling
CRAIG B. HOWLEY, AIMEE HOWLEY, and EDWINA D. PENDARVIS

The Hunter College Campus Schools for the Gifted:
The Challenge of Equity and Excellence
ELIZABETH STONE

Recommended Practices in Gifted Education:
A Critical Analysis
BRUCE M. SHORE, DEWEY G. CORNELL,
ANN W. ROBINSON, and VIRGIL S. WARD

Conducting Research and Evaluation in Gifted Education:
A Handbook of Methods and Applications
NINA K. BUCHANAN and JOHN F. FELDHUSEN, Editors

The Academic Acceleration of Gifted Children
W. THOMAS SOUTHERN and ERIC D. JONES, Editors

Reaching the Gifted Underachiever:
Program Strategy and Design
PATRICIA L. SUPPLEE

Planning and Implementing Programs for the Gifted
JAMES H. BORLAND

The Nature and Nurture of Giftedness

A NEW FRAMEWORK FOR UNDERSTANDING GIFTED EDUCATION

David Yun Dai

Teachers College, Columbia University
New York and London

Published by Teachers College Press, 1234 Amsterdam Avenue, New York, NY 10027

Library of Congress Cataloging-in-Publication Data

Dai, David Yun.
    The nature and nurture of giftedness : a new framework for understanding gifted education / David Yun Dai.
        p.   cm.
    Includes bibliographical references and index.
    ISBN 978-0-8077-5087-2 (cloth : alk. paper)
    1. Gifted children—Education.   2. Teachers of gifted children.   I. Title.

    LC3993.D35 2010
    371.95—dc22

                                                                2010011101

ISBN: 978-0-8077-5087-2

Printed on acid-free paper
Manufactured in the United States of America

17   16   15   14   13   12   11   10   8   7   6   5   4   3   2   1

To the memory of my mentor and friend:
John F. Feldhusen (1926–2009)

Contents

Acknowledgments

MANY OF MY COLLEAGUES took time to provide their personal perspectives on earlier versions of various parts of this book, despite their extremely busy schedules. Their thoughtful comments have helped me a great deal in making improvements on the ideas expressed in this book. They are Don Ambrose, Marc Cohen, Larry Coleman, K. Anders Ericsson, David Henry Feldman, François Gagné, Howard Gardner, Nancy Hertzog, David Lohman, David Lubinski, Dona Matthews, Nancy Robinson, Karen Rogers, Keith Sawyer, Bruce Shore, Dean Keith Simonton, Rena Subotnik, Joyce VanTassel-Baska, Frank Worrell, and Albert Ziegler. Larisa Shavinina provided helpful feedback on a chapter I wrote for the *International Handbook on Giftedness*, of which she was the editor; many ideas developed, expanded, and elaborated on in this book started from there. These distinguished colleagues deserve much credit for challenging me to deepen and refine my thinking, though errors made and opinions expressed in the book are mine. I would like to thank my mentor and collaborator Joseph Renzulli for his guidance and support in the past decade of my scholarly career. I would also like to thank Teachers College Press, particularly Jim Borland, for encouraging me to write this book for the Psychology and Education of the Gifted Series; Brian Ellerback, for sharing his perspective at various stages of this book project; Wendy Schwartz, for carefully going over an earlier draft of the book and providing valuable feedback; and Lyn Grossman, for shepherding the production process.

This book was made possible partly by a sabbatical leave granted by the State University of New York at Albany and a Fulbright research scholarship to China from the U.S. State Department during the 2008–2009 academic year. The research leave proved very helpful for my reflection and contemplation while sorting through some of the critical problems and challenges identified in this book. Thanks are also due to my research assistants, doctoral students, and friends Maynard Lassonde, Graham Potter, Alexander Wind, and Yehan Zhou, for their editorial assistance; to my mother-in-law, Wu Yuqin, and my sister Dai Chenyi for taking care of my children while I was away from home; and to my wife, Lily, and my children, Vivian and Victor, for putting up with my intellectual preoccupations and avocational interests.

Finally, I would like to dedicate this book to the memory of my mentor and friend, John F. Feldhusen. I was saddened by the passing of John in July in the midst of my writing this book. I missed an opportunity, with great regret, to visit with him in Florida last November because of my Fulbright obligation in China. I am indebted to him not only for the ideas I have developed over time and expressed in this book, but, more important, for his fair-mindedness, intellectual vision, and moral courage, which have guided and inspired me through these years of exploration and reflection on critical issues facing the field of gifted education. John always took pride in even the smallest achievement of his students, and it is my hope that this book will in a way continue his intellectual legacy.

Introduction

THIS BOOK IS A RESULT of many years of my reflection and research on the issues raised in an edited volume titled *Rethinking Gifted Education* (Borland, 2003). Conceptions of giftedness have undergone profound change, and many assumptions we have taken for granted for decades have been challenged, including the very notion of giftedness. These changes reflect new understandings of exceptional competence and development, and have implications for how we view phenomena we see as exceptional, or identify individuals we deem "gifted and talented," how we conduct research on them, and how we nurture and cultivate their emergent talents for optimal development of excellence.

What is this thing called giftedness? Many scholars, researchers, and educators have tried very hard to search for a satisfactory answer. Yet conceptions of the nature and development of giftedness vary widely; vigorous debates and disagreements are common among scholars in the field. Disagreements tend to revolve around the issue of the respective roles of natural endowment, environmental experiences, and personal commitment and efforts, arguably the most important ingredients of excellence, academic or otherwise. The search for the road map for excellence is reminiscent of the search for the secret ingredients of becoming an undefeatable kung fu master in the animated movie *Kung Fu Panda*. Some people argue that ultimately it is the work of "nature"—what the person brings to this world, that is, the biological being. For instance, Einstein's brain was scrutinized in every detail (Diamond, Scheibel, Murphy, & Harvey, 1985) in the hope that we would once and for all locate the secret of genius in the brain structure. On the other extreme are people who are deeply convinced that superior accomplishments are mainly a result of experiences and dedicated efforts. Indeed, this is like what is conveyed in *Kung Fu Panda*: the secret ingredient for success turned out to be the audacity of self-beliefs, which is shown in the movie to have transformational power. But how can one be so sure that anyone can be a kung fu master, whether it be a panda, tiger, or crane? Does he or she really have the same potential? How much faith can we place on the notion of mental causation that beliefs and efforts can create miracles? To what extent is cognitive and intellectual functioning subject to conscious awareness and control? Are cognitive functions fundamentally constrained by our biological differences, or transcended by cultural tools and mediated by social and technical support, including formal education and training? The more we seek answers to these questions, the more puzzled we seem to become. In short, we don't have crystal-clear answers to these questions. Efforts to find the Holy Grail of giftedness and build a consensus definition and theory of giftedness have by and large failed and generated much frustration. No wonder that some leading scholars asked, Can we see any light at the end of the tunnel (see Gagné, 1999a)? The field of gifted education started with Lewis Terman's (1925) seminal study of children with high IQ, and high IQ has been a gold standard for identifying the intellectually gifted for the last century. We now seem to stand at another critical juncture in history. Feldman (2003) has this to say about the state of the field:

> It is therefore unlikely that a determined adherence to traditional notions of giftedness as *g* or IQ will be sufficient to sustain the vitality of the field through the 21st century. A more productive strategy might be to integrate the field's traditional commitment to IQ into a framework that is able to organize future efforts. In this respect, we may view the previous 20 years or so of activity in the field of gifted education as a thesis-antithesis period.... The obvious next step is to try to envision what a synthesis of different perspectives might look like. (P. 15)

This book is an effort in the direction Feldman pointed to. In search for a solution to differences among scholars and researchers, I found that all scholars, researchers, and educators have their own ontological biases or commitments regarding the nature of what we hail as gifted and talented and what it takes to achieve excellence in various domains of cultural importance. I attempt to understand their underlying reasoning, and the evidence they have garnered to support their convictions, including how their preferred methodology biases their perspectives in a fundamental way. In my efforts to portray the current state of affairs in this book, I was influenced by Gerald Holton (1981), a historian of science, who argued that "major scientific advance can be understood in terms of an evolutionary process that involves battles over only a few but by no means all of the recurrent themata" (p. 25). Accordingly, this book is organized around three main categories of such themata, or "essential tensions," a term used by Thomas Kuhn (1977) to describe the conflicts that eventually led to the advance of scientific theories and research in history. They are *ontological* issues (what is the nature of manifest gifted behaviors or competencies?), *epistemic* issues (how do we make appropriate assessment, inferences, theoretical analysis, and predictions?), and *normative* issues (what is gifted education for, and what is a desirable state for that matter?). Within each category, I identify three specific, interrelated tensions. The resulting nine tensions form the structure of the main body of this book.

AN OVERVIEW OF THE CONTENT OF THIS BOOK

In Chapter 1, I delineate a brief history of how these tensions evolved in the history of the gifted-education movement in the United States. In the main, my argument is that history has taken a spiral route to understanding the nature-nurture of exceptional competence, from early conceptions of general intelligence as a basis for identification of the "gifted" to the later recognition of a multitude of manifestations of talents, from an emphasis on natural endowment to a focus on the role of nurture, and methodologically from an objectivist stance that takes "gifted child" as a "natural" category of children to the recognition of subjectivity and value judgment involved constructing such a category; now the historical pendulum is swinging back to reconcile their differences. Although the historical unfolding of a social and practical movement such as gifted education is by nature complex and multifaceted, I attempt to show that tensions built up in the field are truly "essential" to gifted education, with ontological and epistemic issues intertwined with ethical and pragmatic concerns.

Beyond the historical narrative constructed in Chapter 1, in Chapter 2, I further attempt to show that the changes in the way we think about giftedness and gifted education is not merely driven by ethical and pragmatic concerns, but reflects changes in its conceptual foundations, particularly changes in how we understand such key foundational concepts as intelligence, development, motivation, context, and how advances in cognitive, affective and developmental neurosciences reinforce these changes. In essence, the current thinking and research point to the incremental (rather than fixed), dynamic, contextual, and multifaceted nature of human potential. To compare and reconcile the traditional and emergent conceptions and approaches, I propose a conceptual, analytic framework wherein I distinguish between ontological and epistemological issues. Ontological issues are about things or objective existence "out there," concerning substantive conjectures, theories, concepts, and aspects of the reality that these conjectures, theories, and concepts are intended to capture, whereas epistemological issues are more reflective, concerning how the researchers, scholars, and educators theoretically and methodologically position themselves, which potentially biases their observations, interpretations, and explanations. The third dimension I identify in the framework is a normative one. The term *normative* here is not used in a descriptive sense, as in such a phrase as *normative development*, but in a prescriptive sense, indicating "what ought to be," instead of "what is," arguably a major difference between social and natural sciences (Simon, 1996). Education is first and foremost normative (ends of education), followed by concerns over effectiveness vis-à-vis desired outcomes (means to achieve ends). Even psychology cannot be completely neutral, free from a normative stance. Developmental psychology, for instance, often takes upon itself to understand and foster optimal human development from the conception of life onward. Thus, the tensions in envisioning and designing gifted education are not only coming from competing evidence regarding differential child development, but also arising from many possibilities of development and what directions are seen as most desirable. In real life, these three dimensions are so intertwined that even a scholarly debate about "facts" can easily turn into a heated ideological battle over "values." Therefore, untangling these dimensions becomes all the more important if we are to reach some level of consensus on a particular issue.

Chapters 3 to 5 deal with three ontological tensions, respectively: nature versus nurture, domain-general versus domain-specific, qualitative versus quantitative differences. The nature-nurture issue has been heatedly debated in recent years (see Dai & Coleman, 2005; Ericsson, Nandagopal, & Roring, 2005, 2007a; Gagné, 2009b; Howe, Davidson, & Sloboda, 1998). The very existence of gifted children by virtue of superior natural endowment has been challenged by those who argue for the fundamental malleability of human potential. One of the purposes of my review in Chapter 3 is to lay out a framework of what constitutes strong and weak supporting evidence for either the nature or the nurture argument. Rather than drawing definitive conclusions about whether nature or nurture prevails, I argue that the dichotomous thinking is problematic in light of how nature and nurture interact in the developmental processes. Instead, I suggest multiple pathways to excellence and equifinality of human potential (different patterns of nature-nurture interaction might lead to similar developmental outcomes). Because of the multitude and diversity of the phenomena of exceptional competence, I argue that midrange theories of a limited scope of generality are more appropriate than all-purpose grand theories of giftedness. For that matter, the lack of intermediate models of how nature and nurture interact given a specific line of talent development hampers progress in the field, theoretically as well as practically.

Chapter 4 can be seen as pivotal for integrating ontological issues and providing a broad framework for a developmental view of giftedness. Although it focuses on the tension of the domain specificity and domain generality of gifted and talented expressions, the purpose of this chapter is to map out parameters of person, domain, and development in a way that could not only help resolve the domain-specificity-generality issue, but also further elucidate the nature-nurture interaction and provide clues about how quantitative differences might give rise to qualitative changes. In this chapter, I distinguish between a structural view of domain specificity generality, focusing on the basic structure of human abilities, and an ecological-functional view, which treats domain-specificity as a set of unique affordances, constraints, and demands imposed by a particular domain of human activity. The trends in recent decades can be characterized as a domain-specific turn, particularly moving away from the notion of general intelligence as an all-powerful influence on performance, though evidence suggests that some abilities are associated with high performance on a wide range of tasks, thus implicating their more pervasive power than that of others. I suggest that an ecological-functional approach, informed by the structural view of human abilities, holds higher promise in helping us resolve the tension between those who emphasize the primacy of "general intelligence" and high IQ as a foundation of intellectual giftedness, and those who stress the pluralistic nature of talents in academic, artistic, and other areas of human endeavor. I further introduce the concept of "developmental complexity" to highlight the fact that functional units operating on tasks have different levels of developmental complexity (in terms of differentiation and integration), depending on the extent of instruction, training, practice, and enculturation as well as adaptive self-organization over time. Talent development can generally be seen as a process of continual differentiation and integration in adapting to domain challenges, resulting in a set of specialized knowledge, skills, and dispositions. I further discuss the development of creativity in terms of person, domain, and development.

Chapter 5 explores an issue that to a great extent determines whether gifted education should be in the form of separate programs, specially tailored to a homogeneous group of children with unique educational needs: Are the differences between the gifted and "nongifted" a matter of degree or kind? I discuss various ways we conceptualize quantitative and qualitative differences, particularly with respect to the cognitive efficiency hypothesis and cognitive sophistication hypothesis, and review empirical evidence for related claims. I conclude that differences can show both qualitative and quantitative aspects, depending on specific aspects involved. I further suggest an alternative way to conceptualize the qualitative and quantitative issue: simultaneously taking several dimensions into consideration in determining the likelihood of qualitative differences and conditions of exceptionality. Taken together, the three ontological issues can be better handled when rich functional contexts, individuality, and developmental changes are brought to focus.

In Chapter 6, I review three "epistemic tensions": (a) how do we come to know someone is gifted, in terms of potential (aptitude) or authentic achievement; (b) how do we study related phenomena or individuals, by starting with universals (i.e., nomothetic) assumptions or with particular (idiographic) observations; and (c) how do we explain these complex phenomena, more statically, as a matter of being (reductionism) or, more dynamically, as a matter of coming into being or becoming (emergentism)? The purposes of highlighting "epistemic" differences is to demonstrate that ontological knowledge claims are subject to empirical verification, which, in turn, is constrained by epistemological and methodological lenses that researchers hold. The three issues are distinct but related. For example, using aptitude measures such as IQ test scores is based on nomothetic or universal assumptions about human traits, and using authentic achievement is more congenial to an idiographic emphasis on particular observations as more "real" or "authentic." The nomothetic approach naturally tends to be reductionistic in that relatively simple rules are regarded as governing complex phenomena, whereas the idiographic approach tends to honor the richness, depth, and complexity of particular gifted and talented manifestations as irreducible to simple rules. To reconcile the differences, I suggest the complementariness of these competing epistemic lenses and angles and further suggest the adoption of the Aristotelian four-cause scheme in formulating systemic explanations.

In Chapters 7 and 8, I turn to gifted education and identify three "normative tensions" surrounding it. As I mentioned earlier, the term *normative* here is used in a prescriptive sense, indicating what "ought to be." Scientific evidence regarding nature-nurture, domain-specificity, or qualitative versus qualitative differences only constrains how effective a particular educational intervention will be, but what we think gifted education should be is very much based on our values and goals. The three normative tensions are the expertise versus creativity tension (e.g., Renzulli's (1986) distinction between schoolhouse giftedness and creative-productive giftedness), the gifted child versus talent development tension, the excellence versus equity tension. I discuss the expertise-creativity tension from both theoretical and educational points of view, pointing to implications for educational strategies such as acceleration and enrichment. The gifted child versus talent development tension has been at the center of many debates on the future of gifted education in recent years (see Delisle, 2003; Morelock, 1996; Subotnik, 2003; Treffinger & Feldhusen, 1996). In important ways, the tension is also associated with the equity versus excellence tension. In Chapter 8, I delineate several voices criticizing gifted education as "elitist" and perpetuating social inequality. I further define excellence and equity more explicitly so that, at the practical level, judgments can be made on balancing these public values and priorities.

While all the "essential tensions" I review in Chapters 3–8 take the form of thesis and antithesis, polarizing existing views is not my purpose; rather, reaching a new synthesis is what I try to accomplish with this book. In Chapter 9, I attempt such a synthesis by proposing a framework of differential development whereby proper analysis and interpretation can be made about a relevant phenomenon, and different levels of analysis can be conducted and integrated in a meaningful way. In essence, the framework I propose stresses the developmental and evolving nature of gifted and talented manifestations, identification, and education in situ, while honoring the tradition of differential psychology by recognizing the fundamental principle of differential development or developmental diversity (different developmental niches, trajectories, pathways for individuals of different capabilities and propensities). It should be noted that the multiple-level framework of differential development presented in this chapter builds on a conceptual analysis of self-organization and self-direction of talent development in Chapter 4 and epistemological considerations discussed in Chapter 6.

Chapter 10 discusses implications of a new synthesis on the ontological, epistemological, and normative fronts for developing a new paradigm of practice for educators as well as professional psychologists with respect to programming, identification, curriculum, instruction, and counseling. For each category, I suggest a set of general principles derived from the framework for guiding gifted education practice in the future. In the main, I envision a gifted education that is open, flexible, tailored to local educational needs, capitalizing on local resources, and recognizing and nurturing a variety of forms and expressions of excellence, an education that is developmentally responsive and socially responsible; that is attentive and responsive to precocious and advanced development; and that encourages and supports strivings for excellence in a personally meaningful, socially equitable, and theoretically sound manner.

CONCLUDING THOUGHTS: THE IMPORTANCE
OF REFLECTIVE PRACTICE

Bertrand Russell once said that if we had definitive answers to some questions, these answers would quickly become disciplinary knowledge and depart from philosophy. What remains in the realm of philosophy are those issues that still don't have definitive answers, and philosophizing about them is still deemed a necessary exercise in order to keep us metacognitively aware of why these issues remain unresolved and how we might go about dealing with ensuing uncertainties. There are two main reasons why science has its limits in helping us solve problems and why metalevel thinking is needed in our field. First, science is good at finding mechanisms and regularities, but it takes philosophical thinking to examine the conceptual structures used in research and practice. One of the tenets of post-positivism is that empirical evidence can inform us as far as it can go, but in many ways, empirical data are not as self-evident as they might appear to be; it takes good conceptualization to put them in proper interpretation schemes. Second, any research endeavor concerned with human conditions and improvement always has to deal with a fundamental paradoxical situation or dilemma: We try to make disinterested and unbiased observations and understand human conditions as objectively as we can. But we are never neutral bystanders, as our purposes ultimately are to improve these conditions; inevitably, what we value or consider desirable states has an impact on our perception and vision of truth. For that matter, the reflective nature of metalevel thinking makes it a good way of organizing our experiences, feelings, and intuitions more rationally, and reflecting on our own values and taking into consideration legitimate concerns that may not be in the list of our preferences and priorities. I cannot claim that my views as expressed in this book are unbiased; my personal biases, beliefs, and values are explicitly stated, particularly in the last two chapters. But I would describe this book as an honest attempt to reach out to scholars, researchers, and educators who might happen to hold different views on giftedness and different philosophies of what gifted education should be about. For that purpose, this book is not meant to be an effort of ideological persuasion, despite both obvious and unobvious biases expressed, but that of exposing implicit assumptions and justifications underlying various positions (including my own) so that readers can exercise their own intellectual judgment on which ones are more viable and defensible alternatives in guiding policy and practice: in what way the field of gifted studies and education can move beyond the ideological differences in serving the common goal of understanding and improving educational and developmental conditions for our precocious and advanced students.

A Brief Intellectual History of "Giftedness"

Things fall apart; the centre cannot hold...
—Yeats, "The Second Coming"

Within the group, some individuals may be more traditionalistic, others more iconoclastic, and their contributions may differ accordingly.
—Thomas Kuhn, *The Essential Tension*

THE TERM *gifted*, or *giftedness*, has never been more problematic than it is today. When Lewis Terman (1925) named his longitudinal project "studies of genius," no one raised any questions about the validity of his argument that the children he identified based on IQ scores of 140 or higher (among other measures and assessments) were an exceptional group worthy of the term *gifted*. From the viewpoint of today's skeptics, however, what is problematic is not the claim that this group of children was highly able, but that the high ability they demonstrated was largely a natural endowment. The fact that most of them were White further raises the red flag to the skeptics, implicating either systematic biases in the measurement or highly favorable socioeconomic home environments. To be sure, the means of identifying gifted children nowadays is more diverse than in Terman's times, and conceptions of giftedness are more pluralistic than ever. This fact reflects current beliefs that giftedness takes many forms and can be expressed in many ways. However, if there are many forms and expressions of giftedness, does that mean that giftedness is an undefinable abstraction, and studies of giftedness is a hopeless cause? Here lie the roots of the crisis in the field: Many stakeholders from the Left to the Right, scholars and researchers included, have experienced a sense of chaos and attempted to seek some order and clarity (e.g., Feldman, 2003; Gagné, 1999b, 2004). Some of them have started to get impatient when it does not seem that we are getting any closer to seeing light at the end of the tunnel (Gagné, 1999a). The purpose of this chapter is not to impose an order based on my own convictions and beliefs, but to go back to the history to seek an understanding of how conceptions of giftedness have evolved over time from the inception of the notion, and what undercurrents are beneath the apparent restlessness in the field. I first briefly discuss why it is highly challenging to infer a quality we deem "gifted" and how the term is used in research and education practices. I then delineate a dialectic history of changing conceptions of giftedness. In particular,

I contrast the traditional "essentialist" perspective with an emergent "developmentalist" perspective on the nature and development of exceptional competence.

THE CHALLENGE OF DEFINING WHAT WE MEAN BY "GIFTED"

Sternberg (1995) summarized lay people's intuitions or folk beliefs about what makes an individual "gifted" with a pentagonal implicit theory of giftedness. According to this theory, in order to be judged as gifted, a person needs to meet the following five criteria:

1. The *Excellence Criterion*, which states that "the individual is superior in some dimension or set of dimensions relative to peers."
2. The *Rarity Criterion*, which states that "an individual must possess a high level of an attribute that is rare relative to peers."
3. The *Productivity Criterion*, which states that "the dimension(s) along which the individual is evaluated as superior must lead to or potentially lead to productivity."
4. The *Demonstrability Criterion*, which states that "superiority of the individual on the dimension(s) which determine 'giftedness' must be demonstrable through one or more tests that are valid assessment."
5. The *Value Criterion*, which states that "the person must show superior performance in a dimension that is valued for that person by his or her society." (Sternberg, 1995, pp. 66–68)

If we interpret *test* broadly enough to include any task performance or manifest behavior, and *dimension* to include authentic domains of human activities as well as psychological constructs such as intelligence or creativity, this list of criteria appears to serve us well regarding whether the label *gifted* is warranted for a person. In actuality, however, these criteria only nominally solve the problem of how "giftedness" is implicitly determined in our natural, nontechnical language. For example, even in scholarly discussion and educational practice, the standards or criteria used to define the "gifted" are somewhat arbitrary (see Hertzog, 2009). A notable practice is that different meanings are intended for the term: It can refer to either psychometrically defined abilities or academic achievement (Gallagher & Courtright, 1986); superior potential or "promise" is inferred when used to describe a child, and eminent accomplishments are referred to when used to describe an adult (Mayer, 2005). However, do these two qualities necessarily implicate each other? Is giftedness, however defined, a necessary condition for excellence in domain achievement? Some critics argue that to the extent it is not a necessary condition, there is no need to invoke giftedness or natural talent as an explanation given an exceptional performance (Ericsson et al., 2005, 2007a).

What further complicates the matter is that the public discourse on giftedness has been historically shaped by multiple stakeholders with different vested interests: some scientific, others ethical and social-political, and still others pragmatic. This is a mixed blessing for the field. On the positive side, the field enjoys its cultural importance and practical significance, as the knowledge it produces has important policy implications and practical utilities in education and training. On the negative side, the discourse has become very murky to the point of compromising its own credibility as a source of reliable knowledge.

Human language itself has contributed to the problem of communication. The term *gifted* can be used *descriptively* and *explanatorily*, and these two modes of expression have different meanings. Descriptive use of the term remains empirical and factual; for example, "She is a gifted musician" can be just an observation, equivalent to saying that "she performed extremely well." Explanatory use of the term, in contrast, implies a causal relationship; for example, "She is a gifted musician" may imply that she possesses a musical talent that leads to an excellent performance. The latter use involves some level of inference and abstraction beyond the observable. Interestingly, many adjectives suffer from the fate of reification; that is, an abstract concept starts to be treated as if it is a real entity or has material existence. Thus, *intelligent* gradually gets hardened into *intelligence*, and *gifted* into *giftedness*; the descriptive becomes implicitly explanatory. The ambiguities involved in the descriptive versus explanatory use of the term in our natural language cause much confusion. This is largely because the word *gifted* is loaded with surplus meanings (Gallagher, 1991; Robinson, 2005), and what is intended and what is not intended in a specific discourse context is not always well articulated. It is easy to relapse from a reasoned argument into a leap of faith in our communication. Some scholars in the field call for an explicit use of the term as explanatory, with *giftedness* referring to "natural abilities" and "talent" referring to systematically developed skills and competencies that build on one or two forms of giftedness (e.g., Gagné, 1999b, 2004, 2005a, 2009a). However, how viable such a distinction is at the empirical and practical level is open to question (Borland, 1999). Moreover, the use of giftedness as a causal agent (e.g., in the phrase "because of one's giftedness") can be criticized as making a circular or tautological argument: to say that one's giftedness gives rise to one's gifted performance is just like saying that someone behaves aggressively because the person is aggressive or possesses aggression: No further insight can be gained about the aggressor (or the gifted).

To make the use of terminology more disciplined, a distinction can be made between *excellence* and *giftedness*. Excellence is a *performance concept*, judged by some performance standards. To be sure, one can question the standards invoked, but usually these standards can be objectively defined and agreed upon. Giftedness, in contrast, is a *competence concept*, involving an inference about the person based on the quality of his or her behavior or performance. This distinction makes it clearer why giftedness as a quality of the person in question is more difficult to define than excellence, which can be more objectively agreed upon. Specifically, defining giftedness entails addressing the following empirical and theoretical questions:

1. Empirically, how do we know that a person is gifted? Which form of assessment is valid and more effective: formal testing or authentic tasks? Should we rely on statistics derived from standardized tests or more up-close clinical judgments? What are the most effective ways of investigating gifted behaviors: psychometric mapping of traits in the population, or tracing unique individual history? And

2. Theoretically, should we see giftedness as context-independent or context-dependent (e.g., "gifted" in one context but not so in others)? How do we explicate the origins and ontogeny of gifted behavior or competence? Should we see relevant phenomena as fundamentally reducible to a set of simple elements or as revealing a form of organized complexity that cannot be explained by simpler elements?

Historically, three core dimensions, intelligence (including specific and general cognitive abilities), motivation, and creativity, have been used to define the substantive nature of giftedness, each constituting a broad, abstract concept itself, which can be further scrutinized in terms of its psychosocial underpinnings (see Robinson & Clinkenbeard, 1998). The order of the three dimensions is not arbitrary. Intelligence (or basic human abilities), psychometrically or otherwise defined, is arguably the most stable of the three and has more transferability in terms of enabling acquisition of new knowledge and skills (Messick, 1992). Motivation is considered more fluctuating and situational, depending on personal experiences and history as well as social contexts (Dai, Moon, & Feldhusen, 1998), though longitudinal stability of motivational patterns was also found (e.g., enduring intrinsic academic motivation; Gottfried, Gottfried, Cook, & Morris, 2005). Last, creativity takes a longer developmental trajectory to develop and likely integrates intelligence, motivation, and personality factors in specific functional contexts and is therefore the least stable and predictable of the three (Renzulli, 1986). The three concepts share a common characteristic with the concept of giftedness: they can refer to either potential (i.e., propensity) or actual behavioral manifestation. However, this is still a highly simplified road map to understanding giftedness. For the purpose of discussion, I follow the widely accepted convention of defining *gifted* as referring to demonstrated excellence through authentic performance or potential for excellence, inferred through aptitude tests, interviews, and clinical observations of behavior and performance (e.g., Marland, 1972; Reznulli, 1978; Ross, 1993).

A DIALECTICAL CYCLE OF CONSTRUCTION, DECONSTRUCTION, AND RECONSTRUCTION OF GIFTEDNESS

The intellectual history of a concept has its own logic. It evolves through human reflective consciousness, sometimes conscience, as an adaptation to new conditions and demands (Toulmin, 1972). I use the term *dialectic* to denote this human tendency for self-correction (including overcorrection), to come back to a better sense of reality through critical thinking and resolution of conflicts of ideas. A concept tends to evolve in this way because of its internal tension, its failure to capture important aspects of what we sense as "truth" or "reality." While this internal tension is essential, various historical circumstances influence the trajectory and timing of conceptual changes. As in the case of a volcano, the tension is always there; however, when it reaches the point of eruption depends on many circumstantial factors that crack the structural and functional stability of the conceptual system. By structuring these events in these three phases, I try to elucidate the larger context or zeitgeist, the underlying motivations, biases, and logic that seem coherent in (a) the *construction* of core values and beliefs concerning the concept of "giftedness," (b) the *deconstruction* of this core, and (c) the *reconstruction* of new core values and belief systems around it.

Giftedness Constructed: Lewis Terman's Legacy of Essentialism

Lewis Terman (1877–1956) was a man of his time, for better or for worse. Francis Galton (1869) envisioned a society or nation where a more distinct role could be conferred upon the intellectually superior to preserve its greatness. Inspired by Galton, among others, Terman launched the first large-scale study of bright youths by introducing massive intelligence testing as a major way of identifying the intellectually gifted. What characterizes Terman's time were his following convictions:

1. Intelligence is a general human quality, and it is largely genetically determined. This is a Galtonian doctrine with connotations of Darwinism: Intelligence is a biological trait heritable through natural selection. Note that in Terman's time, the memory of Gregor Mendel's discovery of genetic inheritance in pea plants was still fresh, further reinforcing this Galtonian conviction that genius is heritable.
2. A hierarchy of intellectually superior, mediocre, inferior people can be established in the society. Herbert Spencer's social Darwinism provided justification for the social strata or hierarchy during that historical period in the United States. A moral imperative shared by Terman and many of his contemporaries was to "better" the human race, eugenics being part of the solution. While Charles Goddard was working at the low end, how to reduce the negative effects of "the feeble-minded" who could not tell right from wrong, Terman mainly worked on the high end, identifying and understanding the gifted (see Hall, 2003).
3. Intelligence as a general personal quality can be measured objectively with the newly invented intelligence test. Terman believed that, with the birth of the first intelligence test in history, created by French psychologists Binet and Simon, the measurement technology was advanced

enough to gauge levels and amounts of this essential quality. The gifted can be operationally defined as the top 1% of the population (roughly at or above an IQ score of 140), as measured by a modified version of Binet and Simon's test created by Terman, a Stanford professor at the time, hence the Stanford-Binet Intelligence Scale.

It is almost bewildering in historical hindsight why Terman and his contemporaries had such confidence in testing and measuring such a complex, abstract human quality. Indeed, they did not even have an elaborated theory of intellectual performance and intelligence, besides its practical importance and potential applications. However, consider the confidence of Charles Spearman (1904) when he titled his now classic article " 'General Intelligence,' Objectively Determined and Measured" (p. 201). The spell of British empiricism in the American culture should not be underestimated. It entails a minimalist (and often radically reductionsitic) assumption of how the real world operates, availability of effective measurement, and efficient mathematical maneuvering of data to find discernable patterns and regularities, all started by Galton (1869). The faith in quantitative measurement at the time (and even today) is illustrated best by Thorndike's famous statement: "Whatever exists at all exists in some amount" (quoted in Mayer, 2003, p. 141). Underlying this conviction was the need for technological control, for good or ill, with measurement as its tool. It is not accidental that Binet had less intellectual impact on the thinking of his American contemporaries, other than contributing a crucial empirical element: an intelligence test. Binet, a more nuanced Continental psychologist, was more intrigued by "idiographic complexity" (Brody, 2000, p. 19) of individual performance (i.e., how exactly a person is performing the task at hand) than mathematical certainty of the normal distribution of human traits like general intelligence and special abilities that fascinated Spearman (1927).

Terman started what might be called an *essentialist or realist tradition* of defining and explaining gifted potential. Essentialism is a belief, first articulated by Plato, that there is a unique essence, form, or quality that gives an object identity, unity, and continuity. Intelligence is, then, seen as a structural, enduring quality of the person (i.e., a trait); thus high-IQ children are seen as possessing this unique quality that sets them apart from their peers. In its most reductionistic form, high intelligence is seen as a natural endowment and neurological advantage (see Geake, 2009). For example, Gagné (1999b, 2004) insists that the term *giftedness* be differentiated from the term *talent* because such a causal structure and ordering of gifts and talents is important from an essentialist perspective. Giftedness or natural endowment can be inferred from exceptional performance as spontaneously developed competencies without systematic, substantial formal training; and talent can be identified if it is systematically developed in a particular line of human endeavor. Although there are many variations, *the basic assumption of the essentialist construal of giftedness is a unitary core of high general intelligence that sets the "gifted" apart from the rest of age peers, not only in terms of high facility in intellectual functioning but also in terms of its profound ramifications for their individuality, such as different ways of thinking, different social-emotional characteristics, different educational needs, and different developmental trajectories and pathways.* The essentialist model of development is how the high level of "raw" intelligence gets "translated" through experience and efforts into specific forms of talent, competence, and expertise in some valued human activities.

Giftedness Deconstructed: Social and Scientific Disenchantment

Even in Terman's heyday, his advocacy for the widespread use of intelligence testing and for identifying gifted children was not going uncontested. In an early nature-nurture debate, many people voiced concerns that IQ testing threatened democracy and diminished the role of education (see Feldhusen, 2003). Lippmann was among the early voices of criticism on intelligence testing; he questioned the scientific validity of IQ tests and, consequently, the ethical implications of making IQ tests "a sort of last judgment of the child's capacity" (Lippmann, 1976, p. 19; see Block & Dworkin, 1976, for the Terman versus Lippmann debate in the 1920s). These voices were a prelude to some of the contemporary criticisms of the gifted movement. More direct criticism of using IQ scores as a benchmark of giftedness was made by Getzels and Jackson (1962), who argued that highly creative children would be excluded when IQ was used as a main criterion for identification of gifted children. However, they only attempted to modify the identification process and broaden the criteria, rather than rock the foundation of conceptions of gifted children. There have been two movements that truly challenge the essentialist conceptions of giftedness; one launched by social critics, and the other by expertise researchers.

Critique from a social constructivist perspective. Social critique of giftedness largely occurs in the context of gifted education in the United States, but it can also be found in other countries with an egalitarian sentiment. The very fact that identification of the gifted was associated with an implicit or explicit social stratification based on IQ reinforced the suspicion that the gifted education movement is a remnant of social elitism. Namely, what were identified as "gifted children" were actually a socially privileged class of children, thus perpetuating the preexisting social inequality (Margolin, 1994, 1996). Persistent efforts to deconstruct the concept of giftedness have been made by Borland (1997a, 2003, 2005), largely from a social constructivist perspective. Borland's main argument is that giftedness is conferred, rather than discovered: We constructed it to serve a social purpose rather than discovered it as an objective reality (Borland, 2003). From this point of view, Borland (2003) puts essentialist conceptions of giftedness into question:

Are these two groups—the gifted and the rest—the discrete, discontinuous, structured wholes this crude taxonomy implies? That is, is giftedness really its own thing, qualitatively different and apart from averageness or normality, making those who possess it markedly different, different in kind, from the rest of humanity? (p. 111)

In essence, Borland argued that the way we define giftedness as an essential quality that sets some children apart from the rest is scientifically unwarranted and practically harmful (particularly for minority, underprivileged students). Borland further resorted to Foucault's argument that knowledge is not neutral but a form of the technology of control typically held by the socially privileged. To push this line of thinking further, we might even extrapolate that the fiction of general intelligence, the psychometric tests, even factor-analytic tools, all conspired to maintain a certain kind of social order. By the same token, the gifted-nongifted comparison research paradigm might have been complicit in further perpetuating the bifurcation of the gifted and the nongifted as two qualitatively different sub-populations, as such comparison is based on the assumption that they constitute two distinct homogeneous groups.

As if to prove Foucault's point that to make knowledge claims is to exert social power, there has been an undercurrent to break the hegemony of the public discourse on intelligence enjoyed by psychometricians. The most prominent examples are Gardner and Sternberg's theories. Gardner's (1983) theory of multiple intelligences has, for good or ill, successfully pluralized the concept of intelligence. Sternberg not only differentiates analytic, creative, and practical intelligences (see Sternberg, 1996a), but also has shown that the concepts of intelligence and giftedness, which are often considered universal human qualities, are fundamentally culture bound, reflecting cultural values, practices, and belief systems (see Sternberg, 2000, 2007a, 2007b). Thus, successful intelligence in different cultures may entail different kinds of human adaptation. Gardner's and Sternberg's theories have profoundly changed the way giftedness is conceptualized. But more important, their theoretical ideas have in effect promoted a more pluralistic value and a more liberal social order (e.g., compared with the conservative position expressed by Herrnstein & Murray, 1994).

Critique from an expertise perspective. In addition to the support from new intelligence theories, the social constructivist critique of essentialist conceptions of giftedness found an unexpected ally from the experimental tradition of cognitive psychology, which sees the world quite differently from the way differential psychology sees it, attributing performance variations to situations and processes, rather than personal dispositions and capacities (Cronbach, 1957). When dealing with issues of alleged gifts and talents, cognitive psychology is mainly concerned with the scientific validity of the claims regarding the existence and importance of native intelligence and natural talents. When Terman defined the gifted as the top 1% of the IQ distribution, there was no scientific justification for why it could not be the top 3% or 10%. Thus, such a practice is of mere pragmatic consideration, rather than scientific necessity (see Chapter 6 for discussion of Type I and II Errors). Grinder (1985), among many scholars, argued that "the psychology of individual differences in intellect, to the extent that its methodology has been dominated by mental tests, never was elevated to the status of a science" (p. 27). While a few psychometrically oriented researchers have attempted to develop a cognitive process account of individual differences in intellectual performance by integrating psychometric and experimental approaches (see Gustafsson & Undheim, 1996; Hunt, 1986, 2006), cognitive researchers have attempted to show that essentialist beliefs about native intelligence and natural talents have no scientific basis (Ericsson et al., 2005, 2007a; Howe, 1997; Howe et al., 1998), and that what used to be attributed to natural talent can now be explained more adequately as a result of years of domain experience and deliberate practice (Ericcson, 2006). These researchers look at contextual experiences for alternative explanations for exceptional competence (e.g., Ceci & Liker, 1986). Although evidence seems to cut both ways, they trust proximal variables (i.e., knowledge and skills that can be linked to performance more directly) more than distal variables (e.g., genetic differences in human abilities). Experimental psychologists typically hold more stringent criteria for knowledge claims and are eager to outlaw the elusive concept of natural ability or natural talent, very much like trying to dispel a superstition from the scientific parlance.

A critique of the critique of essentialist construal of giftedness. Deconstruction of giftedness in a sense demystifies the process of how "giftedness" is constructed, even how we created a fiction of a category of children that came to be accepted over time as an objective reality. On a positive side, deconstruction is a force of antireification and antiessentialism. It has a potentially constructive impact on how we understand giftedness by forcing us to examine our deeply held, often taken-for-granted assumptions. It alerts us to a reality that is more complex and uncertain than we believe. It removes the guise of objective truth regarding intelligence, giftedness, and talent and reveals possible subjectivity, biases, even arbitrariness involved in the construction of these "psychological realities." Most of all, it challenges us to reconsider various theories of giftedness as socially constructed hypothetical models, rather than objective realities independent of the observer or instruments of observation (Borland, 2003, 2005). It reminds us that in the social and psychological sciences, facts and values cannot be clearly separated in our interpretation of the empirical data as they can in the physical and biological sciences. The term *gifted*, for example, is as much evaluative as it is descriptive. However, deconstruction and antiessentialism, represented by Foucault and Derrida, when pushed to an extreme, can also border on nihilism and cynicism: All forms of knowledge are nothing but devices of social control, aimed at gaining economic or political advantages, or merely a language game or academic exercise, with no true meaning or substance. From this extreme point of view, the rationality of scientific endeavor is simply an illusion (see Phillips & Burbules, 2000 for a critique of this radicalism). The temptation in this direction in deconstructivism should be resisted, in my opinion.

On the other front, cognitive science has introduced a new level of rigor and a new set of criteria for judging many claims about giftedness, which are often based on intuitions and implicit assumptions, rather than solid scientific research and evidence. However, scientific adjudication of a possible role of genetically based individual differences for gifted behavior and performance (or the lack of thereof), when pushed to the extreme, can run the risk of radical positivism (e.g., if something cannot be ascertained through controlled experimentation, it is not knowable) and environmentalism (e.g., conditioning, reinforcement, or social learning of various kinds is all we need to explain any human behavior, including exceptional competence). After all, a cognitive science approach to giftedness, expertise, and creativity (e.g., Langley, Simon, Bradshaw, & Zytkow, 1987) has its own conceptual and methodological biases and limitations (e.g., a mechanistic outlook on human functioning, emphasizing "computability," "reproducibility," and the "observable"). Clearly, the challenge is not to throw away evidence regarding individual differences accumulated by psychometric researchers over more than a century, but to understand the discrepancies in the findings of different research traditions and competing theoretical persuasions (psychometric, cognitive, developmental, etc.), and how these discrepancies and conflicting claims might be explained, even resolved, in light of the totality of evidence as well as differences in theoretical lenses and methodologies used. I will discuss these nature-nurture issues in more detail in Chapter 3.

Giftedness Reconstructed: From Essentialism to Developmentalism

As the first person to use an intelligence test to identify gifted children and conduct decades-long follow-up studies on them, Terman has made an impact still palpable today in terms of how we understand giftedness. Some of the basic essentialist tenets of Terman's legacy are still accepted by many contemporary students of intelligence in general and giftedness in particular. For example:

1. Many scholars still believe that general intelligence exists and is a stable quality that has a pervasive impact on one's life (Gottfredson, 1997; cf. Neisser et al., 1996). Carroll (1997) equated general intelligence with the ease of learning: "IQ represents the degree to which, and the rate at which, people are able to learn, and retain in long-term memory, the knowledge and skills" (p. 44). Most agree that there is a distinct genetic component to variations in general intelligence based on behavioral genetics research (Plomin, 1997), though they may not accept the proposition that it is entirely genetically determined, or that there is an inherent racial difference in general intelligence;

2. Many still believe that standardized IQ tests, despite their fallibility, provide the best measures available of this essential human quality, and high IQ is a good indicator of intellectual giftedness, predictive of long-term development and achievement (e.g., Gagné, 2004, 2009b; Gallagher, 2000b; Lubinski, 2004; Robinson, 2005), though they may differ in terms of whether more conservative or liberal cutoffs should be used in identification of the gifted; and

3. Many scholars believe, along with Terman, that high intelligence is a necessary, but not sufficient, condition for ultimate adult achievement and eminence; nonintellective and environmental catalysts play an important role (e.g., Gagné, 2004; Lubinski, 2004). Nonintellective intrapersonal catalyists include motivation and personality, and environmental catalysts include environmental opportunities and instructional and technical support (Gagné, 2004).

However, dissatisfaction with the rigidity of IQ-based definition of giftedness and the central doctrine of essentialist definition of giftedness has also led people to search for alternative ways of thinking about giftedness. Witty (1958), for example, argued for a more inclusive definition of giftedness:

> There are children whose outstanding potentialities in art, in writing, or in social leadership can be recognized largely by their performance. Hence, we have recommended that the definition of giftedness be expanded and that we consider any child gifted whose performance, in a potentially valuable line of human activity, is consistently remarkable. (P. 62)

In this new definition, not only were domains broadened to include artistic and social endeavors, but also criteria for determining giftedness were shifted from test performance to authentic task performance (see also DeHaan & Havighurst, 1957). Historical linkage is discernable between Witty's definition and that offered by Marland's (1972) report, which provided the first "official" definition of giftedness as consisting of several categories of "outstanding abilities" (p. 1). Interestingly, the motivations driving this new approach to giftedness are pragmatic in nature. First, there was an increasing realization that "the gifted and talented come in a tremendous variety of shapes, forms, and sizes" (Passow, 1981, p. 8). Such diversity and heterogeneity of human abilities simply defies the Procrustean bed of IQ tests. Second, intelligence tests as selection/placement tools have little to say about how instruction can be differentiated for a group of children so identified (Lohman & Rocklin, 1995).

Antecedents of the developmental perspectives. It can be argued that two pragmatic movements in educating the gifted prompted the reconstruction of giftedness. The first was the Study of Mathematically Precocious Youth (SMPY) at Johns Hopkins University and subsequently the Talent Search model across the United States (Lubinski & Benbow, 2006; Stanley, 1996). A fortuitous event of trying to meet educational needs of a mathematically precocious child by a professor (Julian Stanley) eventually led to the establishment of the SMPY in 1971 and has proved to be a milestone in understanding and serving gifted children since Terman's (1925) longitudinal study. This model bypassed the IQ criterion altogether and defined giftedness in terms of precocity, based on "out of level" testing; that is, selecting 13- and 14-year-old mathematically precocious students based on their superior performance on Scholastic Aptitude Test–Math (SAT-Math) designed for college-bound high school students. Epistemological and methodological significance lies in the fact that it represented a more domain-specific approach based on precocious mathematical development rather than assumptions of general intellectual advantage. Years later, Keating, quoted by Stanley (1996), reflected on what SMPY brought to the field:

> One of the important principles advanced (in theory, research, and practice) by SMPY is a workable model of educating for individual development, as opposed to categorical placement approaches that dominate most of contemporary education. I think this is a potentially generalizable way of dealing with developmental diversity. (P. 232; see also Keating, 2009)

The second movement was the development of enrichment models for gifted education by Renzulli (1977) and Passow (1981), among others. Just as the Talent Search model is implicitly a developmental model, Renzulli's (1977) "triad model" also treats "giftedness" as a dynamic state: Several qualities need to come together to create a mesh. In his three-ring conception of giftedness, while above-average abilities are stable individual differences, task commitment and creativity are largely developmental tasks and goals that education should facilitate in children, rather than well-formed traits existing prior to educational provision. By the same token, Passow also challenged the standard two-step, identification-differentiation approach. Instead, he suggested that prescribed enrichment be used as a vehicle for identification as much as identification informs enrichment. Thus,

> identification of the gifted and talented is related not only to systematic observation of and intelligent interpretation of observational data, but to the creation of the right kinds of opportunities which facilitate self-identification—identification by performance and product which results in the manifestation of gifted or talented behaviors. (Passow, 1981, p. 10)

In both cases, the pragmatic concern over how to effectively identify gifted children for proper educational interventions has led to new understandings of giftedness as a dynamic rather than static phenomenon, as a functional state rather than a trait. In the same vein, Renzulli (1986) argued that "gifted behaviors take place in certain people (not all people), at certain times (not all the time), and under certain circumstances (not all circumstances)" (p. 76). Contrary to the standard image of high intelligence translated into real life excellence or giftedness translated into talent, these efforts were charting a new way of defining giftedness as a more dynamic, contextual quality. In effect, *this new approach to giftedness as an emergent, changing property of person-environment interaction that grows and becomes more differentiated over time signals what can be called a developmentalist view of giftedness.* However, as should be expected, the pragmatic approaches often fell short of articulating in depth what developmental changes occur and how they occur. After reviewing various proposed definitions, Siegler and Kotovsky (1986) suggested that an optimal approach to theory and research on giftedness is not to take a psychometric, trait approach, but to focus on the developmental processes in an authentic performance context, particularly for those who are "in the process of becoming productive-creative contributors to a field" (p. 434), so that the gap between schoolhouse giftedness and creative-productive giftedness (Renzulli, 1986) can be bridged.

The emergence of developmental models. It was not until the mid-1980s that a significant body of developmental research has accumulated to provide a solid foundation for explicit developmental conceptions of giftedness (e.g., Bamberger, 1986; Bloom, 1985; Feldman, 1986; Gruber, 1981, 1986; Horowitz & O'Brien, 1985; Lubinski & Benbow, 1992). There was a surge of talent development models in the same period (Feldhusen, 1992; Feldman, 1992; Gagné, 1985; Mönks & Mason, 1993; Piirto, 1994; Renzulli, 1994). In general, most developmentalists see giftedness not as a static quality in the head but as a result of the confluence of several forces, endogenous and exogenous, coming together in the right place at the right time. This principle is well articulated in a complex emergenic-epigenetic model that Simonton (1999, 2005) postulated. According to the model, giftedness is relative to the nature of a given domain that offers a specific set of opportunities and challenges to an interested person. Whether gifted behaviors will emerge depend on (a) whether the domain involved is simple or complex, (b) whether the person in question has the right combination of genetic components vis-à-vis the domain, (c) whether these functional components for the domain operate at an additive or multiplicative fashion (see Chapter 5 for a detailed illustration of multiplicative versus additive models), and (d) whether all the components relative to the domain come into place (i.e., developmentally matured) at the right time. In other words, what kind of giftedness will emerge is not prespecified or preordained in biology but determined by a combination of multiple factors: *person* (biology), *domain* (culture), *social context* (age peers), and *developmental timing* (epigenesis). The model also predicts that gifted behaviors are not a constant but can emerge and disappear, depending on individuals' developmental timing and related population characteristics.

Simonton's model, however, still leans toward a biological explanation of giftedness, in terms of the right genetic-based traits coming together at the right time to give expression to a specific talent. Environmental factors still play a back-stage role. In most developmentalist models, however, emergence of giftedness is typically described as an outcome of the confluence of environmental and personal factors, a coincidence (Feldman, 1986). In that sense, no one knows what Bobby Fischer or Garry Kasparov would have been up to if there had been no chess around.

Basic tenets of developmentalism. In its most distinct form, developmentalism has some core assumptions about the nature of giftedness that sets it apart from essentialism:

1. *Giftedness as developmental diversity* (as opposed to the essentialist core of giftedness). This assumption not only treats giftedness as a form of deviation in development, but also implies a variety of niche potentials and developmental pathways that do not share the same essential characteristics, cognitively or affectively. If one further factors environmental conditions and opportunities into the developmental diversity, phenotypic manifestations of giftedness are even more diverse (different domains, different social contexts, and different cultures). Many forms of giftedness belong to what Feldman (1986) called *nonuniversal development*. Nonuniversal development has two important characteristics: First, it has unique individuality in development, a unique set of sensibilities and propensities; second, it occurs only under certain environmental conditions, and in the case of a culturally defined talent, with instructional and training provisions. Hence, other than denoting some form of excellence or potential for excellence (to use Sternberg's excellence and rarity criteria), the concept of giftedness is not unitary and does not imply a set of shared core attributes. Such developmental pluralism is in sharp contrast to the essentialist doctrine that stipulates specific formulas for defining and measuring giftedness.

2. *Giftedness as a developmental state* (as opposed to giftedness as a static trait or a constellation of traits). Developmentalists tend to see giftedness not as biologically constitutional, but rather, as a specific developmental and functional state vis-à-vis adaptive challenges in a specific context and at a particular point in development, subject to further adaptive changes (Matthews & Foster, 2006). Thus, giftedness is seen not as an attribute but as a critical state in some important aspects of development (Ziegler, 2005; Ziegler & Heller 2000), or a point of advanced intellectual or artistic development (Coleman & Cross, 2005; Mönks & Mason, 2000; Robinson, 2005; Subotnik & Jarvin, 2005). In contrast to a trait definition, what is seen as "gifted" is dynamic, contextual, and emergent: through interest and passion, through honing of advanced skills, and through maintaining a creative tension (Dai & Renzulli, 2008). The image of being gifted is no longer a set of static traits but a state of sustained mastery and transformation, and the eventual productive use of knowledge and skills in building one's unique vision of world and life (Feldman, 2003).

3. *Giftedness as a process and product of structural and functional changes through differentiation and integration.* A developmentalist model of giftedness cannot be content with the status of an implicit theory; making assumptions largely based on intuitions and convictions without explicating what develops and how it develops. Such specification can be as detailed at a neural level, such as structural and functional adaptations occurring in the brain as a result of musical training (Schlaug, 2001). Various attempts have been made in the talent development research to specify what is an initial state and what is a developed state that evolved from the previous one (e.g., Bamberger, 1986; Bloom, 1985; Csikszentmihalyi, Rathunde, & Whalen, 1993). The expertise research has also made headway in making explicit the developmental changes in mental structures and functions (see Ericsson, 2006; Ericsson, Nandagopal, & Roring, 2007a).

4. *Giftedness as an interaction of affordances and effectivities (abilities).* In contrast to a structural construal of giftedness, developmentalists tend to see giftedness as functional states that cannot be dissociated with functional contexts. This is in line with the argument advanced by ecological psychology that environmental and social affordances are contingent on the individual's readiness to perceive and act upon them (i.e., effectivities); conversely, the individual's effectivities or abilities are induced and shaped by environmental and social affordances or constraints. Many developmentalists attempt to specify the role of environmental conditions, in interaction or reciprocation with genetic dispositions, in a specific line of the development of exceptional performance and competence (Bloom, 1985; Csikszentmihalyi et al., 1993; Papierno, Ceci, Makel, & Williams, 2005). For some, the task of finding exceptional individuals becomes that of finding exceptional conditions (Sosniak, 2006), the right proximal processes (Bronfenbrenner & Ceci, 1994), and enabling and facilitative conditions (Keating, 2009).

5. *Giftedness as time-sensitive, task-specific performance* (as opposed to an absolute state of being). Developmentalists have introduced the temporal dimension into the discourse and research on giftedness. They attempt to specify developmental timing, sensitive periods, and the age of peak performance in a given domain, to name a few, as significant developmental events that can have make-or-break effects on sustained engagement in a specific line of talent development (e.g., Ericsson et al., 2005; Shavinina, 1999; Simonton, 1999, 2005). Early manifestations of giftedness do not guarantee later success, as task environments at a higher level impose new demands and constraints. As a result, some stand out while others fade away (Lohman, 2005a; Lohman & Korb, 2006). Being gifted has different meanings at different stages of talent development (Dai & Renzulli, 2008; Subotnik & Jarvin, 2005).

6. *Giftedness as an immediate phenomenology* (as opposed to an a priori assumption about the nature of giftedness). A major change from essentialism to developmentalism is an epistemic shift, from an a priori assumption of what

constitutes giftedness to a focus on immediate phenomena of gifted behavior and competence in authentic functional contexts and how it develops. Therefore, the predictive validity of high IQ or other psychometric test scores and justification of their use is no longer a research priority. Rather, understanding the phenomenology of how individuals achieve high-level expertise and creative productivity every step of the way becomes a focus in its own right. The epistemic shift has led to methodological innovations, such as retrospective interviews (e.g., Sosniak, 2006), biographical works (Gardner, 1993; Gruber, 1981), experiential sampling (Csikszentmihalyi et al., 1993). The developing person as a whole becomes the focal point, instead of some isolated variables and abstract concepts such as general intelligence, measured in a decontextualized fashion. Theoretical thinking is no longer ability-centric (e.g., what cognitive abilities the gifted possess), but is integrating cognitive, affective, and motivational processes (e.g., Dai & Sternberg, 2004; Shavinina & Ferrari, 2004; Winner, 1996).

CONCLUSION: THE CONCEPT OF GIFTEDNESS COMES OF AGE

History has taken a spiral route to understanding the nature and nurture of exceptional competence, from early conceptions of general intelligence as a basis for the identification of the "gifted" to the later recognition of a multitude of manifestations of talents, from an emphasis on natural endowment to a focus on the role of developmental processes and contexts, and, methodologically, from an objectivist stance that takes "gifted child" as a "natural" category of children or an "objective reality" to the recognition of subjectivity and value judgment involved constructing such a category, from a focus on traits to a focus on developmental changes. These changes were not only driven by ethical and pragmatic concerns about serving those who demonstrate their high potential and advanced educational needs in immediate educational settings; they also reflect deep changes in how we understand such key foundational concepts as intelligence, development, motivation, creativity, and context. In the next chapter, I will delineate these deep conceptual changes and discuss the challenge of how to reconcile them with the tradition at both theoretical and practical levels in a way that would move the field forward.

Essential Tensions in Understanding
and Nurturing Gifted Potential

The significant problems we face cannot be solved at the same level of thinking we were at when we created them.

—A remark often attributed to Albert Einstein

Major scientific advance can be understood in terms of an evolutionary process that involves battles over only a few but by no means all of the recurrent themata.

Gerald Holton, "Thematic Presuppositions and
the Direction of Scientific Advance"

IN THE PREVIOUS CHAPTER, I delineated a rather simplified picture of how the concept of giftedness has evolved over roughly a century. I alluded to motivations and impetuses driving the conceptual changes, some theoretical and others pragmatic or social-ethical. In this chapter, I first describe deep changes in foundational knowledge undergirding gifted education that call for a new integration in our knowledge base. I then suggest a framework of essential tensions in the field of gifted studies and education and preview the tensions or issues, each of which will be discussed in depth in Chapters 3–8. The aim of identifying these tensions is to integrate the traditional and emergent perspectives on the nature and nurture of excellence.

CHANGES IN THEORETICAL FOUNDATIONS UNDERGIRDING
THE CHANGING CONCEPTIONS OF GIFTEDNESS

Major changes in conceptions of giftedness in the late 20th century reflect our new understandings of the related phenomena. Historically, conceptions of giftedness have relied heavily on the psychological research on intelligence or cognitive abilities, motivation, and creativity (Robinson & Clinkenbeard, 1998). These foundational constructs underlying conceptions of giftedness have undergone significant changes in themselves. New understandings of human development, including the importance of context and neural plasticity, have contributed to the changing landscape of the field of gifted studies.

Intelligence

The term *intelligence* in the technical context of psychological research refers to individual differences in a set of cognitive abilities important for learning and problem solving, such as understanding complex ideas, engaging in various forms of reasoning, and effectively dealing with real-life challenges (Neisser et al., 1996). The gifted-child movement has a close historical tie with intelligence testing (e.g., Terman, 1925). Some basic assumptions behind this movement, though still held in varying degrees by scholars to date (e.g., see Gottfredson, 1997), have been challenged.

The atheoretical nature of traditional intelligence tests. Close scrutiny of intelligence tests raises serious questions about the construct representation and validity of the tests and, consequently, the essentialist definition of giftedness. Stephen Jay Gould, in his book *The Mismeasure of Man* (1981), pointed out the gap between a measured quantity (IQ scores) and the theoretical construct "intelligence," which the test is purported to measure. He argued that the whole enterprise of measuring human intelligence as a normative trait committed the error of reification, seeing something abstract as having material existence. Intelligence seems to be too broad, abstract, and elusive a concept to be amenable to psychometric testing. At face value, standard intelligence tests provide a composite score by sampling a variety of task performance (mostly of an academic kind). This is an empirical approach to test development deliberately used by Binet to represent a wide variety of task conditions for the sake of enhancing its practical utility. However, precisely because of the empirical approach, there is a level of arbitrariness about what to include in such a test; in other words, the measurement is atheoretical. The paradox is that the broader range of tasks a test covers, the better its predictive power across situations (Gustafsson & Undheim, 1996), but the less psychologically meaningful the test becomes (Lohman & Rocklin, 1995).

Causal inferences about predictive relationships. Predictive relationship (i.e., correlation) between intelligence and achievement does not necessarily imply a causal relationship. The traditional IQ definition of giftedness is predicated on the assumption that IQ tests measure natural aptitude apart from achievement, and its correlation with achievement reflects a cause-effect relationship. Now this assumption is challenged (e.g., Lohman, 2006; Sternberg, 1999b). Theoretically, only by holding two persons' experiences constant can one infer differing "natural aptitude" in a specific learning or performance context (Shiffrin, 1996). Mental testing simply does not afford such a stringent controlled condition. New evidence shows that for populations with low socioeconomic status (SES), the heritability estimate of IQ was zero, suggesting that the variation of IQ for those with low SES was largely the result of environmental factors; the opposite was the case for high-SES samples (Turkheimer, Haley, Waldron, D'Onofrio, & Gottesman, 2003). While the finding begs the question of whether SES variations themselves contain a genetic component, and whether dividing subjects based on SES would alter score distributions for subgroups, the study does raise the issue of differential meanings of IQ scores at different levels of SES. It is safe to infer from the study that for individuals from low-SES backgrounds, family and neighborhood make a difference with respect to how well a person performs on IQ tests.

Historically, the causal relationship between intelligence and achievement is inferred from the predictive validity of the intelligence test in question. However, Sternberg (1999b) argued that, even though such predictive validity is well established, no causal priority can be inferred between intelligence measures and achievement measures, because abilities measured by intelligence tests are forms of developing expertise, which itself is a kind of achievement and subject to experiential and environmental influences. Ceci and Williams (1997) provide evidence that schooling has a direct impact on IQ scores. If intelligence test scores have a distinct achievement component, then its high correlation with academic achievement can be seen as indicative of redundancy or overlap of the two types of test rather than a causal relationship. In short, the traditional conceptual and empirical distinction between intelligence and achievement, a distinction crucial for the differentiation of giftedness from talent achievement (Gagné, 2004), has been seriously challenged.

The homogeneity assumption. Children with similarly high IQs do not have the same cognitive profiles. There is emergent evidence that psychometrically defined intelligence is more differentiated at the high end of the spectrum (Hunt, 1999, 2006); that is, at the high end of the IQ distribution (i.e., those with gifted IQs), there are more discrepancies between subtest scores compared to those in the average or low range of IQ scores. Thus, two persons with the same high IQ scores, more often than not, differ in cognitive strengths and weaknesses. One may still see them as equally "gifted" but it means different things to each person, another uncertainty to be reckoned with.

Other issues. Other problems with equating high IQ and giftedness include instrument dependency (i.e., if you change testing instruments, you will identify different individuals as "gifted"), stability of high IQ (e.g., regression to the mean), and different developmental schedules (e.g., early versus late bloomers; see Lohman & Korb, 2006). In sum, what appear to be objectively measured "natural abilities" turn out to depend on many factors, genetic, developmental, environmental, and technical.

New conceptions of intelligence. While the psychometric measurements and theories of general intelligence have been scrutinized, new theories of intelligence have started to redefine the nature of intelligence, considering a broader range of parameters, with profound implications for how giftedness should be defined.

Perkins (1995; Perkins & Grotzer, 1997) identified three broad classes of theories of intelligence (hence, three main sources of intelligent behavior): neural, experiential, and reflective. *Neural intelligence* refers to the contribution of biological variations in neural efficiency, either globally or in a modular form, that supports cognitive functioning. *Experiential intelligence* refers to the contribution of experience and knowledge to crystallized and fluid intelligence, particularly domain-specific knowledge and skills that are highly tuned to particular types of information or environment. And *Reflective intelligence* refers to the contribution of metacognition and reflective self-guidance to intelligent behavior (see also Ceci, 1996, for a bioecological theory). While neural efficiency has been argued for quite some time to be a biological advantage that distinguishes gifted children from their age peers (Gallagher, 2000b; Geake, 2008, 2009), experiential and reflective aspects of intelligence have yet to gain prominence as a basis for giftedness. Although there is research comparing the metacognitive skills of gifted children with those of children who show average ability (e.g., Shore, 2000; Steiner & Carr, 2003), metacognition—a distinct form of reflective intelligence— is not considered a defining attribute of giftedness. What Perkins's eclectic view of intelligence suggests to the field of gifted studies is that conceptions of giftedness should allow for the role of self-engendered cognitive and metacognitive action and environmental stimulation and support. Just as intelligence can be seen as developing expertise (Sternberg, 1999a), expertise can be seen as learned intelligent behavior (experiential intelligence in Perkins's term; see also Ceci & Ruiz, 1993).

This changing conception of intelligence represents a trend away from the essentialist approach toward a more functional approach. Gardner (2003) articulated this new trend succinctly when he identified an alternative definition of intelligence as "fit execution of a task or role" (Gardner, 2003, p. 48; see also Newell, 1990). Thus the Brazilian children who successfully peddled their goods or the professional gamblers who excelled in betting show such "fit execution" regardless of whether they do well on IQ tests. *Conceptualized as such, intelligence denotes a dynamic, effective functional state vis-à-vis an adaptive challenge, rather than a static personal trait, and can be assessed with task-specific criteria rather than a contentious set of tasks presumed to measure a general quality of mind.*

If intelligence is seen not as a trait, but as a functional state, then dispositions such as sensitivity to occasions that call for a particular way of thinking, and inclination to engage in such thinking (Perkins & Ritchhart, 2004), or personality characteristics such as openness to new experience (Stanovich & West, 1997) can influence the quality of thinking (i.e., intelligent behavior). Ackerman (1999; Ackerman & Kanfer, 2004) also highlights dispositional factors by making a distinction between *maximal intellectual performance* typically gauged in testing conditions, versus *typical intellectual engagement* observed in real-life situations.

This functional view of intelligence provides clues about how emergent conceptions of giftedness can go beyond the entrenched ability-centric view to include other aspects of the person, such as cognitive motivation and intellectual character (Perkins & Ritchhart, 2004; Ritchhart, 2001).

Motivation

Motivation can be defined as an internal process that instigates and sustains goal-directed behavior (Pintrich & Schunk, 1996). A motivated behavior is characterized by its *direction, intensity,* and *endurance.* When high IQ is seen as the gold standard for giftedness, motivation might be considered necessary to facilitate the realization of the putative high intellectual potential, but in and of itself is not a defining attribute of giftedness, either because it is an intrapersonal "catalyst" (Gagné, 2005a) or because it is too malleable, too susceptible to contextual influences (Robinson, 2005; VanTassel-Baska, 2005). However, if intelligence reflects a functional state, then motivation and volition must come into play to facilitate effective (sometimes optimal) cognitive functioning (e.g., attentional and process control; Kuhl, 1985).

More important, if experiential intelligence (or arguably, reflective intelligence) is acquired rather than innate, then high intelligence becomes a function of motivation, anything else being equal. Indeed, this view has gained solid empirical support in the motivation literature in terms of whether one construes one's intelligence as a fixed entity or as incrementally developing (Dweck, 1999). The traditional IQ-based definition grows from a clear distinction between intelligence and personality or affectivity. As Snow (1995) and Lohman and Rocklin (1995) point out, such an artificial boundary between the two categories is set up for the convenience of research and does not reflect how a person functions. Cognitive capacity and processes cannot be dissociated so cleanly from emotion and motivation (see Dai & Sternberg, 2004; Shavinina & Seeratan, 2004). A view of "pure" cognitive capacity would have us believe that cognitive capacity is a fixed quantity; motivation is merely a motor, energizing cognitive activity and releasing cognitive capacity to a certain degree. However, the current state of knowledge suggests that motivation, through its attentional and emotional mechanisms, quantitatively changes cognitive capacity (Hidi, Renninger, & Krapp, 2004) as well as alter cognitive functioning in a qualitative manner (Dweck, Mangels, & Good, 2004).

When situated in ecologically valid contexts, motivation is inevitably involved in highly effective behavior, from skilled memory (Ericsson & Lehmann, 1996) to racetrack gambling (Ceci & Liker, 1986). Some theorists regard affect as a quintessential feature of giftedness, such as in overexcitability (Tieso, 2007). In some domains, affect and motivation may be more important than cognitive abilities, prompting, for example, some scholars to highlight "the rage to master" as the defining quality of artistically gifted children (Winner, 1996).

Granted, motivation is often situationally determined; but if one can relinquish the ability-centric view of giftedness, and reconsider the deeply entrenched notion that giftedness is located in the head, or that it has a unitary essence, then it is not difficult to afford motivation a central role in the making of giftedness. To some extent, integration of motivation into conceptions of giftedness affirms the importance of context in gifted-level attainment.

Creativity

Although creativity is multifaceted, involving person, process, and product (and some may add content and context), in order to be deemed "creative," an idea expressed, an action taken, or a product fashioned should be novel and valuable (or effective) for its purposes within a specific functional context (Simonton, 1999). Various conceptions of giftedness either consider creativity a personal quality enjoyed by some individuals (hence, the creatively gifted; Gagné, 2005a; Torrance, 1972a) or a desired developmental outcome (Renzulli, 1999; Subotnik & Jarvin, 2005). Early conceptions of creativity were deeply influenced by Guilford's (1967) notion of divergent thinking, and Torrance's theory of creativity and the related instrument *Torrance Tests of Creative Thinking* (Torrance, 1966) were often used for identifying the "creatively gifted."

The early distinction between intelligence and creativity with respect to definition and the identification of gifted children (see Getzels & Jackson, 1962) seems to be a mixed blessing. On the one hand, it broke the dominance of the IQ definition of giftedness and highlighted the untenable, narrow view of intelligence tests as the sole measure of human cognitive potential. On the other hand, it perpetuated the notion that creativity involves a unique type of cognitive processing or capacity, qualitatively different from what we use for carrying out intelligent thoughts and actions. Furthermore, creativity is seen, just like early conceptions of intelligence, as a personal trait, and thus can be dissociated from content experience and domain knowledge. Although the person account of creativity (i.e., some people are more creative than others, or even "creatively gifted") may still have currency, and divergent thinking tests show some predictive validity with respect to adult creative accomplishments (e.g., Cramond, Matthews-Morgan, Bandalos, & Zuo, 2005; Torrance, 1972b), it is now widely accepted that real-world creative productivity is a long-term proposition (Csikszentmihalyi, 1996; Feldman, 1994; Simonton, 1997). A process account is needed to fully explicate how creative potential is developed and actualized.

And slowly we are learning more about the developmental processes leading to creative expressions and products. Many factors, other than personal traits, contribute to creativity:

- Truly creative work can be done only after many years of skill development, coupled with a driving engagement to keep learning and growing

(Csikszentmihalyi, 1990; Gruber, 1986), and creative transformation rarely occurs without intimate domain experience and substantial mastery of a domain (Weisberg, 2006);

- High-level creative work often reveals unique styles of functioning such as relying on visual imagery (Miller, 1996), and metaphorical and analogical thinking (Holyoak & Thagard, 1995);

- The creative process involves a critical tension between the known and unknown, the old and the new, a tension that keeps one "at the edge of chaos" (Dai & Renzulli, 2008). It takes some form of organized persistence to navigate the treacherous intellectual terrain in a domain of knowledge, leading to new discovery and theory (Gruber, 1995).

- Envisioning new possibilities in a domain involves some domain-specific intuitions and therefore is at least partly domain specific (Feist, 2004; Weisberg, 1999; see also Sternberg, Grigorenko, & Singer, 2004).

- Creativity often includes chance encounters in the real world or chance connections in the mind, encounters and connections that yield surprisingly unique combinations and permutations of existing elements and novelty, what Simonton (2003) calls a "constrained stochastic process" (p. 475).

- Oftentimes, discovery and invention are not the product of a solo act of an individual mind (the traditional conception), but that of synergistic interaction (Dunbar, 1997), what Sawyer (1999) called the "collaborative emergence" of creativity (p. 450). Cognitive diversity within a collaborative group matters in generating novel and high-quality thoughts (Page, 2008). In that sense, creativity is fundamentally a social process (Moran & John-Steiner, 2003).

These new understandings of the developmental and contextual nature of the creative process are trickling down, slowly but surely, to conceptions of giftedness.

Development

A general developmental view of giftedness (i.e., exceptional competence) is that giftedness results from an interaction between biological predispositions and environmental forces: It emerges through development (Coleman & Cross, 2005; Horowitz, 2000; Keating, 2009). This argument is consistent with the proposition advanced in developmental biology that individual development, or ontogeny, is better characterized as probabilistic epigenesis rather than unidirectional determinism (Gottlieb, 1998).

   Although increasingly the roles of nurture and environment in intelligence, creativity, and giftedness are being acknowledged, developmental process accounts of the epigenesis and development of gifted behaviors or minds are sorely lacking. Longitudinal research on gifted children has mainly been concerned with prediction of long-term outcomes, to ascertain either that gifted children can be identified early or whether certain predicted outcomes can be substantiated so as to validate the predictor measures. At best, predictive studies help identify certain enabling and constraining conditions; developmental processes are simply defaulted, rather than carefully mapped out from an initial state to a more advanced state at the individual level. "For the field of gifted education to fulfill its potential, however," as Feldman (2003) argued, "processes of development in person, domain, and culture will have to move to center stage, organize the conversation, and become the most important criteria for assessment of the strength of talents and gifts" (p. 21).

A key to understanding giftedness is to stop taking various forms of its conception for granted and instead start treating the very notion of "giftedness" as problematic, in the sense that its nature, origins, and ontogeny (individual development) need to be understood and explained in detail. Simonton's (1999, 2005) emergenic-epigenetic model provides a framework for understanding giftedness and talent development as a complex process of combinations of multiple genetic traits finding good fits in a certain talent domain in an epigenetically timely fashion. Feldman's (1994) theory of nonuniversal development provides a framework that is particularly suitable for explaining developmental patterns that occur to only some individuals in some social contexts.

The meaning of the term *development* is also undergoing changes. From an organismic view, development means "unfolding" of an organism from its rudimentary to mature form based on some preexisting developmental timetable; thus, Piaget (1972) called his theory *mental embryology*, specifying how an organized structure becomes increasingly differentiated through a more or less fixed developmental schedule. In this sense, the best metaphor is a seed, with proper soil, air, and temperature, germinating and growing and transforming into a full-blown plant. A talent used to be thought of as just like a seed, a natural potential to be realized. Alternatively, development can be truly an *emergent phenomenon*; that is, many factors, endogenous and exogenous, collectively contribute to the emergence of new forms or properties, and none of them acts as a dominant force (Feldman called it *confluence*; see Feldman, 1986; see Sawyer, 2003, for a discussion of development as emergence). Furthermore, factors leading to the emergence of the same form or properties (e.g., demonstrated high intelligence or talents) do not need to be the same for different individuals (Papierno et al., 2005). General systems theory calls this principle *equifinality* (see Wachs, 2000). This principle is in contrast to the essentialist assumption of an essence underlying an object that always holds its identity, unity, and continuity. Such a new understanding of development provides a good way to understand and reconcile oppositional positions in conceptions of giftedness (e.g., nature versus nurture, normal versus abnormal, domain specific versus domain general). This view of development as emergence will be expounded on in Chapter 9.

Context

The term *context* is used here to refer to a broad array of boundary conditions that constrain how giftedness is expressed. It includes immediate social situations; the nature of the task, domain, and field one encounters; and on a large time scale, zeitgeist, historical periods, and culture. Very few would reject the notion that high-level performances and talent expressions entail some contextual support such as opportunities to learn and required levels of social and technical assistance. However, people have rarely thought of context as a constituent of giftedness until recently (e.g., Barab & Plucker, 2002; Ziegler, 2005).

Task conditions as context. Context as constituent of giftedness means several things. First, *context* refers to the set of conditions residing in the task or domain, not in the person. Thus changing the conditions (e.g., lowering the basket for basketball games) will change the criteria for picking "gifted" basketball players (height may no longer be an advantage and, indeed, may become a handicap) (Lohman, 2005a; Ziegler, 2005). Domain-bound or contextually bound giftedness contrasts sharply with conceptions of generic giftedness (intellectual giftedness, creative giftedness, etc.). The second meaning of context as constituent of giftedness is that affordances and constraints of a task condition shape gifted expressions epigenetically, thus contributing to gifted development (Dai & Renzulli, 2008). For example, when one plays a musical piece, the music in return helps one to construct basic musical perceptions (e.g., tonal systems, rhythmic patterns), aesthetic appreciation, and artistic expression. The third meaning of context as constituent of giftedness concerns performance situations that activate a particular set of knowledge from long-term memory, skills, and dispositions. Thus, Brazilian children peddling goods in the street and engaging in sophisticated, though informal, mathematical thinking are unable to do the same mathematical thinking when the problem is presented in the format of school math (Carraher, Carraher, & Schliemann, 1985). This is an illustration of a "situated" skill set, one that is highly tuned to specific situations.

Changing prerequisites as context. Another kind of context boundedness concerns changes in prerequisites for outstanding achievement. In the 19th century, for example, scientists without superior mathematical ability could make groundbreaking contributions to understanding genetics and evolution. However, to make comparable contributions today, one needs high-level mathematical ability (Siegler & Kotovsky, 1986). Similarly, in order to be a top-notch physicist today, a person needs to master computer simulation skills that were unknown to earlier generations of physicists (Ziegler, 2005).

Sociocultural conditions as context. Social and cultural contexts constitute another important class of context. First, social-structural variations (physical living conditions, opportunity structure, availability of educational resources, etc.) may either facilitate or hinder the development of human potential or gifts and talents in the formative years (Bronfenbrenner & Ceci, 1994). The presence and levels of social capital may either depress or nourish talent development (Putman, Leonard, & Nanetti, 1994). The most recent study of three cultural groups, Asian Americans, Jews, and West Indian Blacks, by Nisbett (2009) shows compelling evidence for the role of culture in stretching the limits of human intellectual potential. Social affordances and collective power may create a "critical mass" that ultimately accounts for some creative accomplishments (Keating, 2009; Sawyer, 1999). Second, variations of cultural norms and regulations may render differential standards of excellence or conceptions of what constitutes high human potential and essential personal qualities such as "giftedness" (Sternberg, 2007a). As most of the skills, talents, and expertise that humans develop are biologically secondary (Geary, 1995), the nurturing of specific forms of talent and creativity is fundamentally an enculturation process, involving developing a specific set of values, attitudes, thinking styles, worldviews, and modi operandi (Zuckerman, 1983), entailing technical support (Ericsson, 2006) and mentorship (Subotnik, 2006) at various junctures of talent development. With access to previously unimaginable technological support and sophisticated training techniques nowadays, a person can develop a caliber of performance in some domains that would otherwise be impossible; thus, some music pieces once deemed too difficult to play except by the most accomplished musicians are now regularly played by students of musical conservatories (Ericsson, 2006). Rapid scientific and technological advances over the past century show that not only has the bar been raised for excellence in most domains, but also there are technical support systems that continually stretch the limits of human potential; the bars are being raised and surpassed even as we are discussing this matter.

Cognitive, Affective, and Developmental Neurosciences

There is a long history of scientific attempts to trace gifted behaviors (i.e., the functional) to exceptional brains (i.e., the structural) (see Gould, 1981; Obler & Fein, 1988). A case in point is the enormous interest in Einstein's brain as if its morphology and anatomy might reveal the secret of his genius (see Diamond et al., 1985). Beyond naive or scientific curiosity, neurobiology and neuropsychology have been used to inform inquiry into biological substrates of exceptional minds, not only for those who hold a strong belief in the genetic or innate basis of gifted qualities, but also for those who believe that giftedness is fundamentally nurtured. Neuroimaging techniques such as fMRI increase the possibility of acquiring insights into the mind-brain and nature-nurture relationships with respect to exceptional competence.

There are at least three areas of gifted psychology to which neuropsychological research has made or can potentially make significant contributions. First, brain research can inform us of possibly unique structural and functional organizations of the brain that give rise to specific forms of talent or superior general intellectual functioning. Geschwind and Galaburda (1987), for example, hypothesized that asymmetry of hemispherical growth or anomalous hemispheric dominance may lead to distinct talents, a phenomenon they called the "pathology of superiority" (p. 65; see also later discussion of research on nature versus nurture). O'Boyle's (2008) more recent work on the mathematically gifted provides new insights about qualitative differences in brain functioning between the mathematically gifted and their average counterparts. For children with "dual exceptionalities" (both gifted and otherwise exceptional, such as possessing attention deficit disorder or a learning disability), neuropsychological evidence can be particularly illuminating. Recent efforts to define and measure giftedness in terms of overexcitability in the tradition of Dabrowski's theory (Tieso, 2007) will find an ally in affective neuroscience (Davidson, 2001; Panksepp, 1998). Indeed it can be argued that the best measure of overexcitability should be some form of physiological measures such as event-related potential (ERP) rather than self-report or self-rating. For example, the P300 amplitude (Stelmack & Houlihan, 1995) could be targeted as an indication of overexcitability to a given set of stimuli relevant to the domain of interest.

Second, brain research has started to map out the neurochemical machanisms of cognitive functions responsible for creative problem solving and discovery or invention. For example, the link between working memory and the cerebellum has been hypothesized to contribute to mathematical intuition and discovery (Vandervert, 2003). Intuition, arguably crucial for understanding giftedness and creativity, has previously appeared impervious to psychological investigation. This is changing as increasingly sophisticated neuroimaging techniques enable observations of the activity of the living brain. By the same token, developmental psychologists have been demonstrating that positive affect has an influence on cognitive flexibility and creativity (Fredrickson, 1998); we can observe this process at work in the brain thanks to neuroimaging techniques that permit the mapping of a dopaminergic pathway linking the level of dopamine to the anterior cingulate gyrus (Ashby, Isen, & Turken, 1999), which is specialized for many higher-order functions, such as error recognition, emotional control, problem solving, and cognitive flexibility (Allman, Hakeem, Erwin, Nimchinsky, & Hof, 2001).

Third, developmental neuroscience can be used to shed light on the nature-nurture issue. For example, using brain-imaging techniques to track longitudinal patterns of children and adolescents' cortical development, Shaw et al. (2006) found that children with high intellectual ability tend to have a prolonged period of thickening of the cortex compared with their age peers, which the authors interpreted as probably resulting from a genetically programmed difference. In contrast, in a highly influential research program, Schlaug (2001; Bangert & Schlaug, 2006) found anatomical differences in the brains of professional musicians compared with those of nonmusicians, which likely reflects brain adaptations caused by long-term musical training and practice (see also Greenough, 1976).

Although the cognitive and affective neurosciences are still in their early stage of development, and the research described here is still a work in progress, interdisciplinary approaches that integrate neuropsychological and behavioral aspects of gifted competence and its development promise to make significant strides, even breakthroughs, in demystifying giftedness (see Kalbfleisch, 2009).

In sum, the current knowledge about intelligence, motivation, creativity, and the role of context and development has significantly broadened the intellectual horizon with respect to the nature and nurture of giftedness. Specifically, the traditional accounts of giftedness that emphasizes "natural," enduring qualities of the person need major revision in light of the preponderance of evidence for the role of contexts and development in the evolution of intelligence, motivation, and creativity. A new synthesis is needed the bridge the traditional and the emergent understandings.

TOWARD A NEW SYNTHESIS

Although the trend toward a more contextual and developmental approach is unmistakably clear, disagreements are far from resolved; this is particularly true when there is a lack of integration between the established and emergent perspectives and models. Coexistence of many competing ideas and conceptions is likely to be a normal state of the field for many years to come. A broadened knowledge base does not mean that the traditional conceptions and theories are all obsolete and should be replaced with new ones. Rather, it means that the old needs to be reinterpreted and repositioned in the totality of our understandings. Thus, what I suggest for the field is not a complete overhaul or radical paradigm shift, but a new synthesis that conserves what is useful in the tradition but recasts it in the light of new understandings. Rather than seeing the old and new as "incommensurable," as Kuhn (1962) suggested about different "paradigms," I argue that it is possible to formulate a metalevel framework of different perspectives on the nature and development of gifted competence, which would give some degree of coherence and commensurability to the seemingly incoherent and incommensurable ideas. In this section, I attempt to provide such an overarching framework under which different ideas and their theoretical validity and practical viability can be compared and assessed.

Holton (1981) argued that science is more than an impersonal, mechanical exercise of hypothetical-deductive logic and inductive reasoning based on empirical evidence. There is a third force other than inductive and deductive logic, a more subjective one: scientists' ontological convictions about certain phenomena and commitments to pursuits along these lines of inquiry, what Holton dubbed *themata*. More formally, themata are thematic dimensions or continuities along which people place their ontological commitment and allegiance in a domain or about a class of phenomena. For example, Holton identified in Einstein's beliefs about the universe a deep commitment to unity, continuity, logical parsimony, necessity, and mathematical certainty (p. 15), which set him on a conflicting course with those thinking along the line of quantum mechanics, such as the probabilistic nature of quantum dynamics, discontinuity in measurement. Similarly, scholarly conceptions of giftedness represent a form of motivated reasoning of various persuasions on epistemic, ethical, political, or pragmatic grounds, constrained by logic and evidence (Kunda, 1990).

Unlike Kuhn (1962), Holton (1981) believed that scientific advances are better characterized as evolutionary rather than revolutionary, continuous rather than discontinuous, as the notion of incommensurability implies. In other words, the Kuhnian notion of a wholesale gestalt change or "paradigm shift" disguises the complexity of the issues involved (see also Toulmin, 1972, p. 128). Instead, Holton (1981) believed that "major scientific advance can be understood in terms of an evolutionary process that involves battles over only a few but by no means all of the recurrent themata" (p. 25). He further suggested that scientific advances may not hinge on consensus building, as Kuhn (1962) argued, but on "an enterprise whose saving pluralism resides in its many internal degrees of freedom" (Holton, 1981, p. 25). By the same token, scholars, researchers, and educators who have an interest in gifted children and gifted education also hold their explicit or implicit beliefs, and these belief systems also form "themata" on key issues and along some central dimensions (Ambrose, 2005).

Natural and Normative Aspects of Giftedness and Gifted Education

Simon (1969/1996) distinguished between two modes of investigation, depending on whether a phenomenon is a natural one (e.g., mechanics or thermodynamics) or involves human-made designs and artifacts (e.g., a bridge or computer), which serve specific human adaptive purposes and goals. Simon called the latter *the sciences of the artificial*. He argued that natural science involves discovering a few simple, objective, universal laws and regularities underlying myriad natural phenomena; the sciences of the artificial, in contrast, are mainly concerned with "how things ought to be" or desirable states (p. 4). In short, the focus of the sciences of the artificial is *optimal design*. To be sure, the sciences of the artificial cannot do without natural science; in order to build a bridge, we need to obey the laws of mechanics, among others; in order to speed up CPU on a computer, we need to study how microphysics works. In other words, the sciences of the artificial are constrained, but not dictated, by natural science.

Education is prominently concerned with "how things ought to be." Goals and curriculum structures of education constitute a distinct normative or value aspect of that human endeavor. The pedagogical tools and other support systems constitute a design or engineering aspect, and a particular group of learners (children) involved in education constitutes a material basis as well as a form of agency. Whether the tools and systems will be effective in achieving the set goals is constrained by the children's abilities and motivations or general readiness for benefiting from the education provision in question.

Enter giftedness. How much of its manifestation and development is a "natural" phenomenon, how much of it involves nurture or the "artificial" (goals and values, and purposive acts, along with tools and systems, including parenting), and how much of it involves interaction and optimal match between the natural and the artificial? The traditional domains in which we identify the "gifted," such as academics and the arts, all belong to the artificial, as they are human-made cultural systems with their symbols and meanings markedly human rather than "natural"; competencies in these domains are biologically secondary (Geary, 1995). Of course, you may quickly point out that while these systems are "artificial," the ease of assimilating them has something to do with "the natural": the person as a biological being. Therefore, some people argue that giftedness is fundamentally an enduring personal quality. Some further point out that individual difference constructs, such as intelligence, talent, motivation, multiple exceptionalities, and creativity, have their biological substrates. Except for radical environmentalists, most people would acknowledge some degree of constraints imposed by nature (biologically based differences) regarding how fast and how far one can go in a specific line of talent development. This is the "nature" side of the story. However, from day one, when parents ask their child to sit on the piano bench to start a piano lesson or teach the child how to move a knight on the chessboard, he or she is engaged in a designed, goal-directed activity, one that is structured in a way that facilitates learning and growth. Thus, talented piano or chess performance implicates *cultural designs*. The very notion of "giftedness" is constructed to highlight the cultural significance and importance of some aspects of exceptional competence, in children and adults alike. There is no escaping the dual nature of the field of gifted studies.

Triumphs and Perils of Multiple Conceptions of Giftedness

It is, therefore, no wonder that we have had a proliferation of ideas and models of giftedness in the field. Regarding the nature and nurture of giftedness, there are scholars who have a strong belief that giftedness is by and large a neurobiological advantage vis-à-vis specific or general functional and developmental contexts (e.g., Gagné, 2004; Geake, 2009). There are others who remain agnostic in terms of biological origins of giftedness (e.g., Renzulli, 1999) and still others who view gifted competence as fundamentally an evolving process (e.g., Feldhusen, 1992; Feldman, 2003; Subotnik & Jarvin, 2005) or achieved state (e.g., Barab & Plucker, 2002; Ericsson et al., 2007a; Mayer, 2005). There are good reasons for such epistemic diversity or pluralism. For one, gifted manifestations are diverse, and their etiologies and ontogenies are likely diverse as well. Therefore, diverse, sometimes competing, belief systems may serve their respective phenomena, targeted individuals and groups, and relevant stakeholders well and thus complement each other (in this sense, a truly "saving pluralism" at a epistemic or pragmatic level).

However, the downsides of having many rival ideas and advocates are also obvious. We can easily get tangled up with ideological battles, and specific contexts that make a particular theory relevant can get lost. A more productive strategy is to turn ideological differences into more nuanced, tractable scholarly exchanges, which potentially lead to some degree of consensus and agreement. Although leaving "many internal degrees of freedom" (i.e., allowing the coexistence of different ideas and not treating them as definitive; Holton, 1981, p. 25) may still be useful for a field that is still mapping its territory and developing its identity, it seems important to walk a fine line between hasty consensus seeking, on the one hand, and the anarchy of proliferations and conflations of ideas and models, on the other. One way of doing this is to identify a set of themata or central issues regarding (a) *ontological issues*: how we conceptualize the nature of giftedness; (b) *epistemological issues*: how we empirically assess and investigate related phenomena and ground our knowledge of claims; and (c) *normative issues*: how we should cultivate human exceptional competence.

A FRAMEWORK OF ESSENTIAL TENSIONS

In the following section, I sketch a conceptual framework of the key themata. As one shall see, some of them are epistemic issues, and others concern values and purposes. I suggest that these themata constitute essential tensions revolving around the concept of giftedness and that finding proper solutions or at least easing these tensions would help us achieve some degree of synthesis and move the field forward (see Table 2.1).

Ontological Tensions

Ontology, as a branch of philosophy, is concerned with the nature and kinds of existence or reality (structures, properties, relations, etc.). Ontological commitments or convictions are researchers' deeply held beliefs about the nature of the phenomenon under investigation and the internal workings of objects involved (Lakatos, 1978). They consist of tacit and articulated theoretical assumptions and principles, which guide research hypotheses and questions and help determine where they can expect the best payoffs if they place their "bets" (committing their energy and resources in a particular research direction and designing a particular study). Einstein's belief that there is a fundamental unity in scientific laws is an ontological conviction. Spearman's (1904) belief that there is a g factor is an ontological conviction (the covariance found in the factor analysis of measures of multiple tasks is by no means self-evident for the existence of a general intelligence). Gagné's (1999b) belief that giftedness precedes talent development is an

Figure 2.1. Major tensions and themes in gifted studies.

ONTOLOGICAL TENSIONS		

Being	Versus	Doing/Becoming
Giftedness is possessed; giftedness is biologically constitutional, an enduring personal quality that ultimately explains gifted behavior and outstanding achievement over time.		Giftedness is achieved; giftedness is an emergent property and functional state of person-environment transaction and interaction, and a result of learning, practice, and social and technical support, subject to further development and change.
Domain-General	**Versus**	**Domain-Specific**
Giftedness is not inherently confined to any single domain, because general cognitive abilities can be flexibly channeled and utilized in multiple ways, depending on environmental circumstances and motivations.		Giftedness is domain specific, because each domain has its own unique set of demands in terms of sensitivities, inclinations, and abilities, which are tuned to a particular set of objects, symbolic meanings, and underlying relationships.
Qualitative	**Versus**	**Quantitative Differences**
Gifted individuals are different from their average peers *in kind*, because the structural and functional organization of their minds is different, and their developmental trajectories are unique.		Gifted individuals differ from their average peers only *in degree*, because they only show relative strengths and advantages rather than absolute ones.

EPISTEMOLOGICAL TENSIONS		

Aptitude Test	Versus	Authentic Achievement
Potential for excellence (i.e., giftedness) is best evidenced in performance conditions that can differentiate high potential (aptitude) from high achievement.		We will never know whether a person is "gifted" or holds unusual "potential" unless the person demonstrates superior mastery of skills and knowledge in an authentic domain or functional context.
Nomothetic	**Versus**	**Idiographic**
Manifestations of gifted behaviors are subject to a set of hidden but universally valid laws and principles; therefore, we can determine who are gifted and how the gifted develop by applying these universal rules and principles.		Manifestations of gifted behaviors are diverse and unique phenomena and have their own underlying logic, not subject to predetermined universal principles; therefore, the uniqueness of each manifestation needs to be closely examined in order to shed light on its nature.
Reductionism	**Versus**	**Emergentism**
The complexity of gifted manifestations can be explained by simpler components at a more basic level of analysis; higher-level phenomena can be causally reduced to lower-level components, structures, and processes.		The complexity of gifted manifestations reflects higher-order organizational principles in the organism and functional regularities that are context dependent, and there are emergent properties that cannot be reduced to isolated lower-level components.

(*continued*)

Figure 2.1. (*continued*)

NORMATIVE TENSIONS		
Expertise	**Versus**	**Creativity**
High-level expertise (proficiency) in a given domain should be the hallmark of giftedness and goal of gifted education, because only this form of excellence can be scientifically verified and educationally promoted.		Creative productivity (innovation) should be the hallmark of giftedness and the goal of gifted education, because giftedness is not about mastery of the already known, but about exploring, discovering, and inventing the unknown.
Gifted Child	**Versus**	**Talent Development**
Gifted children should be the center of our focus and the sole rationale for the existence of gifted education; their special educational needs and unique patterns of personal growth should be the driving force in educational programming and intervention.		The evolving process of talent development should be the central focus of gifted education; gifted education should provide maximal opportunity for those who show manifest or emergent talents and are interested in developing their talents to the fullest of their capacities.
Excellence	**Versus**	**Equity**
Identifying and cultivating high potential for excellence is a society's responsibility for the welfare of individuals as well as for society at large. Developing excellence reflects a cultural value that is important for a viable democracy and advances in human civilization.		Singling out the alleged "gifted" for special treatment and privileged access to opportunity to pursue excellence perpetuates existing social inequality and creates a new social "elite," thus violating the democratic principle of equal rights and opportunity.

ontological conviction. To a great extent, ontological commitments also compel researchers to choose particular methodologies amenable to testing related hypotheses. There are three major ontological tensions regarding exceptional competence, each branching out to several specific questions.

The nature-nurture tension. Can superior performance in various domains ultimately be traced to natural endowment, that is, individual differences in genetic and biological-constutitional makeup? To what extent can it be explained by experience, effort, specific types of practice, and contextual support, including instruction and mentoring? How do nature and nurture interact in contributing to the emergence of intelligent behavior, motivation, domain expertise, and creativity and possibly ultimate eminent achievements? As it currently stands, *the tension is between two groups of scholars who hold competing ontological commitments: either defining giftedness as an enduring personal quality or defining giftedness as a functional state, situated in particular sociocultural and developmental contexts.*

The nature-nurture tension is the most fundamental of all ontological tensions revolving around the issue of giftedness. The task of explaining (not merely describing) "gifted" manifestations, whether biased toward "nature" or "nurture," amounts to specifying mediating mechanisms and processes in the influx of a multitude of enabling and constraining forces, both endogenous and exogenous. The nature-nurture tension arises mainly because different researchers place their "bets" differently in mapping the complex structure-function, person-process-context, and functioning-development relationships responsible for the emergence of exceptional competence or giftedness, some stressing the power of natural endowment, and related cognitive and learning mechanisms, and others emphasizing the role of environmental experiences, extended intentional learning, and social and technical support.

The domain specificity versus domain generality tension. As there is no such thing as domain-free achievement, the focus of this tension is (a) to what extent an individual's potential is omnipotent in terms of its capability of learning different things and adapting to a wide range of functional niches with equal facility, and (b) to what extent giftedness is sensitive to a particular class of stimuli, and specific to a particular niche or class of activities, and if so, (c) to what extent cognitive structures and mechanisms attuned to a given domain are preordained or canalized in its development. In other words, *should gifted behaviors be seen as a fundamentally domain-specific or domain-general phenomenon?*

This question can also be broken down to domain generality/specificity of intelligence (human abilities), motivation (inclinations for a particular class of stimuli and activities), and creativity (insights and intuitions), respectively. Casting this question in the framework of the nature-nurture question, we may ask, To what extent does the individual's biological environment, through its brain mechanisms, selectively attend to, choose, and organize environmental features in forming a unique developmental trajectory (a domain-specific view); and to what extent does the biology of brain organization show versatility, through its neural plasticity and cognitive flexibility, in response to environmental opportunities and challenges (a domain-general view)?

The quantitative versus qualitative differences tension. This tension focuses on the following question: Are those who have demonstrated gifted-caliber competence or achievement fundamentally different from the rest of the population in terms of how they perceive, feel, think, learn, and develop and consequently in terms of their educational needs? In what sense and to what extent does gifted development constitute an *exceptional* condition, a condition that warrants special attention, treatments, and interventions?

From a person-centered (i.e., the gifted child) perspective on giftedness, *does exceptional competence reflect some structural and functional organization of the mind that is different in kind rather than in degree compared with others?*

From a domain-centered (i.e., talent development) perspective on giftedness, *does the development of exceptional competence in a domain inherently involve qualitatively different (and sometimes unique) pathways and trajectories, or is it just a little sooner, a little faster?* The question is also related to the domain-specificity issue. If gifted potential is highly sensitive to domains, then the gifted person is likely to show unique organization of cognitive and affective structures and functions, and unique developmental trajectories and pathways, qualitatively different from "normal" people. Conversely, the effects of gifted potential, if highly domain general, would be quite pervasive across a range of contents and performance conditions, but would not be as dramatic for any single domain, as effects of domain-specific structures and mechanisms would. Taken together, the three ontological issues have deep implications about how gifted children should be understood and identified and how gifted education should be conducted to cultivate high potential.

Epistemological Tensions

Epistemology concerns the validity of ontological or knowledge claims and the cognitive foundation of knowing. That is, in what way can one verify and ascertain the truthfulness of particular claim? Strategically speaking, what are the best ways to assess and study specific phenomena that would yield valid and verifiable knowledge? Regarding human exceptional competence and unusual promise, there are three prominent questions:

1. What constitutes best evidence for "gifted" competence or potential (i.e., how to recognize it)?
2. How do we come to assess and study individuals who have demonstrated exceptionally high competence or are apparently in the process of developing exceptional competence and domain excellence (i.e., how to approach relevant phenomena)? And
3. How do we identify causal factors and mediating mechanisms leading to exceptional competence and domain excellence (i.e., how to explain and predict it)?

The following three tensions correspond to these three questions, respectively. As we shall see, ontological beliefs influence epistemological stances. For example, the beliefs that we can eventually pinpoint specific genes or neuroanatomical structures for exceptional competence lead researchers to adopt a more analytic, reductionistic research approach. Conversely, specific methodological tools and infrastructures subserving epistemological stances can also drive research toward certain ontological conclusions. Thus, the method of case studies used by Feldman (1986) led him to develop a confluence, or coincidence, model of the development of child prodigies.

The aptitude test versus authentic achievement tension. Scholars in the field differ on whether giftedness can be better determined through testing of aptitude or putative "potential," or actual excellent and exceptional achievement and performance in an authentic context by age-appropriate standards. It reveals a tension regarding how giftedness is technically defined; how it manifests itself; and how we go about determining its presence, nature, and degree.

The issue at hand is which measures or assessments best meet the criteria of rarity, demonstrability, productivity (Sternberg, 1995), authenticity, and reproducibility (Ericsson et al., 2005, 2007a), among others. For aptitude tests, the question is how well they can predict developmental and educational outcomes and whether they are warranted as measures of "learning potential." For authentic performance or achievement, the challenge is to separate what has been achieved (outcome) and how it is achieved (process).

The nomothetic versus idiographic tension. The aptitude versus authentic performance tension partly reflects a tension regarding how we approach and study exceptional competence. As a general mode of investigation, nomothetic and idiographic approaches represent two different ways of "carving the nature at its joints." Nomothetic approaches make general assumptions about how the world functions and derive deductive consequences of "natural laws" or universal principles for a given population. In contrast, idiographic approaches use an inductive approach, identifying unique patterns, configurations, and regularities based on intimate observation of a set of particular cases and instances (Allport, 1937). Consequently, nomothetic approaches are variable based, focusing on a few relevant parameters of interest at a time, whereas idiographic approaches are person centered, looking at how the person functions and grows within a specific contextual and temporal frame. For nomothetic methods, decontextualization is necessary for generalization. For idiographic methods, contextualization is necessary for a nuanced understanding of individuality and functional contexts. Physics is a classic example of the nomothetic approach, with controlled experimentation as its canonical research paradigm, and anthropology is a classic example of the idiographic approach, with ethnography as its main research paradigm.

Applying this to the issue of giftedness, people with a nomothetic perspective make universal assumptions about what giftedness is and what attributes define giftedness. In comparison, people with an idiographic perspective see giftedness as involving unique individual functioning and development, thus not easily fitting into any general differential or developmental theories.

The reductionism versus emergentism tension. If the nomothetic-idiographic tension concerns whether one starts with universals or particulars, and how uniqueness can be preserved in search of generality, the reductionism-emergentism tension concerns what levels of analysis and explanation are appropriate given a behavioral and psychological phenomenon, and whether a reduction is appropriate in the midst of complex higher-level dynamics and organization of many interacting elements.

A general question in the field of giftedness research is whether manifestations of gifts and talents or outstanding eminent achievement can be explained using the conventional analytic methods by breaking them down to simpler components or whether there is higher-level organizational complexity that is better explained by an emergent, evolving process that cannot be reduced to lower-level components, and higher-order organizational principles that reflect a new level of organized complexity.

Normative Tensions

The term *normative* here implies "norms" and "standards" and "values" that guide human practice, indicating "what ought to be" (i.e., prescriptive) rather than "what is" (descriptive). No scientific evidence, however compelling, can dictate what gifted education should look like, just as physicists are not in a position to instruct bridge engineers what a bridge should look like. Purposes of gifted education, or whether we should have a provision of gifted education at all, are negotiated within a community by its stakeholders for the sake of its well-being, individually as well as collectively. However, any debates about purposes and designs of educational provision should be constrained by our scientific knowledge (including knowledge of the effects of various human-made artifacts, such as educational and instructional designs). One of the purposes of discussing these normative issues is to clarify where our understandings of the nature and nurture of exceptional competence should inform and guide evidence-based, theoretically sound practice and where science stops and social and ethical principles start to rule. In the proposed framework, the following three normative tensions are identified, based on (1) the expertise versus creativity tension: whether gifted education should be more ambitious, aiming at creativity, or more modest, focusing on proficiency; (2) the gifted child versus talent development tension: whether gifted education should be focused on the well-being and personal growth of the child or on long-term talent development; and (3) the excellence versus equity tension: whether gifted education undermines the value of *equity* while serving the goal of *excellence*.

The expertise versus creativity tension. Mature "gifted" accomplishments belong to two broad categories: expertise and creativity. To use Gardner's (1997) words, people in the "expertise" category are *masters* who have perfected their respective trades to an extremely high level (Ericsson, 2006), and people in the creativity category are *makers*, who have significantly transformed an intellectual or practical domain or artistic ways of expression and moved a field forward, or even created a new field (Sternberg, 1999b). Accordingly, designs for outstanding accomplishments can have a more ambitious scope (creativity) or more modest goal (expertise or proficiency). A tension exists between gifted-education practitioners who are aiming at developing high-level expertise and talent, and those at creative productivity. A major issue is to what extent they entail two differing kinds of personality, differing developmental trajectories and pathways, and two different sets of parameters. Alternatively, as some researchers argue, high levels of expertise and creative productivity entail similar developmental processes and pathways.

The "gifted child" versus talent development tension. As I alluded to in Chapter 1, the impetus toward talent development has an underlying social imperative; that is, serving a broader range of students who, through diverse pathways, have demonstrated their potential along specific lines of talent development. However, from an educational point of view, practitioners differ on whether gifted education should have a focus on the person (or the whole child) or the talent(s) children demonstrate, whether the focus should be on how to address their "social-emotional needs" or on how to develop their talent(s).

The issue depends on whether we take a categorical approach (i.e., understanding "the gifted child" as qualitatively different from the rest of the population) or whether we take a domain-specific approach (i.e., a child can be gifted in history but not gifted in mathematics, or a child can be academically "gifted" but not otherwise different from his or her peers).

The talent development movement puts more wagers on designing optimal conditions for a particular line of talent development, using the professional standards in a given domain for judging the progress and merits. In contrast, the "gifted child" movement places more wagers on assumptions of uniqueness in the psychological development of gifted children and their educational needs.

The excellent versus equity tension. Conceptually, promoting and rewarding excellence does not necessarily impede social equity in terms of equal access to opportunities and resources for achieving excellence. However, when equal access to resources and opportunity is hindered, excellence can often be achieved at the cost of equity. This tension, compared with the previous two normative tensions, has least to do with scientific evidence and most to do with social conditions and value systems (conflict of values). At the level of public policy, there is always the issue of how to balance the need for excellence, on the one hand, and equity, diversity, efficiency, and choice, on the other.

In Chapters 3–8 I will review and elaborate on these tensions in depth. As we shall see, untangling these different issues is important for clarifying many debates in the field. Within and across the ontological, epistemological, and normative dimensions, each tension has implications for others. One of the purposes of my review is to show that out of the seeming chaos of a dazzling array of ideas, there is order. Sorting through these tensions will clarify, if not resolve, major differences regarding what we know about the nature and nurture of giftedness and excellence (ontological issues), how we come to know it (epistemological issues), and where we are going in educational policy and practice (normative issues).

From Nature or Nurture to Nature in Nurture

Some are born great, some achieve greatness, and some have greatness thrust upon 'em.

—William Shakespeare, *Twelfth Night*

By natural ability, I mean those qualities of intellect and disposition, which urge and qualify a man to perform acts that lead to reputation. I do not mean capacity without zeal, nor zeal without capacity, nor even a combination of both of them, without an adequate power of doing a great deal of very laborious work.

—Francis Galton, *Hereditary Genius*

THE TERMS *nature* and *nurture* both mean a variety of things. The line between the two is not always clear cut. Galton (1874) defined "nature and nurture" succinctly: "Nature is all that a man brings with himself into the world; nurture is every influence from without that affects him after his birth" (p. 12). Technically, of course, what counts as nature versus nurture is more complex and nuanced; a fetus could be exposed to a variety of external influences through the child-bearer, some nutritious, comforting, and healthy and others toxic, agitating, and developmentally damaging. Any alleged "natural" human abilities, barring some reflexlike responses, are always mediated to some extent through nurture (Dai & Coleman, 2005). But suffice it for this discussion to start with such a simple definition. We can roughly see the nature-nurture issue as boiling down to the relative importance of *being* versus *doing/becoming* (Delisle, 2003; Subotnik, 2003).

Historically, how a very few individuals were able to achieve marvelous feats in the arts and sciences has long been explained as a matter of *being* rather than *doing/becoming*; Namely, these individuals possessed some unique traits that allow them to excel in their respective endeavors. However, skeptics of this view often quickly see the "doing/becoming" side of the story. A case in point was a friendly altercation back in the 19th century between Charles Darwin and his cousin Francis Galton regarding the nature of greatness and excellence. In a letter to Galton, Darwin conveyed his "nurture" beliefs that "excepting fools, men did not differ much in intellect, only in zeal and hard work." Galton rebutted with a note saying that "character, including aptitude for hard work, is heritable like every other faculty" (quoted in Gould, 1981, p. 77).

The modern form of this debate manifests itself in several ways. As in other fields of psychology, scholars of giftedness have tended to be polarized regarding the nature-nurture or being-doing issue. Some people believe that the ultimate an-swer to the mystery of exceptional competence lies in brain structures and native biological differences (Gagné, 2005a; Geake, 2008; O'Boyle, 2008), and there are also staunch champions of gifted development as a personal enterprise, involv-ing purposeful endeavor for a prolonged period of time (Ericsson, 1996; Erics-son, Charness, Feltovich, & Hoffman, 2006; Gruber, 1986). Within the circle of gifted education, it is the issue of stressing the unique traits of gifted children or their unique developmental trajectories (Delisle, 2003; Robinson, Zigler, & Gal-lagher, 2000) versus emphasizing a child's active engagement and achievement in specific lines of talent development as a sine quo non of giftedness (Coleman & Cross, 2005; Subotnik, 2003). In its most radical form, the nature-nurture ten-sion regarding giftedness can be represented as a thesis (argument) and antithesis (counterargument) as follows:

Thesis:
Giftedness is possessed; giftedness is biologically constitutional, an endur-ing personal quality that ultimately explains gifted behavior and outstand-ing achievement over time.

Antithesis:
Giftedness is achieved; giftedness is an emergent property and functional state of person-environment transaction and interaction and a result of learning, practice, and social and technical support, subject to further devel-opment and change.

The policy and practical implications of the nature-nurture debate are pro-found. For example, whether there should be separate gifted programs for gifted children very much depends on how we understand the relative importance of "being" versus "doing/becoming." In the following section, I first lay out a frame-work of what constitutes strong and weak supporting evidence for either the nature or the nurture argument and evaluate specific claims against existing evidence. I then discuss methodological biases that create research findings in support of nature or nurture arguments and suggest that there may be multiple pathways to excellence. Instead of drawing definitive conclusions about whether nature or nurture prevails, I propose a systems perspective that emphasizes the interactive nature of nature and nurture in the developmental processes.

FRAMING THE NATURE-NURTURE DEBATE

To set the stage for discussing the nature-nurture debate on exceptional compe-tence, it is useful to review intelligence theories, as these have long been the foun-dation upon which giftedness is defined, since Terman (1925). Perkins (1995) identified three broad classes of theories of intelligence: neural, experiential, and reflective (see Chapter 2, the "Intelligence" section, for definitions). While neural intelligence represents a distinct contribution of "nature," the other two, experiential and reflective intelligences, more or less involve "nurture," including formal instruction, training, and mentoring, as well as personal efforts to monitor and guide one's own thinking. Therefore, when giftedness is concerned, the issue is not whether "nurture" (or doing) plays a role in developing exceptional competence, but whether "nature" is a critical (sometimes indispensible) factor in facilitating the development of exceptional competence.

The nature argument of exceptional competence hinges on three main hypotheses and related evidence: (1) *biological-constitutional* (*including genetic*) *differences in mental structures or functions* (*person measures*), (2) *a rapid rate of learning* (*process measures*), and (3) *exceptional asymptotic performance* (*outcome measures after a given period of learning and training*). The logic works like this: If we can show that two persons start at different baselines, develop at different rates, and end up at different places, we can infer through the observed correlations that baseline differences potentially account for process and outcome differences, *everything else being equal*. This is an assumption underlying most placement/prediction models of giftedness research (e.g., Lubinski & Benbow, 2006).

The nurture argument takes two forms: either to provide *negative* evidence (null findings) that the three "nature hypotheses" do not hold, or to provide *positive* evidence that nurture (learning, practice, technical and social support, etc.) changes constitutional differences and rate of learning and is ultimately responsible for high-level performance or achievement. This might be called a classic form of the nurture-nurture debate. There is also a more contemporary form of the debate, namely, whether giftedness should be regarded as residing in the head or mind after all and whether exceptional performance is fundamentally "situated" in specific functional contexts, "distributed" across the person in question, the task at hand, and the tools and resources (broadly defined) available (Barab & Plucker, 2002; Plucker & Barab, 2005). The argument that exceptional competence is "situated" in a context undermines the notion that a person can be "gifted" regardless of specific performance "niches" and social-cultural contexts. In the following section, I will focus on the classic form of the debate and then briefly discuss the challenge from a "situative" perspective.

The Nature Argument I: Giftedness as a Biologically Constitutional Advantage

Since Galton (1869) launched the first study of the genetic basis of genius and claimed that "nature prevails enormously over nurture" (1883, p. 241), behavioral genetics research has developed more sophisticated designs and procedures that help tease apart different kinds of genetic and environmental contributions to variations in behavioral and psychological traits. In addition, neuropsychological and behavioral research provides corroborating evidence. At least three types of evidence have been used to support the argument that natural endowment is a basic determinant of exceptional competence: a genetic basis of human exceptionality; neuroanatomical and neurochemical substrates of exceptional cognition and learning; and clinical, anecdotal evidence of exceptionalities involving superior competence.

Evidence of Genetically Based Biological Differences. The argument that early manifestation of exceptional competence or later outstanding achievement involves natural endowment has been closely associated with behavioral genetics, particularly with respect to the *heritability* of intelligence or general cognitive ability, psychometrically defined and measured (Plomin, 1997). The basic technique of this approach is to use various twin designs (identical twins versus fraternal twins or siblings, identical twins reared apart, etc.) to tease apart variances of a given behavioral and psychological trait that can be accounted for by genetic differences versus by environmental factors (Plomin, DeFries, Craig, & McGuffin, 2003; Scarr, 1997). More recently, efforts have also been made to map out specific genes that might be responsible for major psychological traits. There are several findings that support a distinct genetic basis for intellectual and academic competence: (a) Genetic differences explain at least half the variation in cognitive ability measures; (b) heritability estimates (an index of the proportion of variance on a trait explainable by genetic factors) for intelligence are larger in adolescence and adulthood than in childhood, suggesting a pervasive genetic influence throughout life span (Plomin & Spinath, 2004); and (c) many factors traditionally considered environmental influences (e.g., some features of home environment, the type of friends a person has) have been found to have a genetic component; that is, through passive, evocative, and active correlations, individuals with specific genetic dispositions are likely to be selected in, or actively select, certain environments (Scarr, 1992; cf. Dickens & Flynn, 2001). If variations in different human competences have been found to have a distinct genetic component, it is not difficult to extrapolate that, at the two extremes of the human ability spectrum, genetic contributions are likely to carry more weight. Here is the logic: If the environments are "normalized" for most individuals (except for cases of physical and mental deprivation, social barriers for specific social groups, and cultural impoverishment during a specific historical period), cases of exceptional talent intelligence or severe mental retardation likely reflect individual variations (i.e., enduring individual differences) rather than environmental variations. Of course, the conclusion will not hold when unequal access to resources and opportunities is prevalent within a population.

Although the behavioral genetic evidence seems compelling, some qualifications are in order. First, the behavioral genetic research is completely "decontextualized." For example, whether heritability of a trait is evenly distributed in a population is an open question. A recent study looked at variations in socio-economic status (SES) as a moderator of the heritability of IQ (Turkheimer et al., 2003). For the upper-SES group, they found that the variation in IQ can be explained mainly by genetic differences. However, for the low-SES group, almost all variation in IQ can be attributed to environmental differences; the heritability estimate for the latter group was in fact zero. It is uncertain, of course, whether SES itself contains a genetic component (thus, using SES as a moderator might have inadvertently discounted genetic contributions), and whether dividing groups according to SES created truncated distributions of IQ. Nevertheless, the finding suggests that the variation in IQ scores on the lower end of SES may have different etiologies from score variations at the higher end of SES and implicate a distinct effect of environmental compensation (e.g., parental and social interventions despite low SES). Conversely, there are theoretical grounds for the prediction that when environmental support and educational resources become abundant, it would augment, rather than reduce, heritability estimates for the observed variation in intellectual competences (see Bronfenbrenner & Ceci, 1994; Ceci & Papierno, 2005; Gustafsson & Undheim, 1996).

Second, behavioral genetics studies provide circumstantial, but not direct, evidence for a genetic basis for superior performance. For example, Ericsson et al. (2007b) pointed out that no twin studies have included a sufficient number of high-performing twins represented in the samples to permit an estimate of genetic contributions to exceptional competence. Also, attempts to locate a specific group of genes responsible for above-average general cognitive ability have not yielded convergent supporting evidence (Hill et al., 1999; Petrill et al., 1997; Plomin et al., 2001).

Third, data generated from behavioral genetics research are "crude" estimates of effects based on technical partition of variance. Indeed, the method can be criticized as artificially separating the genetic and environmental contributions in terms of percentages of variance as if genes and environments could act independently of each other (Horowitz, 2000). Fourth, findings of the behavioral genetic research merely allude to potential sources of performance or behavioral variation; no mechanisms and processes are elucidated. Analogous situations can be found in medical research, wherein an illness (e.g., a specific type of cancer) has been found to have a genetic influence, but the what, when, how, and why of the alleged genetic influence are largely unknown.

Neuroanatomical evidence. A second line of research supporting a biological basis for exceptional competence taps into structural and functional organization of the "gifted brains." Domain-general approaches search for structural differences in some identified gifted individuals' brains for clues to some broadly defined functional advantages, such as intelligence and creative thinking. Geake (2008), for example, defined creative intelligence as the capability for fluid analogizing and found a correlation of .89 between a neurophysiological (fMRI) measure of fluid analogizing and paper-and-pencil IQ measures. By the same token, Haier and Jung (2008) reported a series of studies attempting to map structural and functional aspects of the brain responsible for superior performance on intelligence tests such as Raven's Advanced Progressive Matrices. Their findings suggest that "smart brains" are smart not because they work harder but because they work more efficiently (e.g., activating fewer brain areas; hence the *neural efficiency hypothesis*). Other studies compared identified gifted and unidentified children under neutral (i.e., baseline) and varied task conditions (Jaušovec, 1997; Jin, Kim, Park, & Lee, 2007; Jin, Kwon, Jeong, Kwon, & Shin, 2006; Liu, Shi, Zhao, & Yang, 2008; Zhang, Shi, Luo, Zhao, & Yang, 2006) and found measurable differences on EEG and event-related potential (ERP) measures, though patterns of data are not as consistent, probably because of different tasks involved, procedures used, and small sample sizes that introduced sample characteristics and random errors (see Geake, 2008, for a review). Research on handedness (e.g., Casey, Winner, Benbow, Hayes, et al., 1993) has also achieved some success in mapping out structural differences in brain morphology that potentially explain functional differences for some of the intellectually gifted. However, Piro (1998) found no significant difference in the prevalence of left-handedness between a group of gifted children (ages 8–14) and their average counterparts.

It is too early to tell whether the observed neural correlates of high functioning indicate a neural causation. For example, we might infer that a structural preference for right hemispheric activation leads to functional advantages in information processing and problem solving. However, explaining the correlation the other way around is also plausible, for example, a learned behavioral preference for visual imaging and analogical thinking can lead to specific patterns of neural activation. Nevertheless, evidence from developmental neuroscience seems to suggest that there are neuroanatomical differences between the intellectually gifted and average individuals, which potentially explain some of their performance differences. A recent study (Shaw et al., 2006), for example, shows that, compared with their average counterparts, individuals with "superior intelligence" (with an IQ range of 121–149) had prolonged cortical development, with cortical thickening peaking at much later ages (11 years of age, as compared to 6 years of age for "normals"), and that this extended brain development was correlated positively with a measure of intelligence. Shaw et al. interpreted this prolonged cortical thickening as indicating a unique maturation process that was probably genetically controlled. However, Passingham (2006) called for caution about this explanation and suggests that the "superior intelligence" group may have experienced more enriched environments, which might also account for the prolonged brain changes. Without further evidence, it is reasonable to hold a tentative view that developmental trajectories of the intellectually gifted may be genetically influenced, if not determined.

Search for neuroanatomical evidence also takes alternative paths to investigating more narrowly defined abilities and talents. Perfect pitch (the ability to name or sing a pitch on an absolute scale without training) is a most researched phenomenon. Individuals who demonstrate perfect pitch have shown a stronger structural asymmetry in the brain than nonmusicians or musicians without perfect pitch (Schlaug, Janke, Huang, & Seinmetz, 1995). Musically gifted children also show physiological differences in perception of emotion in speech (Dmitrieva, Gel'man, Zaitseva, & Orlov, 2006). There is a longitudinal study under way, trying to mapping out early biological markers of musical talent (Norton et al., 2005). The search for a neuroanatomical basis of a specific talent operates under the assumption that a certain structural and functional organization of the brain makes the person more responsive to specific types of environmental stimulation or better equipped to process specific classes of information. For example, a developmental advantage in enhanced right-hemispheric function has been found to undergird the mathematically gifted, enabling and predisposing them to use visualspatial mode of processing (O'Boyle, 2008). Although it is uncertain whether all mathematically gifted children fit this characterization (e.g., Threlfall & Hargreaves, 2008), it helps to establish a well-reasoned structure-function link, necessary for a "natural talent" account of exceptional mathematical competence. It should be noted that neuroscientific studies of giftedness and talent are preliminary in nature and more research is needed to verify the findings and refine the theoretical predictions. (For an introduction of neuroimaging techniques in research, see Kalbfleisch, 2008.)

Clinical and anecdotal evidence. A third source of evidence comes from case studies in natural or clinical settings. Various forms of precocious development provide evidence for a biological-constitutional basis for general or domain-specific advantages in specific lines of talent development. The domains of music, arts, chess, and mathematics provide the most distinct cases of child prodigies (Feldman, 1986), presumably because these domains have visual-spatial and "formal" features amenable to the intuitive grasp of some talented young children and do not rely as much on social and school experiences for building their respective cognitive/affective infrastructures and knowledge bases. Some clinical cases of disorders also provide windows of opportunity through which a genetic or neural-biological basis of some talents can be subjected to investigation. For example, there are many cases of individuals with dyslexia showing a consistent pattern of deficiencies in linguistic functioning and augmented nonverbal performance (e.g., visual-spatial memory and nonverbal intelligence; see Winner, 1997). There is evidence that dyslexia is highly heritable and its brain morphology shows distinct structural and functional properties (see Vellutino, Fletcher, Snowling, & Scanlon, 2004). In the same vein, some scholars (e.g., West, 1991) reasoned that Einstein's delayed language development and the superior ability for spatial imagery were intrinsically related and contributed to his creative imagination (see also Miller, 1996). It is not unusual that certain abnormal development is associated with superior abilities, so much so that Gershwind and Galaburda (1987) named this phenomenon "the pathology of superiority" and speculated that "minor malformations may often be associated, not with abnormal function, but with distinctly superior capacities in certain areas" (p. 65).

The Nature Argument II: Ease of Learning and Asymptotic Competence as Hallmarks of Giftedness

In response to Ericsson's (1996) challenge to the "natural talent" explanation of high-level expertise, Shiffrin (1996) suggested two criteria for determining whether expertise was the result of extended deliberate practice or "natural talent": *rate of learning* and *asymptotic performance* after a period of learning and practice. Differences in the rate of learning given the same amount of training and practice would indicate that some individuals are indeed "talented" as indicated by their fast pace of learning. An asymptote is the peak level of performance an individual can reach given a sufficient amount of training, after which little meaningful gains can be made despite continued efforts. He also suggested that the only way this "nature argument" might be tested would be in controlled conditions where amounts of training and experience were held constant and where sufficient time and training were given to allow subjects to reach their maximal performance (i.e., asymptotic competence). There are experiments in which children's rates of learning are compared on various cognitive tasks. Children with high IQs typically have much steeper learning curves (i.e., learning faster) compared with their average counterparts (e.g., Jackson & Butterfield, 1986; Kanevsky, 1990). Further, they did better in making the transferral of learning to novel, dissimilar situations (Borkowski & Peck, 1986). Haier and his colleagues (see Haier, 2001; Haier & Jung, 2008) provide so far the most compelling evidence that ease of learning (how well subjects can reason their way from simpler matrix questions to complex ones) has to do with individual differences, not practice. Individuals who scored the highest showed the greatest decreases in brain activity after the practice period, suggesting that they achieved learning with higher facility (selecting more effective and efficient strategies in solving the problems at hand, becoming attuned to task constraints more quickly, etc.).

    Rate of learning. Ackerman's (1988) research on the simulation learning task on air traffic control came close to meeting Shiffrin's criteria, as one can assume that air traffic control is new to most people, if not all, and the simulation condition in the lab affords controlling for the time spent on the learning task. Ackerman used perceptual speed and general intelligence measures to predict rate of learning after multiple trials. The main finding of his research was that differences in general intelligence (IQ measures) predict how fast individuals learn (i.e., rate of learning) to some extent (but the size of the correlations was moderate) at the initial stage of learning (early trials); but as subjects gained skills at air traffic control, predictive power of the measure of general intelligence diminished. This finding suggests that rate of learning can be determined by both nature (ability) and nurture (experience), and as a person's knowledge and skills build up, learning is starting to depend less on general processing advantages and more on the domain-specific knowledge and skills an individual has acquired in the practice trials (see Ackerman, 1999). This conclusion, if found to be prevalent across domains, would significantly weaken the natural-endowment argument, as it alludes to the law of diminishing returns regarding the role of general ability.

Individual differences in rate of learning can be easily observed in natural settings but their causes are difficult to determine. Using the developmental standard score norms of the Iowa Tests of Basic Skills (ITBS), Gagné (2005b) described a fan-spread effect whereby academic achievement in Grades 1 to 9 show a widening of the achievement gap within each cohort. More pertinent to the current topic, he showed that by Grade 3, the most academically talented students had caught up with average ninth-grade students, and from fourth grade up, there was a 50-point spread within the top 10%, and by ninth grade, a 50-point spread can be observed within the top 2%.

Gagné attributed this effect mainly to the advantage of general intelligence or the ability to learn, which is, according to him, a hallmark of giftedness (Gagné, 2005a). Gagné (2005b) argued that since this fan-spread effect is resistant to intervention, it should be considered "akin to a law of nature" (p. 151). The theoretical argument that the observed widening gap is largely caused by general intelligence, or the ability to learn is a high-level inference or speculation, not self-evident in the descriptive data presented in the study. Presumably, a multitude of factors can influence rate of learning in natural settings: school motivation, domain-specific predilections, prior knowledge, general ability, different developmental stages of the competence in question, and social contexts (e.g., home environments), some of which may have genetic contributions, but many reflect environmental influences.

Nevertheless, the fan-spread effect is consistent with McCall's (1981) scoop model, which views mental development as following differential and divergent trajectories, starting around 6 years of age, attributable to both genetic and environmental influences. Gagné's argument is also in line with findings that genetic contributions to intelligence and academic achievement permeate human development throughout adolescence and adulthood (Plomin et al., 2003; Plomin & Spinath, 2004).

Asymptotic competence. While the rate or ease of learning indicates facility, asymptotic competence is the maximal performance one can attain on a given task. A further implication is that one's performance has reached its maximal *capacity*, "where he cannot by education or exertion overpass," to use Galton's (1869) words (p. 15). Galton assumed that each person has a *mental capacity* *constraint* for high-level achievement, and the variation in capacity limits is highly heritable. Although it is conceivable that such capacity limits vary greatly from individual to individual, Galton's conviction that a capacity for genius is tractable through family lineage is questionable. Rothenberg and Wyshak (2004, 2005) tracked the family backgrounds of Nobel laureates and other eminent writers and scientists, and found no evidence of direct inheritance of creativity in their parent generations. Nevertheless, Galton's assumption for the existence of capacity limits is widely accepted by contemporary scholars and researchers. Namely, when all the support is given and efforts made, there will be a moment when one hits the point of diminishing returns, even to a point where effort no longer yields any significant gain or payoff. Individual differences in this putative capacity reflect a heritable variable and biological constraint (e.g., Bronfenbrenner & Ceci, 1994). An example of possible asymptotic performance or competence is performance on scholarly aptitude tests such as the Scholastic Assessment Test (SAT) or Graduate Record Examination (GRE). An assumption underlying these tests is that one cannot, simply by exertion (e.g., overlearning and overpreparation), get to the ranks of top performers; there are limits on how far one can go, regardless of how much effort a test taker puts in. To some extent, tests such as Raven's progressive matrices can be seen as a test of the asymptotic competence: As test takers progress to increasingly difficult items, they will eventually reach a point of impasse or performance bottleneck, indicating that they probably have exhausted their cognitive means. Experimental research using the asymptotic performance paradigm is rare. Baltes (1998) reported a research program using a "testing the limits" procedure by which subjects were asked to use a memory technique until their memory performance reached their limits (i.e., asymptotes). He found that practice clearly raised subjects to a high level of expertise on this task. Individual differences in rate of learning and asymptotic performance were also observed. Indeed, counterintuitively, over a period of extended training and practice, individual differences in some cases were even increased rather than reduced, an effect that echoes observations of the growth in natural settings (Gagné, 2005b; see also Ceci & Papierno, 2005).

When applied to high-level expertise or creative productivity in real life, "testing the limits" becomes difficult. Indeed, we may never know where the alleged capacity limits are for particular individuals, as rarely do individuals have the opportunity to "max their potential," let alone measure it. Professional sports or games (e.g., chess or Go) provide an exception, wherein a person's best records can be reliably documented over time, and performance asymptotes measured and analyzed. Beyond the measurable levels of expertise or reproducible superior performance (Ericsson et al., 2007a), knowing the limits of real-life accomplishments or the existence of such limits at all is even more difficult. For example, Lubinski, Webb, Morelock, and Benbow (2001) divided the top 1% of the out-of-level SAT-Math scorers into four quartiles. They compared the top and bottom quartiles (i.e., those who had scored above the 99.75th percentile, and those between the 99th and the 99.25th percentile) in terms of doctorates earned, patents obtained, and tenure secured in the top-50 American universities. The results showed that the individuals in the top quartile achieved these criteria (doctorates, patents, and top-50 tenure) at double or triple the rate of those who scored in the bottom quartile (who had attained extraordinary scores relative to the age peers). Even if we take these indices as proxy measures of asymptotic competence, the statistical estimates of probability simply say that those who had the higher SAT-Math scores tended to achieve higher academic status and productivity; nothing can be inferred about their differences in "capacity limits" (or learning curves, for that matter), as we don't know whether those achieving less has in fact reached their limits or failed to attain higher status for other reasons (effort, support, chance, etc.).

Inherent difficulty in determining rate of learning and asymptotic competence vis-à-vis a given line of talent development. As I alluded to in the above discussion, there is inherent difficulty in testing this nature argument experimentally. First, it is practically impossible to set up an experiment for multiple years and track rate of learning in a domain while controlling for attrition or extraneous variables that would confound the results. However, without tracking a sufficiently large sample of individuals for a prolonged period of time, we cannot determine whether rates of learning differ between individuals at a given stage of expert development. For example, we don't know whether differences in general intelligence would significantly constrain how fast a person can acquire skills and expertise (i.e., rate of learning) beyond the limited training period in Ackerman's (1988) air traffic control experiments.

Second, it is difficult to tease apart the effects of motivation (effort and persistence) and effects of "natural ability" on rate of learning. To be sure, Haier's (2001) experiments convincingly showed that "smart brains" work more efficiently (i.e., less glucose consumption in the brain), not harder, thus indicating ease of learning in the exact sense of the term. However, it does not mean one cannot work harder to effect changes in rate of learning (making performance more efficient, more strategic, more automatized). You can, of course, control the time spent on task, but you cannot control the engaged effort exerted or not exerted by research participants, particularly when the experiment is a prolonged one.

Third, most talent domains of interest to educators of the gifted are semantically rich or knowledge rich, and it is always impossible to separate the role of experience-based content knowledge (and intelligent thoughts) and that of processing abilities as responsible for the ease of learning. Baltes's (1998) testing-the-limit experiment used a knowledge-lean memory skill and Ackerman (1988) used a more complex learning task, air traffic control simulation. As Ackerman's research shows, domain knowledge and skills likely relieve processing demands, as indicated by decreased correlations over the training period between general intelligence and task performance, a finding consistent with the theoretical prediction of cognitive psychology (Anderson, 1987).

Arguments Against the Nature Argument
Regarding Exceptional Competence

The recent challenge to the natural-endowment argument or the notion of existence of gifts and talents from a scientific point of view mainly comes from a prominent group of cognitive researchers specialized in how expertise is developed in various domains, led by Anders Ericsson (see Ericsson et al., 2007a). Their views can be summarized as two main arguments: (a) There is no solid empirical evidence supporting natural-endowment accounts of *reproducible* exceptional competence, and (b) there is good evidence for the nurture argument (Ericsson et al., 2006; Ericsson et al., 2007a; Howe, Davidson, & Sloboda, 1998). Since the second point is less controversial, I focus on the first argument that there is no empirical evidence supporting the "natural talent" or "gifted" explanations. The argument hinges on what constitutes "natural endowment" and what counts as supporting evidence.

What counts as evidence for natural endowment. Critics of gifted and talented explanations tend to interpret *natural endowment* to mean innate structural differences; therefore, the "admissible" evidence has to be either genetically based neuroanatomical structures or certain phenotypes (physical and psychological manifestations) that directly reflect genotypes (genetic kinds). In the previous section, I review some supporting evidence. Even though the neuroanatomical evidence may not be conclusive, evidence of the variation in ease of learning, and a distinct genetic component of the ability to learn, is sufficient to support the "natural endowment" argument.

When the critics claimed that there is no evidence for "natural talent," they assumed that a talent, if it exists, should be preformed or genetically preordained; in their words, "it originates in genetically transmitted structures" (Howe et al., 1998, p. 399); "early ability is not evidence of talent unless it emerges in the absence of special opportunity to learn" (p. 403); if talent exists, we should witness "sudden emergence of high levels of performance" (Ericsson et al., 2007a, p. 31), and "clear superior performance before the start of training" (p. 35). Certain biopsychological traits and pathological symptoms, such as Down's syndrome, can indeed be directly traced to genetic origins, but none of the talents in cultural domains can be seen as "innate" or genetically preordained. Thus, the assumption represents an extreme innatist position that very few scholars in the field hold. As I have discussed earlier, more appropriate evidence for talent is rate of learning and, if feasible, asymptotic competence (as manifested in competitive sports and games).

Innate constraints on how far one can go. Although Ericsson is skeptical about the existence of the "natural endowment" responsible for development of exceptional competence, his main concern is not whether natural talents or high-intelligent people exist, but whether they really matter as much as many giftedness researchers believe. Specifically, Ericsson and his colleagues (2007a) hold an argument against Galton's supposition that there are innately determined constraints on how far one can go (i.e., the limits or asymptotes of competence for particular individuals) along a specific line of talent or expert development. I pointed out in the previous section that the notion of an asymptotic competence or capacity limit is theoretically conceivable, but empirically difficult to assess in real-life circumstances. Gagné (2009b) suggests that we use general intelligence scores as a proxy measure of capacity limits: "General intelligence creates major *quantitative*, thus practical, constraints to achievements. ... As the level of intelligence decreases, the upper limit for achievements in many fields also decreases" (p. 173). This suggestion is debatable, as there is no way to demonstrate the predictive efficacy of general intelligence measures with respect to the learning and developmental capacity limits vis-à-vis demands of a domain. However, as Simonton (2007) argued, a relative advantage in the rate of learning is sufficient for a "natural-endowment" account of expert development, and there is no need to assume, let alone empirically "prove," an innate constraint on asymptotic competence as a basis for a natural-endowment argument.

The Nurture Argument: Giftedness as the Result of Deep Engagement in a Specific Line of Talent Development

Strong versions of the nurture argument take any natural-endowment accounts of exceptional competence as a myth or attribution error (e.g., Tesch-Römer, 1998). A weak version of the nurture argument acknowledges that there might be individual differences in abilities and predilections for certain domains, but with sufficient motivation, personal determination, and extended deliberate practice, any healthy individuals without apparent mental and physical deficiencies can achieve marvelous feats. Ericsson seems to hold the latter position (e.g., Ericsson, 1998). The nurture argument is often supported by the aspects of evidence and reasoning described below.

Training and practice change brain structures and functions. The argument finds some support from Schlaug's (2001) studies of professional musicians, whose brains show distinct anatomical differences from nonmusicians, and who also show a pattern of brain activation different from that of nonmusicians when processing music (Gaser & Schlaug, 2003). Although the role of the genetic predispositions of these musicians cannot be excluded, a more plausible explanation of the anatomical differences of the brains of professional musicians is extended music training and practice. For example, in a neuroimaging study of right-handed string musicians, the cortical region representing the left hand (but not the right hand) is larger than that of nonmusicians, likely because of highly trained, skillful left-hand fingers. Analogously, in an experiment training monkeys to discriminate two vibrating stimuli applied to one finger, after several thousand trials, the cortical representations of the trained finger became more than twice as large as the corresponding areas for other fingers (see Kandel & Squire, 2001). Evidence for structural and functional organization of the brain in adaptation to musical training and development are further corroborated by cross-sectional and longitudinal evidence of effects of music training on children's brain and cognitive development (Schlaug, Norton, Overy, & Winner, 2005). The argument is consistent with a view of probabilistic epigenesis, which sees gene expressions not as unidirectionally determining psychological structures and behavior but as interacting with behavioral and neural activity in a bidirectional way, thus susceptible to environmental and experiential influences (Gottlieb, 1998). Three qualifications are in order. First, the evidence does not negate possible genetic differences that provide a relative advantage for some children in music learning. Increases in the group mean scores after training do not mean elimination of individual differences represented as standard deviations. Second, the nurture-changes-nature argument is predicated on brain plasticity; the brain plasticity is not unlimited and may be sensitive to developmental timing as well. Third, instrument playing has a distinct psychomotor component, and we don't know much about how exercise of higher-order mental functions such as abstract symbol manipulation, reasoning, and problem solving can change neuroanatomy or neurophysiology in the same manner as we found for psychomotor functions.

Deliberate practice provides a parsimonious account of mediating mechanisms leading to higher levels of expertise (Ericsson, Krampe, & Tesch-Römer, 1993). Deliberate practice is a highly focused, intensive form of practice, with a purpose to improve specific aspects of performance in a skill domain. Thus, what matters is not the sheer amount of practice but the quality of practice. Ericsson distinguishes between *ordinary practice* and *deliberate practice*. With ordinary practice, most people can achieve a level of skill that is "good enough" for daily functioning but hard to surpass without dedicated efforts. Only deliberate practice can move people beyond this performance bottleneck. Fischer and Pipp (1984) made a similar distinction between functional and optimal levels of skill development. Ericsson and his colleagues conducted both correlational and experimental studies on this critical mediating mechanism in a variety of domains of expertise and found high correlations between the amounts of deliberate practice engaged and levels of performance reached (Ericsson, 2006; Ericsson & Charness, 1993; Ericsson & Lehmann, 1996). A recent case study of how the American novelist John Irving took painstaking efforts to perfect his craft of creative writing provides yet another illustration of the power of deliberate practice (Amabile, 2001). Much of creative writing involves a labor of love and incessant self-perfection, rather than instant inspiration, according to Irving. Deliberate practice provides a mediating mechanism for the transition from one state to the next, higher state of competence (S[i] to S[i+1]; see Ericsson et al., 2007a).

While deliberate practice is without doubt a necessary condition for developing high-level expertise, is it a sufficient condition? One possibility is that there is a self-selection effect; namely, those who chose to engage in deliberate practice were the most promising ones in their respective fields, and thus the apparent effects of deliberate practice were confounded by their abilities and dispositions (Sternberg, 1996a). Only controlled experiments can untangle this dilemma. A second question is, Are there internal constraints on deliberate practice, besides the opportunity and external support for extended deliberate practice? Ericsson et al. (1993) identified individual differences in temperament as potentially determining how likely it would be that one would engage in deliberate practice for a prolonged period of time; they acknowledged that temperamental differences may have a genetic component. In light of different rates of learning, reviewed earlier, one may argue that intelligence can also constrain the process and effects of deliberate process, particularly when the domain of interest has high cognitive complexity (Carpenter, Just, & Shell, 1990; Stankov, 2003). While the notion of deliberate practice captures the nature of practice in performance domains wherein fine-tuned execution of technical routines is required (e.g., performing heart surgery or executing a figure-skating routine), it may not be specific enough to capture the process of reasoning and complex problem solving in domains of productive thinking where problems are often ill defined and "open ended" (see Chapter 4 for a distinction between the production versus performance mode of functioning).

Motivation modulates cognitive functioning and leads to higher levels of attainment. It is well established that motivation can enhance cognitive functioning through more focused attention and intensive efforts (Dai & Sternberg, 2004; Dweck, Mangels, & Good, 2004; Hidi, 1990). Two motivational factors are particularly related to ease of learning and asymptotic performance: interest and persistence (or task commitment; Renzulli, 1986). Interest facilitates attention and deep processing, and organized persistence overcomes information overload and leads to new paths of solution (Dai & Renzulli, 2008). Gottfried et al. (2005) identified in their longitudinal study a group of children with slightly above average IQ scores, who consistently showed high levels of intrinsic academic motivation throughout their elementary and secondary school years and much higher academic achievement than average peers. They dubbed these children "motivationally gifted" (Gottfried & Gottfried, 2004) in contrast to "intellectually gifted." They justified the distinction on two grounds: First, only a very small number of the motivationally gifted were also intellectually gifted, meaning those whose IQs were 130 or higher; second, the measure of intrinsic academic motivation accounted for the variations in academic achievement over time above and beyond what was accounted for by IQ scores. Research findings of adult expertise in race-track gambling also highlight the role of motivation and deliberate practice for developing high-level skilled reasoning regardless of how these experts measured up on IQ tests. These professional gamblers were capable of highly sophisticated reasoning in their gambling practice but varied greatly in their performance on an intelligence test for adults (Ceci & Liker, 1986). Arthur Ashawlow, a Nobel laureate physicist, remarked, "The labor of love aspect is important. The successful scientists often are not the most talented, but the ones who are just impelled by curiosity. They've got to know what the answer is" (quoted in Amabile, 2001, p. 335). Many case studies of eminent writers and scientists also show the essential role of intrinsic motivation and task commitment (see Csikszentmihalyi, 1996).

In the context of the nature-nurture debate, an emphasis on motivation puts more bets on "doing" than on "being" for explaining giftedness and serves as an antidote to the dominant ability-centric conception of giftedness. However, motivation (e.g., persistence) can also show "nature" at work, as motivation also has a dispositional component, as shown by Gottfried et al. (2005), including its temperamental underpinnings (Chess & Thomas, 1996; Ericsson et al., 1993). The argument for a distinct role of motivation brings us back to Galton's premise: There is a limit to how far we can go. Some psychometric researchers and sociologists tend to believe that this capacity limit is marked by one's IQ test scores (Gagné, 2009b; Gottfredson, 1997; Herrnstein & Murray, 1994). *Evidence seems to support a multifaceted, pluralistic, equipotential, rather than essentialist, view of human potential; that is, human potential can be expressed in many ways and there is no sure way to determine its capacity; advantages afforded by natural endowment are relative, rather than absolute, ones.*

There are less extreme theories that put in perspective the importance of natural endowment while emphasizing sustained mastery efforts. The *threshold hypothesis* states that there are basic threshold requirements for high-level achievement in a domain; but beyond the threshold requirements, relevant traits (e.g., extremely high IQ) would quickly reach the point of diminishing returns (i.e., significantly decreased cognitive and learning advantages; see Hunt, 1999). In Renzulli's (1999) three-ring model, using above-average, rather than superior, cognitive abilities as a criterion implicitly suggests this threshold effect. In an early study, Reis and Renzulli (1982) used a more liberal cutoff (top 10%) for identification of the gifted and found that the gifted so identified did equally well on outcome measures compared with those identified with more stringent cutoffs (e.g., top 3%). The threshold hypothesis has also gained currency in popular media and writings on outstanding accomplishments (e.g., Gladwell, 2008). Similarly, the *partial compensation hypothesis* states that motivation and effort may partially compensate for less than superior levels of ability (Schneider, 2000), which is consistent with Gottfried et al.'s (2005) notion of the "motivationally gifted." However, some findings appear to refute the threshold or partial compensation hypothesis. Lubinski et al. (2001), for example, showed that even among the top 1% scorers of SAT math at the age 13, educational and career achievement tracked for the next 25 years is closely correlated with whether they belonged to the top or bottom quartiles. Ability differences predicted creative productivity even when people with the same terminal educational degrees were compared (Park, Lubinski, & Benbow, 2008). It should be pointed out that in the above studies, SAT-Math, not general intelligence tests, was used. Supporting the threshold hypothesis regarding the role of general intelligence, there were anecdotal cases of two youngsters (William Schockley and Luis Alvarez) who failed to qualify for the gifted identification in Terman's (1925) study because of their lower than satisfactory scores on the Stanford-Binet intelligence test but went ahead in their adulthood to win Nobel prizes in physics, which arguably has the most stringent requirements in terms of abstract and analytic thinking.

Knowledge overcomes basic processing constraints and transforms intellectual functioning. Cognitive psychology has repeatedly shown that knowledge, once acquired, helps people overcome information-processing demands so that there are rarely occasions where people have to exercise "raw intelligence," as it were. Chi (1978) compared a group of skilled chess-playing children with a group of adults who had no chess-playing experience on their performance on memory tasks involving or not involving chess knowledge. When memory materials involved chess positions, the children outperformed the adults, but when more neutral materials, such as digit span, were tested, the adults outperformed the children. This *expertise effect* has been replicated across many domains (see Ericsson et al., 2006). Some intelligence researchers cited working-memory differences as a critical underpinning of individual differences in cognitive tasks such as reading comprehension or reasoning (Just & Carpenter, 1992; Kyllonen & Christal, 1990). The underlying assumption is that basic cognitive capacities constrain one's intellectual operations. Yet Ericsson (1998) argued that expert performance reflects "the acquisition of qualitatively different skills and representations that allow expert performers to bypass information-processing constraints imposed by basic capacities" (p. 413). In other words, the baseline differences in cognitive capacities, if any, do not matter if one can use deliberate practice to acquire proper skills and cognitive representations. One can also add that formal instruction and training play no trivial role in developing expert skills. The nurture part of giftedness, such as how deep conceptual learning and the development of expertise can be facilitated through instruction (Bonsangue & Drew, 1995; Schoenfeld, 1992; Wineburg, 1991), is often ignored altogether when giftedness is conceptualized as a property of the person involved.

A Summary of the Competing Arguments for Nature Versus Nurture

The logic of the nature argument is that if we can identify consistent individual differences in rate of learning and ultimate accomplishments beyond chance, and if these differences can be linked to some ability differences that have a distinct genetic component, then the natural-endowment argument is supported. The logic of the nurture argument is based on the demonstration that there are proximal mediating mechanisms (various forms of "doing" accounts) leading to high-level expertise, which are powerful enough to render any baseline differences insignificant and baseline capacity explanations (various forms of "being" accounts) superfluous. Both arguments have supporting evidence, yet the respective evidence is not so certain as to leave no room for alternative interpretations. In essence, "the nature camp" (the *pronat*, to use a term by Gagné, 2009b) fails to convince "the nurture camp" (the *antinat*) that a certain form of "natural abilities" is a *necessary condition* for developing high-level talent or expertise (given that predictive relationships in the behavioral sciences are merely stating a probabilistic co-occurrence, not a necessity). For the latter, many alleged "natural talents" amount to hearsay (e.g., Howe et al., 1998). Conversely, "the nurture camp" fails to convince "the nature camp" that rigorous training and practice; strong commitment; as well as the technical and social support of teachers, mentors, or coaches, are all it takes (i.e., constitutes a *sufficient condition*) to become top-notch performers and major contributors to a field, whether in academic, artistic, technical, or social-practical domains.

For the champions of giftedness, ignoring many real-life instances of natural talents and superior minds is just too convenient a strategy in the name of rigorous science (Gagné, 2007, 2009b). However, regardless of how problematic the expertise perspective on giftedness may be, given the history of neglecting the "doing" part of gifted performance while taking for granted that various aptitude tests are measures of "natural ability," the nurture argument serves as a necessary antidote, an opportunity for reflection and examination on our deepest assumptions. Overall, there does not seem to be a single "gifted" core that unfolds over time to manifest itself in "gifted children." Just as some may be "intellectually gifted" and others may be "motivationally gifted," some children are gifted by natural endowment (being), and others become "gifted" through interests and dedicated efforts (doing/becoming). Sources and ontogeny of high human potential or promise seem to be too diverse to fit into any essentialist theoretical model.

Person Versus Context Accounts: Is Exceptional Competence "Situated" or "Distributed"?

A more contextual view of competence would view giftedness and talent as residing in the person-task interface rather than inside the mind, let alone reducible to some biological origins (Barab & Plucker, 2002). For example, Brazilian children peddling goods in the street could do "street math" that demonstrated mathematical sophistication and inventiveness; yet when presented with equivalent "school math" versions, these children got nowhere (Carraher et al., 1985). Professional gamblers can engage in highly sophisticated reasoning for betting decisions, which sometimes involve manipulating more than seven variables simultaneously. Yet some of them failed to do much simpler reasoning tasks on standardized intelligence tests (Ceci & Liker, 1986; Ceci & Ruiz, 1993). *What the situative perspective stresses is the fundamental embeddedness of intelligent thoughts in the dynamic task context* (Rogoff & Lave, 1984; van Geert, 2002). There are two implications of this "situative" perspective for understanding giftedness. First, giftedness or degree of giftedness is relative to context. Formally identified gifted children through testing may not be gifted "in the wild" (Hutchins, 1995). There is no context-free gifted competence. Second, acquiring exceptional competence is tuning to a specific task environment, with its unique affordances and constraints; that is, a task environment not only allows you to exercise certain sensibilities and capabilities useful for achieving the task goals, but also structures and shapes your sensibilities and capabilities to meet the demands imposed upon you. For example, when learning batting in baseball, you have to be tuned to the speed of the forthcoming ball and coordinate your visual judgment and motor action (swing) to make a "nice cut." To play a ball game well, having a feel for the game is important, knowing things around or "withitness" is important, and the tacit knowledge of know-how is important. To generalize from this observation, knowledge is situated in the functional context in which learning takes place, rather than dispensed into the head, only to be retrieved later when called on (Bereiter, 2002). When applied to giftedness, the situative perspective stresses the irreducibility of lived experiences in situ (being there) as a basis for intelligent thought (Clark, 1997; Perkins & Grotzer, 1997; Sternberg, 1985). A corollary is that judgment of exceptional competence in that context (a talented baseball player, musician, or mathematician) can be made only by people who are also well versed in that task environment, using the standards and criteria accepted in a relevant professional community (Csikszentmihalyi, 1996). The strengths of the situative perspective lie in its emphasis on context and perceptual and enactive experiences. Where it falls short is that, after all is said and done, we might still have the mystery of how a Roger Federer or Michael Phelps came about. At the end of the day, biologically constitutional individual differences still have to be reckoned with as an explanatory factor, at least for extreme cases of talent.

Methodological Considerations of the Nature-Nurture Debate

The nature-nurture tension not only reflects different ontological convictions and commitments, but also reveals inherent epistemological and methodological differences that "bias" researchers in favor of a particular way of generating and interpreting data (see Chapter 6 for in-depth discussion). In the following section, I discuss two conceptual and methodological issues: prediction versus backtracking and trait-level description versus process-level explanation.

Prediction versus backtracking. The placement/prediction approach is a prospective mode of inquiry: identifying a set of characteristics as important and verifying in the future whether they indeed are associated with certain desirable outcomes. In this mode of inquiry, giftedness is defined as aptitude or potential.

Terman (1925) started this research paradigm. More broadly, any studies that first determine predictor variables that define a subgroup or subpopulation and then use a set of criterion measures to validate the predictors belong to this type of research. Most of the gifted-"nongifted" comparative studies share this family resemblance.

In contrast with this prospective, predictive mode of inquiry, the looking-backward approach used by the expertise researchers is a three-step "backtracking" mode of inquiry: (1) Superior expert performance is captured and reliably documented in the laboratory using tasks representative of core activities in the domain; (2) process-tracing method and measures are used to identify mechanisms that mediate the reproducibly superior performance; and (3) the factors responsible for development of the mediating mechanisms are studied by retrospective analysis of training activities, such as deliberate practice (Ericsson & Williams, 2007). In short, the question is that given an authenticated, reproducible high-level competence, what mechanisms best explain such a feat? Here, giftedness is defined as achievement or high-level expertise.

Note that these two modes of inquiry do not necessarily contradict each other, but they do use very different criteria as "condition of satisfaction" for supporting their respective theoretical conjectures and arguments. For predictive studies in behavioral sciences, any prediction that is made is by nature probabilistic, not deterministic. Therefore, the threshold for a "proof" is low: As long as the researcher establishes some respectful predictive efficacy of certain predictor measures, she can declare success. Besides, longitudinal, predictive studies cannot be too specific about what outcomes will be and what intermediate processes are involved. In contrast, studies that use the backtracking mode of inquiry are more targeted, attempting to find out specific mechanisms for a specific type and level of attainment. They look at processes and contexts closely tied to performance conditions and therefore biased toward identifying proximal rather than distal determinants, in favor of "doing" rather than "being" part of giftedness. But most of all, these two methods use differing definitions of "giftedness," one as "aptitude," and the other as high-level achievement, leading to drastically different conclusions.

A thought experiment may help make the above point clear: Suppose we have two teams of researchers, one on giftedness as potential and the other on giftedness as eminent achievement. Both teams are equipped with the best tools, instruments, and resources possible. The "potential" team conducts an exhaustive talent search, aimed at identifying a group of children who are highly promising for a specific line of talent development and following them for 30 years. The "eminence" team starts a research project 30 years later, identifying a group of adults who have already achieved eminence in the same domain. The research question is, What is the likelihood that a child included in the first study also ends up in the second study? In other words, how well does high aptitude predict eminent achievement? How large an overlap would we expect between the two groups of participants? Suppose that the early identification has a 50% success rate in predicting eminence in adulthood (i.e., there is a 50% overlap in group membership). The "potential" team would declare a huge success, as the prediction rate is beyond the population base rate by enormous measure. However, for the "eminence" team, this record is far less satisfactory, as the other 50% of eminence cases remain unaccounted for by the predictive measures; a satisfactory scientific account of the excellence attained in adulthood should explain 90%, if not 100%, of the relevant cases. The "potential" team might argue that there are many life circumstances that might have derailed half these children from achieving the level of competence the other half have attained, or that if the research team were to delay their identification for 3 years, they would have made more "hits" and fewer "false positives." But for the "eminence" team, this still does not answer the question of how the other half apparently without the right "aptitude" managed to become top-notch performers and contributors. Consequently, the best answers to the question of why some individuals end up in the "eminence" study is to study these individuals who have made eminent contributions, not the group of children who are identified as most likely to achieve eminent contributions. A key question is, Were the half of "less successful" children "gifted" in the first place? Because of the different definitions and criteria used, the two teams would have different answers. The "potential" team would say yes based on evidence of "aptitude," and the "eminence" team would say no (or at least remain agnostic) because they did not deliver what they promised. Thus, differing perspectives and methodologies are partly responsible for the drastically different conclusions. Beyond these definitional and methodological differences, different theoretical interests, trait description versus process explication, also lead to different conclusions.

Trait-level description versus process-level explication. Population or Darwinian thinking hinges on relative or comparative advantages through natural selection. Population thinking by nature characterizes "natural endowment" as a relative, rather than absolute, advantage. For that purpose, defining norms and deviations for human traits is important. Talent development, on a large social scale, can be seen as a cultural selection process whereby certain traits gain cultural distinction whereas others are marginalized or even die out. The social-cultural selection process is probabilistic rather than deterministic. Also, the well-known Matthew Effect makes the cumulative-advantage argument more compelling than any strong nativist arguments (see Ceci & Papierno, 2005; Papierno et al., 2005).

It is not accidental that a strong objection to giftedness as natural endowment came from experimental cognitive psychology, which traditionally favors process accounts of human behavior and performance rather than person accounts (Cronbach, 1957; Lohman, 2001). Trait-level description is often seen as lacking in scientific rigor when used to explain gifted and talented behaviors (Siegler & Kotovsky, 1986). More refined scientific procedures are advocated by expertise researchers, such as more objectively defined metrics for assessing excellence or superior performance, reproducible evidence of superior performance in controlled settings, and more controlled research on mechanisms and processes that explicate how one gains specific levels of competence over time (Ericsson, 1996, 2006; Ericsson & Williams, 2007).

It should be noted that process accounts do not always provide satisfactory answers to questions regarding trait differences. In the intelligence-component approach, for example, underlying components and processes identified by researchers often fail to account for a satisfactory proportion of variation in intelligence measures (see Lohman, 1994a). One reason may be that macro- or molar-level trait descriptions in the mode of population thinking on the one hand, and micro- or molecular-level cognitive processes in the mode of controlled experimentation, on the other, simply represent different time scales and units of human behavior and action (Newell, 1990). Without a clear solution to the problem of levels of analysis (see later discussion in Chapters 6 and 9), they help create what might be called alpha and beta biases in respective research designs and data interpretation scheme. *Alpha biases* (or biases toward personal attributions) refers to a tendency to make dispositional attributions given a pattern of data. Thus, the correlation between intelligence tests and academic achievement is interpreted to mean a causal relationship when the two measures might just have a large overlap in construct representation or item similarities and redundancies. *Beta biases* (or biases toward process attributions) refers to a tendency to make more situational attributions. Thus, if the amounts of deliberate practice are correlated with high-level expertise in a monotonic fashion, then the two must be causally related, when there might well be a third variable accounting for both deliberate practice and achievement, such as aptitudes. The reason why biases can be built into our theorizing is that all these theoretical accounts, whether in favor of nature or of nurture, are constructed, albeit empirically supported, models of the realities, not realities themselves.

THE INSEPARABILITY OF NATURE AND NURTURE:
AN ALTERNATIVE PERSPECTIVE

Although behavioral geneticists argue that it is misleading to pit nature against nurture, or vice versa, thereby creating a false either-or dichotomy (e.g., Plomin et al., 2003), developmental psychologists (Horowitz, 2000, 2009; Lerner, 2004) criticize the behavioral genetics methods, which mechanically parse genetic and environmental influences on a given developmental outcome without considering the person, contexts, processes, and developmental timing. This criticism is echoed by some developmental biologists who do not consider genetic influence as unidirectional and deterministic, as prescribed by the central dogma of molecular biology. Rather, gene expressions are seen as bidirectional, susceptible to influences from other levels of the developmental system (cell, tissue, organism) and organism-environment interaction (behavioral and neural-cognitive activity) during the process of individual development (Gottlieb, 1998). Thus, many aspects of human development, particularly psychological aspects, are seen, not as genetically determined but as epigenetic (i.e., acquiring characteristics not pre-specified in the genes) and probabilistic (e.g., depending on environmental stimulation, behavioral experiences, and developmental timing).

This way of thinking of human development as "*probabilistic epigenesis*" (Gottlieb, 1998, p. 792) has yet to penetrate into the way we think about giftedness, as many still think that genes start everything in a unidirectional manner. For example, Gagné's (2004) Differentiated Model of Giftedness and Talent (DMGT) posits giftedness as a well-formed entity with which one is genetically endowed before significant interaction with the environment. Then this giftedness gets transformed through endogenous and exogenous "catalysts" into systematically developed talents in culturally defined domains. There are two main assumptions that are at variance with the notion of the probabilistic epigenesis of development. First, the gifted quality in the DMGT model is static, predetermined by genetic makeup. Even if we take IQ as a marker of intellectual potential, both brain and behavioral genetic research show that intellectual performance is not stabilized until around the onset of adolescence, partly because of the prolonged brain maturation of the more able (Plomin et al., 2003; Shaw et al., 2006). Shaw et al., based on their longitudinal brain-imaging study, concluded that "the neuroanatomical expression of intelligence in children is dynamic" (p. 676). The second assumption of the DMGT model is that the process of transformation of giftedness into talents is unidirectional. Development here only means that with proper soil and fertilization, the seed of giftedness will grow into proper social

Figure 3.1. Probabilistic-epigenetic framework: Depiction of the bidirectional and coactional nature of genetic, behavioral, and environmental influences over the course of individual development.

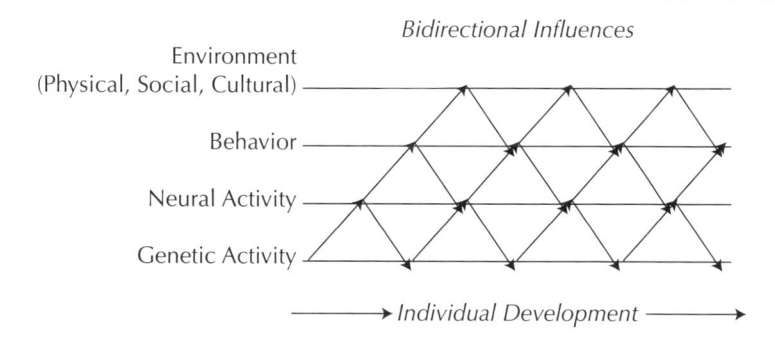

From *Individual Development and Evolution: The Genesis of Novel Behavior* (p. 186), by Gilbert Gottlieb, 1992, New York: Oxford University Press. Copyright © 1992 by Gilbert Gottlieb.

forms and uses, and natural potential will be actualized. *From a bidirectional view of development subscribed by the probabilistic-epigenetic theory of development, gifted potential is not an inborn quality to unfold but fundamentally emergent through experiences and development, subject to further change, for better or for worse.*

Ironically, even the staunchest champions of the nurture argument, who argued for the lack of evidence for talent or genetically imposed constraints, fell into the trap of such deterministic, unidirectional thinking about "natural talent." For example, they argued that in order to ascertain the role of natural endowment, evidence should be present for the role of genes or genetically based structures that are pure and clean, not "contaminated" by experience (e.g., Howe et al., 1998). It can be argued that, in most situations, nature (genetic influences) cannot demonstrate itself unless through nurture (e.g., experience and structured environments). Multiple phenotypes (e.g., manifest physical or behavioral/mental traits) of the same genotype can be developed, depending on the interaction of the organism with its environments at a specific point of development (Gottlieb, 1998).

Given this new understanding of the relationship between nature and nurture, time and resources may be more fruitfully devoted to the issue of how nature and nurture reciprocate and otherwise interact to produce exceptional competence through development. Dai and Coleman (2005) identified three stages of theoretical thinking on the nature-nurture issue. In the first stage, nature and nurture are regarded as separate entities or factors; the question is the share of contributions by each to the individual's development. In the second stage, nature and nurture are still seen as separate forces, but they are conceptualized either *quantitatively*, as reciprocating with each other in amplifying developmental variations (see Dickens & Flynn, 2001), or *qualitatively*, interacting with each other in producing something neither of them alone will produce (see Papierno et al., 2005). In the third stage, nature and nurture work within the same developmental system, such that how the brain builds up its infrastructure and instruments for a specific talent while interacting with a certain structured task environment, and how relevant components are assembled, reassembled, and controlled to produce superior performance are fully accounted for.

Wachs (1992) identified three types of person-environment covariance. *Passive covariance* occurs when certain personal characteristics tend to be correlated with environmental features; thus voracious readers are more likely to be born into intellectually rich home environments. *Evocative covariance* occurs when certain characteristics tend to evoke specific environmental reactions and actions; thus, children who show a propensity for a specific line of culturally valued endeavor (e.g., music or mathematics) are likely to evoke positive responses from adults (e.g., getting more encouragement to develop their talents). *Active covariance* occurs when children seek specific types of environment to the benefit of their own proclivities and optimal development; for example, those who enjoy arts are more likely to select specific environments, or even create their own, that favor or afford the expression of their artistic interests. Note that these three types of covariance or correlation are described by Scarr (1992) as indicating gene-environment correlations. If probabilistic epigenesis is a better explanatory device for human development, then, genes do not directly "interact" with the external environment; rather, genes express themselves by producing specific proteins in response to specific types of neural and behavioral activity vis-à-vis environmental stimulation (see Figure 3.1). Certain traits (e.g., sensation seeking) have direct genetic origins (see Zuckerman, 2004). Other traits are polygenic; that is, they are multiply determined and no single correspondence can be found between traits and genes.

Lack of Intermediate Models That Integrate Structure and Function, and Person and Process in Talent Development

From a scientific point of view, the current problem regarding the nature-nurture of giftedness is the lack of intermediate models, that is, models that connect and integrate being and doing/becoming, and the person on the one hand and social and developmental contexts on the other. Gagné's (2004) DMGT model of how giftedness (i.e., natural endowment) gets "transformed" into systematically developed talents in culturally valued domains does not contain any specification of fine-grained intermediate processes and levels (e.g., how exactly the transformation takes place). In hindsight, the field of giftedness research is deeply rooted in faculty psychology and the psychometric tradition (including mapping human abilities through the factor analytic technique; e.g., Carroll, 1993). It has limited communication with modern cognitive psychology that emphasizes the transformational power of knowledge representation in reasoning and problem solving (Ceci & Liker, 1986; Chi, Feltovich, & Glaser, 1981), and modern developmental psychology, which emphasizes a systems view of development (Bronfenbrenner, 1989) and dynamic skill development situated in adaptive contexts (Fischer & Bidell, 2006). Going beyond psychometrics (and population thinking) to make truly developmental-differential accounts of gifted development needs support from modern cognitive and developmental psychology and from cognitive and affective neuroscience (e.g., Panksepp, 1998).

In search of fine-grained differential-developmental accounts of what develops and how *differential development* occurs every step of the way, we need to consider constitutional (endogenous) and environmental (exogenous) forces as integral parts of a developmental system and how a developmental niche is created and maintained through multiple selection processes at various critical developmental junctures (Dai & Renzulli, 2008). To avoid fruitless debates on the nature-nurture of giftedness, we need to give up ambitious attempts to develop grand theories (theories that try to explain everything), and instead seek more modest, midrange theories (Merton, 1973). Midrange theories have limited generalizability in terms of nature and nurture contributions or interactions vis-à-vis particular types and levels of excellence involved, but explain specific types of talent development well (e.g., prodigies in music, talented young mathematicians, precocious development of scientific thinking, early creativity in painting as compared to a more mature one, or expertise in chess, to name a few). Such midrange theories would particularly seek understandings of how mental structures and functions develop in the brain in coping with task demands and how person, content, and process interact in a specific context of development. Theories developed this way would not only be in a better position to explain the nature and nurture of exceptional competence in specific lines of talent development, but also be more useful for identification and intervention/programming (see Chapter 4 for more elaboration).

Objective and Subjective Stances on Talent Development: Do Intentional States Matter?

From a more general epistemological point of view, scholars who hold a "being" view of giftedness tend to hold an objectivist view of giftedness and talent development. In contrast, models that stress "doing/becoming" permits a distinct role of subjective experiences (see Cross, 2003). Most of these subjective experiences (emotions, feelings, ideas, and desires in our consciousness) are *intentional states* that signify the meanings of person-object, person-person or person-self relationships. When your hand accidentally touches the stove and experiences a burning sensation, this sensation relates you to the stove in a new way (it can be dangerous despite its utility). This directed nature of conscious states is called *intentionality* in philosophy and has a direct bearing on how we cognitively represent the world in its relations to the self (Damasio, 1999; Searle, 2004). Incidentally, intentional states should not be equated with "intentions," though an intention is an intentional state. Intentionality so defined is a broader concept; a belief that the earth is round is not an intention, but it is an "intentional state," because of its referential quality and its subjective nature.

The most simple and obvious form of the nature-nurture controversy is the respective role of ability and effort, or Edison's famous dictum about the role of inspiration and perspiration. Abilities are often regarded as not easily influenced by conscious efforts. Indeed, sometimes intentional states are constrained by ability; for example, not everyone can develop "the right feel" for a particular piece of music, just as very few can achieve the kind of mathematical intuitions John Nash did, albeit these feelings and intuitions are distinctly intentional states. Even motivational states, such as desires and interests (e.g., intellectual curiosity), can be seen as constrained by cognitive abilities. However, it is also obvious that mental exertion (i.e., efforts) and reflective control of one's learning and performance significantly contribute to self-engendered skill and knowledge development, even one's intelligence (Perkins & Grotzer, 1997). Unless one argues, along with Galton (1869), that level of effort a person is willing to exert, like ability, is also highly heritable and thus is merely nature's trick to make someone work harder, intentional states are a critical source of power to be reckoned with in their own right (Bidell & Fischer, 1997), rather than epiphenomenal or trivial, only to be *explained away* by some deeper "natural" forces. A case in point is deliberate practice, which is strongly advocated by Ericsson (2006) as a main mechanism for skill development beyond the ordinary range. Deliberate practice by definition is a form of mental exertion involving intentionality (goals, beliefs, deployment of attention and efforts, etc.). Although Ericsson et al. (2007a) acknowledged that deliberate practice can be constrained by both internal and external factors, including temperament, which is considered an enduring aspect of personality, there is a distinct purposeful and volitional aspect, as deliberate practice is not intrinsically enjoyable and can easily break down without social support and determination (Ericsson et al., 1993).

Intentional states are not epiphenomenal, as many self-related beliefs are known to have social cognitive origins and known to influence one's performance and choice in a nontrivial manner. For example, intentional states such as self-efficacy appraisals (Bandura, 1997), self-concepts (Harter, 1999), and possible selves (Markus & Nuirus, 1986) can be conceptually and empirically distinguished from ability constructs. The most instructive case of intentional states influencing cognitive processes is entity versus incremental theories of ability or related mindsets (Dweck, 1999, 2006): When one's control-related beliefs dwindle in the face of setbacks, one's performance also debilitates.

Beyond the ability-effort distinction, both the nature and nurture accounts can easily miss the role of intentional states as responsible for internalizing and transforming cultural knowledge in a personal way that makes creative contributions possible (Gruber, 1986). An account of personal endeavor similar to what Gruber called *organization of purpose* is needed to fully explain talent development. This may be why many scholars in the field felt compelled to make room for a "subjective action space" (Ziegler, 2005, p. 417; see also Shavinina, 2004). Is it nature or nurture? Maybe it is both, connecting both culture and biology. Maybe it is a form of agency in its own right, a force, which, once formed, has its own momentum. What we still don't know is *how much these intentional states are constrained by biology and to what extent they are empowered by culture (through its symbolic and technical tools) to the point of transcending the limits of what genes permit for human development.* However, one thing is certain: If we refuse to get into this subjective realm for the fear of losing scientific objectivity, we will lose substantial explanatory power as far as human development is concerned, especially its culminating form—excellence.

We can also look at the role of intentional states on a large social scale. Consider cultural values regulating intentional states of its members as analogous to natural selection through sexual selection and reproduction. Particular traits highlighted, or the aspects of exceptional competence or expertise extolled by a specific culture, have a distinct value dimension. A telling example is musical training. Many Asian Americans in my local community (including myself) send their children for piano lessons. In most cases, playing the piano was not a choice these children made, so it would be hard to argue that they were born with musical inclinations. Suppose that this were a distinct pattern of upbringing not shared by other cultures; then the overrepresentation of Asian students at Julliard cannot be explained by arguing that children of Asian descent are more musically talented, but has to be explained by resorting to parental values and expectations and child-rearing practices. In this regard, Nisbett's (2009) recent account of three cultural groups in regard to the role of school and culture in promoting intellectual development is quite compelling.

CONCLUSION: MULTIPLE PATHWAYS TO EXCELLENCE

In conclusion, biology is not destiny as far as outstanding accomplishments and excellence are concerned. However, it is not trivial either. I argue that the dichotomous thinking is problematic in light of how nature and nurture interact in developmental processes. Equifinality of human potential that suggests multiple pathways to excellence (different patterns of nature-nurture interaction might lead to the same level of achievement) is often ignored in the field of gifted studies. Because of the multitude and diversity of the phenomena of exceptional competence, I argue that midrange theories of a limited scope of generality are more appropriate than all-purpose grand theories of giftedness. For that matter, the lack of intermediate models of how nature and nurture interact given a specific line of talent development hampers progress in the field, theoretically as well as practically. More specific delineation of a particular line of precocious and advanced development is needed for theoretical justification of a particular identification and education practice, a topic to be elaborated in the next chapter.

Hedgehog or Fox? Domain Specificity Versus Domain Generality as a Joint Function of Person, Domain, and Development

Human beings, viewed as behaving systems, are quite simple. The apparent complexity of our behavior over time is largely a reflection of the complexity of the environment in which we find ourselves.

—Herbert Simon, *The Sciences of the Artificial*

From one point of view, which I associated earlier with the hedgehog, human beings possess extremely general powers, all-purpose information-processing mechanisms which can be put to a large, or perhaps even an infinite, number of uses. From an opposite perspective, that more reminiscent of the fox, human beings (like other species) have a proclivity to execute certain specifiable intellectual operations, while proving incapable of performing other intellectual operations.

—Howard Gardner, *Frames of Mind*

THE DOMAIN SPECIFICITY versus domain generality issue is not as contested as the nature-nurture issue, but is of equal theoretical and practical importance. If giftedness represents a domain-general advantage, widely applicable to multiple domains and fields, then identification should adopt a hedgehog strategy: using one rather than varied criteria. Further, dealing with one's multipotentialities becomes a real issue for gifted individuals in course selection and career planning, and individuals will have to make decisions about how they can maximally use their potential to advance their individual interests and social agendas. Conversely, if giftedness is highly circumscribed human potential (as the term *talent* implies), with high "niche potential" in one domain but low "niche potential" in another, then it would be imperative to match a program with specific individual profiles to maximize the educational benefits to these individuals. This view is consistent with that noted by VanTassel-Baska (2005):

> Conceptions of giftedness that focus on domain-specific considerations hold the most promise for promoting talent development in individuals at all stages of development because of the capacity to make appropriate correspondence between aptitudes and interventions, between predispositions and interests, and between the life of the mind and creating a life in the real world. (p. 358)

Besides the practical importance, *investigation of the issue of domain specificity generality would lead to a more in-depth understanding of the nature-nurture issue by delineating the interplay of abilities/dispositions, environment (including education), and development in shaping a person's life trajectory, from rudimentary forms of emergent talent to full-blown expertise and creative productivity.*

In this chapter, I first point out how the domains of giftedness are defined in educational practice and identify some pitfalls of using convenient, rather than theoretically sound, categories. I then discuss three key aspects in understanding domain specificity generality of high potential: (a) domain specificity generality as an issue of human cognitive architecture or infrastructure; (b) domain specificity as an issue of differential affordances and demands of different culturally created domains; and (c) domain specificity as an issue of differentiation and integration in development over time vis-à-vis specific functional contexts, involving different timing and trajectories. I argue that these three aspects (person, domain, and development) tend to jointly generate domain-specific trajectories while allowing for much developmental flexibility and alternative pathways, depending on life circumstances and timing of certain life events. Finally, I focus on the development of creative productivity as a window of opportunity to examine the viability of domain-general and domain-specific views of creativity.

HOW DOMAINS OF GIFTEDNESS ARE DEFINED

In everyday communication, *domain* is a rather vague term, conveying a sense that certain cognitive capacities or functions are bounded or confined, not universally applicable. Conceptual confusion is compounded when domains or categories of gifted behaviors are based on convenient, implicit models (i.e., folk beliefs) rather than rigorously defined and scientifically supported models and criteria. For example, consider the definition offered in the official Marland Report (Marland, 1972):

> Gifted and talented children are those ... who by virtue of outstanding abilities are capable of high performance. ... Children capable of high performance include those who have demonstrated any of the following abilities or aptitudes, singly or in combination: 1) general intellectual ability, 2) specific academic aptitude, 3) creative or productive thinking, 4) leadership ability, 5) visual and performing arts aptitude, 6) psychomotor ability. (p. ix)

A major problem with such a convenient taxonomy is that the categories are not mutually exclusive or, indeed, rigorously or consensually defined. Leadership has a social as well as expertise/creativity dimension and can manifest itself across domains; creative (or productive) thinking is not a domain of its own but a process, which can be manifested in all domains of human activity. Such convenient categories could mislead educational practice because they are often seen by educators as a scientifically justified typology of giftedness. The conceptual problem is exacerbated by the tendency in everyday, even scholarly, communication to confuse descriptive categories as explanatory factors. For example, multiple intelligence theory (Gardner, 1983) initially proposed seven types of intelligence or talent as forming a basic architecture of human abilities (hence "frames of mind"), each of which is relatively independent, structurally as well as functionally. However, naturalistic and spiritual intelligences were later added as new candidates (Gardner, 1998). Similarly, factor analysis of psychometric tests has yielded numerous ability factors (e.g., Carroll, 1993), and the researchers are eager to put new names and concepts on newly found structural patterns of data. The tendency to postulate a new ability structure purely based on a particular pattern of empirical data renders the determination of domains of human functioning a highly arbitrary exercise.

An alternative approach is to start with simple assumptions and work toward more refined and complex models of domains of human functioning. We can start with biology and ask the following question: Does evolution provide homo sapiens with a general intellectual capacity to deal with enormous novelty, variety, and complexity of its environments or equip it with a variety of talents in dealing with specific types of situations and challenges (Feldman, 2003)? Historically, early *person-centered definitions* of giftedness ("the gifted child" movement; Morelock, 1996) focused on domain-general traits, such as general intelligence or personality characteristics (e.g., capacity, zeal, and the work ethic; Galton, 1869), while later developed *domain-specific definitions* of giftedness focus on diverse manifestations of talents ("the talent development movement"), thus broadening the range of behavioral manifestations deemed "gifted" (Marland, 1972; Witty, 1958). As discussed in Chapter 1, the changes in the field of psychology in general and giftedness in particular over the second half of the 20th century can be characterized as taking a domain-specific turn. Gardner's (1983) theory of multiple intelligences was but a most salient milestone of this movement. Although some theorists claimed that the tension has been effectively resolved by factor-analytically derived hierarchical model of cognitive abilities, incorporating both narrow and broad abilities (e.g., Carroll, 1993; Messick, 1992), scholars still differ on whether gifted potential can be best characterized as a general (widely applicable) advantage or a special one. For example, while the talent development movement has been gaining more of a following, the traditional IQ-based "gifted child" approach still has many adherents (e.g., Gallagher, 2000b; Robinson, Zigler, & Gallagher, 2000; see Morelock, 1996, for a review). Some theories prescribe additional categories of giftedness (e.g., socioaffective), but still hold fast to intellectual giftedness as a unitary category (Gagné, 2005a, 2009a).

If biology represents one end of the continuum of human experience, culture constitutes the other. We can ask, Are cultural domains different in terms of the opportunities and challenges they afford and the developmental processes involved? For example, in an edited volume, Sternberg et al. (2004) especially

focused on whether processes and developmental patterns leading to creative productivity are specific to a narrowly defined area of human endeavor or are domain general. By the same token, Ericsson (Ericsson et al., 2007a) and Weisberg
(2006) took on the issue of whether creative productivity entails domain-specific
expertise. In the context of gifted education, the tension can be expressed in the
following thesis and antithesis:

> Thesis:
> Giftedness is not inherently confined to any single domain, because general
> cognitive abilities can be flexibly channeled and utilized in multiple ways,
> depending on environmental circumstances and motivations.

> Antithesis:
> Giftedness is domain-specific, because each domain has its own unique
> set of demands in terms of sensitivities, inclinations, and abilities, which
> are tuned to a particular set of objects, symbolic meanings, and underlying
> relationships.

DOMAIN SPECIFICITY AND DOMAIN GENERALITY AS AN ISSUE OF THE BASIC ARCHITECTURE OF HUMAN FUNCTIONING: HORIZONTAL, VERTICAL, OR HIERARCHICAL?

There have been major psychometric, cognitive, and developmental research attempts to map out the *frame of mind* in terms of its structure and functions. Over
time, three distinct views have been developed: horizontal, vertical, and hierarchical views of human abilities.

General Intelligence and the Horizontal Mind

Since the inception of the psychometric testing of intelligence, the nature of the
general factor, or g, first identified by Spearman (1904), has been subjected to
much research and debates (e.g., Jensen, 1993, 2001; Sternberg & Grigorenko,
2002; van der Maas et al., 2006). There are as many true believers as disbelievers
and skeptics about the existence of "general intelligence." A typical definition of
general intelligence is "the ability to reason, solve problems, think abstractly, and
acquire knowledge" (Gottfredson, 1997, p. 93), or more narrowly, "the degree
to which, and the rate at which, people are able to learn, and retain in long-term
memory, the knowledge and skills that can be learned from the environment"
(Carroll, 1997, p. 44). The notion of general intelligence is predicated on the mind
as a general, all-purpose information-processing device, from basic attention,
perception, and memory, to complex symbol manipulation, reasoning, problem
solving, and decision making. Such a mind is considered *horizontally* structured,

progressing from simple perception and memory functions to increasingly complex and abstract thinking capabilities (hence, the *horizontal mind*). Based on the assumption of the horizontal mind, psychometric researchers (Cattell, 1971; Horn, 1986) conceptualized a two-tier system, with *fluid intelligence* representing a domain-general capacity for learning and adaptation, and *crystallized intelligence* being the result of exercising one's fluid intelligence and by nature dealing with specific content and being knowledge rich (see also Stankov, 2003; Li et al., 2004). High general, fluid intelligence is assumed to have an enduring, life span influence on skill acquisition (Gagné, 2005a). A learning advantage seems evident based on comparisons of high- and average-IQ subjects on a variety of learning tasks, whether based on behavioral (e.g., Kanevsky, 1990; Kanevsky & Geake, 2004) or physiological (Haier, 2001) criteria. There is also evidence that measures of general intelligence yield higher correlations with learning ability when the complexity of cognitive learning tasks increases (Gustafsson & Undheim, 1996; Skantov, 2003). Presumably, task complexity increases the need for fluid reasoning abilities (Lohman, 1993).

It should be noted that, when evaluating this body of research, the most reliable tests of intelligence like the Stanford-Binet or Wechsler deliberately measure a heterogeneous set of abilities and skills. In that sense, IQ represents a measure of *aptitude complex*, consisting of different but somewhat intercorrelated abilities, rather than a unitary capacity. Thomson (1916) was among the earliest to question the "*g*" interpretation of the intercorrelations of "positive manifold." Measuring individuals' IQ is like ranking universities (Horn, 1986). Although we know that each university has some relatively strong departments and some relatively weak departments (analogous to intrapersonal strengths and weaknesses), we nevertheless highlight the overall efficiency and quality of a university (or a person's intellectual functioning) at the cost of precision and detail. I call such an IQ-based conception of intelligence and intellectual giftedness a *black-box approach*. It does not do much harm, as long as one bears in mind that discrepancies among subtests are more likely on the high end of the IQ spectrum; that is, in the above-average range, two persons with the same high intelligence test score are more likely to have different cognitive profiles (distinct strengths and weakness reflected in subtest scores), and for the below-average range, a *g* factor, indicated by high intercorrelations among subtests, is more distinct (Detterman & Daniel, 1989; Hunt, 1999; Jensen, 2001; Sweetland, Reina, & Tatti, 2006; Wilkinson, 1993); thus a general ability or *g* interpretation of IQ scores is more justified. Jensen (2001), a staunch champion of *g*, concurred with Charles Spearman on the law of diminishing returns for general intelligence in that "the demands of various mental tasks reflect a *g* to a great degree in individuals of below-average ability than in individuals of above-average ability" (p. 9). As we move to the extreme scores such as top 5 or 3%, discrepancies are the greatest, and there is much heterogeneity within the high-IQ group. Of course, correlations between subtests never plunge to zero. If we push the university-IQ analogy a step further, even though there are within-university discrepancies or disparities with respect to the quality of various departments, top universities still tend to have better departments across the board compared to most average universities. Therefore, intercorrelation of abilities or "positive manifold" still holds in many cases for students whose IQ scores are in the gifted range. Some psychometrically oriented researchers feel that such a positive manifold justifies a *g* interpretation at the high end of the IQ spectrum and consequently a general "intellectually gifted" category (see Gagné, 2009a; Robinson, 2005), while others (including this author) are more skeptical, believing that the notion of *g* as a unitary core of giftedness does not resonate with the evidence for the asymmetry of intercorrelations of abilities for high and low performers (see Hunt, 1999). Given the fact that "vocabulary" scores carry the largest share of *g*, we might think of high general intelligence as having a distinct verbal ability component.

Modular Views of Human Abilities and the "Vertical" Mind

An approach to the architecture of human functioning that is diametrically opposite to the domain-general (horizontal) approach is to view the mind as consisting of many modular devices. From this point of view, the brain is literally "vertical," in the sense that there is a division of labor between the left and right hemispheres and among different sections of the brain that are somewhat vertically structured. This view has been championed not only by early brain researchers (see Gazzaniga, 2000, for a review), which inspired Gardner's (1983) conception of multiple intelligences, but also by many evolutionary psychologists (e.g., Cosmides & Tooby, 2003), who proposed *massive modularity* to denote pervasive specialized functions as a result of the evolution of the human species. Neonativists in developmental psychology further proposed innate rudimental principles for knowledge building, such as an intuitive basis of number, force, and agency, and naive or intuitive physics, biology, and psychology. Although there are controversies about how innately specified these devices are (Fischer & Bidell, 2006), it is now well accepted that some domains or types of information are more "privileged" than others for processing. In short, the brain not only processes information in different modes (e.g., verbal versus spatial), but also privileges certain kinds of information (e.g., people versus things). Consequently, individuals develop a special set of cognitive strengths and affective preferences (or interests) (Lubinski & Benbow, 1992; Webb, Lubinski, & Benbow, 2002). Child prodigies in specific domains (Feldman, 1986) are a distinct case of special talents and proclivities.

Strong modular views of the architecture of human functioning, particularly when used to explain competences in culturally created domains, have serious theoretical and empirical difficulties. Granted that there are many specialized brain functions that can be localized (e.g., Broca and Wernick areas for language processing; see Dronkers, 1999), there are also many connections and communications among these putative modular devices. Any complex brain functions such as those responsible for music or language are necessarily performed by distributed but highly coordinated neural systems, rather than isolated modules. To coordinate complex neural and mental actions, executive functions, subserved by frontal lobes, maintain the regulatory power (Goldberg, 2001; Newman, Carpenter, Varma, & Just, 2003). Together, neuroscientific evidence suggests that, even at the brain level, local modularity without some central executive regulation is not tenable, as it can quickly degrade into anarchy when dealing with the complexities and uncertainties of the world. Empirically, neither a strong modular view of distinct, independent abilities nor a strong domain-general view of intelligence as a unitary capacity is supported. This point becomes clearer by noticing that most of these cognitive abilities as measured by extant psychometric tests are biologically secondary and significantly culturally mediated (Geary, 1995). For example, Plucker, Callahan, and Tomchin (1996) tested the multiple intelligences theory using a variety of rating and testing measures. The factor analysis yielded four factors, thus supporting a multidimensional model of human abilities, but not the multiple intelligence (MI) theory per se, as factor loadings did not all follow the theoretical prediction based on the MI theory. However, Pyryt (2000) reanalyzed the data, performing a second-order factor analysis of the four factors, and was able to extract a higher-order general factor (g) that accounts for 56% of the total variance. Although these findings are subject to different interpretations (see Plucker, 2000), the positive manifold (i.e., positive correlations among the four factors) at least suggests shared performance components across the diverse set of tasks used in Plucker et al.'s study, rather than four independent performance modules.

The Hierarchical Solution

The psychometric tradition offers a hierarchical solution to the domain specificity generality by proposing a hierarchical model of broad and narrow abilities based on factor analytic results (Carroll, 1993; Messick, 1992). This hierarchical model refines Spearman's two-factor model of intelligence (a general factor plus task-specific factors), and Cattell's (1971) distinction between crystallized and fluid intelligence. Accordingly, a conception of giftedness can be hierarchical as well.

The hierarchical solution, though more integrated and sophisticated than earlier psychometric theories of human abilities, runs the same risk of reification (i.e., granting certain behavioral or psychological phenomena or data structures a status of ontological existence). Vernon, who was the earliest pioneer of ability classification using factor analysis, had this to say: "I do not think it is correct to say that I regard, or have ever regarded, hierarchy as a psychological model. It is . . . simply . . . a convenient way for classifying test performances" (quoted in Lohman & Rocklin, 1995, p. 450; see also Deary, 2002). Although we might infer the existence of 80 some factor-analytically verified abilities, we have no way of knowing whether they are methodological artifacts created by the statistical technique or reflect the true division of labor in the mind, nor do we know how they develop. More recently, Molenaar (2004) challenged the assumption that interindividual (between-person) measures of variation can be used to infer intraindividual (within-person) variation over time. He showed that the assumption of the homogeneity of mental attributes underlying this psychometric tradition disguises or obscures much heterogeneity of individual functioning and development. Nevertheless, the hierarchical perspective does clarify one point: Some psychometrically defined abilities are more central than others in terms of their correlations across a range of tasks (Carroll, 1993; Snow, Kyllonen, & Marshalek, 1983), suggesting that some abilities are more pervasive in their impact and are more important than others.

Another way of thinking of the mind as hierarchical is to regard its functional properties as having both vertical and horizontal aspects, in the sense that there are vertical structures that represent specific modes of operation (verbal versus spatial) or dedicated to specific types of information (social versus physical), and there are also horizontal processes that organize and coordinate a variety of response components and monitor and control the effectiveness of functioning (Snow, 1992). Thus, the domain specificity of a gifted manifestation is really a matter of identifying performance components that are unique to the task at hand and components that can be used for other tasks (i.e., having higher degrees of generality; Snow et al., 1983). Although Gardner (1983) contended that Piaget focused on logical-mathematical intelligence to the exclusion of musical or interpersonal intelligence, he concurred with Piaget on the more pervasive impact of logical-mathematical thinking compared to other aspects of mental functions. In this sense, there is no "general intelligence" in the sense of an all-purpose intelligent system; but some cognitive functions (e.g., linguistic or verbal ability) are more pervasive in their applications across a range of tasks than others, and superiority in these functions may afford some individuals a distinct advantage across a range of tasks.

Some scholars and researchers have proposed broad categories of giftedness based on assumptions of the architecture of human functioning, such as intellectual, socioaffective, creative, and psychomotor (Gagné, 2004, 2005a; cf. Heller, Perleth, & Lim, 2005, who added music competence). Lubinski and Benbow (2006) have a de facto tripartite model of giftedness, seeing mathematical, verbal, and spatial abilities as three essential abilities, overlapping with three corresponding intelligences posited by Gardner (1983).

A Critique of Static Views of Domain Specificity
Generality of Giftedness

Although approaching the domain-specificity issue from a static structural point of view has its merits, *there are inherent weaknesses in mapping the exceptional mind or brain structurally without looking at how it interacts with the environment, and how it develops over time*. First, models based on such structural views are static; they do not explain how abilities arise and evolve in dynamic task conditions. Such models often amount to simply declaring that a person is mathematically gifted without explaining what is unique about the way this person is dealing with mathematical problems, which sets her apart from others; in other words, it is not capable of identifying and differentiating components that are dynamically assembled and organized to produce an excellent performance.

Second, static models of ability classification are not sensitive to stages of development and levels of developmental complexity; they do not distinguish, for instance, between an ability that is emergent and developing and an ability that is fully developed. For instance, an IQ score of 130 for a 6-year-old versus for a 16-year-old reflects a completely different level of cognitive and developmental complexity, yet the test scores themselves do not indicate any developmental changes from 6 to 16 years of age, because these scores are based on age norms and are not developmentally calibrated to reflect a new level of cognitive capabilities (McCall, 1981), which can be qualitatively different from earlier ones (Piaget, 1950/2001).

Third, they do not differentiate product and process. This point particularly applies to psychometric testing. What a test yields is a score indicating *how well* one performs on the test (i.e., product), not *how* one did it (i.e., process). Particularly pertinent to the domain specificity generality issue, *what* is achieved early on as developing competencies may be specific to a cognitive or culturally defined domain, and *how* it is achieved may not (e.g., see Chapter 3 for discussion of ease of learning).

In sum, the main weakness of the structural (cognitive architectural) approaches to domain specificity generality is its inadequate consideration of functional contexts and developmental processes. Consider the development of language capacity as human symbolic capability, a major higher mental function. Karmiloff-Smith (2004) had this to say:

> Ontogeny [can be] seen as the prime force for turning a number of domain-relevant processes progressively into domain-specific outcomes in the adults. This does not imply that the infant brain is a single, homogeneous learning device. On the contrary, there is, no doubt, much heterogeneity in the initial gross wiring of the brain. But, contrary to what is often claimed, this heterogeneity bears little resemblance to the ultimate functional structures that can only emerge through interaction with a structured environment. (p. 232)

If this is the case for language development, it should be even more true for the development of talents in cultural domains such as music, literature, chess, science, mathematics, and engineering, which are considered biologically secondary and heavily socially and symbolically mediated, in contrast to language capacity, which is considered a biologically primary ability and thus can be acquired without

explicit guidance and instruction (Geary, 1995). In other words, none of the superior functions in these cultural domains is "hard wired." Therefore, *the key to
the question of domain specificity may not be in the biological makeup (cognitive
infrastructure or architecture) but in ontogeny (individual development) and its
social context.*

MEANING OF DOMAIN SPECIFICITY OR DOMAIN GENERALITY AT DIFFERENT LEVELS OF DEVELOPMENT

One method of first approximation is to take a development-sensitive approach to
defining domain-specific and domain-general competencies. This is what Coleman and Cross (2005) did when they defined giftedness as relatively undifferentiated high potential in childhood, more differentiated domain-specific achievement
in adolescence, and highly differentiated expertise and eminent accomplishments
in adulthood (see also Mayer, 2005). It should be noted quickly that "relatively
undifferentiated high potential" does not equate to a unitary whole, or a sort of the
all-purpose functional system, only to be articulated and differentiated through
structured experience. As Karmiloff-Smith (2004) points out, there is much heterogeneity and "verticality." There are elementary, crude, and underspecified predilections and inclinations, but predilections and inclinations nonetheless. A child
who is tuned into musical rhythms and melodies with facility shows such a pre-
dilection, though we cannot say with confidence that the brain system of this
child is prewired for music. Rather, if there is much modularity (a structural and
functional whole) in musical talent, it is an acquired module through the interplay
of predilections, musical experience, intentional learning, and practice (Schlaug,
2001). Based on the stages of development and complexity of nature-nurture interaction and reciprocation, we could tentatively adopt a three-tier classification
of various abilities and dispositions:

1. *Tier 1 abilities and dispositions: the spontaneously developed abilities
   and dispositions* in the early stage of development. A hallmark of these
   abilities and dispositions is that they take *minimal experience* necessary
   for their typical development and calibration (Horowitz, 2000). This is
   the basic infrastructure of human functioning Gardner (1983) referred to
   when he titled his book on multiple intelligences *Frames of Mind*. It is
   similar to Gagné's (2005a) categories of giftedness but more heterogeneous and amorphous with respect to how well-formed specific abilities
   and dispositions are. Evidence for the heritability of these characteristics
   can be garnered to support the contribution of "nature" to these "spontaneously" developed abilities and dispositions (Simonton, 2008).

2. *Tier 2 competences and interests: the significantly "schooled" and systematically developed mind* in the intermediate stage of development. A

hallmark of these competences and interests is that they are significantly mediated by the use of symbol systems and cultural tools and knowledge. Interests are highlighted as they indicate self-differentiation from others as well as within themselves. Tier 2 competences and interests correspond to the notion of talents in Gagné's DMGT model, though they can be domain-specific or domain-general (e.g., learning how to learn).

3. *Tier 3 expertise and identity: the highly "trained," specialized, integrated mind* in the mature stage of development, serving unique functions of adaptation to a particular domain of human functioning, akin to what is intensively studied by Ericsson and colleagues (Ericsson et al., 2006).

Table 4.1 shows levels of developmental complexity in terms of differentiation and integration and the plausibility of inferring levels of differentiation of abilities, competencies, and expertise as a function of one's developmental status. Tier 1 abilities and dispositions are low in differentiation because we not only grant high plasticity and functional flexibility to early childhood, and the more or less amorphous status of these abilities and dispositions, but also allow for higher instability in ability manifestations during childhood. As a child grows into adolescence, we could infer more specialized functional units or even acquired modules as a result of education and training.

I include dispositions, interests, and identity in the mix, depending on developmental stages, largely because these personal elements (e.g., the musical temperament [Kemp, 1996]) are functionally just as important as those we considered cognitive abilities. I prefer to use *personal profile* as a unit of description, not any single dimension of ability. In essence, I attempt to avoid an ability-centric view of human competencies (see Perkins & Ritchhart, 2004, for a critique; see also Feist, 2006) and treat cognitive, emotional, and motivational processes in

Table 4.1. Three-tier classification of abilities, competences, and expertise by level of developmental complexity and corresponding method of assessment.

		Level of Differentiation	Level of Integration	Methods of Assessment
Tier 1	Latent abilities and dispositions Basic functional units	Low	Low	Inferred
Tier 2	Developing competencies and interests Intermediate functional units	High	Low	Observed or inferred
Tier 3	Fully developed expertise and identity Advanced functional units	High	High	Observed

developing, say, math or musical abilities, as intricately intertwined (see Dai & Sternberg, 2004).

Accordingly, we may consider both various highly specialized functions and dedicated mechanisms (e.g., perception of space and depth) and relatively domain-general information-processing apparatus (e.g., working-memory capacity) as constituting Tier 1 abilities, and many temperament-based and content-sensitive personality and motivational characteristics (e.g., sensitivities, overexcitabilities, persistence of interest, specific patterns of preferences for reward structures) as Tier 1 dispositions. We can imagine that, at this level, a child develops over time a miscellaneous and heterogeneous set of abilities and dispositions not well articulated and organized, but already showing potential and direction. Emergent mathematical, narrative, spatial-artistic abilities in early childhood (6–8 years of age, early elementary school years) studied by Porath (2006a) and her colleagues can be seen as situated at this developmental level. Giftedness defined in this stage of development is best characterized as *precocity* (i.e., ahead of age peers in development) vis-à-vis a particular line of talent development.

Built up from Tier 1 abilities and dispositions are a range of higher-order, knowledge-rich functional units (Tier 2 competencies and interests), what Vygostky (1978) called higher mental functions, such as various domain knowledge, reading comprehension, mathematical sense-making and problem solving, scientific thinking and reasoning (theory-data coordination), deductive and inductive thinking, metacognitive knowledge and skills, aesthetic appreciation of various musical and artistic expressions and styles, and various general or domain-specific habits of mind and personal epistemologies (Perkins & Ritchhart, 2004). These cognitive competencies and affective interests cannot be "natural," because each culture clearly shapes the way they develop through its enculturation process (Sternberg, 2007a, 2007b). Thus, an ear for music is an "enculturated" one. They cannot be completely "cultural" either, because variations in these competencies and interests reflect individuals' *signature* ways of responding to and interacting with their environmental opportunities and structures (Mischel & Shoda, 1995), and thus reveal (but cannot be reduced to) biological-constitutional aptitudes and inclinations of the person in question (Gagné, 2005a). Giftedness manifested in this stage of development is best characterized as *advanced achievement* (i.e., more advanced knowledge, skills, and dispositions).

In contrast with Tier 1 abilities and dispositions, but similar to Tier 2 competencies and interests, Tier 3 expertise and identity reflect a highly trained and highly specialized mind. But different from Tier 2 competencies and interests, high-level expertise is a result of prolonged (typically a minimum of 10 years), systematic development of knowledge, skills, and dispositions in a field of human activity as part of one's career, such as academics, arts, business, social service, sports, and technology (Ericsson, 2006; Gagné, 2005a), often accompanied by a parallel development of personal and professional identity. Giftedness defined in this stage of development is based on performance and contributions by the professional standards of excellence.

Now, to map out the developmental underpinnings of these three-tier abilities, imagine that Tier 1 abilities and dispositions are built up from bottom, subserved by the "hardware" of the brain: specific bundled groups of brain cells, neural circuits and networks, modules, and biochemical mechanisms, mediated by structuring experiences. Tier 2 competencies and interests are supported by hardware, but "programmed" by instruction and training to contain many knowledge-rich functional units such as schemas, rule-based operations, encapsulated knowledge units, associative networks of concepts, and theories (Hirschfeld & Gelman, 1994). Tier 3 expertise and identity, in contrast, is highly integrated domain-specific competence, often characterized by a form of knowledge encapsulation that renders expert performance perceptual and intuitive, highly sensitive to specific patterns of data in terms of regularities and anomalies. In principle, the more complex the organization of a specific ability or competence, the more likely it is positioned higher in the three-tier hierarchy.

To illustrate the distinction between precocity and advanced achievement, consider two children, one a 12-year-old and the other a 17-year-old; both scored 650 on the SAT-Math. Without further evidence to the contrary, we could infer that the score of 650 for the 12-year-old likely reflects more of Tier 1 abilities and dispositions conducive to mathematical development, and the score for the 17-year-old likely reflects more of Tier 2 competencies and interests, as well as schooling experience, though both persons could be considered "mathematically gifted." The underlying reasoning is that it would normally take more instructional "programming" for the 17-year-old to reach the comparable level of mathematical skills demonstrated by the 12-year-old. By the same token, one might infer the presence of mathematically relevant modular devices and reasoning schemes for the 12-year-old (Tier 1 latent abilities and dispositions) that permit fast acquisition of mathematical skills reflected in the 12-year-old's SAT math score. As indicated in Figure 4.1, in the assessment process, *advanced achievement* is observed for both children, but a higher degree of *precocity* is inferred for the 12-year-old. However, neither of them can be said to have reached the level of expertise in mathematics, as the SAT-Math likely taps into a diverse set of basic mathematical operations and reasoning, rather than tasks that require an advanced, integrated conceptual and technical mastery of a mathematical topic, which would reflect the highest level of developmental complexity of mathematical skills.

Although we may disagree on whether specific demonstrated abilities and dispositions can be best seen as Tier 1, 2, or 3 abilities and dispositions, the three-tier classification system can serve as a heuristic device for discussing what kind of "domain specificity" or domain generality" we are referring to developmentally, and how abilities and dispositions so defined can serve the purpose of identification and educational programming. For example, when we discuss Tier 1 abilities and dispositions, domain specificity involves understanding of how initial domain-relevant components are self-organized and turned into domain-specific structures and mechanisms (aptitudes), and how the general thought process interacts with content experiences to engender new learning and domain-specific competence. Domain specificity in Tier 2 competencies and interests is concerned with a set of knowledge-rich functional units and skills, which likely have varying degrees of generality and centrality across various domains of human endeavor; thus, one can ask whether metacognitive processes (e.g., awareness of what strategies work and what do not in the problem-solving process) are domain general, as suggested by Sternberg (1985), or whether they are fundamentally constrained by domain knowledge, as suggested by Ceci (2003). When domain specificity in Tier 3 high-level expertise is concerned, we can ask whether relevant knowledge of a domain or subdomain is highly encapsulated to the point of automaticity, impervious to conscious awareness and control, or whether it still entails controlled processes such as careful reasoning and metacognitive control (e.g., decide what to do when given a set of information). To the extent the process is automatic and information encapsulated, it is fixed and unable to show flexibility and generativity in terms of creating novel ideas and perspectives within or beyond the boundary of a domain in question. To the extent it is subject to metacognitive awareness and control, significant novelty and ingenuity in expert thinking is still possible. This framework, albeit still schematic, could potentially facilitate the development of midrange, intermediate models of talent development, which are sorely lacking, as I suggested in Chapter 3.

DOMAIN SPECIFICITY AS A DYNAMIC
BOOTSTRAPPING (FITTING) PROCESS

Each domain of major human activity (i.e., cultural domain) has its own unique set of affordances, goals, demands, and constraints, and therefore individuals, given exposure and opportunity for a wide range of activities, would experience selective affinity with a domain, depending on their propensities and capabilities. The concepts of affordances and constraints are central in ecological psychology. A domain of human activity, say, video games, affords and invites specific actions that bring into play certain human capacities and motives (e.g., imaginative play, spatial reasoning, decision making, competition, and interpersonal communication) but constrains and structures the way these capacities and motives are expressed and cultivated, just as a chair affords the action of sitting but at the same time constrains and structures the way you sit (e.g., compare the traditional European and Japanese ways of sitting, one with chairs and the other without). In colloquial language, affordances and constraints amount to opportunities and demands that a particular environment provide for people who are prepared to meet the challenges involved and reap the benefits of the opportunity. Neisser (1979) identified academic and practical settings as two domains requiring profoundly different kinds of intellectual functioning (hence practical versus academic intelligence). Likewise, one may consider high-level artistry as taking a different set of aptitudes to achieve (Subotnik & Jarvin, 2005). Moreover, the process is not merely a matter of static match or mismatch, but an active, adaptive bootstrapping (fitting) process to enhance one's "niche potential" or fit with a particular task environment. But before discussing this process, it is important to delineate the structure of major domains of human endeavor.

In human daily transactional experiences, ecological domains have to do with physical, biological, social, cultural-symbolic, and inner (self) worlds. Each of these experiences could engender informal learning and intellectual exploration. In formal educational settings, domains are more formally defined as areas of culturally valued human endeavor, with relatively clear boundaries such as humanities versus sciences, academics versus arts. For Csikszentmihalyi (1996; Csikszentmihalyi & Robinson, 1986), such a domain consists of a body of knowledge and cultural practices that, when internalized and personally transformed, renders someone an expert, even a creator, whereas a *field* is the social organization of a domain through its institutions, gatekeepers, accepted standards, and so on. For Phenix (1964), a domain of knowledge is a system of culturally created meanings intended to comprehend a specific set of phenomena, what we call disciplinary knowledge. To start with a broad framework, Tannenbaum (1997) developed a system that identifies three key elements of giftedness: *person* (producer or performer), *domain* (in what content and through what media), and *style* (how it is expressed).

As shown in Figure 4.1, the system distinguishes between "performers" and "producers" at the person level, which further differentiate into four domains of expression; each can be expressed either proficiently or creatively. Domains in this system are mainly intellectual (producers of thoughts), technical (producers of tangibles), artistic (performers of staged artistry), and social (performers of human service). There may be borderline cases (e.g., chess players may be regarded as performers of staged artistry, broadly defined, as well as producers of thoughts; a musician can be both a composer and performer). What is more important, though, is the implications of the framework. For example, if this system is correct, one may argue that experts studied by Ericsson (see Ericsson et al., 2007a) are by and large performers (e.g., performing artists, athletes), or producers of tangibles (e.g., computer gurus), particularly of the proficient, rather than creative, type. Theories developed based on specific modes of functioning, domains, and styles have limited generality, as there are potentially eight divergent patterns of development or trajectories (see Figure 4.1).

Further refinement is possible under this general framework or heuristic. For example, Feldman (2009) proposes a continuum of domain experiences, from universal to unique. On the more universal end of the continuum are Piagetian stages of development of logic and reasoning; moving toward the middle are pancultural

Figure 4.1. Defining who may show signs of giftedness, through what media it reveals itself, and how it can be expressed.

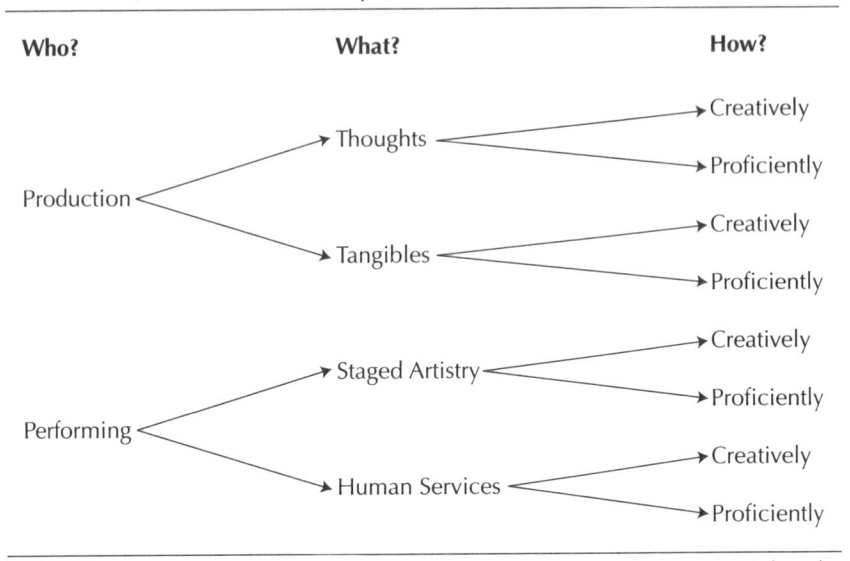

Note: From "The Meaning and Making of Giftedness," by A. J. Tannenbaum, in N. Colangelo & G. A. Davis (Eds.), *Handbook of Gifted Education* (2nd ed., p. 28), 1997. Boston: Allyn and Bacon. Copyright © 1997 by Allyn and Bacon. Reprinted with permission.

domains, such as speech, religion, music, art, and politics, and domains of basic skills expected of all societal members, such as reading, writing, and arithmetic, and domains that are foundations for most jobs and careers, such as American history, algebra, engineering, art. Moving toward the "unique" end of the continuum are domains that reflect specialty choice, such as journalism, tax lawyer, surgeon, martial arts instructor; on the extreme, unique end are idiosyncratic niches people created and even new creation of domains of human activity. The universal-unique continuum is important for one reason: Individual development tends to be more on the universal end first (e.g., picking up basic skills and world knowledge) and gradually branches out toward increasingly specialized modes of functioning. *Increasing differentiation* is a general principle of developmental adaptation, in terms of niches, trajectories, and pathways vis-à-vis social opportunities and demands that are salient at a particular developmental juncture.

Dai (2004a) identified several cognitive dimensions along which domains may differ, such as whether they are formal and analytic or informal and holistic. Also, following Tannenbaum's (1997) nomenclature or classification, performers differ from producers in that performers (surgeons, chess players, performing artists) typically have to make moment-to-moment decisions in dynamic settings with time pressures, whereas producers (scientists, composers, or inventors) are often allowed prolonged deliberation. Consequently, the ecology and demands of these two types of settings are quite different. Of course, diversity exists even within a domain. A good fit for gymnastics (e.g., nimbleness) may not be a good fit for basketball, which requires heights and strengths; therefore, the notion of a generic athletic aptitude is not very useful. A pertinent question is, "Aptitude for what?" (Lohman, 2005a). Consider also experimental versus theoretical physics; evolutionary versus molecular biology; or for that matter, clinical versus experimental psychology. Inclinations and cognitive/affective demands are quite different between these subfields of a discipline. Proximal and task-specific aptitudes are always more meaningful.

A distinct feature of such an ecological-functional approach to domain specificity is its focus on the nature of *doing in a domain*, with all its ecological richness, nuances, and complexities, instead of *being* with the assumptions of structures of human abilities. What one putatively possesses (Tier 1 abilities and dispositions, as shown in Figure 4.1) will naturally reveal itself when one is engaged in domain activities. Defined more formally, *a domain of cultural import is an area of human activity that has a distinct set of affordances and constraints vis-à-vis human abilities and dispositions.* Affordances activate relevant cognitive and affective processes; thus a musical piece affords aesthetic sensitivity, and a complex task affords reasoning. Affordances also indicate the positive or negative valence of a task; interest and enjoyment or anxiety and fear are major indicators. Constraints are specific conditions and demands imposed on anyone who engages in practice in a given domain and reflect the structure and demands of that activity (e.g., the goal structure, knowledge base, and procedural skills involved). It should be noted that constraints do not merely serve as gatekeepers or a set of conditions to be met for successful task performance; in a positive sense, constraints also help *structure* and *modulate* one's abilities in a way that facilitates a specific line of talent development. Affordances and constraints both shape one's development, depending on one's abilities and dispositions, in a process of bootstrapping, which I alluded to earlier and shall discuss in some detail in the following sections.

Mutual Sampling and Self-Organization of Abilities and Dispositions

Imagine that in child development, there are always an array of social or instructional situations that impinge upon the person and activate or invoke specific combinations of abilities and dispositions. Also imagine that the person is also actively seeking and selecting situations and making them personally favored domains of activity. This is a mutual sampling process: The outer environment is sampling the inner environment, but the inner environment is also selectively attending to and choosing the outer environment. This mutual sampling can occur in school environments where instructional conditions favor certain types of abilities and dispositions, whereas learners with certain aptitudes are more apt to advance their knowledge building in only some of their favored subjects (Snow, 1992). As children develop into adolescence and further into adulthood, they become more active in selecting their own environments and create their own "developmental niches," so to speak. Imagine further that such mutual sampling occurs at a neural, even molecular, level. Certain activities call a group of neural circuits into service and, as a result, assemble them into a highly coordinated functional unit, or even a module, whereas certain dominant "overexcitabilities" create what Panksepp (1998) called a "seeking system" that seeks its own favored stimuli. Most problems regarding how Tier 1 abilities and dispositions develop can be explained by this mutual sampling process. To use Tannenbaum's (1997) system, a developing person could gravitate toward tangibles or thoughts, staged artistry or human service. Some individuals are inclined to technical mastery and innovation, and others to conceptualization and understanding of the world (see also Kolb, 1971). Talent in natural language connotes some degree of spontaneity and ease of learning. This can be best explained by self-organization of lower-level units into higher-level function. But the matter cannot be merely an issue of "ability"; we have to look at the whole personality.

Snow's (1992) aptitude theory can illuminate this process. Aptitude à la Snow is proximal, relative to situations; it can include affective and conative as well as cognitive factors, and it can be negative (in which case, the term *inaptitude* is used). For a given domain, one may possess a combination of aptitudes (including possible inaptitudes) vis-à-vis a task environment. The term *aptitude complex* indicates a set of propensities that either work in concert or are at odds with each other in dealing with the challenge at hand (Ackerman, 2003; Ackerman & Kanfer, 2004; Cronbach, 2002; Snow, 1992; Snow, Corno, Jackson, 1996). Indeed, Lohman (2005a) conjectured that oftentimes inaptitudes can drag the person down despite the presence of good aptitudes for a task (see Simonton, 2005, for a similar position). Aptitude so defined is dynamic and evolving, rather than static and fixed; existing aptitude begets new aptitude, and new achievement serves as an emergent aptitude for further learning. Likewise, relatively unschooled talents can also be transformed into schooled competencies (e.g., amateur musicians become professional ones). Aptitudes themselves are not necessarily domain specific in the sense of being dedicated only to a specific domain, but they are *domain relevant* in terms of their applicability and centrality to a given domain (Simonton, 2005; Sternberg, 1986). For instance, spatial ability is not specific only to chess but it is nonetheless highly relevant to the chess domain. Abstract thinking (i.e., performing algebraic operations or discerning relevant variables from extraneous ones) can be used across domains, but becomes domain relevant at a specific stage in the development of domain knowledge, even in domains such as music, which requires a shift from an intuitive mode of processing music to an analytic one (Bamberger, 1986). The four Cs—coalescence, context, conflict, and consistency—posited by Haensly, Reynolds, and Nash (1986), can serve as a guide for determining whether one is fit to pursue a specific line of talent development. The recent Study of Mathematically Precocious Youth (SMPY) longitudinal follow-up studies investigated patterns of numerical, verbal, and spatial abilities by creating a measure of intraindividual ability tilt (i.e., within-person relative strengths and weaknesses; see Lubinski & Benbow, 2000, 2006). Different ability patterns were predictive of domain gravitations (Webb, Lubinski, & Benbow, 2007) as well as ultimate creative accomplishments in arts versus sciences (Park, Lubinski, & Benbow, 2007). Ackerman and Heggestad (1997) used cluster analysis with a large sample of college students and found four meaningful patterns of abilities, knowledge, and interests. These findings show that domain-specific developmental trajectories and pathways are predictable, given a set of abilities and dispositions as antecedents (see also Simonton, 2008; see Chapter 5 for more detailed discussion).

Systematical Development of Expertise and Content-Process Interaction

While mutual sampling can explain the early emergence of talents, systematic development of expertise takes additional considerations. For school-age students, the main task is not the development of advanced expertise but that of a solid knowledge base and domain-relevant skills, as well as higher-order thinking skills mostly pertaining to producing thoughts and tangibles proficiently, and sometimes creatively, and to a lesser degree, to performing staged artistry and human service.

Content-process interaction. Cognitively, the domain specificity/generality tension reflects the content-process conundrum that has not been resolved in psychology to date, that is, to what extent processing is separate from content representation, and the relative importance of content representations and processing constraints, such as reasoning/problem solving. The tension affects how we understand gifted or advanced cognition. For example, when a child is identified as mathematically gifted, is it because the child has developed superior mental models of specific mathematical topics or is it because the child is highly capable of analytic logic and hypothetic-deductive reasoning? Studies of twice-exceptional children provide a unique window of observation onto the domain generality versus domain specificity issue, as they can indicate whether a deficit in a specific domain impairs more general functioning. For example, reading-disabled gifted children have been shown to demonstrate metacognitive insights and strategic behaviors that are more similar to those of their gifted peers than to those of age-peers with a reading disability (Hannah & Shore, 1995, 2007). However, Ceci (2003) shows that metacognition is constrained by domain knowledge and is thus not a domain-free cognitive process. Lohman (2006) has pointed out that the process of reasoning is always sensitive to content, and thus "pure" reasoning abilities are hard to find in reality (let alone measure). In the 1980s, there were many research efforts to pin down metacognition as a key difference between the gifted and "nongifted," leading Siegler and Kotovsky (1986) to ask,

"Is metacognition the 1980's equivalent of g?" Metacognition and cognitive flexibility have also been studied as sources of domain general advantage enjoyed by intellectually gifted children (Kanevsky, 1990; Shore, 2000). Yet the findings are mixed and do not support the notion of an unqualified, context-free general cognitive advantage. It is likely that the more developmentally complex a mental function, the more likely that both domain-general and domain-specific resources are needed. As a simple example, pitch perception is a relatively simple mechanism for music processing, but when rhythms and tonal and stylistic considerations are added to the mix, music processing has to integrate many functional units of varied functional generality to form a whole.

Snow (1992) provided one solution to the content-process conundrum. He suggested that, depending on the nature of a task at hand, there are performance units (crystallized abilities) that have been assembled and are ready to be activated or retrieved from long-term memory when tasks are familiar, and there are performance units that are assembled, reassembled, and controlled online (i.e., on the spot) when the problem at hand is relatively novel and unfamiliar (hence, fluid abilities). Learning in school mostly takes the form of the latter: One needs to assemble existing domain-relevant parts to make a new machinery of functioning, so to speak. Sometimes reassembling is necessary if the task at hand seems to warrant a different approach (think of a teacher pointing out an alternative way of conceptualizing or solving a problem). Teaching is a mirror image of learning: how to help learners assemble (and sometimes reassemble) the old parts in dealing with new challenges. Moreover, control (monitoring, evaluating, decision making) is necessary to ensure the effectiveness of the rendition. In this sense, no matter how much domain-specific strength one possesses, domain-general resources such as metacognitive skills are needed. Indeed, skills in certain domains, because of their cognitive complexity, may never be completely "modularized," as certain control is necessary to ensure that the process is staying on course (e.g., see Wineburg, 1998, for a discussion of historical thinking). Snow's description of fluid ability as assembly, reassembly, and control of performance components is reminiscent of Binet's (1911, cited in Brody, 2000, p. 30) original definition of intelligence as maintaining a direction in understanding the external world, making necessary adaptation based on feedback, and exercising autocriticism or reflective guidance. It also bears resemblance to Sternberg's (1985) distinction between metacomponents and performance components. It does not matter whether a person is developing high level of staged artistry or advanced scientific ideas (or other endeavor); the executive function as a control mechanism seems indispensable. The emphasis on the executive function highlights what people typically do rather than what they can do and thus involves some aspects of personality, which tends to be domain general (see Ackerman & Kanfer, 2004, for a distinction between typical and maximal performance).

Learning and skill development as a reciprocal, iterative top-down and bottom-up process. To delineate a long-term trajectory of systematic development of skills and talents, a distinction between bottom-up and top-down processes is useful. Stanovich (1999) and Kahneman (2003) identified two types of cognitive representations and processes, types they labeled System 1 and System 2. System 1 representations and processes are content specific, fast, and effortless, such as sensitivities, activation of encapsulated knowledge, and intuitive grasp of meanings or underlying structures. System 2 representations and processes are slow, effortful, and likely involve domain general cognitive resources, such as formulating effective internal representations, reasoning about task requirements, sorting out main issues, allocating attention, and monitoring and evaluating performance. Deliberate practice is considered a general mechanism for developing expert performance (Ericsson, 1996), as it has more System 2 characteristics. The content-process interaction is really about how the bottom-up perceptual and intuitive representations and processes interact with the top-down conceptual representations and metacognitive processes (Dai & Renzulli, 2008).

I suggest a reciprocal, iterative top-down and bottom-up process in learning and skill development. In this formulation, bottom-up processes work more or less like Fodor's (1983) input systems, supplying implicit, schematic knowledge representations, such as images, intuitions, and mental models, which tend to be domain specific. Top-down processes work more or less like central processes, imposing conceptual (semantic) structure and logical coherence and monitoring effectiveness and seeking alternatives. Transforming the perceptual into the conceptual ensures deep understanding and flexible use of knowledge (Karmiloff-Smith, 1992), while turning the conceptual to the perceptual facilitates efficiency and automaticity (Sternberg, 1985). *Both bottom-up self-organization and top-down self-direction (in the way Binet defined intelligence) serve the adaptive function of maximally coping with task demands and bootstrapping an effective performance.*

This line of thinking is supported by research evidence on savants (Miller, 2005). For example, autistic savants can display an unusual artistic talent (i.e., strong domain specificity, with modular input), but they typically show "weak central coherence" (Hermelin, 2001, quoted in Miller, 2005, p. 364). This deficiency in formulating abstract or conceptual schemes implicates shortfalls in top-down processes (see also Campione & Brown, 1978, on the case of mental retardation). Without central conceptual frameworks, inconsistencies or lack of coordination among parts can occur (Miller, 2005). Comparisons of work by child prodigies and savants lead to the same conclusion: Truly exceptional competence entails both bottom-up perceptual and top-down conceptual representations and processes (Feldman, 2003). It is conceivable that thresholds of conceptual competence are quite different between staged artistry and production of thoughts, or between production of tangibles and thoughts, or even between production of thoughts proficiently and creatively. Likewise, without the implicit, intuitive basis, conceptual competence may not fly high.

Developmental Timing and Trajectories as a Domain Specificity Issue

Discussion of bootstrapping one's competencies through self-organization and self-direction in dealing with environmental challenges and opportunities is not meaningful without a context of developmental constraints to be reckoned with. These developmental constraints include, but by no means are limited to, (a) the plasticity of the brain and malleability of specific human abilities (and possibly the window of plasticity for a particular ability); (b) the timing of the emergence and differentiation of abilities (increased repertoire of response and skill sets); (c) developmental junctures at which abilities and dispositions become integrated, even encapsulated, into a modulelike functional unit; and (d) ages at which production and performance tend to peak (i.e., reaching asymptotic or peak level) for various domains. In short, developmental constraints concern the timing and trajectories of developing competencies.

Research on the universal end of the universal-unique continuum (Feldman, 2009). Some researchers take a developmental approach to psychometric findings; for example, how the "positive manifold" (i.e., several performance factors are correlated) can be explained dynamically as a result of reciprocal causation and mutual relationships between processes through differentiation and integration rather than by the *g* factor (van der Maas et al., 2006). Other researchers postulate two differing developmental trajectories of fluid abilities and crystallized abilities and how their interplay creates specific patterns of skill development (Baltes, Lindenberger, & Staudinger, 1998). Developmental researchers are also exploring how cognitive aging (a domain-general factor) affects high-level expert performance and creativity (Roring & Charness, 2007), and how domain expertise compensates for the aging effect on fluid intelligence (Masunaga & Horn, 2001).

Among these developmentally oriented researchers, the neo-Piagetian researchers have tried to forge developmental explanation of the ontogeny of gifted cognitions and behaviors. The neo-Piagetian approach postulates that "central conceptual structures" (Porath, 2006a, p. 140) are essential for organizing experiences (such as artistic, narrative, and mathematical), and thus are domain specific, yet these cognitive structures are constrained by working-memory capacity (Case, 1992), which involves brain and cognitive maturation. Using this framework, early emergence of gifted behavior in various domains in childhood has been explored, including spatial-artistic (Porath, 2006b), mathematical (Okamoto, Curtis, Jabagchourian, & Weckbacher, 2006), narrative (McKeough, Genereux, & Jeary, 2006), and comparative performance across these domains (Loewen, 2006). A significant contribution of this body of research is to show how an ability, more or less of the "natural kind" (e.g., social or spatial; Tier 1 abilities; Geary, 2005), interact with culturally created symbolic systems (Csikszentmihalyi, 1996) to form narrative and artistic representations and become Tier 2 competencies. More important, it shows that domain competencies, characterized by their pervasive "central conceptual structures," do seem to have their own etiologies, though constrained by domain-general resources. Taken together, a general message of this body of research is that abilities in childhood are less differentiated (e.g., showing higher correlations across tasks) than during late childhood or early adolescence, when they are afforded systematic exposure to structured school knowledge and instruction, and their abilities (as well as their self-perceptions or self-concepts) become more differentiated. At a later stage, particularly in adulthood, highly differentiated skills, knowledge, and dispositions require integration if a person is to be successful in tackling real-life challenges. By that time, experience-based practical wisdom and expertise may take its hold, whereas fluid abilities, supported by neurobiological mechanisms, may start to decline (Berg, 2000; Li et al., 2004).

Research leaning toward the unique end of the universal-unique continuum. Different from universal approaches that start with what are common developmental parameters for all children, approaches to the unique end start with assumptions about ecologically and culturally defined domain requirements and constraints and then go backward to see what kind of persons are best equipped to deal with the inherent challenges imposed by a given domain. Simonton (1999, 2005) developed an emergenic-epigenetic model of talent development. The emergenic part concerns the right combination of essential genetic traits vis-à-vis a domain; absence of an essential component would make other components inert. The epigenetic part concerns the timing of maturation of these components: whether things come together in the right place (domain exposure and experience) at the right time. The model also works within the framework of population thinking; talent is a relative advantage that can be gained and lost during development, depending on the development of others. In essence, Simonton argues that a model of how a particular talent comes about needs to consider four main factors: domain, person, context, and time. Although biased in favor of a genetic explanation of the emergence of talent, and lacking in interactive and reciprocal terms in describing talent development, the model suggests that epigenetic landscapes for different domains can be quite different, depending on the genetic components that are needed for each domain and the biological clock that regulates the timing of the emergence of these traits. Talent so defined is an emergent module through self-organization, sensitive to developmental timing, not a preordained structure, as assumed by Howe et al. (1998) when they critiqued talent accounts of expertise.

Consider the developmental trajectory Ericsson drew on development of expertise in most domains (see Figure 4.2). It depicts a general onset of skill development at about 10 years of age, which through intensive, deliberate practice, reaches peak performance in about 10 years and then starts to decline around 30 years of age. One may argue that there are significant variations across domains.

Figure 4.2. An illustration of the gradual increases in expert performance as a function of age in such domains as chess. The international level, which is attained after more than 10 years of involvement in the domain, is indicated by the horizontal dashed line.

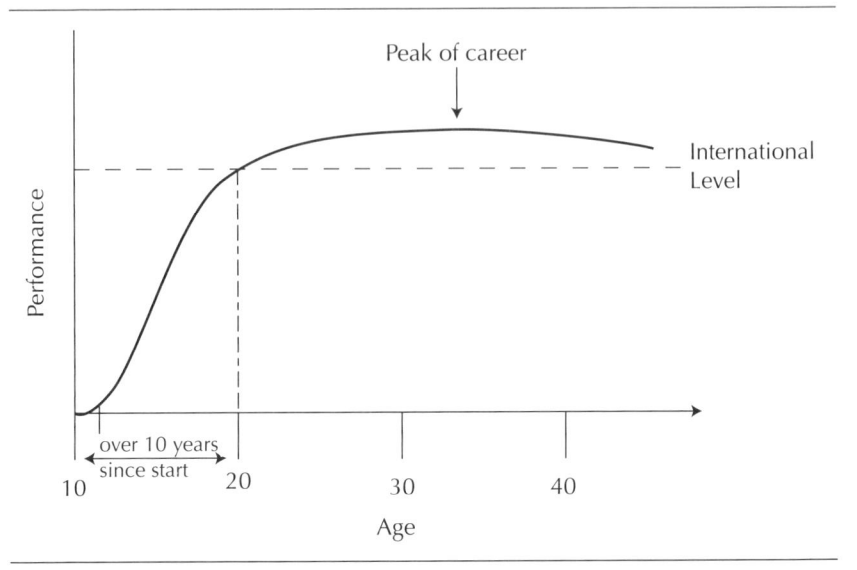

Note: From "Giftedness Viewed from the Expert-Performance Perspective," by K. A. Ericsson, K. Nandagopal, & R. W. Roring, 2005. *Journal for Education of the Gifted, 28,* pp. 287–311. Copyright © 2005 by K. A. Ericsson, K. Nandagopal, & R. W. Roring. Reprinted with permission.

For example, production of original thoughts may take more time to happen than performance of staged artistry. The timing of onset and its importance for later attainment may also vary, depending on the plasticity of relevant brain structures and functions, as well as the nature of a domain. Lehman (1953) provided early evidence for correlations between age and achievement across different domains. Research on child prodigies (Feldman, 1986) also provides important clues to domain specificity in developmental timing and peak performance. Why is it that child prodigies are found mostly in formal domains, such as music, mathematics, and chess (Feldman, 1986)? One possible explanation is the logical, analytic basis in these rule-based (*if-then* productions) domains, providing bottom-up implicit learning (e.g., unanalyzed intuitions and insights) that facilitates advanced mastery at a much faster rate than occurs normally (e.g., Bamberger, 1986). There are deep developmental explanations about why poets reach eminence at a much younger age than, say, playwrights, or why physical scientists make creative contributions to their fields at a much younger age than social scientists. Many conjectures have been offered, including the decline of fluid ability in the aging process (Baltes et al., 1998).

CREATIVITY: DOMAIN-SPECIFIC OR DOMAIN-GENERAL?

In Tannenbaum's (1997) framework or taxonomy of gifted expressions, each domain of competence can be expressed proficiently or creatively. To illustrate the difference between proficiency and creativity, a textbook author can be highly proficient in identifying recent advances in knowledge in a field, even pointing out trends, discrepancies, and unsolved problems. But he or she may not be the one who is capable of envisioning new possibilities, asking new questions, and fashioning novel and valuable solutions that help move the field forward. The tension between domain specificity and domain generality of creativity takes two forms: creative personality and creative thinking.

Creative Personality

The argument for creative personality is an argument for the domain generality of creativity: Creative persons tend to work creatively, regardless of what domains they choose to work with. The counterargument is that a person's special talent, intuitions, and insights into the nature of deep problems in a domain make him or her creative; thus creative expressions are highly confined to a narrow domain.

   Is there some general creative personality that cuts across the board? This is an important question, as whether "the creatively gifted" warrants a separate category hinges on answers to this question (Torrance, 1972b). Reviewing a large body of research on this topic is beyond the scope of this chapter (see Cramond, Matthews-Morgan, Bandalos, & Zuo, 2005, for a recent longitudinal follow-up report; Feist, 1998, for a meta-analysis). A thought experiment is helpful to illustrate the intricacies of the question. Kevin Spacey is an Oscar-winning movie actor, and Richard Feynman was a Nobel laureate in physics. They presumably represent the best creative minds in their respective domains, which differ drastically. But suppose Kevin Spacey happened to be born in Feynman's family and happened to pursue a scientific career, and vice versa for Richard Feynman; would these persons still be creative? My answer is yes to some extent, depending on their attaining the level of expertise needed for the highest level of creative attainment. For example, each of them is (was) intelligent, and yet impulsive and iconoclastic in temperament, playful and adventurous, preferring to stay "at the edge of chaos," a critical edge conducive to creative thoughts (see Dai & Renzulli, 2008). To be sure, acting as staged artistry is not the same as scientific exploration, and there could be domain-specific flair, insights, and dispositions that are not exchangeable between the two persons (see Feist, 2004). But it does not negate the likelihood that a person has a tendency to work creatively, whether he or she is in the acting profession or physical science. To use Sternberg's (1997) theory of thinking style, some individuals, by their natural tendency, tend to be more "legislative," creating their own rules and ways of thinking and doing, regardless of what games they choose to play. In a meta-analysis, when scientific and artistic creativity are compared, Feist (1998) found supporting evidence for the domain generality of creativity, such as the personality trait of "openness to experience" in the five-factor model of personality (McCrae & Costa, 1987). However, scientists and artists also differ sharply on the dimension of conscientiousness, with the former a half standard deviation higher than nonscientists, and the latter a half standard deviation lower than nonartists, suggesting that scientists, when compared to artists, are much more cautious and careful in their respective creative endeavor.

Creative Thinking

The domain-general argument postulates that creative thinking is fundamentally combinatory, drawing on ideas and facets from heterogeneous sources; a corollary is that creative thoughts in a domain benefits from experiences, insights, thoughts, and perspectives from other domains. The counterargument is that creative thinking is highly specialized through socialization; even what is deemed "creative" or even "groundbreaking" is determined by domain-specific criteria.

Several scholars proposed the process of creative thinking as combinatory (Root-Bernstein, 2009; Simonton, 2003). Root-Bernstein (2009) used the term *polymathy* (p. 853) to describe how the creative process is facilitated by borrowing modes of expressions and thinking from other domains (e.g., using artistic modes of thinking in science, or infusing scientific knowledge into artistic expressions). He elaborated on a quote by Max Planck, "The creative scientist needs an artistic imagination," and provided extensive, though correlational and anecdotal, supporting evidence. One Nobel laureate in chemistry (Peter Debye, 1936) reported that his way of generating new insights was to live through the chemical process like an actor and "get a picture of what is happening" (quoted in Root-Bernstein, 2009, p. 860). Indeed, imagination is a form of mental simulation that provides promising avenues to the invisible truth. This is often an untold story of scientific creativity in the archival literature or research conferences. It should be noted that what Root-Bernstein advocates is not some "general creativity" manifesting itself in a multitalented manner; rather, his point is that maintaining strong avocational interests may inadvertently benefit creative thinking (generating novel and useful ideas and products) in one's vocational pursuits. Ultimately, we may realize that for any creative thinking, an analytic, logical mode of operation is not sufficient; an imaginative play that helps create magic synthesis of discrete elements is necessary.

In contrast, the expertise researchers tend to emphasize creativity as inherently a domain-specific phenomenon, entailing a highly specialized way of thinking about a class of phenomena. Weisberg (2006), for example, pointed out two competing propositions regarding the relations between expertise and creativity: (a) expertise facilitates creativity, and (b) expertise impedes creativity. In light of Tannenbaum's (1997) framework, the question is essentially whether attainment of proficiency and creativity represents two different, divergent trajectories or largely one (see Chapter 7 for more detailed discussion). It is argued that expertise is necessary for creative productivity because a well-organized, in-depth knowledge base makes it possible to detect discrepancies and problems in the domain and identify new pathways to solving the problems. This *facilitation hypothesis* is supported by many real-life cases in arts and sciences and controlled research, discussed by Weisberg (1999, 2006) and Ericsson (2006).

As a counterargument, expertise impedes creativity because too much encapsulated knowledge renders an expert entrenched in established points of view and unable to "think outside the box." Experimental research demonstrating the difficulty of breaking a mental set (e.g., Luchins & Luchins, 1970) supports this *impediment hypothesis*. In real life, Max Planck's reluctance to go in the direction that Einstein went and Einstein's rejection of premises underlying quantum mechanics are cases in point (see A. Miller, 1996). Indeed, it is not unusual that scientists "become increasingly ensnared by the ideas that they themselves created" (Simonton, 2002, p. 272). Too much expertise becomes a handicap when rules of a game change, figuratively as well as literally (Frensch & Sternberg, 1989).

To put this debate in perspective, the expertise research tends to focus on domains involving the mastery of performance (i.e., *performance* rather than *producer* type) that requires one to execute a set of skills and routines within a specific time frame, such as instrument playing, figure skating, or the game of chess or go. One may argue that being capable of playing and interpreting a musical masterpiece to near perfection is a completely different matter from being able to create a masterpiece, just as being able to execute a difficult routine beautifully does not equate to being able to choreograph such a routine. For the latter, deliberate practice may not be sufficient. Although one may agree that expertise is a necessary condition for creative productivity (this is even the case for Mozart; see Lehmann & Ericsson, 1998), a theory that provides a compelling account of exceptional mastery of staged artistry or otherwise skilled performance may not be adequate as an account of production of masterpieces and great theories. Biographical analysis shows that personalities and life trajectories of masters and makers seem distinctly different from each other (Gardner, 1997). While masters tended to exclusively focus on one domain, creators tended to hop around different domains, enhancing cognitive flexibility and forging borrowing and cross-fertilization (Root-Bernstein, 2009; Simonton, 1997). Incidentally, novel thoughts and ideas are less "reproducible" than skilled performance.

The nature of domains may also influence the way creativity is expressed. For domains of high technicality (i.e., relying on concepts and instruments that do not have referents in everyday life; e.g., physical sciences, computer language, or information technology), extended, formal instruction and intensive training are necessary for developing high-level expertise. On the other hand, in domains that do not have formal, technical, sequential structure but rely heavily on personal imagination, such as filmmaking, creative writing, or social skills, as in entrepreneurship and social leadership, formal training may not be critical. There are many examples of great artists, actors, inventors, and fiction and nonfiction writers who were mainly self-educated.

The impact of social-historical changes is also noticeable. For example, in an age of increasing specialization and professionalization, "Renaissance men or women" who are as versatile as Da Vinci or Goethe are increasingly difficult to find. Conversely, the social organization of human endeavors is so integrated in our globalized world that collaborative creativity is more common than in the old days, as evidenced by many collaborator winners of Nobel prizes in recent decades. In this kind of collaborative creativity, each collaborator may contribute to the enterprise differently; some may be visionaries who envision new possibilities in a field, and others may be technicians who refine relevant designs and instruments that ultimately make a breakthrough.

CONCLUSION: INTEGRATION OF STRUCTURAL, FUNCTIONAL, AND DEVELOPMENTAL DIMENSIONS

In this chapter, I have discussed structural (person differences), functional (differences in domain activities and requirements), and developmental (developmental timing and changes) aspects of the issue of domain specificity versus domain generality. My main argument is that a dynamic and contextual view of talent development, rather than a static, structural view of individual differences in abilities, provides a more viable account of how domain competence arises, though this functional-ecological view does not contradict the findings that persons with particular patterns or configurations of abilities and dispositions tend to gravitate toward certain domains but not others. In fact, the structural and functional views can be readily integrated in considering how a particular talent emerges and evolves in the developmental process. This account of domain specificity, however, does refute the notion of innate or inborn talents. It suggests that talent development involves a bootstrapping process through the interplay of the person (with a particular pattern of abilities and dispositions), environment (opportunities, resources, and support), and development (self-organized and self-directed changes and timing of these changes). By the same token, when creativity is concerned, the three parameters need to be taken into account: person, domain (context), and development (see Chapter 7 for educational implications). A course of talent development can be charted (and theories developed) by integrating these three factors in a dynamic but tractable manner.

Qualitative or Quantitative Differences?
Person, Process, and Developmental Outcome

The current trends in intelligence and personality assessment allow for the hope of a future integrated understanding of the ways...that each person is like all other people, some other people, and no other person.
—David F. Lohman and Thomas Rocklin, "Current and Recurrent Issues in the Assessment of Intelligence and Personality"

Discontinuous outcomes can emerge from continuous change within a single system.
—Elizabeth Bates and George F. Carnevale, "New Directions in Research on Language Development"

IN THE NATURE-NURTURE debate, we have come across a range of the natural-endowment arguments that people are born different, and some are born "gifted," and others are not. One lingering question related to the alleged differences in natural endowment is, Are these differences a matter of a kind or degree? As Borland (2003) put it, "Are these two groups—the gifted and the rest—the discrete, discontinuous, structured wholes this crude taxonomy implies?" (p. 111). The tension between quantitative and qualitative differences focuses on the following question: In what sense and to what extent does giftedness, however defined, constitutes an *exceptional* condition, a condition that is beyond normality and warrants special attention and interventions? Do gifted children identified as such show a structural and functional organization of the mind that is different in kind rather than in degree from the rest of the population? From a talent-development perspective, does the development of exceptional competence inherently involve qualitatively different (and sometimes unique) pathways and trajectories, which should be the case if talent development is best characterized as "nonuniversal" development? The question is also related to the domain-specificity issue. If gifted potential is highly domain specific, then, the gifted person in question is likely to show unique organization of cognitive and affective functioning and unique developmental trajectories and pathways, qualitatively different from those of other people, including other talented individuals with different kinds of abilities and propensities. Conversely, the effects of gifted potential, if highly domain general, would be quite pervasive across a range of contents and performance conditions, but would not be as dramatic for any single domain, as effects of domain-specific structures and mechanisms would. There is a third possibility, a middle ground, that the differences observed are a matter of degree, and sometime a matter of kind, depending on how we define and measure these differences. The quantitative versus qualitative tension in its typical form can be expressed as follows:

Thesis:
Gifted individuals are different from their average peers in kind, because the structural and functional organization of their minds is different, and their developmental trajectories are unique.

Antithesis:
Gifted individuals differ from their average peers only in degree, because they show only relative strengths and advantages rather than absolute ones.

There are important educational implications of knowledge about whether gifted students differ from their "average" peers qualitatively or quantitatively. If gifted learners differ from their peers only quantitatively, then curriculum differentiation and instructional adaptation to these learners can be made based on existing curriculum standards but tailored to their precocious development and fast pace of learning (e.g., acceleration). If, instead, gifted learners differ from their peers in a qualitative way, then curriculum differentiation and instructional adaptation would take additional considerations, such suiting their highly personalized knowledge, unique strengths, and particular ways of thinking. Indeed, we could even think of a unique "gifted pedagogy" particularly suited to the cognitive sophistication and thinking styles of the "gifted."

BACKGROUND: THE CATEGORICAL APPROACH TO GIFTED EDUCATION

The categorical approach to gifted education is part of an education system in the United States that puts students into a variety of categories, such as mentally retarded, learning disabled, and average. To some scholars and educators, the categorical approach to education amounts to pigeonholing students in an oversimplified manner and is thus not adaptive to a variety of human potentials and developmental diversity (Keating, 2009). An increasing discontent expressed in the circle of education is that a categorical assumption is made about what "gifted" means on the basis of a rather arbitrary cutoff set on some continuous variables of aptitude or achievement (e.g., Berliner & Biddle, 1995; Borland, 2003, 2005; Keating, 2009; Ziegler, 2005; see also Hertzog, 2009). Although not everyone agrees on the categorical interpretation of gifted and "nongifted" differences as "qualitative" ones (e.g., Gagné, 2004; Gallagher, 2000b; Robinson, 2005), many scholars still feel compelled to label different levels of giftedness (e.g., moderately gifted, profoundly gifted, extremely gifted), similar to the practice of labeling different levels of mental retardation (American Association on Mental Retardation, 1992), creating subcategories within the "gifted" category. Others prefer more inclusive cutoffs, implicitly assuming an above-average threshold in ability requirements for a variety of human endeavors (e.g., Renzulli, 2005); beyond this threshold, further finer-grained differentiation may not be theoretically justified or may have limited practical utility. Furthermore, many theorists assume unique developmental experiences as quintessential to being intellectually gifted. For example, there is a group of scholars who see *developmental asynchrony* (i.e., social-emotional and intellectual development fail to align with each other) as an inevitable result of being gifted (see Morelock, 1996). Dabrowski viewed gifted development as involving *positive disintegration* (i.e., a breakdown in identity development that proves beneficial in the long run; see Ackerman, 2009). Robinson et al. (2000) see the gifted as going through more cognitive stages than those of their average age peers. All these theories imply qualitatively different experiences and processes unique to being gifted. However, when various cognitive and affective characteristics of the "gifted" and "nongifted" are compared in empirical research, the picture is far from clear cut; differences found between the gifted and "nongifted" or "unidentified" were better characterized as a matter of degree rather than kind (e.g., Dai et al., 1998; Jackson & Butterfield, 1986; Robinson & Clinkenbeard, 1998; Steiner & Carr, 2003). There is also a gap between what theorists postulate and how "the gifted" is identified in practice. Typically, the theoretical Procrustean bed fits some identified individuals but not others. Nevertheless, qualitative differences seem quite obvious in many cases. Case studies of child prodigies (Feldman, 1986), for example, evidence the early emergence of talents that seem to be qualitatively different from those of normal developmental trajectories. Children with extremely high IQ seem to have unique academic and social experiences and social-adjustment problems (Gross, 1993; Hollingworth, 1942; von Károlyi & Winner, 2005). Children with special talents (e.g., the mathematically gifted) seem to have unique structural and functional organization of mind (e.g., O'Boyle, 2008).

The categorical approach to (intellectual) giftedness and gifted education in practice identifies a generic group of "gifted children" under the assumption that they constitute a homogeneous group that is qualitatively different from others, just like mental retardation constitutes an exceptional condition in terms of the person's functioning as well as education and social interventions. Therefore, gifted children have "special educational needs" by virtue of being "gifted." Given the preponderance of evidence of the heterogeneity or diversity of identified gifted students, the argument for a generic category of "gifted children," who share the same unique personal and developmental experiences and demand the same unique educational interventions, faces serious challenge.

To be sure, being "exceptional" can simply indicate extremity without implicating a separate category or unique essence. Any psychometric measurement assumes the continuity of a measurement scale for a certain behavioral and psychological dimension. Even extreme scores represent quantitative, rather than qualitative, differences. However, it is conceivable that beyond a certain critical point quantitative differences actually reflect structural and functional differences that are qualitative in nature, as in the case of water molecules that form crystals or evaporate under a certain temperature, or some physical and chemical substances that change their properties under extreme conditions. In the following sections, research on possible qualitative differences as inherent personal qualities and behavioral characteristics of the gifted is reviewed, followed by a review of research on qualitative differences as emergent from developmental changes.

IN SEARCH OF PERSONAL AND BEHAVIORAL CHARACTERISTICS AS QUALITATIVE DIFFERENCES

Associated with the categorical approach to giftedness and gifted education, there has been a bulk of research on enduring personal and behavioral characteristics, cognitive, affective, or motivational, as constituting the unique individuality of the gifted. Characteristically, it tends to focus on domain-general features of cognitive and motivational processes. Based on research methodology, we can identify several distinct approaches: metric based, case or clinically based, and phenomenology based.

Metrics-Based Evidence

Metrics-based research assumes certain important dimensions or parameters on which people differ in a nontrivial way. Most research on qualitative and qualitative differences adopts a gifted-average comparison paradigm, not unlike the expert-novice paradigm dominant in the expertise research. There are two broad categories of research, one focusing on differences in *cognitive efficiency* and the other on differences in *cognitive sophistication*, such as cognitive strategy use, rich knowledge base, and metacognition.

Giftedness: Cognitive efficiency or cognitive sophistication? The cognitive efficiency hypothesis assumes advantages that reflect properties of basic cognitive infrastructure or hardware, such as processing speed, cognitive inhibition, and general working-memory capacity. Some researchers identify these basic functional properties as reflecting "a neurological constitution" that allows gifted children "to learn fast, remember more, process information more effectively, and generate more new and unusual ideas than their age peers" (Gallagher, 2000b, p. 6; see also Geake, 2009). We can also add to this list possible modular devices for specific type of information, such as perfect pitch for music or keen spatial perception and visualization. *The cognitive sophistication hypothesis*, in contrast, assumes "higher order" advantages and has to do with knowledge, meta-cognitive insights, effective selection of strategies to attain specific goals, and the productive and flexible use of knowledge in new situations or transfer (Alexander, Carr, & Schwanenflugel, 1995; Rogers, 1986; Steiner & Carr, 2003). The cognitive efficiency hypothesis is generally associated with the psychometric tradition (measuring basic dimensions of information-processing apparatus; e.g., Jensen, 1993; Jensen, Cohn, & Cohn, 1989) and lends itself more readily to a quantitative-difference argument (a matter of degree), barring the case of special modules, which tend to function in an all-or-none fashion (e.g., in perfect pitch, you have it or you don't). The cognitive sophistication hypothesis, in contrast, is largely based on cognitive theories of complex thinking and reasoning processes as adaptations to specific task conditions; therefore, it lends itself more easily to qualitative interpretations, such as strategy and style differences (a matter of kind).

The cognitive (and neural) efficiency hypothesis has been vigorously pursued and has yielded positive findings in support of it. The most compelling evidence supporting the cognitive efficiency hypothesis is the finding that the brains of highly intelligent individuals work more efficiently, not harder, with dealing with novel tasks; as brain activity (i.e., glucose consumption) decreases over time during work on a challenging cognitive task (Haier, 2001; see also Geake, 2009). Other research shows that higher-order mental functions such as fluid analogical thinking and reasoning are supported by the more basic infrastructure of the brain (Haier & Jung, 2008). For example, the ability of reasoning has been found to have a high correlation with measures of working-memory capacity, which belongs to the cognitive infrastructure, a hardware (efficiency) advantage (Kyllonen & Crystal, 1990). Although domain-general advantages offered by cognitive efficiency are distinct, they do not automatically reveal whether they are qualitative or quantitative in nature. From a psychometric point of view, the efficiency measures are continuous ones (i.e., whether some systems work more efficiently than some others).

Different from the cognitive efficiency hypothesis, the cognitive sophistication hypothesis assumes domain-general higher-level thinking advantages. Robinson, Shore, and Enersen (2007), for example, cited Russian psychologist Krutetskii's insights about able pupils that they tend to "see even single problems as part of a class or category of problems" (p. 176), suggesting a distinct power of transfer enjoyed by gifted students. Shore and Kanevsky (1993) reviewed the literature and identified many ways in which gifted individuals differ in thinking processes: (a) They have more extensive knowledge and use it more effectively; (b) they utilize metacognition more efficiently and more often; (c) they spend more time on the cognitively complex parts of problem solving and then quickly solve and report solutions; (d) they understand problems better, especially in terms of commonalities and transfer; (e) they employ assumptions that they systematically evaluate; (f) they are flexible in choosing strategies and points of views; and (g) they enjoy and create complexity and challenge around their tasks (pp. 137–139 see Hoh,

2008, for a recent review). However, the differences vary in size and do not show a uniform advantage.

In a carefully designed study comparing young children (ages 4–5) with high IQ ($M = 154$) and their average age peers, while controlling age or developmental differences by including a comparable sample of 7- and 8-year-old children, Kanevsky (1990) engaged these children in a problem-solving task, Tower of Hanoi. She found quantitatively measurable differences between the two groups of young children, such as move accuracy, hints needed to solve the problem, illegal moves made. Moreover, she also identified qualitative aspects of the observed differences. For one, regardless of age, gifted children were more likely to refuse an offer of help; they preferred to "own" the problem rather than seek external help when the problem at hand got challenging and to enjoy the personal satisfaction of an autonomous solution (see Kanevsky, 1990, pp. 131–135, for more details). As the study involved two age groups, cross-age comparisons reveal important differences related to developmental changes and differences associated with intellectual giftedness. Kanevsky noted that in some cases the 4- and 5-year-old gifted children did even better on some quantitative indices of problem solving than the 7- and 8-year-old gifted children. However, "the IQ-related differences in children's sensitivity to task similarity increase with age" (p. 133), implicating a widening gap in transfer skills over the course of development.

In recent years, the research focus has been increasingly on various forms of cognitive sophistication as defining characteristics of giftedness, such as metacognition and cognitive flexibility (Alexander et al., 1995; Shore, 2000), development of problem-solving strategies (Steiner & Carr, 2003), and dynamic assessment of learning potential (Kanevsky & Geake, 2004). Alexander et al. (1995), Shore (2000), and Steiner and Carr (2003) conducted extensive reviews and suggested that while gifted children do use high-level strategies more frequently and do make more metacognitive comments compared to their age peers, they are not *unique* in using these strategies or achieving metacognitive insights. In other words, the differences found are likely quantitative rather than qualitative. In a recent study, Steiner (2006) videotaped second-grade children as they were playing a computer strategy game. Using Siegler's (1996) overlapping wave theory of strategic development, she found dynamic patterns of changing strategies by gifted students that are consistent with the overlapping wave theory. More pertinent to the discussion of qualitative versus quantitative differences, she found that strategic development of gifted and regular children did not show qualitative differences, as both groups show increases in using more sophisticated strategies over time. However, there are differences in frequencies of strategy use in favor of gifted children, suggesting that the differences are quantitative.

As cognitive sophistication reflects more behavioral, cognitive, and developmental complexity compared with cognitive efficiency, and thus likely reveals more intrapersonal and conextual variability, experimental tasks and assessment procedures used in research have to be more complex to capture the inherent behavioral and psychological intricacies. A distinct methodological feature of Kanevsky (1990), Kanevsky and Geake (2004) and Steiner's (2006) studies is that they made observations and measurements of online strategic behaviors and comments while the subjects were actually performing a task, making it a more authentic assessment than the typical psychometric methods have allowed. However, such measurements, compared to simpler ones (e.g., a measure of reaction time) naturally tap into the "doing" (the enactive component of performance) rather than "being" (simple reactivity) part of superior performance. As Borkowski and Peck (1986) pointed out, the traditional research paradigms tended to focus on "an isolated aspect of learning or cognition, usually studying a single, momentary process and its influence on performance. The past history of each child in the two samples was generally ignored, as were other concomitant intellectual processes" (p. 184). When researchers seek more nuanced understanding of individual performance in situ, which naturally involves characteristic organization of behavior and concomitant affective and motivational processes, rather than merely identifying a single psychological variable such as strategy use, qualitative aspects of differences become more amenable to observation.

For example, there is evidence suggesting qualitative differences in the sense of how gifted children characteristically approach problems (a matter of how, not how much). One instructive finding from this research is that intellectually gifted children spend an equal amount of time or more working on the problem at hand than their average peers, even though they more frequently use high-level strategies (Steiner, 2006); this is true particularly at the explorative and planning stage (Lajoie & Shore, 1986; Shore & Lazar, 1996). Counterintuitively, they are more likely to feel challenged than other students (Bouffard-Bouchard, Parent, & Larivée, 1993), have a more accurate gauge of task difficulty (technically called *calibration*; Pajares, 1996). They are also more likely to rework the problem and show persistence (Bouffard-Bouchard et al., 1993). This suggests that there are a host of variables or factors contributing to the development of strategic behavior in children, not the least of which is motivation and self-regulation, including cognitive engagement, task commitment, and persistence (Dai et al., 1998). As Shore (2000) pointed out, metacognition involves an active (or enactive) state of mind, not just activation of static knowledge in the long-term memory. Although there may not be qualitative differences on any single cognitive or motivational dimension, when multiple factors come into play to produce cognitively sophisticated behaviors, qualitative differences can emerge. In other words, dimensionally speaking, the differences found may not amount to qualitative ones, but in combination, they can create characteristic patterns or styles of behavior, which are uniquely individual.

Aptitude-treatment interaction (ATI) and quantitative and qualitative changes. It is practically more meaningful and useful to understand whether various instructional conditions would produce differential learning outcomes, qualitative as well as quantitative, depending on the ability levels of students. In the ATI paradigm (Cronbach & Snow, 1977), aptitude can be affective as well as cognitive. The gifted-regular comparison paradigm can be seen as an ATI study when instructional "treatment" conditions are involved. Borkowski and Peck (1986) assumed differential training effects on a memory strategy, depending on the gifted and "nongifted" status. Specifically, they hypothesized that, when strategy training was embedded in incomplete instructions ("minimal strategy training"; p. 191), children with superior metamemory (a form of metacognitive skills) should be able to recognize the importance of strategy use and consequently use relevant strategies in new situations whenever strategies are applicable. They tested this hypothesis by randomly assigning a group of 7- and 8-year-old gifted and regular children into experimental (minimal strategy training) and control groups. The most revealing finding of this study was that gifted children, but not regular children, showed strategy transfer with minimal strategy training on a dissimilar task. Kanevsky and Geake (2004) found that the high-IQ (gifted) children needed less tutoring assistance and fewer prompts in reaching solutions to mathematical pattern-recognition problems and evidence knowledge transfer. These findings are consistent with the conjecture made by Krutetskii and echoes the earlier research by Snow (1994), which indicated that students with high IQs tend to function well with incomplete instructional conditions, while students with average or low intelligence test scores tend to work better under more complete instructional guidance and structure. They also support the conjecture that processes that help fill the instructional gaps are metacognitive (Jackson & Butterfield, 1986). While evidence seems to indicate that a metacognitive advantage that gifted students enjoy is a relative, rather than absolute, one, its interaction with the instructional condition can potentially produce learning gains and transfer that can be considered qualitative changes.

Developmental considerations. To evoke the three-tier scheme I proposed in Chapter 4, while we might define cognitive or neural efficiency as reflecting Tier 1 abilities and dispositions that manifest themselves early in development, and likely have a distinct biological-constitutional component, cognitive sophistication likely reflects higher levels of developmental complexity, better classified as Tier 2 developing competencies. Expertise-novice differences are usually qualitative in nature; experts differ from novices not just in the amounts of knowledge they have, but also in domain experience, knowledge organization, and domain-specific metacognitive insights and strategies (Glaser & Chi, 1988). Cognitive advantages, such as neural efficiency or metacognitive insights, enjoyed by gifted children, in contrast, tend to be domain general and thus may be fundamentally a matter of degree. *It can be assumed that the higher the developmental complexity, the more likely the emergence of qualitative differences.* Indeed, emergence of new properties and new organization of behavior is a sine qua non of development

(Fischer & Biddell, 2006). For instance, when one is more metacognitively disposed (e.g., seeing single problems as a class of problems, mentioned earlier), the transfer of learning is more likely across a range of phenomena or concepts. Such conceptual advantage is a central definition of intelligence (Campione & Brown, 1978). However, this kind of qualitative differences is not the same as the differences found in the expert-novice comparison research, wherein differences likely reflect many years of highly focused efforts in a domain (e.g., Ericsson, 2006; Ericsson et al., 1993). Based on the three-tier system, Tier 3 expertise, because of its level of developmental complexity, most likely shows qualitative differences in terms of acquired domains-specific competencies (see Figure 4.1).

When discussing domain-general cognitive efficiency and sophistication as potential sources of qualitative and quantitative differences, we should not forget the task-dependent nature of performance and the role of domain knowledge. Lajoie and Shore (1986) looked at the trade-off between speed (efficiency) and accuracy (sophistication) in the problem-solving behavior of high-aptitude individuals, depending on whether the task at hand is an easy or difficult one (e.g., how close it is to the upper limit of the zone of proximal development). Probably because of this complexity, Kanevsky (1995) proposed a more eclectic model of *gifted learning potential* that includes three components: information-processing efficiency (elementary processes), general knowledge base, and metacognitive knowledge and control (higher-level strategies). They encompass both low-level cognitive efficiency and high-level cognitive sophistication.

Methodological considerations. The gifted-average comparative research paradigm has its own limitations. It is a variant of the intelligence-correlation design (Gustafsson & Undheim, 1996). The purpose of this design is to trace individual differences in products (psychometric test scores) to possible underlying cognitive processes, a meshing of the psychometric and cognitive traditions. The efforts to integrate psychometric research on intelligence and cognitive psychology were inspired by the cognitive revolution (e.g., Hunt, 1986; Snow, 1994). However, traits by nature are broad psychological constructs and thus cannot be completely explained by specific process models (see Lohman, 1994a, 2001). By the same token, attempts to identify a set of core processes defining intellectual giftedness as a unique quality are likely to fail, as there may not be any single process or capacity corresponding to the measurements; in other words, emergent developmental complexity likely reflects the interaction of many factors, endogenous as well as exogenous, motivational as well as cognitive. The gifted-average paradigm is based on an assumption that children of high and average IQ represent two homogeneous groups. However, if there is much heterogeneity in terms of personal history, prior knowledge, personality within the gifted group as well as within the average group, then it is unlikely to find categorical differences between the high and average groups.

Case-Based Evidence

Much evidence supporting a categorical conception of giftedness comes from case studies and clinical observations. For example, the definition of giftedness as *developmental asynchrony* (Morelock, 1996) was partly based on early studies of extremely high IQ children by Hollingworth (1942). Dabrowsky's theory of overexcitabilities and positive disintegration as central to gifted development (see Ackerman, 2009; Mendaglio, 2008) was also based on case studies. Case-based research can focus on behavior and performance, such as early emergence of talents and child prodigies (Feldman, 1986). Qualitative differences can be easily observed when comparison is made with age peers. It should be noted, however, that these differences tend to be highly domain specific. These children may look quite "normal" outside the domains of their talent. Case studies can also focus on brain mechanisms, as Gershwind and Galaburda (1987) did. What they were trying to identify was neuroanatomical and neuro-developmental evidence of certain structural differences in the brain that facilitate specific cognitive functions. This evidence lends strong support to a qualitative-difference argument, as it implicates developmental abnormality, involving brain mechanisms, or even modularity, as a source of qualitative differences.

It is likely that unusual brain development and functions tend to produce special talents. O'Boyle (2008), for example, reported a series of studies that identified a consistent pattern of laterality (right-hemispheric dominance) and interhemispheric communication for the mathematically gifted when they solve mathematical problems. This type of evidence implicates unique organization of cognitive functions in these mathematically talented youths. Although it is not certain whether it is the brain structure that causes behavioral differences (a structural explanation) or whether it is the learned behavior (e.g., using spatial reasoning) that causes hemispheric preferences (a functional explanation; see Sternberg & Kaufman, 1998), the former seems to be a more plausible explanation.

In sum, case studies provide important evidence for the qualitative-difference argument. However, we might argue that case-based evidence provides a weak form of support for a qualitative-difference argument (or a categorical approach), as they may represent only special cases and conditions, rather than being generalizable across the board. One reason is that case-based research as a methodology inherently leans toward some "unique individuality" explanation (see Chapter 6 for detailed discussion). But it is probably also because case studies have tended to focus on extreme circumstances, such as children with extremely high IQs (Hollingworth, 1942), extreme forms of talent, child prodigies (Feldman, 1986), or children with abnormal conditions (e.g., idiot savants; see Miller, 2005), and children with extremely high mathematical talent (O'Boyle, 2008). One might even argue that they are not the kind of children typically identified as gifted in school (or "modal" or typical gifted children; see Coleman & Cross, 2005). For example, when a large sample of 9-year-old, top-10% mathematically able students were compared with 13-year-old average students, no qualitative difference in strategies and approaches was found between the two groups (Threlfall & Hargreaves, 2008). The authors suggested that mathematically able children in this study simply show developmental precocity, rather than unique cognitive styles or developmental trajectories. To be sure, this group of mathematically able students was not as selective as, say, those identified in the SMPY study (Lubinski & Benbow, 2006), and thus less likely to display qualitative differences. Regardless, case-based knowledge has limited generalizability; one cannot generalize a qualitative-difference argument across a whole population on the basis of a few extreme cases. By the same token, gifted education cannot be predicated on evidence of a few cases of exceptional talents. The case-based evidence provides some prototypes of gifted children, which is important in its own right, but does not preclude other forms and ways of achieving excellence.

The Phenomenology-Based Evidence

As I alluded to in Chapter 4, individuality that leads to domain-specific excellence is more than cognitive potentials. It involves personhood in all its richness, complexity, and idiosyncrasies. Several colleagues who got their doctoral degrees from Harvard told me that Harvard professors are quite idiosyncratic. I have heard the same observation about professors at other top universities (e.g., University of Chicago). One of my professors concurred with the comment that they are always "out of the pack." This leads to an important insight: A phenomenology of idiosyncrasies is open to immediate observation by people but elusive to formal measurement. This is because phenomenology-based evidence involves subjectivity of the person (how the person perceives, feels, and thinks) that can only be accessed by a more personal (e.g., first-person) approach (see Cross, 2003). In other words, lived experiences can be detected only through intersubjective communication. At this level, it is not merely one's personality traits that we try to "measure," but also one's personhood (inner feelings and thinking), into which we try to penetrate. By exclusively using standard identifications procedures, we would likely miss these qualities, as the measurement and assessment procedures typically do not capture this more personal aspect of unique strengths (see more discussion in Chapter 6 on the idiographic versus nomothetic tension).

A distinct characteristic of great individuals is that the kinds of inspirations, insights, feelings, and reasoning that drive their work seem to be uniquely their own and not socially shared—that is, idiosyncratic. Darwin envisioned various forms of life as having the same origins. Einstein imagined what would happen if one were moving at the speed of light. In this sense Darwin and Einstein were as idiosyncratic and "bizarre" as Picasso, when the artist was envisioning cubism in painting. Shavinina captured this quality when she defined giftedness as a unique cognitive representation of the world (see Shavinina & Kholodnaja, 1996). Eyscenk (1995) captured part of this individuality when he identified creative personality as having a dose of "craziness" (*psychotic*, in his personality theory), although the psychopathology of this kind of personality is overstated, as the approach to personality tends to conveniently pigeonhole the "inconvenient" individual peculiarities into the extant dimension of personality such as psychosis or other personality dimensions (see Feist, 1998). Most documentation of this personal side of creativity is biographical or autobiographical in nature (e.g., Gardner, 1993; Gruber, 1981). Newton, Kant, Beethoven, Darwin, Einstein, Picasso, Freud, Skinner, Edison, and Tolstoy, to name a few, are among the most celebrated individuals. However, there are many who achieved a lesser degree of eminence but nonetheless lived a creative life, in the way of producing new thoughts, fashioning new products or expressions, and performing great artistry and human service that advance important causes and enrich human life (Csikszentmihalyi, 1996; Kerr, 1985; Kitano & Perkins, 2000). The general findings of the phenomenological research are that, to a large extent, these creative individuals are self-directed. They are fascinated and even obsessed with something that preoccupies their mental lives. They have deeply held convictions and pursue their visions relentlessly. They are sensitive and smart in their own ways but can be clumsy and even obnoxious in social interactions. Indeed, they typically don't do well academically or socially in school (see Subotnik & Olszewski-Kubilius, 1998). They are risk-takers and therefore prone to failure, like their parents (Feist, 1998; Goertzel & Goertzel, 2004), but they have plenty of ego power to sustain their endeavors.

Methodologically, researchers use a variety of "intimate" methods to capture this aspect of unique personhood, such as interviews, experiential sampling (i.e., sampling a person's moment-to-moment feelings and thoughts), and studies of personal diaries. What is of scientific interest is trajectories of personal development, such as development of enduring *life themes* in a person's subjective world and evolving personhood, whether in the direction of human service, artistic expression, or quest for knowledge (Csikszentmihalyi et al., 1993), and in what way some unique visions of the world start to take shape and be articulated or materialized over time (i.e., crystallizing experiences; Walters & Gardner, 1986). It is a case of unique individuality (i.e., idiosyncrasies) or human diversity, when allowed to flourish, becoming a source of creativity and leading to socially recognized excellence and significant contributions to culture and civilization. Things that are initially quite idiosyncratic and private become standards and publicly shared visions and perspectives. As creativity is simply moving from the periphery to the center (Kagan, 2002), the first thing we should pay attention to is the idiosyncratic aspect of one's personality and personhood. A direct practical implication is that identification procedures should be sensitive to this more elusive aspect of human functioning as a source of high potential.

In sum, metrics-, case-, and phenomenology-based evidence can be seen as constituting a continuum of methods to capture the nature of gifted competence, from the most objectivist, universal psychological dimensions to the most subjective and unique human experiences. Perhaps it is wise to adopt an eclectic perspective that sees a gifted person as being like all others, gifted or nongifted; like some similarly gifted; and like no other person (unique individuality).

DEVELOPMENT AS EMERGENCE OF NOVELTY AND QUALITATIVE DIFFERENCES

It is possible that while the makeup of a gifted individual represents only a relative, comparative advantage that is not qualitatively different when this person is compared with "average" peers, the developmental outcomes can be qualitative different. This is an alternative explanation of qualitative differences I alluded to in the previous chapter when I discussed unique developmental niches, trajectories, and pathways as a function of person, domain, and developmental interactions with the environment.

Gagné (2005b) observed a fan-spread effect whereby the academic achievement gap widens among children over time (see Chapter 3). Developmentally, gifted children demonstrate domain-specific competence that is at least 2 years ahead of that of most age peers (Okamoto et al., 2006). At a certain point, the assumption of measurement continuity underlying psychometric measurements may not hold, as qualitative changes likely occur (e.g., transformation of knowledge to a new level of sophistication). There are knowledge gaps analogous to the qualitative differences found between experts and novices (Ericsson, 2006; Glaser & Chi, 1988). If qualitative differences do occur developmentally, we need a model that shows how they emerge.

Gagné (2005b) sees the fan-spread effect as governed by the "law of nature"; thus, *gifted potential* is squarely defined as located within the person, and consequently the fan-spread effect is largely attributable to natural endowment. However, gifted potential can be alternatively defined as *interactive* in the spirit of probabilistic epigenesis (Gottlieb, 1998; see Figure 3.1) and social-cognitive origins of human potential (the triadic reciprocal causation of internal, behavioral, and environmental factors; see Bandura, 1986). The interactive view can be formulated even in a way consistent with Gagné's (2004) DMGT model. For example, consider that quantitative differences in Tier 1 abilities and dispositions (somewhat equivalent to Gagné's natural abilities or giftedness) do not function linearly and independently, but interact with the environmental conditions in a multiplicative way (Papierno et al., 2005; Simonton, 2005), leading to the fan-spread effect (qualitatively different learning or developmental outcomes; Tier 2 developing competencies and dispositions) observed by Gagné (2005b). To illustrate the qualitative developmental changes resulting from quantitative differences, suppose we have three individuals whose cognitive, motivational, and environmental resources (e.g., excellent teachers, instructional support) are represented quantitatively on a 10-point scale as the following:

	Cognitive	Motivational	Environmental
Person A	7	7	7
Person B	7	5	5
Person C	7	5	3

This hypothetical scenario includes three person-situation profiles, with the cognitive factor held constant, but motivation and environmental factors varying across the three cases. The cognitive factor indicates all relatively stable abilities, domain specific or general for the person (specific composition could vary across the three individuals). The motivational factor partly represents the person's dispositions and partly reflects the properties of the task at hand and the social milieu (the intrapersonal and environmental catalysts in Gagné's model). The environmental factor indicates, among others, the degree of optimal educational provisions and supporting social conditions for each person. Let's further assume that contributions of each variable to the developmental potential vary, such that cognitive factor carries the most weight (.5) followed by the motivational (.3) and the environmental factor (.2), in a way prescribed by Gagné (2004). Thus the developmental potential (P) can be estimated as the product of weighted cognitive, motivational, and environmental variables:

$$P = C_w \times M_w \times E_w$$

Estimates of the developmental potential for the three persons are 15.44, 5.25, and 3.15. The differences are quite dramatic, largely because of the combinatory and multiplicative effects. The competitive edge Person A holds over Persons B and C can be seen as a case of quantitative differences (between and among the three individuals) on the three dimensions turned into qualitative developmental outcomes. Imagine further that at a certain point (likely an intermediate stage) in development, motivation (intrinsic interest and organized persistence) becomes more important (and consequently carries more weight) when the task gets challenging, requiring extended deliberate practice and problem solving; cognitive advantages reflected in the initial ease of learning may start to dwindle (Subotnik & Jarvin, 2005). In the meantime, mentorship and cognitive apprenticeship (an environmental variable) becomes increasingly important. The weight these variables carry would change substantially. Suppose that the values of each profile do not change, but the cognitive factor now carries less weight ($w = .3$), while weights for the motivational and environmental factors increase to .4 and .3, respectively. The resulting developmental potential for the three persons would be 12.35, 6.30, and 3.78. If we stretch this way of thinking further in a way Simonton (2005) suggested, the results would be more dramatic, since the absence of one component essential for a domain would nullify all other effective components (mathematically, a zero on any one of the three dimensions would make the product of these numerical values zero). For example, in a person-environment interactive model, absence of a critical environmental component (failure to get mentorship in high school or to obtain access to more advanced learning materials) would also foreclose any opportunity for further talent development.

Granted, the multiplicative model illustrated above is a vast simplification of what happens in real-time dynamics of person-environment interaction. For one, it does not differentiate domain requirements and thresholds. For each domain, cognitive, motivational, and environmental constraints can be quite different. For another, the three variables are not fixed in space and time but are variable in development. Nevertheless, the hypothetical scenario illustrates two points: First, emergent differences in developmental potential can be quite dramatic even among those who have relatively homogeneous cognitive profiles, depending on the interaction of cognitive, motivational, and environmental characteristics. Second, changes in the importance of each factor (different weights it carries) vis-à-vis developmental challenges would significantly alter the developmental potential at a specific point in development; thus developmental potential varies over time, depending on what phase or stage of development one is at.

Argued this way, *qualitative differences can emerge at the critical state of gifted development that generate divergent trajectories, pathways, and developmental niches* (Ziegler & Heller, 2000). Defined as such, it is contextual, emergent, and dynamic (Dai & Renzulli, 2008; see Chapter 9 for further discussion). It can truly take many shades and forms (Passow, 1981).

TECHNICAL AND PRAGMATIC CONSIDERATIONS

Metrics-based research naturally defines and quantifies dimensions of human abilities, skills, and traits as high, median, and low. It can assume the measurements to be *parametric*: They are a set of parameters or key variables that can be used to characterize all members of a population and help predict behaviors of any member based on these variables. In the preceding section, I illustrated how quantitative differences can be amplified by a combinatory or multiplicative factor; namely, personal, behavioral, and environmental variables can interact in a way capable of accounting for the observed widening of individual differences, or the fan-spread effect, a case of quantitative differences leading over time to qualitative differences and discontinuous changes. This kind of emergent qualitative differences can be seen as hierarchical qualitative differences in the sense that the rich get rich and the poor get poorer, creating a divide between the advantaged and disadvantaged (Ceci & Papierno, 2005).

Emergent qualitative differences can also be seen as pluralistic in the sense that development goes in many directions. According to McCall's (1981) scoop model of mental development, starting around 6 years of age, children's development can be characterized as divergent, going in many directions, rather than convergent, in a more-or-less, sooner-or-later invariant sequence, as prescribed by Piaget (1950/2001). Of course, Piaget is right that most children become increasingly competent in organized thoughts or logical thinking as a result of maturation, experience, and formal education. But at the same time, children and adolescents as well as young adults also become more and more divergent in terms of their cognitive strengths, self-concepts, and interests (Ackerman, 2003). In Chapter 4, I discussed a continuum that Feldman (2009) proposed from the universal all the way to the unique of human skill development. He suggested that as we move to the unique side of skill development, developmental niches, trajectories, and pathways become so divergent that over time, each person will have a unique set of knowledge, skills, and expertise. In other words, discontinuous changes occur and the continuity assumption of parametric measurements can no longer hold. To illustrate what I mean, you initially may compare the sizes of two apples, but sooner or later, you realize size no longer matters as you are comparing apple and orange! Therefore, sometimes nonparametric methods are needed. Lubinski, Benbow, and their colleagues, for example, created a measure of within-person relative strengths and weaknesses. Children with different patterns of verbal, mathematical, and spatial abilities measured at the ages of 13 and 14 showed predictable differential career trajectories and adult creative accomplishments in mathematics and science versus arts, and in inorganic versus organic fields (Lubinski & Benbow, 2000; Park, Lubinski, & Benbow, 2007). Ackerman and his colleagues (Ackerman & Haggestad, 1997; Rolfhus & Ackerman, 1996, 1999) provided yet another example of identifying emergent qualitatively different patterns of development in the college years and onward, in terms of abilities, knowledge, self-concept, and interests, what Snow (1992) called *aptitude complex* and Ackerman (2003) called *trait complex*. In their empirical research, four broad trait complexes were identified: social, clerical-conventional, science-math, and intellectual-cultural (cf. Feldhusen, 1992; Tannenbaum, 1997). It is conceivable that college students will still go through the developmental process of differentiation and integration, and it is this developmental process that tends to create distinct developmental niches, which differ qualitatively in terms of affordances and constraints. Thus, the verbally precocious may lean toward intellectual-cultural domains (e.g., humanities), and the mathematically precocious may gravitate toward physical science or technical fields (Park et al., 2007). Therefore, ingredients and processes for exceptional development can also be different, not only between performers and producers and between producers of artistic expressions and academic thoughts (Tannenbaum, 1997), but also between and among producers of thoughts in different academic domains (say, history versus chemistry). In principle, *development of exceptional competence in domains of cultural importance from a life span perspective is the inevitable result of increasing differentiation and developmental complexity.* It is in this sense that developmental diversity and development of individuality are a major source of excellence, be it in the performing or producing mode, in the domain of arts, sciences, or human service, of the proficient or creative kind (Tannenbaum, 1997).

So far I have discussed various human conditions that can be seen as exceptional, in the sense that they indicate qualitative differences from "normal conditions." But exceptionality in the context of education has a fundamentally pragmatic meaning. A student in a regular class may be "exceptional" by virtue of outstanding achievement, but not so when placed in a highly selected class or school (the same can be said about students with special education needs). In other words, what constitutes an exceptional condition is not within the person, but depends on the situation in which the person finds him- or herself. Shore and Delcourt (1996) identified shared and unique aspects of curriculum and pedagogy for gifted and regular students. They identified acceleration, ability grouping, and high-level curricular materials, among others, as uniquely suited for gifted students, and enrichment, developing creative abilities, and mentorship, among others, as effective with gifted students but generally applicable to all students. Tomlinson (1996) posits nine dimensions in which educational and instructional differentiation may be made for gifted learners: (a) foundational to transformational, (b) concrete to abstract, (c) simple to complex, (d) few facets to multifacets, (e) smaller leap to greater leap, (f) more structured to more open, (g) clearly defined to fuzzy, (h) less independence to greater independence, and (i) slower to quicker. They can be seen as dimensions along which all students (including the "gifted") can be properly positioned based on their zones of proximal development (ZPD; Vygotsky, 1978), on how much they will benefit from a given educational experience at a specific point in time. Technically, if the upper bound (i.e., one can successfully perform a task with the assistance of a more competent person) and lower bound (i.e., one can successfully perform a task independently) of the ZPD for a particular learner are significantly displaced out of the ZPDs of most peers, an exceptional need may be present; that is, this learner may need the kind of challenge (the upper bound) that is beyond most peers. However, the exceptionality is not located within the person but in the person-in-context. Imagine that efforts have been made to accommodate all kinds of learners, advanced or slow, within regular classroom; then there is no "exceptional condition," hence no need for a separate gifted program, just as in a full-inclusion class, in which differentiation efforts are made within a regular classroom. Indeed, to some extent the existing curriculum structure reflects the increasing differentiation and diversity of academic advancements over time (more advanced placement [AP] classes, more advanced electives). However, suppose that for some learners, their ZPDs are way beyond what is offered in regular, age-graded classes, and within-class differentiation efforts, because of lack of resources and expertise, fall short of meeting their needs. Then, an exceptional condition exists for these more advanced learners, no less than those in the category of mental retardation or learning disabilities; sometimes even a special magnet school is created for a particular type of exceptionally advanced learners. Thus, *exceptionality in the pragmatic sense is not a personal trait, but fundamentally situational: whether a normal, age-graded educational environment is adequate for highly precocious or advanced children.* Highly advanced children and children with intellectual and specific learning disabilities differ in one important aspect: The need for remediation for the second two is more obvious than the need for sufficient challenge for the first. The need of highly advanced students for sufficient challenge is more easily shortchanged because it is less visible than the deficiency needs in the classroom. However, there are general rules that can be followed. When the ZPD of a child vis-à-vis a particular task shows a much higher upper bound compared to the ZPD of most of his or her age peers, regular educational conditions may not be adequate to meet this student's advancing needs, and exceptional needs become clear. When both person and situation factors are taken into account, a justification can be made for curriculum differentiation, an Individualized Education Plan (IEP), even the raison d'être of a gifted program. Although differential development or developmental diversity may have both quantitative and qualitative aspects, some general rules of thumb or heuristics can be used for gauging the likelihood of qualitative differences in developing exceptional competence when making decisions about curriculum differentiation and educational placement:

- When an observed characteristic shows extremity compared with the norm, it tends to be exceptional in the sense of unique structural and functional organization of mind. This conjecture is partly supported by the evidence that at the extreme end of a normal distribution, dispersion of scores tends to show a pattern best characterized as discontinuous rather than continuous (see Robinson et al., 2000). In other words, assumptions of normality and continuity break down on the extreme. For example, this seems to be the case when comparing mathematically above-average and highly gifted children, discussed earlier (O'Boyle, 2008).
- When there is evidence of modularity or encapsulated knowledge (e.g., perfect pitch or the fast mental calculation found in savants), exceptionality can be inferred. Such evidence includes domain-specific flairs, such as unique intuitions and imaginations about certain physical, biological, or social phenomena or high facility acquiring in academic, artistic, and practical skills. The assumption of this conjecture is that domain-specific mechanisms that facilitate learning and talent development are different from domain-general mechanisms; the former shows System 1 characteristics (fast, not accessible to consciousness and conscious control, etc.), and the latter show System 2 characteristics (slow, effortful, subject to rational analysis, etc.; see Chapter 4 for detailed discussion). On the other hand, as discussed earlier, when domain-general cognitive advantages are concerned, they tend to be less dramatic, mainly because System 2 representations and processes are temporally less stable and situationally more variable.

- When a skill or competence is highly developed through systematic training and practice and shows high levels of developmental complexity (e.g., a well-integrated set of knowledge, skills, dispositions, and interests), as evidenced by expert performance (in chess, physics, arts, etc.), it is likely exceptional (i.e., qualitatively different from less skilled performers). This conjecture is based on the assumption that profound differences exist between those who have spent many years perfecting their trades and those who only managed to develop skills that allow them to function effectively in daily situations. Even the way experts engage in practice is qualitatively different from that in everyday life (Ericsson, 2006). In general, high-level domain expertise reflects uniqueness of development along the universal-unique continuum that Feldman (2003, 2009) proposed.

- When we consider the idiographic complexity of the organization of knowledge, skills, and dispositions in a person, there is always uniqueness in personal functioning and organization of intellect, including how individuals perceive and cognitively represent the world. Cognitive diversity demonstrated by unique individual perspectives is a source of creativity and developmental novelty, a quality that is by nature a matter of kind, rather than degree.

CONCLUSIONS: WHEN "EXCEPTIONAL" IS TRULY EXCEPTIONAL

As pointed out in the previous chapter, superior competence can be subjected to structural (human architecture), functional (domain ecology), and developmental analyses. The interplay of person, domain (context), and development can produce unique domain-specific trajectories. By the same token, when aptitudes or aptitude or trait complexes are better seen as continuous (like other people), and when they should be better seen as discontinuous (like no other person) is an empirical question, and no sweeping generalization either way should be made. However, I argue that, contrary to the homogeneous assumption about "the gifted," there is much heterogeneity and diversity of high human potential in terms of varied developmental niches, trajectories, and pathways, which ultimately account for the emergence and development of many exceptional talents. Therefore, no a priori qualitative differences should be assumed between the two broad, abstract categories of the "gifted" and "nongifted" (often based on cutoff scores arbitrarily set up for administrative convenience) as if they were two homogeneous groups of children. Rather, qualitative differences lie in the very individuality of the person in question, or, to use Feldman's (2003) term, in the "non-universal" (p. 22) or unique aspects of individual development. For that matter, it is conceivable that qualitative differences exist not only between the gifted and "regular" but also within the group of children identified as "gifted."

Ultimately, the qualitative-quantitative difference tension could be addressed by resorting to a developmental solution. The nature versus nurture tension revolving around the "being" and "doing" of superior competence can be resolved by arguing that even though no qualitatively different innate structures exists and we should not expect a sudden emergence of superior performance, the process of "doing" could bootstrap new systems and new talents if there were a right combination of interacting endogenous and exogenous forces. The domain specificity versus domain generality issue can be resolved by arguing that even though domain-general or domain-specific advantages enjoyed by some children may not be qualitative, over time, various abilities and dispositions of different degrees of generality will be coalesced and self-organized vis-à-vis environmental affordances and constraints to create a unique personal life trajectory that has developmental novelty in its own right.

Truth in the Eye of the Beholder:
Differences in Worldviews and Epistemic Stances

Psychologists can't do their work without the rationality assumption of intentional stance, and biologists can't do their work without the optimality
assumption of adaptationist thinking.

—Daniel Dennett, *The Intentional Stance*

Antinomality, in sum, is at the basis of the endemic human need for crawl-
ing into cozy conceptual boxes—any box, so long as it gives promise of
relieving the pains of cognitive uncertainty or easing problematic tension.

—Sigmund Koch, "The Nature and Limits of Psychological Knowledge:
Lessons of a Century qua 'Science'"

IN THE PRECEDING chapters, I discussed three key ontological issues regarding
giftedness, namely, theoretical assumptions or educated guesses about (a) how nature and nurture jointly contribute to exceptional competence at different stages of
development; (b) how domain-specific competencies and creativity are shaped by
the interplay of person, domain, and development; and (c) how exceptional development may emerge as a result of the unique biological formation of the person,
of particular developmental patterns, and of a dynamic fit between a person and
a functional environment. This chapter focuses on epistemological and methodological issues; that is, in what way can we gain valid, generalizable, and verifiable knowledge about these issues? What kinds of broad theoretical lenses and
methodological tools have been frequently used in the field? I attempt to show that
many ontological claims about the nature-nurture debate or other issues are actually dependent on researchers' *epistemic stances*, namely, how they cognitively
position themselves when looking at a particular phenomenon. Epistemic stances
are the lens we use to interpret information and predict how an object would
behave. Epistemology (beliefs and theories about the nature of knowing and the
grounds for knowledge claims) governs methodology (e.g., conducting an experiment or making an ethnographic inquiry). Thus, positivists believe that objective
truth is out there to be uncovered, and only one out of many competing knowledge
claims can be true, while post-positivists believe that knowledge is one way or
another constructed by human beings, and conceptualization and interpretation
inevitably play a role in even the most stringent scientific investigation (Lakatos,

1978; see also Howe, 2009, on the nature of education science). Different research methods are simply cognitive tools and instruments we deem appropriate for investigating certain phenomena and issues.

In gifted studies as well as gifted education, there are three basic issues that call for strategic and pragmatic decisions regarding adopting appropriate epistemic stances and research or assessment methods: (1) What counts as best evidence of "giftedness" and what exactly do we mean by "gifted"? (2) How do we come to know and investigate various "gifted" expressions and manifestations? (3) How do we explain and predict something as complex as development of gifted potential and excellence? In this chapter, I will discuss these three questions respectively, identify inherent tensions in each, and contemplate solutions to these tensions.

WHAT COUNTS AS THE BEST EVIDENCE OF "GIFTEDNESS": APTITUDE OR AUTHENTIC ACHIEVEMENT?

To say someone is gifted is like saying someone is beautiful, which requires clarification, even some defending. Descriptions such as *gifted* or *beautiful* are implicitly comparative and differential (norm referenced); that is, someone is gifted or beautiful, compared, by default, with the less gifted or less beautiful. Semantically, both descriptions are ambiguous, as the issue of how beautiful is beautiful, or how gifted can be considered gifted, is subject to qualitative judgment and pragmatic considerations. Sometimes, it is a subjective judgment based on objectively quantifiable dimensions and scales, and other times the judgment is purely subjective, in the eye of the beholder. At any rate, there is no absolute, objective gold standard for determining these qualities. The description *beautiful* differs from that of *gifted* in that *beautiful* has more concrete referents (e.g., certain facial features and proportions), whereas *gifted* or its equivalents (*superior*, *outstanding*, *excellent*, or *exceptional*) are used to describe something more abstract (intellectually gifted, academically gifted, musically gifted, etc.), inferring mental qualities based on observations. The term *gifted*, as used in contexts of education as well as scholarly communication, has both denotations and connotations. It first *denotes* the superior quality of some performance, which is not as controversial, as it can be subjected to verification by judging the performance against objectively defined criteria. The term further *connotes* high "promise" for further development, which is an inference increasingly controversial nowadays. The essential epistemic tension is between those who believe that the best evidence of giftedness as potential is from psychometric tests of aptitude and those who believe that the best evidence of gifted potential is authentic achievement in a domain. The tension can be expressed in the following manner:

Thesis:
Potential for excellence (i.e., giftedness) is best evidenced in performance conditions that can differentiate high potential (aptitude) from high achievement.

Antithesis:
We will never know whether a person is "gifted" or holds unusual "potential" unless the person demonstrates superior mastery of skills and knowledge in an authentic domain or functional context.

Conceptual and Empirical Issues of Using Aptitude Tests as Measures of "Potential"

Extant mainstream models (e.g., Gagné's DMGT model, and the Munich Dynamic Ability-Achievement Model; see Gagné, 2005a; Heller, Perleth, & Lim, 2005) invariably propose various mental abilities as a *precondition or prerequisite* for later domain achievement, implicitly or explicitly assuming a causal link between abilities and achievement. Aptitude in educational and psychological research is associated with aptitude tests, such as the IQ, SAT, ACT, or GRE, typically used for selection and placement purposes. The first and most important issue concerning using ability or aptitude tests as measures of potential is whether the conceptual distinction we make between aptitude and achievement is valid at an empirical level, namely, whether we can ascertain particular mental capacity as indeed an antecedent of, even a precondition for, actual excellence in a given domain.

Angoff (1988) suggested that we shift the focus from the nature-nurture debate to the issue of stability, malleability, and transferability in conceptualizing aptitude. According to him, while general scholastic aptitude, like achievement, is a developed, rather than innate, quality, it differs from academic achievement in several important ways:

1. Aptitude grows more slowly than achievement, the latter of which is likely a direct result of formal exposure to a specific content area;
2. Aptitude tends to resist short-term interventions to hasten its growth, while achievement is more amenable or receptive to such interventions;
3. Aptitude mainly concerns potential (e.g., rate of learning), and achievement provides a measure of how much is learned;
4. Aptitude tests sample a wider range of behaviors than achievement tests and therefore are indicative of a more generalizable capability than achievement measures;
5. Since aptitude does not particularly rely on formal schooling, evaluation of general intellectual functioning is made possible with aptitude tests

regardless of school experience and achievement (thus, a school dropout can theoretically still get high scores on IQ tests);

6. Aptitude as a measure of potential is still useful, when the learner whose aptitude is being evaluated has not yet been exposed to the learning material.

Although many points of justification that Angoff (1988) offered here for the distinction between aptitude and achievement are debatable (see Ceci & Williams, 1997; Lohman, 2006), to the extent that we still make a distinction between how individuals differ in their ease of learning and performance (process), and how much they have gained as a result of their efforts (product), the aptitude-achievement distinction seems still warranted. As these "aptitude leads to achievement" models have been challenged by the expertise researchers (see Ericsson, 2006), conceptualizing aptitude as a prerequisite for achieving domain excellence hinges on evidence of the predictive validity of measurements involved (i.e., the "productivity" criterion; Sternberg, 1995). Research on the predictive validity of aptitude tests is abundant, and review of this body of research is beyond the scope of this chapter (see Lubinski & Dawis, 1992; Sackett, Borneman, & Connelly, 2008; Schmidt & Hunter, 1998). But suffice it to say that the preponderance of research shows good efficacy and utilities of various aptitude tests for selection and placement purposes. In a recent SMPY follow-up study, for example, within a highly selective group of mathematically precocious individuals who were in the top-1% of quantitative ability (SAT math) among age peers as measured at the age of 13, ability differences of these individuals remained predictive of inventive or scholarly productivity assessed 25 years later, in terms of patents gained or scientific publication. Moreover, the predictive power held even when academic degrees earned by these individuals were held constant (i.e., comparing individuals with the same levels of terminal academic degrees; Park, Lubinski, & Benbow, 2008).

Although evidence for predictive validity of various aptitude tests is quite compelling, there are several concerns over using aptitude measures (particularly general aptitude tests, such as IQ tests) as the sole indicator of giftedness. They include the following:

1. General scholastic aptitude tests (compared to, say, the Iowa Algebra Test or Carroll's foreign language aptitude tests) are typically not fine-tuned to differential domain requirements, and therefore they are relatively poor predictors of domain-specific academic achievement (Lohman, 2005a); different domains likely have different threshold requirements (Simonton, 1999) for mental abilities. Even within academic studies, the demands of each academic domain or discipline can be quite different.

2. Inferring a causal relationship between measures of mental abilities and achievement can be problematic (Sternberg, 1999a), a commitment of

jangle fallacy, that is, labeling one set of instruments as tests of intelligence or ability (or abilities) and the other as tests of achievement, while the two may have a large overlap in construct representation (Kelley, 1927; see Lohman, 2006); measures of both aptitude and achievement likely reflect joint effects of nature and nurture (see Lubinski, 2004), involving knowledge and process skills, both of which are acquired (Lohman, 2005a).

3. Privileging mental ability tests as aptitude measures is often at the risk of downplaying noncognitive personal factors such as intrinsic motivation as a potent force for high-level achievement (Dai, 2004b; Gottfried & Gottfried, 2004). A contextual view of aptitude that situates personal factors such as knowledge, affect, and motivation as well as cognitive potentials in specific functional contexts and at a particular point in development seems more viable (Ackerman, 2003; Cronbach, 2002; Dai & Renzulli, 2008; Matthews & Foster, 2006; Snow, 1992).

In general, domain-general aptitude tests show good predictive validity at an aggregated level, but do not seem to deliver what they promise when it comes to a specific line of talent development and eminent achievement, which is a main concern of educators. Moreover, aptitude tests, when exclusively used for identification, tend to perpetuate an ability-centric view of human potential, as if only those who are tested well deserve special attention, and high potential demonstrated otherwise are considered through this lens as less validated.

Conceptual and Empirical Issues of Using Achievement and Eminence as Measures of Giftedness

On the other side of the story, there are concerns over using domain achievement as the main indicator of giftedness. Using achievement and expert performance as an indication of giftedness (i.e., demonstrated excellence), though authentic and free of some shaky assumptions about "latent capacity" (Ericsson et al., 2005, 2007), naturally biased in favor of those who have the necessary experiential exposure, opportunity, and technical and social support to get that far. It is conceivable that many individuals are "gifted" but lack such exposure, opportunity, and support to demonstrate their high potential. Without the equivalent "opportunity to learn," assessment and related selection decisions would be open to serious question with respect to validity and equity (Gee, 2003). This empirical issue reflects an epistemological dilemma: Teasing apart "natural ability" and developed skills and knowledge is almost impossible; one cannot demonstrate high-level "capacity" in academic or other domains without considerable amounts of exposure, experience, intentional learning, and practice (the same can be said about performance on IQ tests). However, the argument that the only things that matter for high-level achievement are experience, learning, resources, and support also runs counter to a widely accepted notion that there are fundamental individual differences in the *ease of learning*, which is a hallmark of giftedness (Gagné, 2004; see discussion in Chapter 3).

Furthermore, the concept of "latent capacity" or potential, as long as it is seen as multifaceted and dynamic rather than "fixed," still seems useful for several reasons. First, there is compelling evidence for a distinct genetic component for high potential, albeit with a complexity of expression and interaction with environment and development (Simonton, 2005, 2008). Second, it is unrealistic to expect mature, full-blown gifted and talented achievements at a very young age, barring a few cases of child prodigies (e.g., Feldman, 1986). Oftentimes, signs of giftedness and early talent still need to be recognized through testing or observation outside a specific domain of interest (e.g., acuity or sensitivity of the intellectual or artistic sort), so that we still can conceive of unrealized gifted potential or "gifted underachievement" as quite prevalent, rather than an oxymoron. Third, we can make a distinction between content mastery as a product, measured by certain achievement tests, and mental structures and operations (process) leading to the product; it is the latter (processes) that often underlies the concept of gifted potential as indicative of the ease of learning. Of course, content representation and processing skills can never be truly separated, as they are reciprocal (see Chapter 4); more content knowledge means less demand on cognitive elaboration. Thus, as a general rule, the more advanced the knowledge level involved in a task, the less likely we can separate the respective contributions of nature and nurture. And finally, at a pragmatic level, defining giftedness as potential allows for discretion and expert judgment of gifted behaviors and potential in informal settings (e.g., through conversations and anecdotal evidence), without strictly adhering to the domain excellence criterion.

Using eminence as a marker of giftedness has its own drawbacks. Eminence is often based on social prestige and reputation and therefore may or may not reflect true excellence by objective professional standards and scientifically credible evidence, unless social appeal is an inherent part of the criteria for excellence (e.g., arts, oration, social leadership). A major argument from the expertise perspective on "giftedness" is to use "reproducible superior performance" as evidence (Ericsson, 1996, 2006; Ericsson et al., 2007b; Ericsson & Williams, 2007). Although it is questionable whether many of the authentic creative expressions and products are "reproducible" in a controlled setting, the demand for objective, credible standards and criteria is well justified on scientific grounds. It is important, therefore, to use more rigorous criteria and procedures for judging the degrees and levels of excellence, rather than relying on procedures and criteria such as nomination or public accolades (Ericsson, 1996). In folk psychology, for instance, it is often implicitly assumed that if a contribution to human knowledge or artistic expression is highly *important*, then the process leading to the contribution must be superb and the mind that produced this contribution must be proportionally exceptional. Therefore, people are naturally curious about Einstein's brain (Diamond et al.,

1985), as if by figuring out Einstein's brain we would have a measure of the greatness of his mind comparable to the greatness of his accomplishments. Although the importance of a contribution may be traced to greatness of a mind, it is not always the case; the extraordinary importance of a product does not necessarily mean an unusual underlying mental power. Consider the cases of Gutenberg and Newton. It can be argued that although Newton's mind was of a caliber superior to that of Gutenberg's, it is Gutenberg who was ranked as the most influential person for civilization in the past millennium because of his invention of, arguably, the earliest printing press. Although it makes sense to use measures of eminence, such as Nobel prizes, as a way to understand superior minds, we cannot presume that an exceptional outcome (a Nobel Prize–winning discovery) must entail an exceptional mind (the experimental design involved in the discovery must be superb by extraordinary measure). Another reason that eminence may not be the best criterion is the chance factor. Two persons may be equally brilliant or may have equally contributed to a field, but only one has gained fame and social distinction, because he or she happened to be in the right place at the right time. Don Ambrose (personal communication, August 2009) made an observation about the differences between Thomas Edison (1847–1931) and Nikola Tesla (1856–1943). Although Tesla's work seems to have been more insightful and brilliant, Edison's name is much better known and he made a much bigger impact on the world, probably because of his "business savvy" or *practical intelligence* à la Sternberg (1996b). This comparison further shows that eminence itself should not be used as an objective measure of exceptional competence. Beyond the issue of properly using eminence as a criterion, these two brilliant individuals further attest to the heterogeneity of superior or "gifted" minds, even though their excellence is expressed in the same domain of human endeavor.

A Development-Specific Approach to Gifted Identification: Beyond Essentialism

Essentialist conceptions of giftedness hold that a fixed set of essential traits can be extracted to define those who are "gifted." In other words, the concept of "giftedness" or "gifted child" is definable in a canonical manner (e.g., Gagné, 2005a, 2009a). I argue, instead, that the concept of "giftedness" is fundamentally prototypical, even exemplary; that is, instead of reducing the "gifted" to a set of abstract properties (i.e., what constitutes "giftedness"), people use prototypes to identify those who are "gifted." Just as people tend to see sparrows or eagles as *prototypes* of birds (likely using "flying" as a defining attribute) but tend to overlook the fact that ostriches and penguins are also birds, high-IQ children used to be considered prototypical of "gifted children," only for this concept to be replaced later with more pluralistic conceptions of gifted children as a variety of *exemplars* (e.g., Passow, 1981; Witty, 1958). I will revisit this issue when discussing the monothetic-idiographic tension.

From a more pragmatic viewpoint, Coleman and Cross (2005) offered a school-based, developmentalist solution: In childhood, giftedness may be defined as psychometrically or otherwise measured "potential," but as the child reaches adolescence, there should be evidence that the alleged potential is substantiated by age-appropriate accomplishments in specific culturally valued areas of human endeavor. Their definition represents a compromise between aptitude (ability) and achievement. Mayer (2005) extended Coleman and Cross's definition to include adult creative productivity by providing a life span formula that defines giftedness as "an age-specific term that refers to potential for the beginning stage, achievement for the intermediate stage, and eminence for the advanced stage" (p. 439). The three-tier system of increasing developmental complexity I postulate in Chapter 4 (Figure 4.1) roughly corresponds with the three phases of development of gifted potential. The framework I suggest is meant to serve as a heuristic for keeping up with the changing nature of gifted potential, thus avoiding the kind of reification and essentialism that has plagued the field and bogged down research efforts.

As shown in Figure 4.1, Tier 1 abilities and dispositions are a set of nebulous, developing personal traits that can be assessed in early and middle childhood (say, around 6–8 years of age), when performance and behavior likely reflect efficiency in basic functional units and more or less spontaneous, "natural" dispositions, which can be *inferred* only by comparing a child's performance with that of peers of equal experiences and backgrounds in terms of propensity and rate of learning or pace of skill development. This operationalization of "potential" is consistent with the definition of gifted potential offered in the federal Javits Gifted and Talented Education Act as "the potential for performing at remarkably high levels of accomplishments when compared with others of their age, experience, or environment" (Ross, 1993, p. 3). Comparing performance between and among peers of different backgrounds and experiences would inevitably confound interpretations and potentially invalidate the ensuing judgment and raise equity concerns (Gee, 2003).

Tier 1 aptitudes and dispositions are low in differentiation because they demonstrate high plasticity and functional flexibility, as well as higher instability in manifestations during childhood. In view of the limitations of the traditional view of aptitude as a latent capacity or potential, perceived by some scholars as a mysterious quality (e.g., Ericsson et al., 2005, 2007a; Matthews & Foster, 2006), Snow (1992, 1994) offered an alternative view of aptitude as the readiness to deal with situational demands and benefit from situational opportunities. Instead of a wide-open promise or even a blank check, as it were, aptitude so defined is a highly circumscribed, proximal potential, sitting right at the person-situation interface, rather than solely referred to as a personal trait, validated by its predictive validity. In other words, *aptitude, as Snow defines it, indicates the fitness to learn or perform well given a specific functional context, with whatever developed knowledge, skills, and dispositions a person brings to that point.* Such a situational definition of high aptitude not only locates aptitude at the person-context interface but also includes knowledge, affect, and conation as well as cognitive potentials (hence, *aptitude complex*; see Ackerman, 2003; Cronbach, 2003). It is close to domain-specific mastery models in two ways: First, it favors evidence of proximal mastery (the ease of learning given a specific task or level of challenge) over generic aptitude measures such as IQ or other general aptitude tests, so that authenticity of the potential is redeemed; second, it stresses the evolving nature of aptitude as a process of integrating many personal elements vis-à-vis the constraints of a task environment rather than a static personal trait.

As early nebulous abilities and dispositions of varying degrees of generality and specificity are in the process of differentiation vis-à-vis specific functional contexts, we can only infer rather than directly observe them in some well-developed form. For example, a child may show a good grasp of certain mathematical concepts or comprehension of the logic of a narrative, but fall short of full articulation. Thus, identifying some children as "gifted" at this stage is based on fallible inferences; identification of high promise in such a way always has a high degree of uncertainty. Precocity demonstrated by some children may turn out to be short lived, as they might lose their gifted edge over time (Simonton, 2005). What we typically use as identification tools (including IQ tests) are actually screening devices, aimed at selecting those who are *more likely* to succeed in a highly challenging program and eliminating those who are less likely to succeed. In other words, *what is at issue for identification is the likelihood of success in a specific activity or program, not the probability of being "gifted" or "nongifted" (for which no absolute gold standard exists)*. There are both statistical and pragmatic considerations here. Using aptitude assessment boils down to figuring out a trade-off between using relatively liberal criteria and relatively stringent criteria; that is, more liberal criteria or cutoffs would tolerate more "false positives" (committing more Type I errors, that is, accepting more of those individuals who turn out to be mediocre), but prevent "false negatives" (avoiding the Type II error of rejecting those who can succeed in meeting a given challenge), while more stringent criteria or cutoffs tend to minimize "false positives" but permit more "false negatives."

As shown in Figure 6.1, if we move the vertical bar (i.e., cutoff score) further to the right (say, the 95th percentile, as indicated by the dotted line on the right-hand side), fewer individuals would be qualified for inclusion. As a result, the number of "false positives" would decrease, but the number of "false negatives" would increase. Conversely, if we move the bar in the opposite direction (i.e., making the selection criterion less stringent, more liberal and inclusive, say, at the 85th percentile, as indicated by the dotted line on the left-hand side), the number of qualified individuals would increase. So the trade-off is that the number of "false negatives" would decrease but the number of "false positives" would increase (see Hartas, Lindsay, & Muijs, 2008). As a principle, using more stringent criteria is a play-safe strategy that works well for educational institutions but can be costly for some capable but rejected candidates (i.e., "false negatives"). For example, William Shockley, a 1956 Nobel Prize winner in physics, was screened

Figure 6.1. An illustration of use of more liberal versus conservative cutoffs in the normal distribution of a putative potential for identification and selection and the trade-off of related Type I and Type II errors.

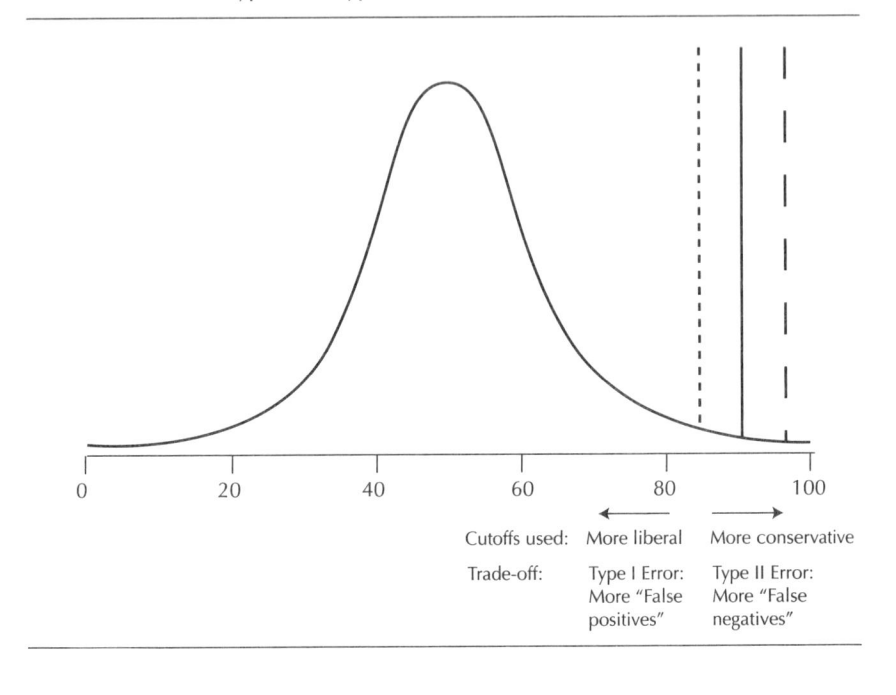

out in Terman's (1925) study because his IQ performance was repeatedly in the range of the 120s, below the bar of 140 (and later 135) set up by Terman.

At a later stage, say, starting around preadolescence or early adolescence (10–13 years of age), it is possible to identify a more developed, intermediate functional knowledge base and high-level processes, which are typically knowledge rich or knowledge enhanced, what I call Tier 2 competencies and interests. A distinct example is mathematically precocious children (Stanley, 1996). Their abilities as measured by the SAT-Math are highly differentiated in the sense that the mathematically precocious not only have developed knowledge about various topics and domains in mathematics, but also have had metalevel, strategic knowledge about the utilities of specific pieces of mathematical knowledge (i.e., cognitive sophistication within the domain can be observed). An accelerated rate of learning of more advanced materials, as well as intrinsic interests, even task commitment, can be observed at this stage. Indeed, distinct aptitude or trait complexes can be identified that set individuals on qualitatively different developmental trajectories and pathways (Ackerman, 2003). *With higher differentiation comes higher certainty of identification.*

However, patterns of abilities, knowledge, and interests at this stage of development still show diversity and heterogeneity rather than highly focused personal pursuits, hence low integration. Highly developed expertise, in contrast, is both differentiated and integrated and thus can be observed and measured with the highest certainty (and to some extent reproducible; see Ericsson et al., 2007a). This kind of developmental interpretation of high human potential avoids the problematic essentialist construal of gifted potential as having a unitary core (general intelligence, or natural talent in a domain) that maintains its identity, unity, and continuity. Furthermore, it is capable of fully accounting for the contextual, changing, evolving, and diverse (heterogeneous) nature of human potential and excellence over the course of individual development (i.e., ontogeny).

HOW WE COME TO KNOW THE NATURE AND DEVELOPMENT OF GIFTS AND TALENTS: NOMOTHETIC VERSUS IDIOGRAPHIC

Relying on immediate observation of authentic performance rather than on inferences about population-based characteristics as measured by aptitude tests leads to another distinct epistemological tension: What methods are more reliable—immediate observation and intensive case studies or studies using large sample sizes, psychometric measurements, and probabilistic inferences? A historical anecdote is telling. When Spearman (1904) declared that, once and for all, general intelligence had been "objectively determined and measured" (p. 201), Binet (1905; cited and discussed in Brody, 2000, p. 19) was not convinced; he argued that two persons who obtained the same test score on some psychometric tests might nevertheless possess different skill sets, which turns out to be the case at the high end of the spectrum almost by statistical necessity. These two early pioneers of intelligence theory illustrate two very different ways or styles of looking at the world. Spearman was a mathematician who valued universality, generality, simplicity, and precision and preferred numbers to immediate phenomenology, with a default assumption characteristic of his time: Intelligence works like a *mental faculty* (Spearman, 1927), a position largely discredited by modern cognitive psychology (see Jensen, 1993; van der Maas et al., 2006). In contrast, Binet was a clinician who was intrigued by nuances and the "idiographic complexity" of the individual intellectual functioning (Brody, 2000, p. 19). Spearman's approach is *nomothetic*, namely, seeking and relying on assumptions of universal laws and principles governing behavioral variations within a population, whereas Binet's approach is more *idiographic*, that is, attempting to understand a particular individual case in all its richness and complexity. Nomothetic approaches examine a forest of trees, some taller than others but all sharing fundamental properties (or common parameters) as trees, whereas idiographic approaches focus on individual trees and their unique structures and functions (and conditions for optimal growth). The terms *nomothetic* and *idiographic* come mainly from early personality research (Allport, 1937). Parallel to the tension between nomothetic and idiographic approaches in psychology is the tension between quantitative and qualitative approaches in educational research (Bredo, 2009; Ercikan & Roth, 2006; Howe, 2009). The nomothetic-idiographic tension can be expressed in the following manner:

Thesis:
Manifestations of gifted behaviors are subject to a set of hidden but universally valid laws and principles; therefore, we can determine who are gifted and how the gifted develop by applying these universal rules and principles.

Antithesis:
Manifestations of gifted behaviors are diverse and unique phenomena and have their own underlying logic, not subject to predetermined universal principles; therefore, the uniqueness of each manifestation needs to be closely examined in order to shed light on its nature.

The following are three key methodological differences between the two approaches:

- *Logic.* Nomothetic approaches are deductive in nature, making general assumptions about human conditions and the way human beings function and derive deductive consequences of "natural laws" or universal principles for a given population. Idiographic approaches, in contrast, use an inductive approach, identifying organized patterns of behavior based on intimate observation of a set of particulars (Allport, 1937), which may explain a particular class of phenomena. Applying this to the issue of giftedness, people with a nomothetic perspective make universal, essentialist assumptions about what giftedness is and what attributes define giftedness. Therefore, the purpose of research is to test the viability of these general hypotheses with representative samples (the gifted and average) in a population. In comparison, people with an idiographic orientation see giftedness as involving unique individual functioning and development, as in child prodigies (Feldman, 1986) and musical talent development (Subotnik & Jarvin, 2005), thus not easily fitting into any general or grand theories of "giftedness." The task for researchers is to identify unique patterns of *individual development* leading to exceptional competencies (e.g., Bloom, 1985).
- *Language.* The language used by nomothetic approaches is analytic and abstract (e.g., general intelligence, mathematically gifted, intrinsic motivation), intended to capture the essential properties of the object under investigation, and the language used by idiographic approaches remain naturalistic, low inference, or phenemic, to use Holton's (1981) term; that is, it comes directly from natural observations and is closely tied to the

empirical instances it is meant to capture (e.g., interest, crystallizing experiences, organization of purpose).

- *Data.* From a nomothetic perspective, regularities underlying diverse behavioral and psychological manifestations are quantifiable and reveal themselves as measurable dimensions and variables that are universally valid and applicable (hence, parametrical). From an idiographic perspective, the functioning person is an indivisible unit of analysis and thus cannot be psychologically dissected into isolated, static dimensions (see Bredo, 2009; Ercikan & Roth, 2006, for a similar analysis in educational research).

Strengths and Pitfalls of Nomothetic or Universalistic Approaches

Making nomothetic or universalistic assumptions about psychological processes and individual differences in intelligence and personality is the mainstay of differential psychology. Its main task is to identify variables that operate within a population. As Novick (1982) stated, "Our success as scientists can be measured by our skill in identifying variables that can be used to define relevant, exchangeable subpopulations" (p. 6). Various ability and personality variables are thus derived through measurement techniques and are considered valid across a population. In other words, they are seen as fixed parameters that permit prediction of how individuals will behave. A distinct advantage of using nomothetic approaches is that once we developed a valid set of parameters and proper instruments to estimate these parameters, long-term prediction and long-range reasoning can be made about how these parameters operate in the real world and what are logical, probabilistic consequences of their operations, without overly relying on the empirical manifestations, which are presumably always amorphous, varied, and elusive to our senses and observations. Physics is a textbook example of such a deductive logic. Starting with Terman (1925), the nomothetic approach to research on the gifted as the mainstream in gifted studies has made major advances, as evidenced by both the gifted-average comparative research (Borkowski & Peck, 1986; Kanevsky, 1990), and longitudinal research (the SMPY study by Lubinski & Benbow, 2006; the Fullerton longitudinal study by Gottfried, Gottfried, & Guerin, 2009), among others.

A potential problem with applying the nomothetic mode of thinking to human behavior is that psychological constructs, such as various forms and types of intelligence and personality, are conceptual instruments we created to describe and organize a set of observations in terms of how these variables may influence individual functioning in a population. A person does not act as a list of variables (Snow, 1995). These nomothetic constructs start to lose their explanatory power when they fail to capture the nuances and complexities of individuality or specific lines of individual development (see Cross, 2003, for a critique of the empirical-analytic mode of inquiry). More technically, the monothetic or universalistic assumption of individual functioning is predicated on evidence that interpersonal variation in human functioning reflects intrapersonal variation, that is, individual organization of behavior and how this organization changes over time. Molenaar (2004) argued that this is not the case and that the entire psychometric tradition fails to capture the intra-individual changes and variability and the ensuing heterogeneity of individual functioning and growth.

As a corollary, a nomothetic approach to giftedness (e.g., operationally defining giftedness psychometrically as a set of general psychological traits) has both strengths and weaknesses. On the one hand, we might assume that extreme conditions of individual functioning should be captured by a psychometric measure if the instrument involved allow for fine-grained differentiation at the high end (i.e., no apparent ceiling effect). On the other hand, we can argue that the highly gifted may evade standard psychometric measurement altogether, because of the unique structural and functional organization of their minds, including the idiosyncratic handling of specific test situations itself. In other words, the nomothetic assumption underlying psychometric-based approaches to giftedness may capture *individual difference* dimensions at the cost of obscuring one's *individuality* (Edelman, 1995; Molenaar, 2004). This is where the idiographic approach comes to claim its own legitimacy as an alternative or complementary approach.

To understand the rationale of a more idiographic, or "clinical" and diagnostic, approach to identification and understanding of gifted potential, a distinction between statistics-based knowledge and case-based knowledge is helpful. Statistics-based knowledge is concerned with characteristics of a population or subpopulation, while case-based knowledge retains the individual's information in all its richness and complexity. While educational policy makers in Washington, DC, or state capitals typically rely on educational statistics in fashioning policy arguments, local schools and classroom teachers are mainly working with individual students and making case-based decisions, such as identifying specific individuals for curricular differentiation or nominating some students for specific gifted programs. An analogy of medical diagnosis and treatment is useful here. Doctors clearly have to know updated medical statistics, such as the prevalence of a particular disease, high-risk subpopulations, or the recovery rate using a particular treatment plan. However, when it comes to a particular client or patient, a diagnosis should always be tuned into the particularity of this person with a unique pattern of complaints, symptoms, and etiologies; the treatment plan should also vary accordingly. Rich case-based knowledge, not familiarity with medical statistics, is what makes medical expertise in clinical settings.

Idiographic Approaches as an Alternative or Complement to Nomothetic Approaches

The nomothetic approach takes an objectivist, mechanistic, epistemic stance, treating the structures and functions of a person as those of an object, following universal laws, acting in a predictable manner based on a set of parameters; thus the subjective, intentional life of a person can be treated as epiphenomenal or inconsequential. In contrast, the idiographic approach always entails an intimate look into the mental life of the person (e.g., including a phenomenological approach; Cross, 2003). Thus, many researchers have proposed constructs, such as *organization of purpose* (Gruber, 1986), *subjective mental space* (Shavinina & Kholodnaja, 1996), or *subjective action space* (Ziegler, 2005), as one of the key ingredients of a model of how gifted competence comes about. For them, unique cognitive and affective experiences and personal ways of perceiving and representing the world are major sources of giftedness (Shavinina & Kholodnaja, 1996). The idiographic approach raises the issue of whether intuition, personal judgment, and other subjective aspects of a personal life should be taken into account in the scientific understanding of psychosocial functioning and development that are as complex as intelligence, expertise, and creativity. Psychologists (including researchers on giftedness) differ in this regard (Kimble, 1984).

The variable-centered, nomothetic approach still represents the mainstream of psychology (Cronbach, 1975; Molenaar, 2004). It is predicated on the assumption of objectivity, quantifiability, and generalizability of psychological traits, processes, and events. Even though IQ scores or personality trait measures such as introversion/extroversion have very different meanings and properties from, say, physical properties such as height or weight, the nomothetic perspective assumes that certain essential mental qualities can have sufficient stability and functionality to allow us to measure them with reliability and make behavioral predictions based on their putative influences. However, the person-centered, idiographic approach, using constructs such as *individualized life tasks* (Cantor, 1990, p. 740) and *personal strivings* (Emmons, 1986), has gained momentum. Molenaar (2004) even proposed statistical techniques that would allow us to bring *the person* back into psychology and reestablish psychology as an *idiographic science*.

We all try to carve nature at its joints. The issue is how to make the cuts that retain complexity and sufficient detail yet show intelligible structures and regularities, the ways that "each person is like all other people, some other people, and no other person" (Lohman & Rocklin, 1995, p. 470). As mentioned earlier, the field of gifted research started with nomothetic assumptions about human traits, such as the assumption that general intelligence is the core of giftedness (Terman, 1925), but increasingly recognized the importance of starting with particulars, the immediate phenomenology of gifted and talented behaviors (e.g., Witty, 1958). Indeed, Terman himself conducted many case studies in later years of his longitudinal study, producing insights that otherwise could not have been obtained (see Terman & Oden, 1959). While the monothetic perspective led to essentialism in conceptions of giftedness and categorical approaches to gifted education in practice, the idiographic perspective opens up new avenues to exploring the many and varied ways in which talents unfold; hence, the prototypical and exemplary conceptions of gifted children and adults, and diverse ways of identifying and serving promising youths.

Strategic Considerations of Using Nomothetic and Idiographic Approaches

As a research strategy, the nomothetic versus idiographic approaches in psychology, just like the quantitative versus qualitative approaches in educational research, can be better seen as a continuum rather than a dichotomy (Ercikan & Roth, 2006), as a dialectic process of data-theory coordination and generalization rather than a static either-or choice (Bredo, 2009). There is a middle ground between universals and particulars, between using a variable-centered approach to identify "exchangeable subpopulations" (gifted, average, mentally retarded, etc.), and a person-centered approach to identify unique individuality (multiple exceptionalities, girls gifted in mathematics, etc.). The aptitude or trait complexes identified by Ackerman (2003) through cluster analysis represent such a midlevel synthesis. Similarly, Muthén and Muthén (2000) offered a technical compromise between variable-centered and person-centered approaches. They recommended using a "latent class" statistical technique (available with the statistic software M-Plus) to identify relatively homogeneous subgroups in terms of differential individual profiles and developmental patterns. Alternatively, Silverstein (1988) argued that to truly resolve the nomothetic-idiographic tension, functional developmental history (FDH) should be used as a unit of analysis. In the same vein, Haensly, Reynolds, and Nash (1986) called for attention to "the dynamic nature of the human response to specific and varied settings" (p. 130). Snow (1995) echoed this sentiment: "It may be that the best way to understand both individual differences and individuality is in the context of development, whereas developmental pathways both general and unique may best be interpreted in the context of differential distributions" (p. xiv; see also Horowitz, 2009; McCall, 1981). The use of FDH as a unit of analysis seems to point in a promising direction. It amounts to *using person-in-context as a unit of analysis rather than locating human behavior squarely as a function of decontextualized personal traits, and looking into intra-individual changes (through time series analysis or microgenetic methods) in adaptive organization of one's knowledge, skills, and dispositions over time.* Dai and Renzulli (2008) proposed three constructs that represent such a unit of analysis that are purportedly capable of capturing the person-context dynamics. *Selective affinity* refers to the way individuals selectively attend to and choose certain aspects of their environments in cultivating their developmental niches or niche potential. *Maximal grip* refers to a process of striving for mastery of a system that cognitively and affectively further propels individuals toward differential development (niches, trajectories, and pathways). *At the edge of chaos* refers to critical points where individuals experience a psychological tension between the known and unknown, the old and new, or two systems of thought, and have to make decisions in dealing with opportunities, risks, and uncertainties engendered by such occasions. These central concepts represent an attempt to preserve the functional integrity, unique individuality, and context dependency of human functioning and development while making generalizable claims about talent development.

Alternatively, *both the nomothetic and idiographic approaches can be used in parallel, illuminating gifted manifestations on different time scales and at different levels of description.* Simonton (1997) and Lubinski and Benbow (2006), for example, developed predictive and explanatory models of creative productivity in which only a small number of parameters are postulated and all the theoretical predictions expressed statistically and empirically testable. In contrast, Bloom (1985), Gardner (1993, 1997), and Gruber (1981) took a much more intimate look at the personal and intellectual lives of those who have made, or were on their way to make, landmark creative contributions, with painstaking efforts to develop a sympathetic understanding of the workings of their minds. Both approaches are needed: nomothetic, trait-based, variable-centered research affords some objective, macro-level, population-based predictions (e.g., Lubinski & Benbow, 2006); idiographic, process-oriented, person-centered research affords deep, micro-level, case-based understandings (e.g., Bloom, 1985; Gruber, 1981). Ultimately they may serve different epistemic purposes and have different practical utilities.

HOW WE EXPLAIN AND PREDICT MANIFESTATIONS AND DEVELOPMENT OF GIFTED BEHAVIOR: REDUCTIONISM VERSUS EMERGENTISM

If the nomothetic-idiographic tension concerns whether one starts with universals or particulars, and how richness and uniqueness can be preserved in search of generality, the reductionism-emergentism tension I identify here concerns what level of analysis and explanation is appropriate given a behavioral and psychological phenomenon. The analytic/reductionist versus constructivist/emergentist tension can be expressed in the following manner:

Thesis:
The complexity of gifted manifestations can be explained by simpler components at a more basic level of analysis; higher-level phenomena can be causally reduced to lower-level components, structures, and processes.

Antithesis:
The complexity of gifted manifestations reflects higher-order organizational principles in the organism and functional regularities that are context dependent, and there are emergent properties that cannot be reduced to isolated lower-level components.

Broadly speaking, the nomothetic efforts to analytically isolate and identify essential elements of human functioning are reductionistic in nature, and the idiographic efforts to preserve the uniqueness of individual functioning is anti-reductionistic (Bredo, 2009). However, reductionism in the context of the nature and nurture of excellence has a particular meaning: it represents a tendency or effort to trace exceptional human performance ultimately to endogenous sources, particularly natural endowment as a distinct material or physical advantage.

Dennett (1987) identified three epistemic stances: understanding and predicting behavior of an object as *physical*, as involving *design*, or as *intentional*. Treating an object as physical is the most concrete; things can be predicted based on mass, velocity, energy, force, and so on. The domains of physics and chemistry take this *physical stance*. In comparison, looking at an object from a design point of view is more abstract: We infer its structures, functions, and purposes. Disciplines that characteristically take a *design stance* include biology and engineering, which help us understand, for example, how a bird is designed, in a evolutionary sense, for flying, or how a clock is designed, mechanically or electronically, to tell time. The most abstract stance is *intentional stance*: We have to infer desires, thoughts, and feelings or various mental states to make good predictions about the behavior of a given object. Minds and some software have this intentional property. Dennett insists that these epistemic stances be used only as cognitive strategies to tackle complex phenomena; they are valid as far as they effectively predict behavior; no ontological claims (i.e., are they "real"?) are intended. For example, we have to think about software and many animals *as if* they possessed "intentions" and "purposes" without claiming that they do form intentions and purposes, like human beings. However, utilities of the three epistemic stances are not just about their predictive efficacy with particular objects or behaviors; a proper epistemic stance helps us grasp the inner workings of a thing, and an improper stance obscures its essence. For example, to understand why a clock stops ticking, you have to take a design stance (e.g., making a guess that "the design may be flawed") and from there work down to the material level (maybe there is some mechanical failure); simply attributing the clock's failure to, say, material wearing (i.e., taking a physical stance) may not find and solve the problem. The mind happens to have all three properties: It is physical in the sense that it is made of billions of neurons energized and connected by complex neurobiological structures and biochemical processes; it has been "designed," genetically and epigenetically, through development and learning, to do various things that have adaptive value; it is capable of reflective consciousness and directing its consciousness toward certain aspects of the world, including oneself (i.e., capable of intentionality). Thus, to understand the superior workings of the mind and assess unusual potential, one has to decide which stance or a combination of stances stands the best chance of uncovering its deepest secrets.

Worldviews (Ambrose, 2000) are similar in a way to epistemic stances (Dennett, 1987). The notion of worldviews can be traced back to Pepper's (1942) world hypotheses. Pepper opposed the objectivity premise of logical positivism by arguing that there is no such thing as "pure" factual data free from interpretation.

He outlined four worldviews or conceptual systems—formism, mechanism, contextualism, and organicism—that serve as "root metaphors" for interpretating a variety of natural phenonema and world affairs. Along this line of thinking, Overtone (1984) identified mechanistic, organismic, or contextualist worldviews as most frequently used in psychology, reflecting our basic or deep assumptions and understandings of human functioning and development. The mechanistic vision of human functioning and development is that of the refinement of machinery. Just like a mechanical gadget, the human functioning apparatus can be taken apart to show how each component works, all following physical laws. For such a system, the addition, subtraction, and rearrangement of components are sufficient to make it work, but no qualitative change can occur in and of itself. The mechanistic worldview aims at reduction, prediction, and control. In contrast, an organismic vision of human functioning and development is modeled after living things such as plants and animals. Living beings progressively undergo transformation or qualitative, discontinuous changes. The process involves "integration of subsystems within larger systems as well as long-term teleological development" (D. Ambrose, personal communication, August 2009). Human beings are even more so; they actively participate in their own development through adaptation, self-modification, self-selection, and self-initiatives (Bandura, 1986; Piaget, 1950/2001; Siegler, 1996). A contextualist vision of human development incorporates organismic principles (e.g., humans as active agents) but see human functioning and development as fundamentally embedded or situated in the person-environment dynamic interactions and functional relationships (Fischer & Bidell, 2006). The person-environment interaction creates developmental novelty that cannot be accounted for by merely mechanistic or organismic principles. In other words, contextual models of human development are interactionist in the sense that the dynamic interaction of the person and the environment is responsible for adaptation and developmental changes (see Piaget, 1950/2001).

Similarities between Dennett's (1987) three epistemic stances and Overtone's (1984) three worldviews are obvious. In fact, one can almost be mapped onto the other. What is important for our discussion, however, is that whatever stance we take, there are methodological consequences, in terms of what kinds of research questions we ask; what kinds of research design we tend to adopt; what kinds of observations, measurement, and documentation we tend to use; what kinds of findings we will get; and ultimately what kinds of interpretation scheme or model we will use given a set of data (Ambrose, 2003b; Bredo, 2009; Ercikan & Roth, 2006). Therefore, adoption of a particular epistemic stance or worldview is a strategic decision one makes, wittingly or not, when facing a phenomenon.

Psychology, as a relatively young discipline, used to emulate physics (some may argue that it still does!). Newtonian physics, with its first principles, has attested to the magical power of reductionism. As a matter of fact, it was so powerful that brilliant physicists such as Planck and Einstein all aspired to unify physical sciences under an even more basic, foundational theory. Planck, for example, warned that "physical research cannot rest so long as mechanics and eletrodynamics have not been welded together with thermodynamics and heat radiation" (quoted in Holton, 1981, p. 18). Despite the unsuccessful attempt in Einstein's later life with his unified field theory, reductionism has proved highly effective when used in physics, but less so in biology, and is increasingly controversial in psychology (see Koch & Leary, 1992). Psychology as a science started out with a strong reductionist orientation (e.g., psychophysics), treating mental events as epiphenomenal of neural-physiological processes. In general, reductionism in psychology is a tendency to trace all complex behaviors and high-level psychological phenomena (including early manifestations of gifts and talents or outstanding eminent achievement) backward to simpler, lower-level components and regularities that constitute higher-level phenomena. In their most radical forms, psychological processes and events can be causally reduced to neural-physiological events and biochemistry, which can, in turn, be reduced to physics (or from cellular to molecular). A less dramatic example of the reductionist approach is to parse variations in intelligence and personality variables into proportions explained by genetics and environment, respectively. Using a more refined scheme, variations in human intellectual performance can be taken apart to show its simpler components (processing speed, working memory, deductive and inductive logic, metacognition, etc.), and explained by genetic and environmental components in an additive or multiplicative fashion (see Scarr, 1997). However, an enduring question, as articulated by Cronbach (1975) decades ago, is, "Should social science aspire to reduce behavior to laws?" (p. 116; see also Koch & Leary, 1992). A stance in radical opposition to reductionism is holism, which insists that a whole is more than the sum of its parts and that the uniqueness of the whole (including individual functioning) should be preserved (Bredo, 2009).

Compared to reductionism and holism, emergentism as a philosophical orientation is relatively new in psychology (Sawyer, 2002). Different from holism, it argues for the material basis of all mental processes and the possibility of analytically collapsing a complex system into different levels of analysis. Different from reductionism, it argues for the emergence of novel properties and increasing organized complexity of a system as a joint function of many interactive factors, endogenous or exogenous, and thus is not reducible to any single factor. For example, evolution can be understood as a self-assembly and self-organization of complexity: living beings have, over millions of years of evolution, surpassed critical thresholds of nervous systems, consciousness, language, and shared technology, which enable *Homo sapiens* to achieve a maximal fit through learning and development in an unprecedented manner. Each threshold represents a new level of organized complexity that is indebted to, but cannot be reduced to, lower-level components. For example, the linguistic, symbolic capability as an emergent property of human functioning entails intentionality or directed consciousness, but cannot be simply explained by consciousness. Emergentism would explain individual differences in complex human behaviors, including intellectual performance and manifestations of talents and creative productivity, as a matter of real-time developmental emergence, a dynamic form of organized complexity (Dai, 2005; Sawyer, 2002). Indeed, the essence of development from an organismic point of view is the emergence of new properties (Overtone, 1984). While Jensen (1993, 2001) and other differential psychologists are seeking the biological underpinnings of intelligence by obtaining physiological measures such as neural conduction velocity (see also Geake, 2009; Vandervert, 2009), Gruber (1986) dismissed such a reductionistic account and characterized Darwin, Piaget, and other epoch-making creative lives as self-construction (i.e., doing/becoming) of the extraordinary. Reductionists and emergentists are trying to answer the same question of how human exceptional competence and creative productivity comes about, but going in opposite directions. As another example, after the three-ring conception of giftedness, Renzulli (2002) still found something wanting and went ahead to propose a set of personal constructs, such as optimism, courage, sensitivity to human conditions, and sense of destiny, as necessary motivational forces that lead to major creative contributions to society and humankind. Behind the nature-nurture, being-doing/becoming debate also lies an epistemological tension, differences in what Kimble (1984) identified as two cultures in psychology: scientism and humanism (see also Koch & Leary, 1992). Given these competing views and the opposite directions in which researchers go in finding answers to the same question, how are we ever going to find a solution that can satisfy both? I believe that the only way to resolve differences is to resort to a systems approach. Fortunately, four explanatory factors proposed by Aristotle may help us untangle the intricacies involved in a tension between reductionism and holism or emergentism.

Aristotle's Four Types of Causes or Explanatory Factors: Beyond Reductionism and Holism

In *Physics* and *Metaphysics*, Aristotle suggested four types of causes or explanations we use to understand why things turn out the way they do (see Cohen, 2006). *Material causes* address the question of "what is it made of?" *Formal causes* address the question of "what is its form or structure?" *Efficient causes* address what makes it happen, in other words, the question of "how is it produced or how did it come into existence?" Finally, *final causes* address the question of "what is it for?" Consider building a bridge. A bridge is made of steel and concrete, among other materials (material causes); it is constructed based on a blueprint that defines its structural and functional properties (formal causes); it is produced through human agency, such as labor, engineering expertise and creativity, and technical equipment (efficient causes); and it is made to facilitate traffic and transportation (final causes). Taken together, we can state the four causes in the following manner: A thing comes into existence or is produced when matter (materials) is turned into a certain structure (form) through some agency (mechanism) based on telos or some functional purpose. The material and formal causes (matter and form) are static explanations, and efficient and final causes (agency and purpose) are dynamic explanations (Cohen, 2006). Relevant to the issue of differential development are two questions: First, how do we explain the process of becoming or "coming into being" of human development, from a relatively amorphous existence in terms of mental structures to a highly differentiated, organized, talented being? Second, to what extent is human development like the production of an artifact, such as building a bridge, and to what extent is it like a natural, organismic growth such as the growth of a tree or fruit? As we know, the types of explanation we come up with for human-made artifacts can be quite different from those for organisms such as plants or animals (see Cohen, 2006; Simon, 1996). To use a simple example of how a person who was "unmusical" becomes highly musical, there are two types of static explanations. The first type infers that the person may have some hardware advantages (e.g., fast processing speed, keen pitch perception) that facilitate learning in music (e.g., ease of learning). This is an endogenous material explanation. The second type infers possible biologically hardwired structures dedicated to music or innately programmed rules or principles governing the processing of musical information (e.g., perfect pitch, rhythmic pattern recognition). In this case, formal causes residing within the person are implicated (i.e., there are structural and formal advantages). In explaining differential development, those in the tradition of psychometric and differential psychology (e.g., Gagné, 1999b, 2009b; Plomin, 1997) tend to give material explanations of giftedness as a general natural endowment (i.e., material causes) without further commitment to innatism (i.e., formal causes) that postulates biologically preordained, specialized structures such as modularity for music or other cultural domains.

Those with an emergentist or holistic stance tend to resort to more dynamic causes of differential development, such as *how* a person who was unmusical, through exposure to, and training in, music, becomes musical (efficient causes), and *why* the person has to be musical in the first place (final causes). It does not mean that emergentist explanations necessarily negate reductionist explanations. Rather, they resort to higher-level organizational principles, such as reciprocal interaction of the person and a task environment and self-organization in the process of developmental transition from State A (e.g., being unmusical) to State B (being musical). Thus, to go beyond reductionism and holism is to figure out how these four explanatory factors might piece together the entire puzzle of differential development of interest (e.g., musical or mathematical development). To put all our bets on the table and keep all options open, I suggest that the four causal elements be regarded as coming from both the inner environment of the person (endogenous) and the external environment the person finds himself in (exogenous), and thus can be presented in a 2 x 4 matrix (Table 6.1).

As shown in Table 6.1, *endogenous material causes* include genetic variations, biological infrastructure (including developmental changes in neuroanatomy

Table 6.1. Endogenous and exogenous factors contributing to development of excellence, based on Aristotle's four causal or explanatory factors.

Explanatory Factors	Endogenous	Exogenous
Material causes	Genes, neurobiological infrastructure	Technical and cultural resources
Formal causes	Self-organization Meaning making	Structuring or scaffolding environment
Efficient causes	Developing abilities, modules, and skills Action, self-initiative, and motivation	Incentives, values, technology, and more competent others
Final causes (*Telos*)	Self-actualization	Social and cultural vitality

and biochemistry) that supports various mental functions. *Exogenous material causes* include technical and cultural resources that support specific human endeavors. Formal causes can also be either exogenous or endogenous as well. On the endogenous (person) side, one "formal" factor is a "dumb" mechanism, namely, self-organization of, say, music perception in making adaptation to inherent constraints such as the tonal system; thus an unmusical person became musical without awareness of how it took place. The other "formal" factor is a "smart" mechanism, meaning making: the symbolic capability of mentally representing musical forms, expressions, and meanings, as well as making fine discrimination and generalization of properties of various kinds of music (e.g., jazz versus classical music); thus an unmusical person can articulate what music is and how it works as a system. Note that I do not postulate any modular devices exclusively dedicated to music or other cultural activities as a formal cause, as I do not believe that a biologically preordained structure exists for a cultural artifact like music (or mathematics, for that matter). In other words, the module for music (or for other domains), if any, is made through experience, not born. Besides the *endogenous formal causes*, there are also *exogenous formal causes*, including particular structuring and scaffolding environments, as Vygostky (1978) suggested with respect to construction of any higher mental functions. I argue that for culturally created and semantically rich domains, exogenous formal explanations are crucial and indispensable. As for what makes differential development actually happen (efficient causes), I list developing abilities, skills, and modules, as well as motivation and emotion as *endogenous agency*, and incentives, cultural values, supporting technology, and more competent others as *exogenous agency*. It is at this level of analysis that material and formal causes, endogenous and exogenous, mesh together. Last, for the "final causes," it is open to debate what constitutes "telos" for development of high-level competence and excellence. I list self-actualization as the ultimate *endogenous purpose* for striving for excellence as Maslow (1970) prescribed (wittingly or not), and social and cultural vitality as the ultimate *exogenous purpose* or reasons why a society goes to great lengths to promote, nurture, and celebrate various forms of excellence.

Listing these possible explanations as either endogenous or exogenous has its own pitfalls, as if our skin were a boundary between nature and nurture, between the subject and object. If Vygotsky is right, most things that we think belongs to "nature" are actually nurtured and later become our "second nature" through internalization. As we move along in development, it is increasingly difficult to separate nature and nurture, the endogenous and exogenous, without significantly distorting how nature and nurture together dynamically bootstrap a developmental trajectory and pathway. Nevertheless, Aristotle's four-cause framework permits a more systemic view of how humans develop and puts the tension between reductionistically and holistically inclined researchers in perspective. Depending on domains (e.g., arts or sciences), type (e.g., performer or producer), and level of excellence (e.g., world class versus natural or state level), plausible explanations one can draw from this table may vary, calling for domain-specific, midrange theories rather than grand theories of talent development.

To put reductionist and emergentist explanations in a larger scheme of the four causes, those with reductionist orientations in understanding gifted competence tend to seek explanations that are endogenous (within the person) and static (i.e., re-sorting to material and formal explanations), and those with holistic or emergentist orientations tend to be more concerned with dynamic causes (efficient and final), higher-order interaction of endogenous and exogenous factors, and emergent properties and relationships. It should be noted that there are two kinds of reductionism. The first kind is *eliminative reductionism* in the sense that it tries to explain away other causes as plausible, in the form of "nothing but neurocognitive efficiency" or "nothing but genes." The second type of reductionism is *noneliminative* in that observed variations of interest are partly attributed to lower-level elements (e.g., cognitive and neural efficiency or genes) without eliminating the need for higher-level explanation (see Searle, 2004). If reductionism is seen only as part of cumulative research efforts to understand some of the pieces illustrated in Table 6.1 out of the whole puzzle, then the cycle of research will take a spiral turn to include and integrate other elements, rendering the contributions and limits of reductionist findings clearer. It seems that an eclectic, multifaceted view of human potential better explains the complexity of the emergence of gifted and talented behaviors. Multiple worldviews and epistemic stances, thus, can be seen as complementary in tackling the complexity of phenomena involved (Ambrose, 2003b). Three basic classes of the theory of intelligence that Perkins (1995; Perkins & Grotzer, 1997) identified, biological, experiential, and reflective, can be recast and refined in the Aristotelian four-cause framework to facilitate a more systematic view of how human competence (including an exceptional one) develops and evolves over time. Ultimately, the success or failure of a theory depends on its ability to make ever more refined theoretical predictions and explanations. Newtonian physics may provide a good prediction of the trajectory of a falling apple, but not a falling leaf; for the latter, a more nuanced understanding or complex model (e.g., involving aerodynamics) of a falling object is needed. What we need in the field of gifted studies are theories that are simple enough to capture the main elements involved and complex enough to elucidate the way they work together to produce particular developmental outcomes (see Chapter 9 for an integrated framework).

CONCLUSION: TOWARD A METHODOLOGICAL SYNTHESIS

In this chapter, I attempt to demonstrate that what is seemingly factual and objective evidence for giftedness is based on a set of research practices with conflicting definitions and assumptions; what are seemingly factual and objective ontological statements about the nature of gifted potential or gifted competence are never free from some epistemological lens of interpretation and explanation. Identifying the nature of our work as fundamentally constrained by our epistemological beliefs does not necessarily lead to a relativist stance regarding knowledge claims. Rather, by pointing out the strengths and weaknesses of each method we use, each lens we adopt, we will be in a position to see where each of them can find a good niche in helping us understand the nature of giftedness, where each of them falls short on epistemic or pragmatic grounds.

The tension between those who view population-based high "aptitudes" as indicative of "high potential" and those who view superior authentic performance and achievement as the best evidence of "gifted" potential reflects different levels of trust or confidence in the observation of superior performance in authentic settings versus making inference about potential based on contrived testing. I argue that retaining the concept of high aptitude as differentiated from achievement is still warranted, though aptitude should be seen not as static and context free, but as dynamic, evolving, and context bound. As for the nomothetic-idiographic tension, I suggest several available options to make both approaches part of the ongoing, complementary efforts to preserve individuality and contextual dependency while making generalization. A way to achieve a methodological synthesis is to identify proper units of analysis that permit observation of giftedness in the making; that is, how exceptional development occurs in situ. Finally, there will always be reductionist efforts to pin down lower-level components that are responsible for gifted development and emergentist efforts to identify higher-level interaction and organization, and emergent properties. A systems perspective will help us to know how cumulative research can make a spiral turn in putting different pieces together. Seeing giftedness as an emergent and evolving quality that is fundamentally relational and situated vis-à-vis a particular environment at a particular point in development is as important as seeing it as having many lower-level components supporting its realization. Aristotelian four causes are useful for facilitating a more systemic view of talent development, under which midrange, more circumscribed theories of high-level competence and excellence can be developed.

Ends and Means of Gifted Education

Everything is good as it leaves the hands of the Author of things; everything
degenerates in the hands of man.
                        —Jean-Jacque Rousseau, *Emile, or On Education*

The yeast of education is the idea of excellence, and that comprises as
many forms as there are individuals to develop a personal image of excellence. The school must have as one of its principal functions the nurturing
of images of excellence.
                        —Jerome Bruner, *On Knowing: Essays for the Left Hand*

IN CHAPTER 2, I argued that gifted education is constrained, but not dictated, by
what we know about the nature and development of gifted behavior and exceptional competence. I also argued that we should be aware of where the role of
scientific knowledge in gifted education stops, and ethical, social, and pragmatic
considerations become major considerations in designing gifted education. In
other words, there are boundaries of how far science can go in telling us how to
conduct gifted education and design its programs. In this and the next chapters, I
will try to elucidate aspects of gifted education that can be informed by scientific
research and are contingent on evidence-based understandings, that is, how the
implementation of programming goals we espouse for gifted education are constrained by scientific research and understandings. At the same time, I will also
identify aspects of gifted education that concern different "values" and can only
be negotiated and agreed upon by its stakeholders, or relevant communities. The
focus here is on two issues that have to do with the primary purposes of gifted
education: (a) expertise versus creativity, and (b) the gifted child versus talent
development.

A FRAMEWORK FOR UNDERSTANDING GIFTED EDUCATION

In the discourse among educators and researchers, the term *giftedness* is used in
two ways, sometimes in a scientific discourse (e.g., what is the nature of "giftedness") and sometimes in a normative way (e.g., how we develop this desirable
quality; for example, see Renzulli, 1999). The two uses of the term reveal a basic
understanding of giftedness as a dynamic and evolving, rather than static and

fixed, quality. They also reveal two alternative research strategies. We can focus on its nature, in which case our task is to understand its workings and development; this is a basic science part of our research endeavor. Alternatively, we can focus on its nurture, in which case our task is to make research and development (R&D) efforts with the aim of promoting high-level excellence for those students who show great promise in that regard; this is a more applied and practical part of research closely related to gifted education (see also Winner, 2000). Gifted education as an educational design has the following properties:

1. It is based on our understanding of what a child can be, if properly nurtured; therefore, it involves future developmental states we deem desirable for a child, which are never specified or preordained in the nature of the child, but appropriate given his or her demonstrated potentials.
2. It involves social and ethical considerations; we view gifted children as precious resources that need to be protected and cultivated for the vitality of the society as well as the self-actualization of the individuals involved. All children should have opportunity to develop and demonstrate their potential.
3. It involves pragmatic considerations, such as availability of resources (time, money, expertise), and how available resources can be used effectively and efficiently.

Legitimate scientific arguments supporting specific provisions of gifted education boil down to two issues: whether they are consistent with what we know through research about the developmental trajectories of specific groups of children (Point 1 above), and whether they have proved to be effective and efficient in producing desired outcomes specified in the programming design (Point 3). In comparison, curricular goals we set up for particular programs (Point 1) and ethical and social concerns (Point 2) involve value judgment and can be negotiated only by stakeholders of gifted education; for example, how inclusive gifted education should be, and whether the goals of gifted education should be pluralistic or uniform. As can be seen in the following substantive discussion, differentiating these aspects of arguments is important for an intelligible scholarly discourse on gifted education.

THE EXPERTISE VERSUS CREATIVITY TENSION

Is gifted education aimed at developing an advanced knowledge base and expertise or creative productivity? There are clearly normative and pragmatic aspects of this tension. Most gifted programs are working with children and adolescents whose "giftedness" is best characterized as the "proficiency" kind (indicated by some test scores or grades) rather than the "creativity" kind (indicated by behaviors and products) and whose advances in academic programs are more likely of the former kind rather than the latter. Renzulli (1986) dubbed this kind of test-taking (including taking intelligence tests) and lesson-learning abilities "schoolhouse giftedness" (p. 57). However, there is a general feeling in the community of gifted education that goals of talent development in school should go beyond mere expertise to reach creative productivity (Renzulli, 2005; Subotnik & Jarvin, 2005). In contrast to schoolhouse giftedness, "creative-productive giftedness describes those aspects of human activity and involvement where a premium is placed on the development of original material and products that are purposely designed to have an impact on one or more target audiences" (Renzulli, 1986, p. 58). Although these two aspects of education do not need to be antithetical or mutually exclusive, they reflect different emphases in curriculum and instruction. This is the perennial content-process conundrum with which gifted educators have attempted to come to grips. The conceptual tension of expertise versus creativity exists between educational and psychological researchers who focus more on mastery of existing bodies of knowledge, skills, and expertise, and those who focus more on thinking, problem solving, and creativity. Gifted-education practitioners also espouse differing educational agendas, some aiming at developing high-level expertise and talent, and others at creative productivity. The conceptual tension between desirability of expertise and creativity in gifted education can be expressed as follows:

> Thesis:
> High-level expertise (proficiency) in a given domain should be the hallmark of giftedness and the goal of gifted education, because only this form of excellence can be scientifically verified and educationally promoted.

> Antithesis:
> Creative productivity (innovation) should be the hallmark of giftedness and the goal of gifted education, because giftedness is not about mastery of the already known, but about exploring, discovering, and inventing the unknown.

In the following section, I first describe the debates in the research community on the nature of expertise and creativity, which forms a scientific basis for making claims about the viability of specific educational approaches. I then compare two major educational strategies, acceleration and enrichment, in addressing the educational goals of developing expertise and creativity. I end this section with some general conclusions and observations regarding how our knowledge of expertise and creativity sheds light on educational planning and programming.

Debates Among Expertise and Creativity Researchers

Mature "gifted" accomplishments belong to two broad categories: expertise and creativity (Tannenbaum, 1997). To use Gardner's (1997) words, people in the "expertise" category are *masters* who have perfected their respective trades to an extremely high level (see Ericsson, 2006), and people in the creativity category are *makers*, who have significantly transformed an intellectual or practical domain or artistic ways of expression, and moved a field forward, or even created a new field (Sternberg, 1999b). Both forms of excellence, high proficiency and high innovation, are considered valid long-term goals for gifted education (Tannenbaum, 1997).

In a response to Ericsson's (1996) model of carefully charted pathways to expertise based on controlled experiments and systematic observations of the performance and practice of experts (using verbal protocol analysis), Simonton (1996) delineated a vision of the development of creative productivity that is drastically different. From Simonton's point of view, charting the ontogeny (i.e., individual development) of creative productivity entails a different set of parameters from what expertise researchers have prescribed. In his conception, initial creative potential and the onset or debut of a creative career (when the first creative "hit" is made) are two important parameters for determining a person's life span trajectory in terms of creative productivity. If Simonton is right, then educators of the gifted have to consider creative potential as an important selection criterion if creative productivity is the goal of their programs. Also, they have to consider how to enhance their creative potential, to increase the likelihood of an early debut of a creative career.

However, in the view of many cognitive psychologists, Ericsson included, trajectories leading to creativity that are not all that different from those leading to domain expertise (see Ericsson, 2006; Weisberg, 1999). For example, Watson and Crick discovered the double helix, a major breakthrough in molecular biology and genetics, as a result of their high levels of domain-specific expertise, extensive search, and collaboration with colleagues, including building on other researchers' ideas and strategies, such as model building techniques (see Weisberg, 2006, pp. 775–776). In short, these psychologists feel that the distinction and differences between high-level expertise and creative productivity is overstated. According to Ericsson (2006), the explanatory power of deliberate practice involved in building up one's knowledge base, expertise, and ultimately, creativity, significantly downplays the importance or necessity of assuming some a priori creative potential as a precondition, and the sharp distinction between processes differentially leading to expertise versus creativity. On the other side of the story, Simonton (1996) argued that eminent creators, like Einstein, sometimes show less expertise than their less illustrious colleagues: "What was crucial was not how much he knew, but rather how he organized his knowledge, including how that information meshed with a distinctive style and worldview" (p. 228). In sum, creativity depends not as much on the amounts of knowledge one accumulates as on how information and knowledge gets transformed and integrated in a personal framework. As Root-Bernstein's (2009) case studies show, strong cross-disciplinary and avocational interests may be crucial for novel ideation and creative visions.

Creativity: Parameters of Person, Domain, and Process

Despite the differences, there seems to be a consensus in the research community that creativity is a much more complex concept than was envisioned in the early years as mainly involving divergent thinking (Guilford, 1967; Torrance, 1966). Indeed, some scholars even argue that we really cannot tell which children are "creatively gifted," as children are not yet in a position to produce anything truly "creative" by professional standards or show such promise (Csikszentmihalyi, 1990; but see Cramond et al., 2005; Feldman, 1986). It is generally agreed that creative productivity is a long-term proposition, and truly creative work does not just take "sudden insight" (the "aha" moment) or a unique set of thought processes (e.g., divergent thinking), but involves knowledge preparation over time, as well as a prolonged process of prodding, mapping, framing (or reframing), and refining. Styles of work, a disposition for novelty, as well as perseverance, also count (see Chapter 4). To avoid a misleading bifurcation of expertise and creativity, a more refined distinction between adaptive expertise and routine expertise serves a good purpose (Hatano & Inagaki, 1986). Bransford and colleagues (see Bransford, Brown, & Cocking, 1999) proposed two dimensions: efficiency and innovation. When one strikes a balance between efficiency (achieving mastery and automaticity) and innovation (making transformations and generalizations), one is more likely to become an adaptive expert. When one exclusively focuses on efficiency, one tends to become a routine expert. When one attempts to be innovative without achieving efficiency, one is likely to remain a confused novice. Thus, adaptive expertise entails a balancing act. Metacognitive awareness and control of what one is learning (e.g., understanding the conditional utilities of specific pieces of knowledge) seems to be needed for achieving adaptive expertise (Weisberg, 2006). Sometimes one has to give up well-mastered skills in order to try new ways of doing things, or take a metacognitive distance from one's entrenched beliefs to facilitate alternative ways of thinking about an object or phenomenon.

In the same vein, Dai and Renzulli (2008) proposed a model of long-term developmental trajectories based on whether a person is building his or her knowledge along the trajectory of conventional expertise or striving for innovation through the transformation of knowledge and skills at critical junctures in talent development. Differential development in this regard depends on person, domain, and process.

Person. People who prefer to stay "at the edge of chaos" and be trailblazers are likely to show an early onset of creativity. People who prefer to master the existing systems would likely follow a conventional path to expertise. There are critical points at which a person has to decide how much innovation is "too risky," as being innovative also means stepping into the world of the unknown and the uncertain, with a high likelihood of failure. The more daring would radically depart from the tradition and those with a conservative leaning would likely show their creativity by refining and perfecting the existing system (Sternberg, 1999a). In any person, there exist two opposite forces, a force for experience-producing and differentiating, and a force for experience-organizing and integrating. For example, intellectual curiosity is a disposition that helps produce new experiences and expanding oneself, while intellectual cautiousness is a disposition that helps safeguard and maintain the stability of the developing person (Dai & Renzulli, 2008). This personal dynamic is responsible for many decisions a person makes at critical junctures of his or her development. For example, Bill Gates and Steve Jobs forewent prestigious college credentials in pursuing their unique life path, the path less traveled.

Domain. Domains and disciplines vary in terms of how early training can begin and the amount of training that is required for high-level achievement (Simonton, 1996). In other words, *how early creative productivity can emerge is constrained by the onset and duration of knowledge and skill preparation for that specific domain or discipline.* There are domains more formally organized as a field, with well-defined rules, standards, boundaries, players, and gatekeepers, and there are domains whose social organization (i.e., field) is relatively loose, and standards for excellence are not uniformly defined. For more formal disciplines and domains (e.g., classical music, academic disciplines, or medicine), substantial expertise (i.e., mastery of a canonical set of knowledge, skills, and values) may be necessary before one can be creative in that domain. For other domains such as creative writing, business, or pop music, where technical mastery may not be as rigorously structured as in more formal disciplines, creativity may not require extensive development of expertise or formal education and training. Sometimes a lack of technical proficiency can be a good thing for innovation, as in the case of Van Gogh's painting, partly thanks to his lack of rigorous training in realist painting techniques. In school subjects, there is a contrast between the sequential, formal nature of mathematical curriculum and development, and the less structured and formal nature of language arts, with natural and social sciences probably sitting in between. As a rule of thumb, the more technical and abstract a domain is (mathematics, physics, classic music, etc.), the more stringent the training requirements, including the extent to which formal education or training is required. In these domains, an early onset of talent development may be desirable, given the prolonged period of honing the necessary skills to be creative. Therefore, educational programming and instructional design aimed at expertise or creativity should observe this domain-specificity principle.

Process. The way an intellectual or artistic activity is structured by educators and experienced by children influences how they feel and think about the task at hand. In the context of education, curriculum and pedagogy play a major role in giving the learner a sense of what is desirable: mastery or going beyond. It can be argued that going beyond mere mastery is what gifted education is all about; that is, in order to cultivate a person's potential for creative productivity, it is crucial to develop in the person a sense of what is possible with newly acquired understandings and tools, and what remains unknown, and what still lies ahead, not just what one can reproduce given a set of instruction. Thus, even acknowledging that a substantial body of knowledge and technical proficiency need to be mastered and achieved before a person can make a creative contribution in his or her career, it does not mean that the person cannot develop a creative mindset, capable of productive, rather than merely reproductive, thinking.

It is also worth noting that efficient mastery in terms of achieving knowledge encapsulation, technical precision, and skill automaticity may be of differential importance at different stages of talent development. Slowing down and analytically controlling the quality of mastery is desirable at later points (Bamberger, 1986). Quick and easy learning will give way to meticulous efforts for technical precision and expressive perfection (Subotnik & Jarvin, 2005). In favor of the *expertise-facilitates-creativity hypothesis* discussed in Chapter 4, intensive efforts at mastery are necessary for the personal transformation of knowledge, in the sense that a striving for high-level understanding pushes one toward "the edge of chaos": detecting gaps, discrepancies, or imperfection in the existing system, which calls for creative solutions (Dai & Renzulli, 2008; Runco, 1994). But unless a person is willing to break the mental set and deviate from entrenched viewpoints, no creativity will occur (Sternberg, 1999a).

Considerations for Educational Strategies and Practices

In light of the above discussion, the goals of developing expertise and creativity have slightly different yet complementary pedagogical ramifications. Development of expertise typically goes through steady professional routes of sustained or extended mastery, with its emphasis on technical precision and nuanced understandings of specific concepts and theories (i.e., knowing how to play the "game"). Development of creative productivity, in comparison, involves more individuality (such as self-direction, risk-taking, and a sense of destiny) and integration of various sources of knowledge (which could be multidisciplinary) in a personal style or framework, including the blurring of boundaries of knowledge to achieve a creative synthesis. These two aspects of development complement each other. Knowing that a developmental trajectory toward expertise and creativity depends on the interaction of person, domain (content), and process, we can map out this interaction in the context of programming in gifted education.

Person and identification. In the gifted-education community, there is a widely held belief that students identified as gifted academic learners are not necessarily the most promising ones in terms of creative productivity. It is this misgiving that seems to have motivated a distinction between a mastery type of giftedness (or schoolhouse giftedness) and a creative type of giftedness (e.g.,

Callahan & Miller, 2005; Renzulli, 1986; Tannenbaum, 1997). Indeed, retrospective accounts of schooling experience by eminent creative scientists and writers suggest that schooling in general was not a particularly pleasant and productive experience for many of them (Subotnik & Olszewski-Kubilius, 1997). In general, creative individuals tend to structure their own lives and actively seek developmental opportunities instead of being structured by others, as illustrated by a remark credited to Mark Twain: "I have never let my schooling interfere with my education." The most successful individuals in adulthood whom Terman identified in his longitudinal study (Terman & Oden, 1959) also shared similar personal characteristics, the ones that might not be congenial to typical school structures in terms of a fixed curriculum and didactic pedagogy, as well as the age-graded social organization of schooling. Most schools are of a "conventional type," rigidly structured for administrative convenience instead of flexibly adapting to the growth needs of each child. The distinct profile of eminent individuals in their school years has implications for identification, particularly if the goal of gifted education is to develop creative productivity. The traditional test score–determined identification may not be adequate in identifying children with creative potential (Getzels & Jackson, 1962). The traditional divergent-thinking tests are still useful for identification, but other important characteristics, such as self-directedness (e.g., the ability to work independently) and task commitment, also need to be considered if programming is aimed at identifying and nurturing creative potential.

Domain experience and advanced and personalized curriculum. In terms of learning subject matters in school, the pace and content-process dynamics of learning are two major issues to consider. Regular schools often fall short of serving gifted students well on two counts: efficiency and quality. Age-graded classrooms could shortchange gifted learners by teaching to the "average," leaving gifted and talented learners unchallenged and bored (Archambault et al., 1993; Rogers, 2007). Various forms of subject- or discipline-based acceleration allow advanced learners to move along at their own pace, and provide sufficient challenges to keep gifted learners engaged, rather than turning them off, as it were. For example, through within-class grouping, advanced learners are able to learn materials or engage in research activities particularly suited to their levels of mastery and ability. Curriculum compacting could be done to facilitate such curriculum differentiation (Renzulli & Reis, 1997). In more technical domains such as the physical sciences and information technology, we can ask, Is the curriculum sequenced and structured to ensure a solid mastery, and is it rigorous enough for technical precision and deep conceptual understanding? It is likely that, in these academic domains, creative productivity can emerge only through deep content knowledge and understanding, and high-level technical proficiency, building on existing ideas, models, theories, and tools (Sternberg, 1999a).

In domains that are seemingly more accessible to lay audiences such as history and literature, we can ask, Is there a sufficient emphasis on the underlying conceptual structure of the discipline? Are there sufficient amounts of inquiry-based learning, such as case studies, class discussion, and research-based learning (Aulls & Shore, 2008)? For example, a deep understanding of what facts count as having historical significance, how historical accounts are constructed and reconstructed, and how to make systematic historical inquiry, is not something always at the center of history curriculum in secondary schools. As a result, even talented high school students known for their penchant for history typically tend to take an uncritical view of historical accounts and historical writings and miss the subtext or tacit message these writings conveyed at the time they were produced (Wineburg, 1991). Likewise, in science teaching, the conventional curriculum that encourages reproductive thinking in terms of remembering facts, concepts, and theories or performing "canned" experimental procedures has to give way to a new vision of science curriculum for productive thinking, in terms of grasping the nature, structure, and processes of doing science in authentic problem-solving situations (Duschl & Duncan, 2009; Robinson et al., 2007, chapter 19). In essence, acquiring deep disciplinary knowledge and expertise itself is much more important than the regurgitation of facts and concepts; it takes productive thinking and creative interpretation of the meanings of the knowledge system involved. We can also ask whether there are sufficient amounts of integrated, interdisciplinary, and thematic activities that allow learners to pursue intellectual interests of their own, which might not fit neatly with the mandatory curriculum. Ultimately, the quality of gifted education should be assessed at least partly in terms of how much expertise one demonstrates vis-à-vis a domain or discipline and how much creative potential (if not "truly creative" products) a learner demonstrates in the way of the productive and integrative use of knowledge in formulating his or her own thoughts and fashioning products that are distinctly his or her own.

    Process and pedagogy. Curriculum addresses the question of *what* to develop in students and what kind of structure and sequence of learning experiences can bring students to that desired point. Pedagogy, in contrast, addresses the question of *how*: how a unit is taught and how thinking and reflection are engaged through teaching and designed activities. If efficiency and sufficient challenge are two criteria governing the appropriateness of curriculum for a particular learner, the quality of learning experience can be ensured only when both pedagogical and curricular considerations are given full attention. It is useful to think of the dialectic of freedom and discipline that Whitehead (1929) formulated as a way of balancing content and process in teaching and learning. Whitehead argued that the initial learning of a new concept or theory should be playful and imaginative, to avoid cognitive rigidity. Then technical precision should be enforced to ensure disciplined, accurate understanding and use of knowledge. And finally, learners are encouraged to generalize and extend their newly equipped knowledge so that knowledge truly sets them free to explore new frontiers rather than only sets boundaries on their minds. To use more current terminology, both critical and creative thinking should be engaged. To think critically (i.e., exercising mental discipline) about certain content issues or knowledge is to rely on pertinent and sound criteria when judging the merits of a piece of information or the validity of a concept or theory (Kuhn, 1999); to think innovatively and imaginatively means to stretch the mind to envision new possibilities with what one already knows. Here both content and process are important so that not only knowledge is gained; so is metalevel awareness of what the knowledge allows one to do, and how it fits into a personal network of enterprises (Gruber, 1986). Only by exercising both critical and creative thinking can one develop truly adaptive expertise and creative productivity. It seems that inquiry-based learning is a mode particularly suitable for this purpose, given gifted learners' metacognitive ability to effectively use instructional guidance to scaffold their learning and make transfer or generalization (Aulls & Shore, 2008; Borkowski & Peck, 1986; Kanevsky, 1990; Snow, 1994).

Acceleration and enrichment as two main educational strategies for gifted students. Unlike subject-based acceleration, which is confined to domains of strength and interest for specific learners, grade-based acceleration (e.g., grade skipping, early college entrance) allow learners to advance more quickly to later stages of academic and career development (Colangelo, Assouline, & Gross, 2004). From the viewpoint of one's long-term development, acceleration efficiently utilizes time in school and may facilitate an early debut of a creative career (e.g., early college education, early advanced degrees). Enrichment often serves as a less "radical" approach, in the form of pull-out programs where students meet once or twice a week to pursue their intellectual interests, engage in project-based activities, or exercise critical thinking or leadership. Although there is nothing wrong with the pragmatic way of conducting gifted education based on local resources and circumstances, enrichment programs are often at risk of being downgraded to superficial activities that disconnect from what students experience in regular classrooms or do not really challenge gifted learners to think more rigorously and creatively in a discipline. What should be at the core of enrichment experiences is an extension above and beyond regular curriculum to promote gaining depth and breadth of the knowledge to which one is exposed, or exploration of new frontiers of knowledge (e.g., informatics, genomics, or nanotechnology). Thinking skills can be developed only when students are thinking about something. We now know that thinking cannot be "content free," and content knowledge always assists in reasoning and thinking processes (Lohman, 2006). Therefore, it does not matter whether an exceptionally advanced learner is in an enrichment program, is being accelerated in some way, or remains in the regular classroom. How to balance content and process in teaching is a fundamental task facing all teachers, particularly teachers of highly able students. It is not how much students know about facts, but how they are enabled to think in a disciplined or expert fashion (i.e., developing an appropriate modus operandi) that ultimately allows students to think in a productive and innovative way.

THE GIFTED CHILD VERSUS TALENT DEVELOPMENT TENSION

Two competing visions of gifted education have endured to date, one focusing on a particular group of children with putative special needs (i.e., the gifted-child movement), and the other focusing on identifying and developing emergent talents deemed important for society as well as the individuals involved (i.e., the talent development movement). Although the talent development movement has an underlying concern about achieving excellence while ensuring equitable access to good education, which will be discussed in the next chapter, there are intrinsic reasons why the talent development approach has evolved in recent decades as an alternative to the "gifted child" approach to gifted education. One reason is, as I mentioned in Chapter 1, a domain-specific turn in theory development, of which the multiple intelligence theory (Gardner, 1983) is an epitome. Another is the rise of developmentalism, with its emphasis on development of high-level abilities and competencies as an evolving process and therefore open to multiple pathways (Feldman, 1986; Horowitz, 2009). To a large extent, the tension between the gifted child and the talent development approaches reflects the three ontological tensions (nature versus nurture, domain specific versus domain general, and quantitative versus qualitative) and the empirical support these competing views garner (see Chapters 3–5). The tension between the two visions or paradigms of gifted education can be expressed in the following way:

Thesis:
Gifted children should be the center of our focus and the sole rationale for the existence of gifted education; their special educational needs and unique patterns of personal growth should be the driving force in educational programming and intervention.

Antithesis:
The evolving process of talent development should be the central focus of gifted education; gifted education should provide maximal opportunity for those who show manifest or emergent talents and are interested in developing their talents to the fullest of their capacities.

Theoretical trends and advances aside, there are deep social reasons for these movements, since scientific evidence, however convincing, does not dictate human practice. For example, knowing that some people have inherited diseases does not make it less compelling to find a cure for these diseases; in this sense, biology is not destiny. By the same token, that some individuals fall short of superior levels of human abilities does not make it less compelling to find a way to capitalize on their unique strengths and develop their talents. Natural science can be harnessed in enhancing human potential and well-being, but by itself does not say anything about what we should or should not do. Therefore, whether we adopt the gifted-child or talent development model is very much a human decision based on values and purposes. This is the normative side of gifted education. Namely, the gifted-child movement stresses the intrinsic value and needs of being gifted, whereas the talent development movement stresses the value of nurturing specific emergent and evolving talents as cultural capital.

A brief review of the history of the gifted education movement in the United States is helpful for clarifying how the purposes of gifted education were defined. In its early inception, social Darwinism was a dominant ideology influencing the practice of identifying "gifted children," a new invention at the time, not unlike the invention of "adolescence" as a transitional developmental stage between childhood and adulthood in the industrial age. Galton's (1869) work on the genetic basis of geniuses was not merely an exercise of intellectual curiosity, but was driven by the motivation to preserve the greatness of a nation. For Lewis Terman, who conducted the first large-scale longitudinal study of gifted children identified mainly through an IQ test, children with high IQs were not just "smarter" than others, but indicative of a better fit through evolution. Betterment of the human race was an underlying motivation for many social activists in the early 20th century, including scholars like Terman and Goddard (see Hall, 2003). In contrast, Hollingworth (1942), whose research focused on children with IQs above 180, started a new tradition of stressing the unique needs of gifted children for their own sake: helping extremely bright children with social-emotional difficulties, a predecessor of the contemporary "developmental asynchrony" definition of giftedness (Morelock, 1996; Silverman, 1993). In the late 1950s, when Sputnik stunned Americans, and later in the 1970s and 1980s (e.g., with the publication of the national report *A Nation at Risk* in 1983; see National Commission on Excellence in Education, 1983), economic and technological competitiveness and other national interests provided a strong impetus for the gifted-education movement.

The normative tensions involve human purposes. If the expertise-creativity tension concerns what is a desirable state of gifted education in terms of its ultimate goals, preparing well-trained professionals and "quota talents," to use Tannenbaum's (1983) terms, or higher-level creative thinkers and performers, the tension between the gifted-child and talent development approaches concerns whether gifted education should serve the intrinsic needs of gifted students per se or aim at meeting societal needs as well as promote personal fulfillment. We can roughly discern four arguments for the raison d'être of gifted education:

1. *The cure-for-cancer argument* asserts that gifted children we identified stand the best chance of becoming cutting-edge researchers and innovators who will help us solve urgent problems facing the world and improve human conditions (Renzulli & Reis, 1991). This is a legacy of Sputnik. It is by and large a social and economic exigency argument based on the social efficiency and productivity model of education: that is, gifted children are precious "natural resources" that should be fully protected

and cultivated for the social good. Naturally, it leans heavily toward mathematics, science, engineering, and technology, or what is now called STEM education (see Subotnik et al., 2009), which is arguably more "instrumental" to social and economic development.

2. *The enhancing-social-capital argument* asserts that we should enhance the moral qualities of the most able in a population so that the society in general can benefit from their leadership and integrity (Gardner, Csikszentmihalyi, & Damon, 2001; Putnam et al., 1994; Renzulli, 2002). This argument is concerned less with the economic competitiveness of a nation and more with increasing the social capital for the sake of the society. Gifted programs based on this argument feature leadership and character education more prominently (e.g., Karnes & Bean, 1995).

3. *The personal fulfillment argument* asserts that gifted education should be concerned mainly with how gifted children can live a satisfactory and fulfilling life rather than meet societal demands. This is a more individualistic argument, based on theories of personal fulfillment and self-actualization (e.g., Grant & Piechowski, 1999; Piechowski, 2009; Roeper, 2006). Although this argument is less "utilitarian" and emphasizes personal dimensions that are less practically oriented (e.g., spirituality), there is an implicit social motivation: preserving and developing the most "refined minds" (i.e., the gifted minds) is a way of preserving fine culture. Although very few today would see gifted education as a way of improving the human race as its early predecessors did (e.g., Terman, 1925), the idea that gifted educators should be good shepherds of fine minds and culture is deeply rooted in gifted education (Tannenbaum, 1998).

4. *The unique-needs argument* asserts that gifted children have unique affective and cognitive developmental experiences and therefore deserve an education that addresses their unique educational needs (e.g., Silverman, 1993; Winner, 1997). This argument treats gifted students as a special education group similar to that of the intellectually disabled (i.e., a categorical approach), and sees gifted education as more or less a branch of special education, assuming unique educational and counseling needs of these children. A distinct example is the definition of giftedness as "developmental asynchrony" wherein cognitive and social development are not in sync, so to speak, leading to emotional issues and problems (see Morelock, 1996). Cases for the unique-needs argument include multiple exceptionalities, multipotentialities, the extremely gifted, and possibly gifted underachievement, among others. This argument can be traced to the early history of studying the unique personality of creative individuals (Eysenck, 1995) and extremely high IQ children (Hollingworth, 1942).

The first two arguments (the cure-for-cancer argument and the enhancing-social-capital argument) are more congenial to each other, as are the last two arguments (the personal fulfillment argument and the unique-needs argument). The first two are more "socially oriented" and more of the "talent development" breed, and the last two are more "individualistic," focusing on the uniqueness of being "gifted." To be sure, at a practical level, a gifted program may use more than one argument as its rationale and can encompass both individual and social dimensions. However, different emphases and different levels and criteria of selectivity often put them on a collision course. Sometimes the term *paradigm* is used to describe talent development models as an alternative to the "gifted child" approaches (Borland, 2003; Feldman, 1992; Renzulli, 1994; Treffinger & Feldhusen, 1996). Although it is important to distinguish between "research paradigms" and "paradigms of practice," these two modes of gifted education practice do show some paradigmatic quality in terms of coherent sets of phenomena studied, theoretical assumptions made, and systematic emphases in a particular set of goals for gifted education. Figure 7.1 list some of the contrasting features of these two approaches.

Table 7.1. A comparison of the gifted child focus and the talent development focus

A Gifted Child Focus	A Talent Development Focus
Highlighted phenomena and constructs	
Gifted underachievement	Diverse learners, diverse talents
Twice exceptionalities	Strengths and weaknesses (profiling)
The extremely gifted	Various cognitive and learning styles
Conceptual foundations	
Exceptionality assumed	Exceptionality not assumed
General intelligence (g) emphasized	General intelligence downplayed
A more exclusive category of people	A more inclusive category of people
More homogeneity	More heterogeneity
Person centered (the whole child)	Domain centered (specific talents)
Educational goals and strategies	
Meeting unique needs	Meeting emergent needs
Personal growth a priority	Skill/talent development a priority
Personal standards of excellence	Objective standards of excellence

Targeted Groups of Children for Service: Inclusive or Exclusive, Homogeneous or Heterogeneous?

A hallmark of talent development models is their openness to a variety of populations and talent profiles of individuals, as long as they show strengths in a particular line of development valued by the society. Talent domains featured in school can be mainly academic (mathematics, humanities, natural and social sciences, etc.; Subotnik & Coleman, 1996), or include artistic, vocational, and personal-social domains (Feldhusen, 1992). In general, the talent development approach gives legitimacy to a wider range of students for participation in gifted education and a wider range of talents and talent expressions formally or informally observed (Feldhusen, 1992; Renzulli & Dai, 2003). In contrast, the gifted-child approach, in Terman's (1925) tradition, is more stringent in defining who are "gifted," and more selective in identification criteria. Theoretically, a "gifted child" does not need to be a high academic achiever (otherwise topics like gifted underachievement would not make sense). In practice, however, IQ or academic achievement cutoffs at 95th or 97th percentile are often used in conjunction with teacher and parent nominations. A challenge for the gifted-child approach is that there is no well-justified rationale for a particular cutoff used, other than resource considerations (e.g., admission slots available for a particular gifted program). One could argue that the more selective identification criteria would enhance the chance of success in highly challenging gifted programs, with limited resources concentrated on fewer "hopefuls" rather than dissipated when too many are competing for very limited resources (Gallagher, 2000b). In other words, efficiency is a main consideration. Yet it can also be argued that a more inclusive system of gifted education would allow for more diverse talents and talent expressions to manifest themselves, and because of its openness and inclusiveness, various forms of excellence are more likely to be recognized and nurtured. There is always a trade-off between the two when educational productivity or effectiveness is concerned (see Chapter 6 for the discussion of Type I and II errors in using more stringent or liberal selection criteria).

Basic Assumptions About Giftedness: A Fixed Category of Individuals or a Fluid Developmental State?

Whether a more exclusive or inclusive system is used depends on one's beliefs about the nature of giftedness and talent (an epistemological issue) and the purposes of setting up special provisions of gifted education in the first place (a normative issue). Thus, there are both epistemological and normative differences between the gifted child and talent development approaches.

Criticism of a categorical approach to the "gifted child" and gifted education results from various developmental considerations. The gifted-child approach privileges early bloomers (precocious children) who show signs of promise much earlier but may or may not demonstrate excellence in any meaningful way later on. Research efforts to distinguish "giftedness" (some qualitative differences that set gifted children apart from others) from "precocity" (early development) have not been successful so far (see Robinson, 2006; Shore, 2000). From a measurement point of view, regression to the mean, as well as measurement errors, renders any unequivocal identification of the "gifted child" problematic, as a child can be "gifted" at one time but not "gifted" after a while (Lohman & Korb, 2006). The complexity and uncertainty of development still outwits the predictive power of current human sciences. Put differently, like a story that unfolds before your eyes, development has such a dynamic quality that emergent novelty can only be captured when it emerges. The inherent uncertainty of evolving human abilities and talents renders any "scientific" prediction of long-term developmental outcomes a fallible exercise.

Developmental changes are connected with another factor: motivation. Many scholars stress drive and persistence (Subotnik & Coleman, 1996; Winner, 1996), task commitment (Renzulli, 1986), and intrinsic motivation (Feldhusen, 1986; Gottfried & Gottfried, 2004) as integral parts of being "gifted." Developmental researchers have long pointed out the "developmentally instigative" quality of motivation, in that it facilitates the acquisition of knowledge and skills (Bronfenbrenner, 1989). Although there are disagreements about whether high cognitive abilities should be privileged over motivational factors as worthy of the label "gifted" (see Dai, 2004b; Gagné, 2009b; Gottfried & Gottfried, 2004), there is no disagreement that motivation plays a crucial role in talent development. Indeed, some scholars argue that motivational factors play an increasingly important (sometimes make-or-break) role as a person moves to more challenging phases of talent development (Bloom, 1985; Ericsson et al., 1993).

Exceptionality Assumed or Not Assumed

A key difference between the two models or paradigms of practice is that exceptionality (i.e., qualitative differences between the gifted and the "nongifted") is assumed in most gifted-child models and not assumed in talent development models. As Treffinger and Feldhusen (1996) argued, "The trend towards talent development involves the important but challenging realization that the use of the term 'gifted' as a specific category or type of child is untenable or indefensible" (p. 184). Defenders of the gifted-child approach typically use studies of twins and child prodigies to show the genetic basis of superior potential (Gallagher, 2000b). However, the standard image of gifted children as a homogeneous group, often with IQ as a stand-in for general intelligence, raises the issue of whether the group so identified can live up to high expectations for excellence (Subotnik, 2003). High IQs (say, with a cutoff of 97th percentile) clearly predict good academic performance and later job performance to a point, but they don't predict eminent achievement as well when compared with more domain-specific measures such as SAT-Math, as shown by several major longitudinal studies (e.g., Lubinski & Benbow, 2006; Park et al., 2008; Subotnik et al., 1993; Terman, 1925). Moreover, gifted children so defined can hardly fit into various theoretical prescriptions, whether it be Dabrowskian overexcitability (Ackerman, 2009) or "developmental asynchrony" (Morelock, 1996). It is not that these theories are wrong, but that the gifted-child approach has an extra burden of proof that gifted children identified in school are indeed unique and homogeneous in their cognitive and affective profiles, developmental trajectories, and pathways, and consequently unique in educational needs, and there even exists a "gifted pedagogy" that works best with gifted children (see Coleman, 2003; Kaplan, 2003, for discussion). Without clear evidence, the "exceptional needs" of the "gifted child" remains a theoretical proposition rather than a verified reality. It is for this reason that the gifted-child paradigm is criticized as a mysterious model (Matthews & Foster, 2006); a social construction with unwarranted assumptions made about uniqueness, homogeneity, and exceptionality of children so identified (Borland, 2003); a categorical approach oblivious of the developing nature of the child (Keating, 2009).

The talent development approach is more defensible than the gifted-child approach, not because of its superiority but because it is based on a much simpler assumption that can be met more easily: *Some children show strengths and interests (or even emergent excellence) in certain areas of human endeavor and should be supported to further develop their talents that are culturally and socially important as well as personally meaningful and rewarding.* There is no need to assume that these children belong to an "exceptional" group with exceptional needs and thus deserve some extended or special educational services. By nature, talent development programs can have a flexible entrance and exit policy and strategy (Subotnik & Coleman, 1996; see Renzulli & Reis, 1997, for a Revolving Door Model of Identification), and does not have to stick to any rigid cutoffs and selection criteria. Indeed, if the ease of learning is a hallmark of giftedness, formal testing may not even be necessary, as experienced and trained teachers can easily spot gifted learners in classroom interaction or in the process and product of relevant projects (Winner, 1997). Action and dynamic assessment information as well as performance information in the past can readily assist in curriculum differentiation or identification of candidates for talent development programs in a flexible manner (Renzulli & Reis, 1997).

Educational Goals and Strategies: Child Centered or Talent Focused?

The four arguments presented earlier show distinct differences between the gifted child and talent development approaches regarding the purposes of gifted education. The unique-needs argument focuses on helping gifted children overcome possible barriers, internally or externally, and the personal fulfillment argument is concerned with supporting children's growth as they are searching for meaning and identity for their lives. The well-being and optimal personal development of these children is the main goal of gifted education; whether they have the potential to become eminent achievers or how much progress they have made in talent development is of secondary concern. Indeed, for some of the advocates of the gifted-child approach, when gifted children are allowed to explore selves and develop and follow their passions, talent development, even eminent achievement, will naturally follow (Piechowski & Grant, 2001). In comparison, the talent development approach (the cure-for-cancer argument and the increasing-social-capital argument) is more "instrumental" and outcome driven, aimed at preparing a pool of candidates and hopefuls for future leadership and excellence on major areas of human endeavor valued by the society. Consequently, for the "gifted child" advocates, an ideal curricular model of gifted education is that of liberal education (to "liberate the mind") or "whole child" education. For talent development advocates, specialization and deep engagement in a specific line of pursuit is a main educational focus (see Coleman & Cross, 2005, pp. 266–269, for a distinction between a "talent/multiple abilities" model and a "whole child" model of education). Two issues follow: Should we develop the gifted child or the gifted mind as a whole or focus on developing a particular talent; put differently, should we structure gifted education around the child or around domains?

There is clear value in emphasizing the free exploration of knowledge in a personally meaningful and integrated way and development of life themes and personal enterprises, unconstrained by the boundary of disciplines. Indeed, a refined mind should be both intellectual and aesthetic and appreciate arts as well as sciences. People who engage in both scientific and artistic ways of thinking enhance their chance of making creative contributions (Root-Bernstein, 2009). However, there is also clear importance in timely specialization, particularly in more abstract and technical domains, in order to enhance a person's chance of an early debut of a creative career (Simonton, 1999). The answer to this question is not taking either side but balancing the depth and breadth of knowledge pursuits. An example of combining both arts and sciences is seen in the Israel Arts and Science Academy, where students are specialized in specific disciplines or art forms, yet have the freedom to pursue interests that are not their majors (see Israel Center for Excellence through Education, 2009). In principle, a talent development program should be rigorous enough, be based on professional standards, and encourage deep disciplinary engagement, yet allow for interdisciplinary explorations and applications in a personally meaningful and integrated way. This is particularly important in the 21st century, when the disciplinary boundaries are increasingly blurred, and many urgent world problems and issues call for integration of the knowledge of both social and natural sciences. Besides, the whole-child approach puts more emphasis on affective goals, such as the exploration of personal meanings through talent development and the search for identity and destiny, and the talent development approach places more emphasis on tangible advances in talent domains and cognitive gains. These two aspects of talent development should go hand in hand (Dai & Renzulli, 2000; Folsom, 2006).

Self-Directed or Adult Structured and Standards Driven?

School is a social institution structured by adults to prepare children for their future roles as effective individuals and responsible citizens. Although adult-structured, standards-driven programming and curriculum is a mainstream approach, it has long been contested, starting with the French philosopher Jean-Jacque Rousseau's *Emile* (1762/2003)—or even earlier. Rousseau's general idea is that if children are allowed to freely explore the world and themselves, they will eventually find goodness in themselves and hear their calling. To some extent, the idea of *positive disintegration* (a breakdown in identity development that proves ultimately beneficial for personal growth) proposed by Dabrowski (see Ackerman, 2009; Laycraft, 2009) is also in keeping with this line of thinking about the personal development of gifted children. For some advocates of the "gifted child," gifted development has its own logic; therefore, gifted education should not impose artificial standards on gifted children and push them toward achievement or excellence by adult standards. Indeed one criticism leveled against the talent development approach is that it is too driven by achievement and "success," and too little by the inner growth of a child (Grant & Piechowski, 1999; Roeper, 2006). For advocates of talent development, standards are necessary for ensuring the quality of gifted education; without standards of excellence, there is no way to judge the effectiveness of education and student progress toward goals of excellence.

Should we have clear standards of excellence (at both entry and exit points) for gifted programming, and consequently program evaluation? Should excellence be defined personally or by some publicly verifiable criteria? If an identified gifted child is not willing to make a firm commitment to talent development or is not willing to take a leadership role, is this person still admissible to a gifted program? If a gifted-education program addresses only the personal needs of identifiable gifted children without distinct goals and standards for excellence, is it still a defensible and viable gifted program? To answer these questions, it is important to put them in their proper social contexts. It is perfectly fine for a private advocacy group to have an exclusive focus on the well-being of gifted children. However, if tax money is involved in setting up a gifted program or service, which is often the case in public school systems, some accountability to relevant stakeholders is in order, that is, why extra money should be spent on these children but not other children, if goals of excellence are not stressed and standards of excellence not articulated and enforced. For most educators, a gifted-education program or service should be held accountable for whether it provides a challenging curriculum that is commensurate with the capabilities of a particular group of gifted learners and whether it is effective in achieving its goals and standards (see Borland, 1997b).

Sometimes the real issue is not whether excellence should be our goal, but how to effectively achieve the goal of excellence. It is, of course, impossible to have a successful gifted program if many gifted children are in effect dragged into the program kicking and screaming, as it were. They should have a right to opt in or out. Besides abilities and skills, the admission policy should consider factors such as whether a child is passionate about what he or she is good at and whether he or she is willing to commit time and effort in a gifted program designed to develop his or her talents. Capacity, zeal, and willingness to work are all indices of aptitude vis-à-vis a challenging program or provision.

As a corollary for designing curriculum and instruction, there also should be deliberate considerations of how to balance the seriousness of children's work (e.g., identity development) and the playfulness of their endeavors (e.g., enjoyment and intellectual curiosity), so that optimal motivation is maintained (Rea, 2000) and talent development and personal growth go hand in hand (Dai & Renzulli, 2000; Piechowski & Grant, 2001). Finally, standards of excellence should be socially and culturally important, publicly verifiable, and personally meaningful.

CONCLUSION: INTEGRATION OF INDIVIDUAL AND SOCIAL ASPECTS OF TALENT DEVELOPMENT

There is no disagreement that gifted education is aimed at providing opportunity, resources, and support to those who show the promise and readiness to pursue excellence in their respective endeavors at a level commensurate with their capabilities. The expertise-creativity tension can be eased or resolved if we recognize the role of person, domain, and process: (a) the diverse paths of individuals toward high-level expertise and creativity, (b) differential domain requirements and constraints in terms of knowledge and skill preparation for creative productivity, and (c) skill development processes that could integrate deep disciplined understanding (content) and imagination of new possibilities with the knowledge. The gifted-child versus talent development tension boils down to the issue of whether the educational focus should be on the intrinsic needs of the person in question or on the talent growth and domain contributions in the long run. Translated into curriculum and instruction, the question is whether we should nurture the person or teach the subject (content knowledge and skills), whether the curriculum should be structured around a domain or the person. One way to resolve this issue is to conceptualize domain excellence and personal excellence as two sides of the same coin. Domain excellence is indicated by skilled, expert-like performance or productive thought in an either proficient or creative manner (Tannenbaum, 1997). Whatever the case, the performance or product needs to be authentic and have a potential social impact. To achieve expertise in a particular domain, a specialized, highly focused curriculum works better. However, based on our knowledge of the interaction of person, domain, and process in the development of creativity, to achieve creative synthesis at a personal level, a more open and integrated curriculum is desirable in facilitating personal integration and knowledge transformation. Cognitive and affective goals should go hand in hand (Folsom, 2006). To enhance the chance of gifted students becoming good leaders in their respective fields of endeavor, compassion and responsibility can be part of the explicit or implicit curriculum of personal growth (Piechowski, 2009; Renzulli, 2002).

Gifted Education in Broader Social Contexts: Excellence at the Cost of Equity?

I recognize the general and systematic idea upon which a great people direct all their concerns. Aristocratic nations are naturally too liable to narrow the scope of human perfectibility; democratic nations, to expand it beyond reason.

—Alexis de Tocqueville, *Democracy in America*

Schools cannot equalize children; schools can only equalize opportunity.
—Leta Hollingworth, "Provisions for Intellectually Superior Children"

WE LIVE IN A WORLD that is based on the principle of equal rights and opportunity for all. In the zeitgeist of an egalitarian, classless world, any group that is apparently privileged for no justifiable reason would evoke resentment, and any remarks that seemed to degrade a particular group of people would trigger an uproar. Such was the case when then Harvard president Lawrence Summers (2005) suggested possible "innate" or "intrinsic aptitude" differences between men and women, as an explanation for male dominance in mathematics and sciences at top universities in the United States, or when James Watson, the DNA double-helix co-discoverer and a Nobel laureate, suggested a genetic intellectual inferiority in Africans as a possible explanation of why the social policies of helping them did not seem to work (Reuters, 2007).

In a democratic nation that has a history of racism, sexism, or other forms of social injustice, there are justifiable concerns about whether only some groups of individuals have privileged access to opportunities and resources for achieving excellence and cultural distinction, while others are marginalized or disfranchised. We know that racial and gender differences in psychological functioning and development are highly complicated issues, despite many scientific efforts to understand them. But here is the crux of the matter. Regardless of how true or how erroneous the remarks of Summers or Watson were, any assertion regarding fundamental individual and group differences in human abilities can be disquieting to the public psyche and seem at odds with the conviction that all humans are born equal and should be treated equally. Indeed, some psychologists have felt compelled to argue that there is no credible evidence for alleged "innate" sex differences in mathematics and sciences (Spelke, 2005), or even the very existence of "natural talents" (Howe et al., 1998; Ericsson et al., 2005, 2007a). For those like Herrnstein and Murray (1994) who try to perpetuate the notion of hierarchically stratified society based on IQ or some alleged genetically based traits, with smarts ruling the dumb and dumber, there will always be a countermove to deconstruct it as an ideological ploy for social control or a plain social conspiracy. For those scientists who have a profound appreciation of individual differences, any denial of the existence of talents and fundamental individual differences in intellectual functioning flies in the face of the compelling evidence from more than a hundred years of psychometric and developmental research on intelligence and personality (Gagné, 2009b). Conversely, for scientists and practitioners who have a deep appreciation of social injustice and various social impediments to human development, including the IQ mythology manufactured behind the scientific facade of *The Bell Curve* (Herrnstein & Murray, 1994), seemingly objective portrayals of human conditions can send toxic messages and lead to malpractices that potentially undermine the healthy texture of democracy (Berliner & Biddle, 1995; Sapon-Shevin, 1994). Here, the limits of scientific perspectives become poignantly clear. First, the behavioral and social sciences are concerned with living human beings with feelings, intentions, and will power, not objects; in these sciences, there are more uncertainties and unpredictability about human development, compared with the physical sciences. Even what researchers say can influence the behavior of the observed. Second, facts and values can never be completely separated in the behavioral, educational, and social sciences (Bredo, 2009; Howe, 2009), as the behavioral and social sciences have a fundamentally normative side; seemingly purely descriptive psychological concepts, such as intelligence and talent, are implicitly evaluative, with ethical and social significance in practice. Third, behavioral and social scientists have their own political sympathies. It is fair to assume that whatever political persuasions scientists identify themselves with, left or right, their intention is to build a society that is good for all, based on their understandings of human nature. But the fact that scientists, like other members of society, have their own subjective convictions, preferences, values, and biases makes it hard to separate, in their belief systems, value judgments and scientifically credible knowledge claims. Therefore, it is not difficult to understand why many scholars and educators hold diametrically opposite views of gifted education.

In the previous chapters, I distinguished between epistemic (cognitive) and normative (value) reasons for different attitudes toward gifted education. Epistemic reasons involve the nature-nurture issue, among others, and related empirical support, discussed in length in Chapters 3–5. In history, there have been many staunch champions of environmentalism, such as John Watson and his radical behaviorist colleagues, who have argued that human behavior (or development) is all about "nurture," and human malleability is almost boundless. Here is Watson's (1930) famous quote:

> Give me a dozen healthy infants, well-formed, and my own specified world to bring
> them up in and I'll guarantee to take any one at random and train him to become

any type of specialist I might select—doctor, lawyer, artist, merchant-chief and, yes, even beggar-man and thief, regardless of his talents, penchants, tendencies, abilities, vocations, and race of his ancestors. I am going beyond my facts and I admit it, but so have the advocates of the contrary and they have been doing it for many thousands of years. (p. 82)

Indeed there are just as many champions of genetic origins of high potential, such as Francis Galton, who would argue that "nature" prevails enormously over "nurture." Lurking behind these epistemic differences are normative value differences as to whether everyone is entitled to develop excellence in some way, whether resources are fairly and equitably distributed for that purpose, or whether we even need the concept of excellence or comparative merit at all in an egalitarian society (e.g., Reich, 1970; cited in Tannenbaum, 1998, p. 25). Inherent in gifted education is a tension between excellence and equity (Renzulli & Reis, 1991), which can be expressed as follows:

Thesis:
Identifying and cultivating high potential for excellence is a society's responsibility for the welfare of individuals as well as the society at large. Developing excellence reflects a cultural value that is important for a viable democracy and advances in human civilization.

Antithesis:
Singling out the alleged "gifted" for special treatment and privileged access to opportunity to pursue excellence perpetuates existing social inequality and creates a new social "elite," thus violating the democratic principle of equal rights and opportunity.

GIFTED EDUCATION UNDER SIEGE

Somewhere in the mid-1990s, several books singled out gifted education as culpable for holding back education reform efforts in the United States. Sapon-Shevin (1994, 1996), one of the most vocal critics of gifted education, argued that "gifted education as it is currently defined and implemented in this country is elitist, meritocratic, and constitutes a form of educational triage" (1996, p. 195). In Sapon-Shevin's depiction, gifted education is a safe haven, particularly for White middle-class parents, within what is perceived as a disastrous public education system. Gallagher (1996) vividly characterized this resentment as if gifted education were a lifeboat that only a few privileged ones had a chance to jump into while the *Titanic* of American education was sinking! Regardless of whether Sapon-Shevin portrayed a too rosy picture of gifted programs (see Borland, 1996) and a too gloomy picture of public education in general, gifted education was blamed (or scapegoated, as some might argue) for the alleged or actual low-quality public education. The logic of Sapon-Shevin's argument seems to be that gifted programs hold up high standards and have reaped the benefits of striving for excellence, because excellence is seen as a privilege of "the gifted," leaving the regular classes (teachers and students alike) complacent with mediocrity. In comparison, Berliner and Biddle (1995) were more upbeat about public education in general, as they dismissed the myth of a poor public education as "a manufactured crisis." However, they equally criticized gifted education as a putdown on general education in that it de facto creates a social divide between the elect (i.e., the gifted) and the damned (the regular or nongifted; see Berliner & Biddle, 1995, pp. 208–210).

In short, criticism of gifted education as elitist and standing in the way of education reform is based on two elements: First, gifted programs are in effect an offshoot of the tracking system, which privileges the already socially privileged, and is at odds with reform efforts to detrack students into heterogeneous classes; second, it offers a very few gifted students enrichment experiences that should be open to all, therefore violating the principle of equity based on the conviction that all students can learn and should have the opportunity to develop high-order skills (Shepard, 2000). The anti-elitist sentiment is understandable if one realizes that in the U.S. educational system, minority students are overrepresented in special education and underrepresented in gifted education (Donovan & Cross, 2002). In one district of New York City, for example, 80% of students who participated in gifted programs were White, though it was a district in which 80% of the students were children of color. The racial and socioeconomic disparity in gifted education was exacerbated by the fact that in some school districts there was manipulation of entry to gifted programs by economically advantaged parents, facilitated by complicit school and school district authorities (Fruchter & Siegle, 2004). In confronting the criticism of gifted education from outside, leaders within the gifted-education community are divided in how to position (or reposition) gifted education in the midst of the criticisms and controversies. On the more conservative side, Gallagher (2000b) argued that gifted children are real, not a fabrication, and the very existence of these children warrants a special provision of gifted education. Benbow and Stanley (1996) responded to the criticism of gifted education as elitist by pointing out the inequity for high-potential students caused by the extreme egalitarianism in the United States. Specifically, they pointed out six symptoms of this extremism: (a) pitting excellence against equity, (b) anti-intellectualism, (c) the dumbing-down of the curriculum, (d) equating aptitude and achievement testing as elitism, (e) the attraction to fads by schools, and (f) the insistence of schools to teach all students from the same curriculum at the same level. On the more liberal side, Renzulli (1994, 1999, 2002) called for developing talents for all, using more inclusive, diverse, domain-relevant criteria, rather than restricting gifted programs to a narrowly defined category such as high-IQ children. Treffinger and Feldhusen (1996) suggested we abandon the label *gifted child* and the corresponding categorical approach and instead treat talent potential as fluid and developing through education and proper nurturing. Borland (2003) concluded, in line with Sapon-Shevin (1996, 2003), that gifted education as currently practiced, for all its good intention, further perpetuates social injustice. Borland suggested that we should have gifted education that provides differentiated opportunities to able students without separate, generic gifted programs especially set up for the so-called gifted. Bernal (2003) echoed this sentiment when he argued that gifted education should be more future oriented; it should no longer serve a fixed category of children deemed "gifted" but should instead educate *for* developing talented young adults.

Ideological differences also permeate scholarly inquiry into the nature of giftedness and talent. Coleman, Sanders, and Cross (1997) identified three modes of inquiry in the field of gifted education, empirical-analytic, interpretivist, and transformative, respectively, each carrying specific tacit assumptions about the nature of giftedness and talent. People who believe in *the empirical-analytic mode* see giftedness and talent as quantifiable psychosocial phenomena, which can be studied using objective methods, not unlike those used in natural science. Thus, universal criteria can be determined about who are gifted and what kind of education is good for them. In contrast, people under *the interpretivist mode of inquiry* see giftedness and talent as socially constructed by specific cultural groups for social purposes, which can be best understood by tapping into the meanings and purposes relevant parties and stakeholders attach to the term *gifted and talented*. Thus, the nature and education of the gifted and talented are based on consensus by stakeholders, rather than on universal principles and criteria. Finally, people who use *the transformative mode of inquiry* view giftedness and talent as defined by the most powerful and influential to the possible detriment of the marginalized, whose gifts and talents lie outside those parameters set up by the powerful. These three modes of inquiry carry different values and beliefs regarding what "ought to be," and none of these modes of inquiry can claim to be value neutral (see also Ambrose, 2000). The empirical-analytic mode of inquiry I rely on in my review of the ontological and epistemological issues in previous chapters is not immune to the value issue, as the very notions of giftedness and talent, as well as psychological constructs such as intelligence, creativity, expertise, motivation, are not only descriptive categories and dimensions; they are all value laden or implicitly evaluative. As shown in these modes of inquiry, even the research methods reflect deep ideological differences, with the empirical-analytic mode of inquiry guarding the tradition of gifted education and the interpretivist and transformative modes of inquiry undermining the basic assumptions of objectivity and universality held by the empirical-analytic mode.

DEFINING EXCELLENCE AND EQUITY AND FRAMING THE DEBATE

Equitable access to excellence is an emotionally charged, politically sensitive issue. The contested nature of gifted education makes it even more important to define clearly what we mean by excellence and equity, respectively, and when and how they constitute competing values and priorities in practice and public policy, lest we get tangled up with unproductive ideological battles and either-or, dichotomous thinking.

Webster's Ninth New Collegiate Dictionary defines *excel* as "to be superior to; surpass in accomplishment or achievement." Several characteristics of excellence are distinguishable. First, excellence is an inherently norm-based and merit-based concept, implying a distinct comparative advantage or merit in a domain of human performance, though degrees and levels of excellence may vary (e.g., a national-level versus an international-level player). Second, as superior achievement, excellence is not possessed, but earned. Therefore, while sharing characteristics with the concept of "gifted" as being "superior" and "rare," excellence is more of a performance concept, denoting superiority or outstanding quality by certain widely accepted performance standards, whereas the term *giftedness* is often seen as an attribute of the person in question (e.g., "A gifted musician gave an excellent performance"). *In the educational context, excellence can be defined as superior achievement in academic, artistic, social, and vocational domains, among others, by age-appropriate standards.* It can take the form of highly skilled performance (a chess champion, a piano virtuoso, etc.), creative products (a scientific theory, a novel, etc.), or distinct leadership in some worthy human endeavor (environmental protection, visionary governance, etc.). At any rate, excellence is a less ambiguous term, and an instance of excellence is more easily recognizable and agreed upon than the question of whether a person is "gifted." Third, excellence, like the term *gifted*, is fundamentally value laden, indicative of superior achievement in domains valued by a culture and important for improving human conditions. Gifted burglars or computer hackers are perfectly conceivable, but few, if any, would cite their feats as instances of excellence and treat them as paragons of the gifted.

Most would agree that to maintain the strategic and developmental vitality of a nation as well as the self-fulfillment of individuals, the pursuit of excellence in academic and other domains of sociocultural importance should be one of the main goals of education. Most would also agree that one of the main goals of gifted education is to allow those students who have demonstrated emergent excellence or high potential for excellence to move faster and deeper in developing their talents, at a pace and level appropriate to and commensurate with their capabilities, advanced knowledge, and levels of commitment. Very few would argue that the promotion of excellence is an unworthy goal for school merely because it would support, highlight, and reward the high achievement of a small number of students, potentially at the cost of self-esteem and resentment for a majority of students. For those who do argue that the goal of excellence should be scratched out from school, there is indeed no place for gifted education. However, if we accept the premise that the pursuit of excellence should figure prominently in school, there is a place for gifted-education services (with or without gifted programs). The equity issue, then, is how we ensure that all students have a fair opportunity to participate in an education aiming at excellence, whether in regular classrooms or in pull-out and self-contained programs.

Webster's Ninth New Collegiate Dictionary defines *equity* as "justice according to natural law or right; *specif*: freedom from bias or favoritism." Thus, equity mainly concerns individual rights; fairness in opportunity for self-development and pursuit of happiness, broadly defined; and freedom from social discrimination. To build a consensus about the pursuit of excellence with equity, it is helpful to start with some general principles.

First, everyone has the right to pursue excellence in areas that he or she finds personally meaningful and rewarding. Therefore, all students should be given the encouragement, resources, and necessary support to excel in school in domains of their choosing, particularly in academics. However, no one is obligated to pursue excellence to the best of his or her ability. It is conceivable that some highly intelligent and "gifted" students may decide to just get by in school or pursue personal interests outside school. Some help would surely be warranted to get these gifted underachievers "fired up" about schoolwork, but excellence is a commitment and personal decision that cannot be forced upon anyone. An equitable gifted-education policy should consider motivation and commitment as an important factor of one's readiness for pursuit of excellence so that we don't easily reject highly interested and committed students on the grounds that they fall short of meeting some test score criteria and accept those "eligible" but lukewarm ones.

Second, there are a wide range of options and opportunities for the pursuit of excellence, including but not limited to "gifted programs." Many individuals recalled having teachers and tutors in and outside schools, while in elementary or secondary school, who inspired lifelong interests and passions in them, leading to their eminent adult accomplishments (see Bloom, 1985), and many of these teachers are regular classroom teachers or not associated with gifted programs. Nonetheless, the nature of their work is not that different from that seen in gifted programs. It does not make sense to think that if one does not participate in gifted programs, one would miss out on any opportunity to pursue excellence. It is conceivable that some individuals pursue their passions and talents outside the classroom or school and eventually are recognized as making great contributions to respective domains. It should not surprise us if we find out that quite a few eminent contributors to the sciences, the humanities, the arts, and technology never attended gifted programs in school at all. By the same token, we cannot infer that if a school does not have a gifted program designated for the "gifted," then the school is not promoting excellence or cannot provide educational services to promote and nurture excellence.

Third, there is a continuum of services that constitutes gifted education, ranging from enrichment to acceleration, from offering curriculum compacting and differentiation (with challenging learning materials commensurate with one's capabilities) within the regular classroom, all the way to self-contained classes, programs, and schools (Benbow & Stanley, 1996; Renzulli & Dai, 2003). The pursuit of excellence through these options should be flexible and open enough to allow maximal participation and rigorous enough to ensure efficiency and quality. For various enrichment curricular activities (independent or collaborative projects, field trips, etc.), the threshold for extra service or entry to special programs can be quite low so that most willing students can participate, and for others such as Talent Search programs (Swiatek, 2007) or early entrance to college for the mathematically or verbally precocious, the threshold can be very high (e.g., 99th percentile; Stanley, 1997). Selectivity of specific programs depends on program goals (e.g., the nature and levels of excellence a program targets) and logistic considerations (e.g., available resources, including expertise). Selectivity is an inherent feature of gifted programming or services aimed at helping advanced students to strive for higher-level achievement and excellence and thus should not be the reason for "elitist" charges, as long as the selection process is open to all, and selection criteria are intrinsic to the nature of excellence in an area of human endeavor.

From general principles to specific considerations, there are at least three issues relevant to equity in gifted education: (a) fair opportunity to participate in gifted programs and services aimed at developing high-level achievement or excellence (including ensuring a level playing field for all); (b) equitable curriculum provision and resource allocation for different classes and programs, particularly when homogeneous grouping is practiced; (c) nondiscriminating, nondebilitating psychosocial conditions, which suggest that possible negative effects of identification (including labeling some children "gifted" and others "nongifted") and selection practices on self-concept, self-esteem, and self-efficacy, particularly for unidentified students, should be minimized.

Fair Opportunity for Participation in Developing Excellence

Equity of selection procedures and criteria: What count as good measures of potential for excellence. Since most gifted programs involve a selection or identification process, as stipulated by state policy, selection criteria are often faulted for creating a questionable "gifted" category of students for special service and "preferential" treatment. Some critics believe that there is no sure way to identify at an early age those who are truly gifted or talented (e.g., Berliner & Biddle, 1995; Howe et al., 1998). Besides, generic gifted programs are often based on blanket statements and vaguely defined or unwarranted assumptions about the unique needs of gifted students.

To understand this critique of the gifted-education movement, we have to put it in historical context. The traditional "gifted child" model is often perceived as an integral part of the social efficiency model of education, based on the industrial-factory metaphor of educational productivity, whereby tracking is used to sort out who will go to college and pursue advanced degrees and go ahead to become lawyers, doctors, and engineers, and who will go to the vocational track for less prestigious careers and jobs (Borland, 2003; Sapon-Shevin, 1996; Shepard, 2000). This tracking practice is often justified by alleged inherent individual differences in general intelligence, which in large part determines success or failure in one's life and career paths (Gottfredson, 1997). The technology of intelligence testing is seen as culpable for sorting and stratifying children for these purposes (Shepard, 2000). For many social critics, "the gifted child" is a fabricated product, a social construction based on IQ testing that tends to perpetuate a myth of the inherent limits of one's educational and developmental potential, implying an "uphill battle" for those at the low end and "all yours to lose" for those at the high end of the spectrum of general intelligence.

The very notion of education hinges on the concept of human potential, particularly the potential to learn and grow; that is, given putative potential X, we could reasonably assume that education could bring the person from the current state to a future, desired state (i.e., acquiring some desirable characteristics such as certain skills, knowledge, and identity). When Terman (1925) decided to conduct a follow-up study on 1,500 Californian children with IQs of 135 or above into their adulthood, he apparently believed that this group of children held the highest promise of achieving excellence and eminence in adulthood. It is open to debate what constitutes a good measure of "potential," which is likely contextually determined, depending on a combination of factors, such as personal characteristics, the nature of domains, stages of development, and targeted levels of achievement (see Chapter 4). Nevertheless, it is widely accepted that given the same opportunity and resources to develop talents and expertise, outcomes are likely quite different, because of differences in capacity (ability), zeal (i.e., passion), or willingness to work (i.e., work ethic), to use Galton's (1869) triadic conception of genius (what would be called "giftedness" today). In his now classic book, *A Theory of Justice*, Rawls (1971) also carefully qualified "fair equality of opportunity" to mean that *similarly able* people should have similar life chances by eliminating the effect of social contingencies. Although there are critics of gifted education who argue not only for equality of opportunity, but also for equality of educational outcomes (e.g., Schulz, 2005), Sapon-Shevin (1996) justifiably pointed out that "arguments framed in terms of justice are complex because they often fail to discriminate between the goals of equality of access, equality of services, and equality of outcomes. . . . Few educators would advocate equal treatment if by that we meant giving every child the same kind of educational experiences at the same pace, using the same materials, and so on" (p. 198). Thus, the argument is not that every child is gifted and thus every child is entitled to gifted education, which would effectively eliminate the need for any kind of gifted education. Rather, the key question is, What constitutes a scientifically credible and socially fair basis for judging one's potential to learn, grow, and excel?

Main theoretical differences within the psychological and educational research community are (a) whether human potential should be seen as fixed or fluid and malleable (i.e., absolute state of being or a developing state; see Chapters 1, 3, 4, and 5), (b) whether it should be seen as unitary or multifaceted (see Chapter 4), and (c) what constitutes evidence for high potential or promise (see Chapter 6). My review in these chapters shows that the field is moving increasingly toward recognizing the fluid and multifaceted qualities of high potential and its contextual, dynamic, and emergent nature (Dai & Renzulli, 2008); consequently it is moving away in practice from heavily relying on decontextualized tools such as IQ tests as the sole basis of assessing this potential (often in a once-and-forever fashion), toward using more proximal, authentic assessment of one's functioning in situ (i.e., in more authentic rather than contrived performance situations). Indeed, researchers are now more concerned about how an identification/assessment system operates to serve its purposes of proper educational placement and interventions that match the identified advancing needs of students than how a particular test captures the elusive quality of "giftedness" (Matthews & Foster, 2006; VanTassel-Baska, 2006); in other words, a specific test is used as an information-gathering device, along with other tools, in facilitating an assessment of the likelihood of success of a student for a particular educational challenge, rather than a litmus test of "giftedness."

Based on this understanding of the assessment of human potential, a more circumscribed interpretation of high IQ is warranted: Instead of buying into the omnipotent, "blank check" notion of IQ power, one should use IQ or various general scholastic aptitude or ability tests, not as indicative of the inherent limits of human potential, a view fairly criticized by Ericsson et al. (2007a), but as one of the indices of the likelihood of future success in academic domains, given their close association with academic achievement in general and theoretically more generality and pervasive influence across a wide range of tasks compared with other ability constructs (Gustafsson & Undheim, 1996; Lubinski, 2004; see also Sackett, Borneman, & Connelly, 2008), while acknowledging that they do not predict domain-specific achievement as well, compared with domain-specific measures of aptitude (Lohman, 2005a; see discussion in Chapter 4), and they do not predict eminent accomplishments in adulthood (Subotnik, 2003).

From an educational point of view, a major limitation of using high IQ or other general aptitude measures as a rationale for differentiated educational treatment is the lack of clear educational justification. It is built on a problematic assumption, pointed out by many (e.g., Borland, 2003; Sapon-Shevin, 1996), that the group so identified is a homogeneous group. When domain knowledge, special penchants, and interests are considered, they are clearly not (see Chapter 4). Consequently, the argument that all children with high IQ scores have the same "educational needs" is not very compelling. To be sure, extremely low IQ scores would suggest a possible instance of intellectual disabilities that calls for intervention and remediation, as the very first intelligence test was intended (Binet & Simon, 1916); but what high IQ means educationally is less obvious, because the putative growth potential or high promise is more elusive and abstract than "deficiency needs" indicated by extremely low IQs. This is why Matthews and Foster (2006) called the traditional IQ-based or other general aptitude–based models of giftedness "mystery" models (p. 64). As an alternative, they proposed a mastery model of giftedness that defines giftedness as "exceptionally advanced subject-specific ability at a particular point in time such that a student's learning needs cannot be well met without significant adaptations to the curriculum (p. 65). Their suggestion is to avoid the use of the elusive and ill-defined term *potential*, but instead define more specific educational needs in specific content areas as they emerge in educational contexts. This way, not only is it much clearer what education needs are, given a child's advanced level of academic development in specific school subjects; there is also much clearer coherence between definition, identification, and programming. Such a model of gifted education would be much more defensible compared with some generic gifted-child models, though the extent to which one's educational needs become so "exceptional" that they warrant a special educational provision needs to be specified in practical settings. In effect, Matthews and Foster cast talent development approaches into a special education mode, and by so doing appealed to the value of equity (gifted children have special educational needs just as children with autism or learning disabilities do), rather than the value of excellence, which most talent development models highlight (e.g., Subotnik & Coleman, 1996; Treffiger & Feldhusen, 1996). The methods to implement this gifted-education model is analogous to the recent movement in special education called "response-to-intervention" (RTI), in which whether a child truly has special needs and whether he or she gets adequate educational treatment in regular classroom can be assessed to determine whether special services were warranted (Vellutino, Scanlon, Small, & Fanuele, 2006). In general, special education models of gifted education tend to be reactive in the sense of responding to emergent needs of individual students, while talent development models are more proactive in the sense of setting goals for systematically developing talents and creative productivity based on educational priorities and talent pipelines as perceived by school districts, states, or nations. Nevertheless, both are based on the same understandings of the evolving, incremental nature of learning and development and the contextual dependency of human abilities. They both believe that these understandings of human potential should provide a sound basis for equitable, defensible provisions of gifted education (Matthews & Foster, 2006; Treffinger & Feldhusen, 1996).

Diversity and equity. Lack of proportional representation in the gifted education of ethnic minority students (barring Asian Americans), students with limited English proficiency, and students from economically disadvantaged families is a main concern for advocates of equity and educational equality (Ford, 2003; Frasier, 1997; Graham, 2009). Critics point out that procedures commonly used to select students for gifted programs, for example, using standardized IQ or achievement tests, are inherently biased against minority students, causing the disparity in gifted programs and ultimately perpetuating inequalities that already exist in society (Berliner & Biddle, 1995; Ford, 2003; Naglieri, 2008; but see Cleary, Humphreys, Kendrick, & Wesman, 1975; Sackett et al., 2008). For conceptual clarity, a distinction should be made between *test bias* as a technical term and *consequential validity* of using particular tests. As *Standards for Educational and Psychological Testing* (American Educational Research Association, American Psychological Association, & National Council on Measurement in Education, 1999) states, "While group differences in testing outcomes should in many cases trigger heightened scrutiny for possible sources of test bias, outcome differences across groups do not in themselves indicate that a testing application is biased or unfair" (p. 75). For example, one cannot jump to the conclusion, based on the fact that African American players are overrepresented in the National Basketball Association (NBA), that its selection system is biased against, or unfair to, other ethnic groups. Technically, a test is biased against a group as a selection criterion if it significantly underpredicts a criterion outcome of interest for that group. For example, if IQ test scores significantly underpredict African American students' academic achievement compared with, say, that of European American students', we can say that there is a test bias against African American students. Research examining possible differential item functioning of a variety of aptitude tests generally does not find the presence of the alleged test bias (e.g., see Sackett et al., 2008). Different from *test bias* in this technical sense, which mainly concerns whether a test is doing its job as intended by the test user, or inadvertently disfavors certain groups for extraneous reasons irrelevant to its intended purposes, *consequential validity* is concerned with broader social and practical implications of using particular tests, thus dealing with both intended and unintended consequences of using a particular test for social purposes. Messick (1995), who first proposed the concept, defined consequential validity as an appraisal of "the value implications of score interpretation as a basis for action as well as the actual and potential consequences of test use, especially in regard to sources of invalidity related to issues of bias, fairness, and distributive justice" (p. 745). If IQ and other aptitude tests cause disproportional overrepresentation of students of wealthy families and underrepresentation of students of poor families and certain ethnic groups, there are ethical and social consequences of the fact that the rich get richer and the poor get poorer, even if the tests involved do not show apparent "test bias" in the technical sense (Ceci & Papierno, 2005). Contrary to this common perspective, Benbow and Stanley (1996) suggested that if these aptitude tests are more pervasively used than is the case in current practice in selection and admission decisions, minority groups would be more equitably represented; in other words, these tests have "equalizing" power. Nevertheless, the overwhelming concern seems to be the "oppressive" effect of the tests.

The call for alternative ways of identification aimed at selecting more minority students for gifted programs has been addressed by many research efforts since the 1990s (see Frasier, 1997), partly funded by the Javits Act, a federally funded program in the United States to support research on identifying and serving traditionally underrepresented groups in gifted programs, particularly economically disadvantaged, limited English proficient, and disabled students (NAGC, 2009). At least three alternative approaches were used for identification and selection purposes: (a) identifying diverse abilities and talents rather than the generic "gifted," (b) assessing ease of learning using dynamic assessment, and (c) using nonverbal tests as an attempt to identify more minority students. As an example in the first approach, DISCOVER was an assessment system developed in the early 1990s (see Maker, 1996), largely based on the theory of multiple intelligences (Gardner, 1983), using multiple assessment tools and techniques, including classroom- and performance-based observation rather than relying on standardized tests. In comparison, the use of dynamic assessment methods in identifying gifted students is based on the assumption that traditional standardized tests tend to be tailored to mainstream culture and may not be appropriate as identification tools for minority students. The key to dynamic assessment is its focus on the process and progress of mastery as a marker of learning potential rather than on what a person already knows or is capable of doing. Dynamic assessment is more diagnostic, showing what a person can do with instructional hints and support and where is the zone of proximal development (ZPD) upper bound (i.e., what a person can do with instructional support) for a particular learner; it typically takes the form of a test-intervention-retest sequence, using test-retest difference scores to indicate the ease of learning as a marker of high potential (Kirschenbaum, 1998; see also Kanevsky, 2000). Like any new alternatives, dynamic assessment has its own challenges. Lohman (personal communication, May 2009), for example, expressed his reservations about dynamic assessment for both statistical and psychological reasons. Statistically, test-retest difference scores are most reliable only when the pre- and postmeasures show low correlations, in which case the postmeasure would carry the load as truly indicative of "progress," or ease of learning. Psychologically, it assumes that content knowledge (e.g., what one already knows) and process (e.g., how fast one can acquire a skill) can be assessed independently, which is never the case, as the former will inevitably influence the latter (his reservations on the use of nonverbal ability tests for identification are partly based on the same concern over treating knowledge and process as independent of each other; see Lohman, 2005b). Nevertheless, dynamic assessment is more "situated" than standardized tests, and its careful use for diagnostic and placement purposes enriches our understanding and assists in determining a person's learning potential in situ.

Another alternative approach is to use nonverbal ability tests for identification, which has been more frequently explored, researched, and contested in recent years. A main rationale for using nonverbal tests in gifted education is that African American and Hispanic students would have the same likelihood of earning high scores as their European American counterparts, hence their chances of being considered for gifted programs. An underlying assumption is that, while verbal and quantitative abilities are typically developed through schooling and other enriching educational experiences, thus disadvantaging relatively poor, cultural, and linguistic minority groups, nonverbal tests of general ability tend to be "culture fair," less "contaminated" by differences in cultural experiences, or less confounded by the issue of language proficiency (Naglieri & Ford, 2003). In a critique of Naglieri and Ford's study, however, Lohman (2005b) argued that a preponderance of evidence on nonverbal ability tests suggest the implausibility of identifying equal or more equitable proportions of diverse ethnic, language, or low-SES groups through the use of nonverbal ability tests. He further argued that use of nonverbal ability tests as a primary means of identification would neglect those who either exhibited academic excellence or were more likely to benefit from educational enrichment.

The issue of validity claims about using nonverbal tests for identification, just like using dynamic assessment or classroom-based performance observation, is a complex one, involving technical analysis of tasks involved, evaluation of specific test items, and proper sampling of relevant populations (see Naglieri & Ford, 2005, for a response to Lohman, 2005b). At any rate, exploring alternative means of identification to achieve diverse student representation in gifted education is a valuable endeavor, as long as it can show that those identified can benefit equally from specific programs and can excel equally compared with those who are identified using more traditional instruments and criteria (see Borland, 2008). In a recent study, VanTessel-Baska, Feng, and Evans (2007) compared academic progress over a 3-year period of gifted students who were identified using more traditional procedures (i.e., using test scores) and those identified using performance-based measures. Using performance-based measures, particularly the nonverbal version, did increase the percentage of students from low-SES homes (by 3%) and African American students (by 5%). When it came to academic performance over time in their relevant programs, traditionally identified students did better than students identified through performance tasks, suggesting a better predictive validity of the traditional, rather than alternative, approaches. The authors argued, based on their findings, that merely increasing the number of minority students is not sufficient, as they may represent different ability profiles that warrant educational differentiation of a different kind compared with traditionally identified students. In other words, further clarification is needed of what kind of potential for excellence students so identified demonstrate and in what way it predicts success by some standards of excellence over time through appropriate educational experiences offered by specific programs (see Borland, 2008, for a more comprehensive treatment of the topic of identification).

Although they differ on how nonverbal ability tests should be used in identification, Lohman (2005a), and Naglieri and Ford (2005) agree that both *demonstrated excellence* (i.e., high achievement) and *potential for excellence* should be considered in the identification and selection process, particularly when minority students are involved. The notion of potential for excellence, and its corollary—using measures and criteria other than academic achievement—is preserved precisely because many students from underrepresented groups have yet to have the opportunity to develop the academic skills that would enable them to demonstrate their excellence. It is important to understand the existence of *chronic involuntary underachievement* that is experienced by disadvantaged groups (Siegle & McCoach, 2009) because of their less than adequate home, neighborhood, or school conditions, such as a lack of inspiring curriculum and teachers, or language deficiencies (see also Hébert, 2001). Giving the opportunity to the most promising members of these underrepresented groups to catch up is necessary before we can truly claim that we have a level playing field for all players. As Ceci and Papierno (2005) pointed out, "Just as a nation does not want to rob itself of creating the best scientific, management, and engineering elite among its higher functioning group, it would likewise not want to lose out on many potential leaders, scientists, and so forth, whose talent may be [*sic*] not be realized because of external constraints" (p. 158).

Seeking excellence with equity and diversity in mind entails a delicate balancing act. The U.S. Supreme Court rulings on the University of Michigan's affirmative action cases in 2003 (Gratz v. Bollinger, 2003; Grutter v. Bollinger, 2003) are instructive in this regard. The Court upheld the University of Michigan Law School's admission policy, which considered race as a "plus" factor in admission decisions, ruling in *Grutter* that diversity of a student body is a compelling state interest because it presumably brings educational benefits of cross-racial understandings and breaking stereotypes, among others, and "better prepares students for an increasingly diverse workforce, for society, and for the legal profession." In *Gratz*, a parallel case decided in conjunction with *Grutter*, the Court held the admission policy of the University of Michigan College of Literature, Sciences, and the Arts (LSA) to be "unconstitutional" because its automatic assignment of 20 points to any minority undergraduate applicant (1/5 of the points needed for admission) violated the Equal Protection Clause of the U.S. Constitution. The ruling points out that "the LSA's 20-point distribution has the effect of making 'the factor of race ... decisive' for virtually every minimally qualified underrepresented minority applicant." Both the Law School and LSA of the University of Michigan are highly prestigious programs with limited but coveted admission slots. The Supreme Court ruling on the Law School case, drafted by Justice Sandra Day O'Connor, who cast the deciding vote to support the Law School policy, is revealing in showing Justice O'Connor's ambivalence toward race-conscious admission policies; the document ends with the following statement: "Race-conscious admissions policies must be limited in time. . . . The Court expects that 25 years from now, the use of racial preferences will no longer be necessary to further the interest approved today" (Grutter v. Bollinger, 2003). Justice O'Connor apparently realized that a racially preferential policy in the name of diversity is a double-edge sword and can potentially discriminate against nonminority applicants and thus threaten the very notion of equal rights, protected by the Constitution. In the

LSA case, wherein racial preference was more distinct in the admission policy, infringement upon the principles of both excellence and equity was quite blatant to the opponents of this policy. Note that the rationale for affirmative action in university admission policy is twofold—to diversify the student body and to remedy the impact of racial discrimination in history, so that all racial and ethnic groups can have an equal footing in society over time. In a sense, what educators of the gifted are trying to do with underrepresented minority groups is similar to what affirmative action is intended to accomplish: balancing excellence with equity. It is not easy to juggle these priorities, as every decision we make could affect individuals' lives one way or another, sometimes in a profound way, for better or for worse.

It is important to note that identification itself will not solve the problem of the underrepresentation of minority students in gifted education if the lack of "opportunity to learn" (Gee, 2003) inside or outside the school is still prevalent. There is a limit to how much gifted education (or school in general) can do to remedy the situation (Robinson, 2005). Given the importance of person-environmental interaction in human development, a lack of early stimulating, developmentally instigative environments and development-producing experiences can have a far-reaching impact on the emergence of gifted and talent behaviors as well as the long-term developmental trajectory of a child.

Curriculum Differentiation and Fair Allocation and Distribution of Educational Resources

Critics of gifted education (Berliner & Biddle, 1995; Margolin, 1994; Oaks & Wells, 1998; Sapon-Shevin, 1994; Schulz, 2005) faulted curriculum and instructional differentiation (i.e., adaptations tailored to particular learning needs or situations) for the gifted as being fundamentally a tracking practice; that is, giving qualitatively different educational experiences to students of different tracks based on some assumption of fundamental differences in developmental potential between them, resulting in an unjustified stratification and social divide. Many argued that most enrichment programs that are suitable for gifted students are also good for students who are not identified as gifted (Berliner & Biddle, 1995; Sapon-Shevin, 1996). It is important, therefore, to have a clear understanding of why curriculum differentiation is needed for gifted students and in what way it can be justified based on the principles of both excellence and equity.

Critics of gifted education offer different reasons, sometimes quite drastic, for why gifted-education provisions are problematic. For example, Margolin (1996) made a cogent point when he argued that historically, gifted education put too much emphasis on cultivating personal characteristics that are presumably conducive to creativity and leadership and gave too little attention to teaching and learning disciplinary knowledge. It highlights an entrenched problem in gifted education of treating higher-order thinking as independent of deep content knowledge, as if one can exercise critical and creative thinking without a solid knowledge base. To some extent, it also reflects the unresolved issue of domain-versus person-centered gifted education and the tension between personal growth and talent development models that I discussed in the preceding chapter. But Margolin seemed to have an extra ax to grind—the main purpose of his book (Margolin, 1994) was to advance a thesis that gifted education is really about creating or maintaining a dominant social class; its practice throughout its history has been simply "a pedagogy of privilege," the flip side of the "pedagogy of the oppressed" (p. 164). In other words, gifted education, according to Margolin (1996), is part of a political machinery aimed at maintaining and perpetuating a social order that keeps the lower class and the powerless where they are, while solidifying the position of the wealthy and powerful.

The methodology used in Margolin's (1994) critique is a blend of historical ethnography and cultural criticism. While the narrative Margolin constructed is coherent and highly intriguing, it begs the question of whether this coherence is achieved at the cost of credibility. His conclusion that "nothing's changed" (Margolin, 1996, p. 169) since the inception of the gifted-child education movement in 1920s in the United States obfuscates decades of efforts, starting at least in the late 1950s (e.g., Witty, 1958) to make gifted education more diverse, accessible, and equitable. For example, Renzulli's (1977) enrichment triad model can be seen as an early attempt to maximize participation in developing higher-order thinking skills. Tomlinson and Callahan (1992) explored how gifted education practices might benefit regular classroom teaching and learning for all. The whole talent development movement I reviewed in Chapter 1 has been aimed at diversifying the talent pool as well as identifying multiple pathways to realize students' potentials, rather than protecting the interest of a few socially privileged individuals.

Schulz (2005) offered a view of gifted education similar to Margolin's in the current Australian context. Schulz's methodology was discourse analysis, based on interview protocols she collected. As with Margolin's critique, it is difficult to tell in Schulz's exposition the line between serious scholarship and outright political advocacy. In comparison, Sapon-Shevin's (1994, 1996) critique is based on the notion that what is good for gifted students is good for all students. "Gifted programs often result in the resegregation of schools: white students are in gifted programs and students of color are in the mainstream. The benefits provided by such programs-smaller classes, more enthusiastic teachers, rich curriculum, more individualization—are all changes that would benefit all students" (Sapon-Shevin, 1996, p. 199). Berliner and Biddle (1995) made a similar argument that curricula that are supposed to be authentic, novel, and challenging, involving problem solving and high-order thinking for the gifted, should be open to all. The same argument was made by those who advocated detracking as a way to solve the problem of educational disparity by raising standards for all (Oaks & Well, 1998). Sometimes, detracking means intentionally creating heterogeneous classes and eliminating all form of homogeneous grouping within or between classes, as in the case of cooperative learning (Slavin, 1990). However, some leading scholars in gifted education quickly pointed out that in the name of cooperative learning, whereby the more able are supposed to help the less able, the cooperation can border on exploitation (Robinson, 1990, 2003), an issue of equity and fairness on the other side of the story to be reckoned with.

To put this debate in perspective, grouping based on levels of ability, skills, prior knowledge, motivation, and so on, is a strategy to deal with a fundamental flaw of modern age-graded schooling, which operates under an unwarranted assumption about the developmental and educational comparability of age peers. In actuality, age-graded schooling is not based on scientific knowledge of child development, but largely serves the administrative convenience of school as a social institution. From a pedagogical point of view, grouping, for good or ill, is designed to make teaching and learning more efficient, in terms of appropriate levels of difficulty in curricular materials and appropriate pedagogy vis-à-vis levels of understandings, ways of thinking, and motivation for a particular group of students, what Shulman (1987) called pedagogical content knowledge. That all children can learn and excel does not mean that all children will learn the same way, at the same pace, and achieve the same level of excellence. Differentiation in curriculum and instruction, which sometimes involves various ability grouping arrangements, rather than a one-size-fits-all education, is a way to deal with student differences and diversity. Therefore, one has to be careful not to over-politicize a pedagogical issue. In a response to Oaks and Well (1998), Reis et al. (1998) distinguished between *tracking*, which is the permanent assignment of students to classes for teaching, and *grouping*, which is a more flexible arrangement of students according to student levels of abilities, knowledge, and motivation. They concurred that tracking based on ability or achievement can be problematic; however, various grouping arrangements are often necessary for differentiation purposes. In a sense, offering electives and advanced placement (AP) classes for advanced students is also a form of grouping for more specialized or advanced training and development. It is part of the curriculum that is tailored, not to the person per se, but to the level of achievement he or she has attained, indicating the promise of rising to new heights of excellence. Unlike the controversial tracking practice in the United States and many other nations (e.g., Germany's three-track system), this kind of educational arrangements and provisions for advanced students is fully justified (Coleman & Cross, 2005). It would be ludicrous to demand that, since a few mathematically advanced students find a calculus class challenging and rewarding, all students should have the same curricular experience and reap the same benefits.

In all fairness, critics of gifted education such as Sapon-Shevin (1996) or Oaks and Well (1998) acknowledge the value of differentiation or educational adaptation to individual differences in levels and pace of learning; equality does not mean that all students should be treated the same way. What they ask for is not "equal treatment" but "equally good treatment" (Sapon-Shevin, 1996, p. 199).

"The key issue is whether gifted programs provide differentiation that is clearly linked to the child's difference (in the same way that we are justified in giving a larger portion of food to a 12-year-old than to a 4-year-old) or whether the differentiation is not only based on faulty questionable assumptions about inherent differences among children but also results in further, continuing, and more deeply embedded and significant discrimination in the future" (Sapon-Shevin, 1996, p. 199). In fact, defenders of gifted education also acknowledged that some generic enrichment programs with vaguely defined needs of gifted children are indeed not tailored to any well-defined and justified educational needs and can be ineffective and potentially inequitable (e.g., Benbow & Stanley, 1996). A central question is, Is there such a thing as "gifted curriculum" or "gifted pedagogy" that is uniquely suited only for "the gifted"? The notion of a "gifted program" or "gifted curriculum" implies that gifted children as a homogeneous group have homogeneous educational needs regardless of particular patterns of knowledge, abilities, and interests and personal styles. The emergent consensus in the field of gifted education seems to be that although we have more advanced curriculum and more tailored pedagogy to suit the needs of advanced learners at a particular stage or phase of their development, we don't have a curriculum uniquely tailored to the generic category of the gifted and a pedagogy that only works for "the gifted" (see Coleman, 2003; Kaplan, 2003; Shore & Delcourt, 1996; Tomlinson, 1996). While arguing that goals and guiding principles for gifted education and general education are fundamentally similar, Tomlinson (1996) posits nine dimensions on which educational and instructional differentiation may be made for gifted learners: (a) foundational to transformational, (b) concrete to abstract, (c) simple to complex, (d) few facets to multifacets, (e) smaller leap to greater leap, (f) more structured to more open, (g) clearly defined to fuzzy, (h) less independence to greater independence, and (i) slower to quicker. They can be seen as dimensions along which all students (including the precocious and advanced) can be properly positioned based on their zones of proximal development, on how much they will benefit from a given educational experience at a specific point in time. Thus we should avoid two extremes: One extreme is to think of gifted education and general education in a dichotomous way, as two separate entities, and the other extreme is to make a blanket assumption that what is good for gifted students is good for all students. Neither would serve the goals of excellence and equity.

As a theoretical basis for differentiation, besides the rate of learning, we can also hypothesize that the educational benefits of various curricular experiences for a given student follow the same rule of diminishing returns as postulated in economics. For some individuals, the point of diminishing returns is reached more quickly than others, meaning that beyond the point a given educational provision may not produce meaningful learning gains and skill development (i.e., one is reaching an asymptote; see Chapter 3). For some individuals, more advanced materials and learning experiences continue to yield payoff. A premise underlying this hypothesis is, of course, that there are fundamentally individual differences in learning potential given a wide range of available educational opportunities and experiences. And contrary to a common belief that education is an equalizer in the sense of diminishing individual differences in achievement, educational experiences and broadly based social interventions can amplify and increase individual differences (Baltes, 1998; Bronfenbrenner & Ceci, 1994; Ceci & Papierno, 2005; Gustafsson & Undheim, 1996).

If we accept the premise that equality of opportunity does not mean the same treatment for all, and equal learning opportunity will not yield equal outcomes, then differentiated curriculum and instruction should be tailored to individuals' learning potential as evidenced by one's demonstrated levels of knowledge, skills, and motivation (i.e. aptitude complex; see Ackerman, 2003; Cronbach, 2002). In the absence of such evidence because of lack of exposure and opportunity, some aptitude tests (verbal or nonverbal) may be used. It should be pointed out quickly that this learning potential should not be equated with any single test score, IQ or otherwise, though general aptitude tests still have their utilities for educational placement. A person's readiness for a particular learning opportunity depends on a host of personal and contextual variables and is at least partly domain specific. In short, a more defensible (and equitable) practice is to judge the likelihood of success for a particular educational provision based on the current level of abilities and mastery related to the subject taught, rather than putative, abstract notion of generic learning potential (Matthews & Foster, 2006).

Based on appropriate assessment, a continuum of educational provisions can be made, some suitable for many and others suitable only to a relatively few (Renzulli & Reis, 1997; Shore & Delcourt, 1996). In talent development models, advanced levels of knowledge and skills in a discipline or domain become a justification for extended curricular experiences usually not available in regular classrooms (Matthews & Foster, 2006; Subotnik & Coleman, 1996). Special arrangements for precocious and advanced learners, such as acceleration and flexible grouping, do not necessarily mean additional educational expenditure, though more administrative flexibility and instructional adaptation is called for (Benbow & Stanley, 1996). Many accelerated arrangements, programs, and schools, because of the shortened schooling, can be a money-saver (Benbow & Stanley, 1996; Robinson, 2005). To be sure, sometimes self-contained programs and schools are created to address educational needs of the advanced such as Talent Search programs and special schools (Benbow & Stanley, 1996; Stanley, 1997). These programs and schools may have higher requirements for teaching staff, but are not necessarily more costly compared with regular programs and schools.

Incidentally, it is worth noting that merit-based programs or honors college at a university level tend to be less controversial. But since K–12 education in most developed countries is supported by tax dollars (except private elite boarding schools; see Gaztambide-Fernández, 2009), whether resource distribution is fair is a politically sensitive issue. For example, a decision to set up a selective governor's academy in a state very much depends on the state legislators' (and their constituents') values and priorities. The issue of resource allocation and distribution involves the politics of balancing various concerns and priorities and thus cannot be solved by educational research. However, a sound decision is constrained by what we know about human potential, individual differences in this regard, how effective a given educational provision would be for a particular group of learners, and what kind of social and economic returns one can expect. Indeed, depending on where policy makers put their stake, education interventions can potentially widen the achievement gap rather than reducing it (Ceci & Papierno, 2005). In short, research helps address the question of *effectiveness*, but it is up to the relevant stakeholders to decide whether a particular educational provision, including gifted education, serves a valuable and worthy cause.

Psychosocial Conditions as an Equity Issue

Opportunity and curriculum issues aside, critics of gifted education are often concerned about the psychosocial impact of gifted-education practice on students not identified as gifted. Sapon-Shevin (1996) argued that unidentified students suffer emotionally as a result of their separation from gifted programs, and lack of social interaction and mutual acceptance disrupts the learning community of a school. As I point out in Chapter 1, the social construction of "the gifted child" was largely indebted to massive intelligence testing initiated by Terman at the beginning of the 20th century. Even then, Terman was confronted by opponents who were seriously concerned about the ethical and social implications of making IQ tests "a sort of last judgment of the child's capacity" (see Lippmann, 1976, p. 19). Here, whether Terman was right or wrong in considering high-IQ children as "gifted children" par excellence is not the issue. What is at issue is the use of the generic "gifted" category to classify children into "gifted" and "nongifted" and its possible Pygmalion (i.e., self-fulfilling prophecy) effect on those who failed to make the cut. A case in point is William Shockley. The Shockley story illustrates well why psychosocial issues become an equity concern.

Shockley was a candidate for Terman's (1925) study of high-IQ children (i.e., the gifted), and his IQ score of 125 (on the Stanford-Binet) fell short of meeting a cutoff of 140 and later 135 set up by Terman. Shockley's mother suspected an error in her son's testing and requested a retest, but his second and then third test scores were still in the range of the 120s. By Gagné's metric-based system of levels of giftedness (Gagné, 2005a), Shockley would be classified as "mildly gifted." As a result, Shockley did not become one of the "Termites," as the participants of the Terman study were jokingly called, but he went ahead anyway to win a Nobel Prize in physics for developing the transistor, which revolutionized the electronics industry, a feat that arguably none of the Termites have achieved.

Here, the issue of interest is not the limits of the IQ or any psychological test in predictive efficacy, but that of the social attribution and self-attribution process related to dichotomizing students into two categories using quite arbitrary cutoffs.

Shockley seemed to be resilient enough to come out unscathed, though his mother was a bit distraught and frustrated. But what would happen if Shockley and his mother bought into the notion that Shockley was indeed not "gifted" and his parents conceded that indeed they had unduly high expectations of their son? What is clearly pertinent is that failing to make the cut and fit into the "gifted" category could cast a shadow on one's self-concept and put a damper on one's aspiration, particularly when IQ was thought in folk psychology to be a natural endowment (you are born with a certain amount of IQ) and indicative of limits of one's potential. Dweck (1999, 2006) convincingly shows in her research the impact of one's view of intelligence and ability as fixed versus incremental on people's goals, efforts, and persistence in the face of setbacks. Therefore, labeling some children as "gifted" and others as "nongifted" could send an unintended but nonetheless wrong message to students that only those students who are designated as "gifted" are privileged by God's gifts, as it were, to do something others cannot. Steele (1997) also shows the negative effect of "stereotype threat" on one's performance in academic or other pursuits; namely, the feeling that you belong to a social group that has a reputation of not doing something well can depress your relevant performance, particularly when the task involved is challenging. Given the importance of social environments in facilitating emergent talents, any educational and social practice that prematurely puts people in broad categories (disabled, average, gifted, etc.), potentially leading to lowered aspirations for people who are unfavorably designated, should raise concerns about equity (see Ambrose, 2000, for a more formal presentation). For example, the practice of tracking or labeling a handful of students "gifted" as if there were a generic category of such can have such an effect. In both examples, of course, situations and psychosocial influences can be complex, and negative effects can be inflicted on both the "gifted" and unidentified students. "The gifted" so labeled may feel threatened, because if they failed to demonstrate their superior ability in classroom, the suspicion that they were fakes would loom large (Dweck, 1999). In participating in gifted programs or selective schools, one can also experience reality shock and a shrinking self-image: A big fish in a little pond suddenly turns small in a big pond, with many bigger fish out there! (this is called the big-fish-little-pond effect; see Dai & Rinn, 2008; Marsh, Trautwein, Ludtke, Baumert, & Köller, 2007). However, by and large, concerns are more on the other side, that is, for those who end up in a lower track or get a message that by default they are not "gifted." By the same token, any theory or theoretical conjecture expressed by socially influential people should be carefully examined if it tends to perpetuate stereotypical images of particular social groups based on race, gender, or other social markers, as inferior in some fundamental way, such as in the case of Watson and Summers's respective remarks on racial differences in intelligence and women in math and science, mentioned at the beginning of this chapter. It is not that these theories are necessarily false scientifically or in a statistical sense, or that they are just simply "politically incorrect." Rather, it is the ethical implications of the possible negative psychosocial impact these remarks could have on youths who are developing their identity and need guidance and encouragement to develop their aspirations as well as their skills and talents (Worrell, 2007). It is ironic that Shockley became an IQ convert in his later years, probably influenced by Arthur Jensen, and made a strong argument about the supposed inferior intelligence of people of African descent compared with the intelligence level of Caucasians, and even advocated voluntary sterilization for those whose IQ was below 100. To be sure, we can still exercise our academic freedom and openly debate regarding, say, whether there are important biological differences that lead gifted girls and women to careers other than those in math and science (see Ceci, Williams, & Barnett, 2009; Dai, 2002, 2006; Pinker & Spelke, 2005; Spelke & Grace, 2006; Summers, 2005). But statistics, however compelling, cannot directly lead to conclusions about particular individuals. Unlike sociology, which is mainly concerned with groups and group-related regularities and principles (e.g., see Herrnstein & Murray, 1994), education is fundamentally about individuals. There are philosophical and psychological reasons why individuals' potential should not be seen in a deterministic way.

According to Scheffler (1985), human potential is fundamentally related to the freedom and ability to exercise the power of personal agency. The purpose of education is to empower one's learning and give one the power of self-development and the freedom to determine what sort of characteristics one will have and what kind of person one will be. Therefore, an educational practice that claims to know the degrees of one's potential, thereof, is not only arrogant but also limiting in realizing human potential (Renzulli, 1986). It is not accidental that Rawls's (1971) theory of justice puts self-respect and the liberty to explore selves as a central issue of justice. Philosophical arguments aside, human development has such complexity and uncertainty that no single predictor or even a conceivable combination of multiple predictors can fully predict developmental outcomes. By the same token, excellence in various domains of human endeavor is not predetermined, but influenced by multiple factors, personal, contextual and developmental. On both philosophical and psychological grounds, protecting and enhancing students' sense of personal agency is a moral imperative of any education system. It does not mean that we should eliminate advanced placement programs, gifted programs, and selective schools for the sake of not hurting anyone's feelings and dampening anyone's spirits. It does mean, however, that our educational practice should not create psychosocial impediments, such as pigeonholing students into different categories in a way that creates unproductive, and often times detrimental, social stereotypes.

GIFTED EDUCATION IN BROADER SOCIOCULTURAL CONTEXTS

Ceci and Williams (2005) showed that social interventions (including education) would help the have-nots (i.e., the cognitively disadvantaged) gain, but such interventions would help the "haves" (i.e., cognitively advantaged) gain even more;

efforts to bring those in the bottom up to close the achievement gap are unsuccessful because of the Matthew Effect (i.e., a comparative advantage tends to self-propagate so that the rich get richer). The resentment of educational reformers against gifted education could be somewhat mitigated by realizing that fairness and equality do not mean that all students can attain the same level of academic excellence; the reformers have to reckon with the reality that education tends to increase, rather than decrease—let alone eliminate—individual differences because of the differential learning payoff. Blaming the efforts to help precocious and advanced students for increasing the achievement gap between the "haves" and "have-nots" is unproductive. As Silverman pointed out, "Holding back the brightest students will not magically help the slower ones; bringing the top down does not bring the bottom up" (cited in Benbow & Stanley, 1996, p. 256).

Sergiovanni, Kelleher, McCarthy, and Wirt (2004) identified four public values guiding educational policy and decision making: excellence, equity, choice, and efficiency. Balancing acts are needed because exerting one value tends to infringe upon other values. For example, the No Child Left Behind (NCLB) Act under the Bush administration can be criticized as seeking equity and efficiency at the cost of excellence and choice. Excellence is compromised as billions of dollars in public money have been spent to develop basic skills and lift up those at the bottom at the cost of neglecting high-order skills and high-achieving students (see Loveless, Farkas, & Duffett, 2008). The NCLB initiative also threatened the value of choice, as it was quite heavy-handed in its implementation; local input and decision-making power were restricted. For gifted education, excellence is always the main goal and top priority, though equity, choice, and efficiency should be taken into consideration.

How to juggle these values and priorities? Unfortunately, there is no fixed formula. But we can call upon all practitioners in the field to adopt a value-conscious, reflective approach to gifted education, what I call Responsive and Responsible Educational Practice (RREP). An educational practice is *responsive* to the extent that it socially and instructionally supports emergent talents, interests, and excellence in school subjects or other important cultural endeavors and skill domains, in a proactive as well as reactive manner. An educational practice is *responsible* to the extent that it is equitable as well as efficient, fully accountable in terms of equitable access as well as its effectiveness and efficiency in promoting and producing excellence. All existing practices can be scrutinized according to this RREP principle. Educational innovations in gifted education can be fashioned based on the principle.

CONCLUSION: EQUAL OPPORTUNITY, BUT NOT EQUAL OUTCOMES

There is compelling evidence of individual differences in the rate and asymptote of achievement in academic, artistic, and practical fields. However, there is no evidence that a potential for excellence in various domains of human endeavor is predetermined or preordained by genetics. There is no sure way to tell who will be the most successful, given a line of human endeavor in adulthood, though short-term and long-term prediction can be made about the trajectories and pathways based on proper assessment (Lubinski & Benbow, 2006). Therefore, a once-and-for-all identification/selection system is scientifically untenable and ethically problematic. Checking for progress should be conducted continually to ensure appropriate placement, and a fair and flexible entry-and-exit policy should be put in place for quality control of particular programming efforts.

Equity in the educational context means equitable and fair opportunity to develop personal excellence, not equal outcomes of excellence, or the same treatment for all. Therefore, there should be an assessment system that assists decisions based on advancing needs of students, solidly grounded in evidence of emergent excellence or potential for excellence for a particular human endeavor, not on some vague or unwarranted assumptions about a generic category of "the gifted."

Gifted education should be about excellence, not about "giftedness." The fact that someone demonstrates excellence or potential for excellence in an age-appropriate manner warrants educational attention and investment in a society that values excellence. Strivings for excellence are a personal decision and choice, usually encouraged and supported by familiar and communal environments and social institutions that value excellence. As a corollary, excellence is earned; being "gifted" does not entitle a person to privileged access to gifted education; passion for and commitment to excellence in areas of one's choosing is an essential element.

Arguments against gifted education as elitism in a wholesale fashion are made at the cost of loss of talent. Conversely, dogmatic adherence to a view of a stratified society based on IQ or other fixed categorical approaches is also highly problematic, because it is based on the faulty assumption that some standardized aptitude tests can tell us in a once-and-for-all fashion who has the highest potential and who will be most successful. A new paradigm is needed that is supported by scientific evidence and meets the moral imperatives of excellence and equity.

Toward a New Synthesis in Understanding Gifted Development: A Framework for Gifted Studies

The idea that development could actually transform a person's gifts has not had much currency in the field to date, and the failure to embrace a more profound concept of development is at the heart of the current tension in the field as well as the key to its future.

—David Henry Feldman, "A Developmental, Evolutionary Perspective on Giftedness"

Growth is the key ingredient for the generation of snow-crystal patterns.... Even the tiniest protruding points will grow faster than their surroundings and thus protrude even more. Small corners grow into branches; random bumps on the branches grow into side branches. Complexity is born.

—Kenneth Libbrecht, "Snowflake Science"

IN CHAPTERS 3, 4, and 5, I discussed three key ontological issues regarding the nature of giftedness: nature-nurture, domain generality or specificity, and quantitative-qualitative differences—asserting that how we conceptualize giftedness along these dimensions directly affects the way we think about educational programming. At the same time, as I demonstrated in the preceding chapters on the means and ends of gifted education and the issue of excellence and equity, all the issues involved reflect values shared and contested within the community of education as well as society at large. However, they hinge on beliefs about the nature of human potential and various manifestations of excellence. In this chapter, I propose a unified framework that moves away from dichotomous thinking about the nature-nurture, domain-generality or -specificity, and quantitative-qualitative issues, and toward a model of contextual and developmental emergence and evolution of excellence.

Lohman (2006) suggested that theories of ability and achievement develop across four somewhat sequential levels. Level 1 is "naive nominalism," whereby tests of ability such as intelligence tests are seen as measuring genetically based capacity; Level 2 contains an awareness of the ability/achievement overlap and an understanding that abilities are developed through interacting with environments, rather than provided innately; Level 3 focuses on "island kingdoms" and the exploration of a multitude of isolated endogenous and exogenous causes for high abilities; and at Level 4, system theories and complex integrated models are developed to explain how high abilities evolve. Based on current theoretical perspectives and empirical evidence, giftedness as demonstrated competence is best understood from a Level 4 vantage point, as a complex process of becoming and growing, rather than an absolute or fixed state of being.

As I pointed out in previous chapters, giftedness is a competence concept and can be contrasted with excellence, which is a performance concept. Excellence is manifest, while giftedness or superior levels of competence can be inferred from some evidence of excellence. Evidence can take a variety of forms. A child who answers a set of IQ questions brilliantly or who figures out a novel way to solve a math problem provides evidence of excellence by age-appropriate standards, from which "giftedness" might be inferred. But increasingly we are finding that that "giftedness"—if any—is unlikely to be demonstrated to the same extent or in the same way if the same child's performance or competence is assessed 5 years later or in different situations (Gottfried, Gottfried, & Guerin, 2009; Lohman & Korb, 2006). *The invariance or fixed quality of giftedness across tests, domains, situations, and time, as assumed by Level 1 theorists, is untenable and unwarranted.* For example, an IQ score of 130 obtained at the age of 16 means different things, developmentally and functionally, than the same score obtained at the age of 6, even though the relative standing (against age norms) that the score represents is the same (McCall, 1981). This leads Carroll (1997) to propose a developmental definition of mental-age IQ scores as "a measure of the rate at which the child's *mental age* improves as a result of exposure to the culture and learning from it" (p. 38). "Mental age scores indicate the absolute amount of progress *achieved*, by whatever means (genetic or environmental) in attaining the mental skills and knowledges [*sic*]" (p. 37; emphasis added). To be sure, it is open to debate whether IQ scores should be better seen as highly enduring or malleable mental qualities (i.e., whether they should be treated as competence or performance; see Ceci & Williams, 1997) and whether the putative ability so measured is "general" enough to warrant the name "general ability" or even "general intelligence" (see Chapter 4 for discussion). However, one thing is certain: Intelligence, as a mental property, however defined, is subject to developmental changes, qualitatively (i.e., discontinuously) as well as quantitatively. In that sense, intelligence is an attained, rather than biologically preordained and fixed, state. In other words, it is an emergent property of the developing person that keeps evolving and changing while interacting with and adapting to specific functional environments. By the same token, to paraphrase Carroll's remarks on intelligence, gifted competence can be inferred by the amount of progress achieved, by whatever means, nature or nurture. Therefore, the most important theoretical issue is not what "giftedness" is as a trait or a constellation of traits, but the process of giftedness in the making.

GIFTEDNESS IN THE MAKING:
BASIC TENETS OF DIFFERENTIAL DEVELOPMENT

Charting the developmental process of becoming exceptionally competent instead of identifying essential traits has been recommended in the concluding chapters of each of the two editions of *Conceptions of Giftedness* edited by Sternberg and Davidson (Mayer, 2005; Siegler & Kotovsky, 1986) and in volumes exploring giftedness from a developmental perspective (Balchin, Hymer, & Matthews, 2009; Feldman, 2003; Horowitz, Subotnik, & Matthews, 2009). It is also consistent with the consensus definition that Mayer (2005) suggested, that is, to "view giftedness as an age-specific term that refers to potential for the beginning stage, achievement for the intermediate stage, and eminence for the advanced stage" (p. 439).

How might we visually represent giftedness in the making? Such a chart would have to include what we know about key dimensions of human development, incorporating the dynamic, open, living systems that affect human development, including *functional, developmental,* and *temporal* dimensions of human functioning (Dai & Renzulli, 2008; cf. Ford, 1994) (see Figure 9.1).

Figure 9.1. Schematic representation of three critical dimensions of human functioning and development. The oval indicates a unit of analysis that intersects the three dimensions. The arrows signify the dynamic nature and direction of the three dimensions.

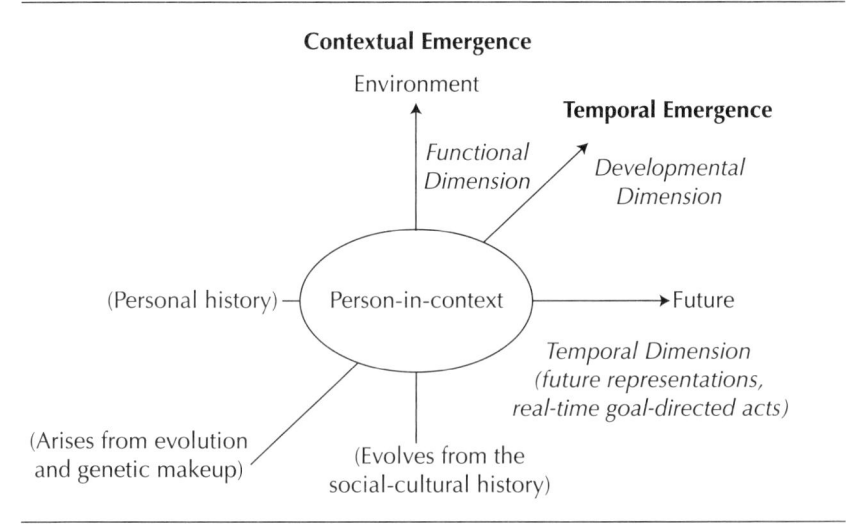

Note: Originally published in Dai & Renzulli, 2008.

The Functional, Temporal, and Developmental Dimensions

As shown in Figure 9.1, there are three dimensions that jointly define a particular functional and developmental state of the person in question:

- *Functional dimension.* In Figure 9.1, the vertical line refers to the person-environment functional relations and the nature of an individual as an open, self-organizing, self-directed, adaptive system, constantly exchanging energy and information with its environment, capable of changing itself as well as its environment. Consider a simple example of an infant attempting to reach out and grasp a toy. An infant and a toy here constitute a functional relation: A toy *invites* grasping, so to speak (sometimes called an *affordance*), but it also poses challenges to an infant (or, *task constraints*). What we characterize as gifted and talented behavior or performance always involves a set of functional relations, particularly the effectiveness of the person's functioning vis-à-vis the affordances and demands of a specific task environment, supported by the social-cultural history of human endeavors. In educational settings, such functional relations mainly concern the readiness or proneness of particular individual learners to make learning gains from particular instructional conditions (Snow & Lohman, 1984).
- *Temporal dimension.* The horizontal line indicates the temporal dimension of a dynamic system: Transactions and interactions between an individual agent and a task environment take place through time. The temporally evolving nature of these interactions can be represented as a *trajectory* through a state space. For example, an infant may initially fail to grasp the toy in question, but with improved visual-motor coordination over time, the child finally succeeds (Smith & Thelen, 1993). The arrow here indicates two things: the temporal sequence or time series of an action, and the future-oriented, goal-directed nature of human behavior; that is, a self-directed human agent anticipates future states of an action (even for an infant or toddler, what developmental psychologists call *means-end readiness or sensitivity*) and behaves accordingly (e.g., making self-corrections based on feedback). Thus, what we characterize as gifted and talented behaviors or competences are not only situated in functional relations (i.e., having a functional dimension) but also have a temporal trajectory (evolving from the past state and moving toward a future state).
- *Developmental dimension.* The diagonal line indicates the developmental dimension. I define *development* as incremental or qualitative changes occurring within the developing person, on various time scales, while he or she is interacting with a specific task environment. Thus, an infant's engagement in coordinated motor acts promotes the development

of coordination skills (to use Piaget's term, a "grasping scheme" is developed). Although biological maturation contributes to his or her growth, it is contingent on experience, learning, and cultural provisions, which play an indispensable role in how far human competence of the intellectual, artistic, or practical nature develops. Therefore, development involves gradual and orderly changes as a result of physical maturation as well as adaptive interactions of the individual with an environment (the functional dimension) over time (the temporal dimension).

The Contextual, Emergent, and Dynamic (CED) model maps out the interaction of these three dimensions (see Dai & Renzulli, 2008). Namely, (a) differential development of competence is situated in functional contexts; (b) person-task interactions and transactions have a characteristic temporal trajectory; and (c) competence is thereby understood as the emergent self-organized complexity of human behavior. *From this perspective, manifested gifted competencies are emergent properties of person-task transactions and functional relations over time, which are subject to further change (including discontinuous one).* As shown in Figure 9.1, I think of the emergent person-task relationship properties as *contextual emergence*, and the development of new cognitive structures (e.g., modules, schemas, mental models, theories) and affective features (i.e., proclivities, interests, identity) over time as *temporal emergence* (Dai, 2005). This general principle applies to the whole range of phenomena associated with exceptional competence, from the achievements of child prodigies to adult eminent accomplishments.

Basic Tenets of Human Development

Thus, the development of gifts and talents follows the usual general principles of the human living system (open, dynamically self-organizing and adaptive, and intentional), rather than being exceptional to these general principles. Extreme forms of differential development—including but not particular to gifted and talent development—are consistent with the following basic tenets of human development:

- *Flexible agency.* Unlike the makeup of other animals, which have relatively fixed, preformed developmental pathways, human biology affords individuals a certain degree of neural plasticity and cognitive flexibility in their development. Although there is surely much heterogeneity in the developing brain and surely many dedicated learning and functioning mechanisms that help human beings cope with specific challenges (language, social interaction, spatial navigation, etc.), the human ability to acquire novel, complex skills through adaptive learning and extended periods of special training and development is a major mechanism for skill and talent development. In short, human beings are not just *rigid, reactive* creatures, but rather *flexible, creative* beings.

• *Differential development.* Individual human beings have both genetically shared and individually unique predispositions, propensities, and potentialities. As a general rule, individuals tend to gravitate toward capitalizing on their strengths and comparative advantages in carving out their developmental niches. However, specific developmental paths and trajectories are contingent on a person's environmental experience and learning. Early upbringing, socially structured activities, and fortuitous encounters all play a role. Given the same environmental circumstances, genetic predispositions bias the developing person in certain directions and pathways, but in and of themselves do not determine developmental outcomes. Given the same genetic makeup (e.g., identical twins), different opportunity structures and environmental experiences help shape differential developmental pathways and trajectories. In short, differential development is a joint function of genetic and environmental variability (Gottlieb, 1998; McCall, 1981).

• *Self-organization and temporal emergence.* Many aspects of mental functioning show *dynamic instability* and are capable of self-engendered adaptive changes (e.g., error detection and self-correction) to enhance the individual's effectiveness in specific contexts and result in emergent patterns of behavioral and psychological complexity. It is important to note that self-organization here is a *spontaneous* formation of patterns or pattern changes that occur as the person-environment interaction temporally unfolds: "There is no 'self' inside the system responsible for emergent pattern[s]. Rather, under certain conditions, the system organizes itself. There is no ghost in the machine, instructing the parts how to behave" (Kelso, 2000, p. 65).

• *Self-directedness.* Self-directedness is a principle applicable only to *intentional* living systems. Although there is no homunculus (miniature person) inside the head pulling the strings, and no ghost in the machine, human beings are capable of regulating and directing their own behavior according to their intention and determination so that some degree of unity, identity, and continuity can be maintained. Because of their self-awareness, reflectivity, and symbolic capability, human beings are able to reconstruct the past, represent the present, and model the future (Edelman, 1989). They can exercise self-direction and self-regulation through feedback control of the implementation of current goals or feedforward anticipation of future states and possibilities. It is in this sense that some developmental theorists consider humans as producers of their own development (e.g., Lerner & Busch-Rossnagel, 1981); self-directedness and the ability to mentally represent, and strive for, a future state is a unique form of agency not shared by other creatures, whose lives are mostly defined

by moment-to-moment existence, albeit with some capability of selecting their habitats for the viability of their long-term survival and reproduction.
• *Balancing instability and stability.* This is a challenge that any complex, open living system has to face. The openness creates both opportunity and hazards. To be viable and creative, complex living beings have to avoid rigidity on the one hand, and chaos on the other. They have to be sensitive to new opportunities and possibilities in order to be adaptive and innovative, yet stable enough to function properly and not get overwhelmed by the bombardment of new information and stimulation. In Michael Crichton's (1996) words, "There is enough innovation to keep a living system vibrant, and enough stability to keep it from collapsing into anarchy" (p. 4). In order for extreme developmental complexity and novelty to occur (e.g., to be creative), however, "self-organized systems may even tune themselves to stay near critical points" (Kelso, 2000, p. 68).

In short, the five tenets of human development—flexible agency, differential development, self-organization and temporal emergence, self-directedness, and the balancing of stability and instability—are applicable to all kinds of developmental trajectories and pathways, including the development of gifted competencies. The development of excellence, no matter the line of human endeavor, does not deviate from these basic tenets, but rather highlights them.

How do we investigate the development of exceptional competence in a way that is consistent with these principles? The answer is to identify the units of analysis and research methodology that allow us to observe these principles *in action.* Specifically, we need to look at functional relationships of the person with *that individual's* environments, social, symbolic (or semiotic), as well as physical. This process may take place at the microlevel (days and weeks) or macrolevel (months and years, or even decades).

IDENTIFYING EMERGENT AND EVOLVING PROPERTIES BASED ON LEVELS OF ANALYSIS

How does a contextual, emergent, and dynamic model differ from the traditional models? Historically, studies of giftedness were deeply influenced by (even entrenched in) the psychometric tradition, with its underlying nomothetic assumption of universally valid human traits. Its practical consequence is a categorical approach to identifying and educating "the gifted" based on arbitrarily determined cutoffs on certain test scores. While both the CED and traditional models are attempts to understand developmental diversity and psychological individuality, the CED framework I delineate here attempts to capture the *developmental processes.* The CED framework also relies on a conception of levels of analysis I have suggested for studying the emergence of gifted behaviors or competencies (Dai, 2005).

Levels of analysis are epistemic tools or devices used to analyze complex systems, which are best conceptualized as multilevel phenomena (Newell, 1990; Rasmussen, 1993). The human being is a complex system and consists of numerous complex subsystems or sub-sub-systems. Human development, when conceptualized as a system change, involves many levels of analysis, from molecular and cellular to tissues, organs, neural circuits, and modular systems; from biological to social-cultural; from the individual to the collective; and temporally, from simple formation of functional units to increasingly complex differentiation and organization of knowledge and skills, from small time scales or units (minutes and hours) to large time scales (years and decades) of developmental changes. The levels of analysis I propose here are informed by three epistemic stances proposed by Dennett (1987): the physical, design, and intentional levels of explanation, discussed in Chapter 6; by Pylyshyn's (1984) model of cognitive architecture; and by Newell's (1990) model of human functional hierarchy and related time scales (see Dai, 2005). It also draws on a model of personality development proposed by McAdams and Pals (2006), who differentiated four levels of differential personality development.

The basic assumption or premise of this framework is *differential development*, that is, self-development of individual human beings tends to go in many directions in terms of competencies, interests, preferences, and values. This approach synthesizes differential (individual difference) psychology and developmental psychology; the former has never adequately dealt with developmental issues, and the latter has never adequately dealt with individual differences in development, including development of giftedness and talent (Horowitz, 2009; Roberts & Pomerantz, 2004). The tendency of differential development is undergirded by the tenets of self-organization and self-direction, among others discussed earlier. The framework is meant to explain differential development in all its manifestations, including, but not limited to, the development of exceptional competence and excellence. Differential development can be subjected to four levels of analysis: (a) disposition and aptitude (biological-constitutional or physical level), (b) characteristic adaptations (design or program level), (c) construction of self and future (intentional level), and (d) the differential role of social-cultural environments (activity level) (see Figure 9.2).

Level I: Dispositions and Aptitudes (Biological-Constitutional or Physical Level)

Much of the research on giftedness has been in the tradition of differential psychology and psychometrics and can be characterized as describing traits that define giftedness at the biological-constitutional or physical level. McAdams and Pals (2006) are mainly concerned with broad personality traits that are functional in social situations. Psychometric research on human abilities focus on cognitive traits, broad or narrow (e.g., Carroll, 1993). While both are characteristically

Figure 9.2. The human functioning hierarchy mapped on the epistemic/methodological continuum.

Epistemic Lenses	Methods	Human Functioning Hierarchy
Constructivism or emergentism	Complex units of analysis; multilayered, nested, higher-level organization	Activity level
		Intentional level
		Design or program level
	Simple units of analysis; decomposable, constituent, lower-level components	Biological-constitutional or physical level
Atomism or reductionism		

metric based, and inherently comparative (i.e., norm referenced) and differential, personality traits are often defined as bipolar (e.g., you are either more extroverted or more introverted), while ability traits are seen as unipolar (e.g., you have a relatively high or low IQ). This level of analysis corresponds to Tier 1 abilities and dispositions discussed in Chapter 4, which can be inferred through testing and observation.

Following the conventional use of the terms, *aptitude* is more of an ability concept (e.g., working memory capacity, reading proficiency [Just & Carpenter, 1992; Kyllonen & Christal, 1990]), and *disposition* is more of a personality concept (e.g., sensation seeking [Zuckerman, 2004] or overexcitability [Ackerman, 2009]). Most psychological traits of the ability or personality type are emergenic and epigenetic. That is, there is no one-to-one correspondence between specific genes and certain psychological traits. Rather, it is a combination of genetic expressions vis-à-vis environmental stimulation and behavioral interaction that gives rise to a particular phenotype (psychological trait; see Simonton, 2005). For a trait to be important to a specific line of advanced development or, to use Bronfenbrenner's (1989) words, for a trait to be "developmentally instigative" (p. 219), the following conditions have to be satisfied:

- *Biological constitutionality.* A personality or ability trait is considered *constitutional* if it is a stable and enduring characteristic of the person as a biological being, not easily altered by changing circumstances and environments. It could be directly based on a particular genetic makeup, or emergenic (polygenic) and epigenetic, whereby phenotypes can vary depending on when and how genes get activated and expressed in bidirectional interaction with other genes and with other levels of the developmental system (Gottlieb, 1998). Heritability of a particular trait can be used to support the biological constitutionality, though some biopsychological traits are nongenetic but developmentally calibrated (Gershwind & Galaburda, 1987; Simonton, 2008).

- *Predictive validity.* There should be evidence not only for its stability in order to justify the "constitutional" nature of a trait (e.g., high IQ or introversion), but also for its predictive validity vis-à-vis some meaningful outcome measures, such as achievement in a near or far future, in order to satisfy the demonstrability and productivity criteria (Sternberg, 1995).
- *Internal validity.* Since achievement can be influenced by many endogenous and exogenous factors, the best evidence for the role of a trait is to show the extent to which a trait influences the rate and asymptote of learning in a domain in a relatively controlled setting (Shiffrin, 1996). Without such evidence, strong arguments for the causal role of a particular trait (e.g., high IQ) cannot be made; for example, the strong predictive relationship between IQ and academic achievement does not necessarily represent a causal relationship but could be at least partly explained by the overlap of the tasks sampled (Sternberg, 1999b).
- *Psychological mechanisms.* Although a trait may be relatively domain specific (e.g., sensitivity to music, or a flair for cracking codes) or relatively domain general (e.g., working memory capacity, analytic reasoning), it must be functionally meaningful vis-à-vis a task situation; that is, there must be strong reason to believe the ability or disposition in question facilitates performance in the situation in a major way (necessary or central for the execution of a task at hand; see Sternberg, 1986).
- *Boundary conditions.* A trait may be differentially important, depending on stage of development and functional contexts (Ackerman, 1999; Lohman, 2005a; Simonton, 1999; Subotnik & Jarvin, 2005). For example, high facility in analytic reasoning may be very important in mathematical problem solving, but less so for social problem solving; intuition-based ease of learning may be highly important in early stages of development but less so for later stages. In short, the conditions under which a trait is effective need to be specified.

Trait-level explanations of gifted competencies as differential development are in effect *material and efficient explanations* based on the Aristotle's scheme of causes or explanatory factors discussed in Chapter 6, and thus reductionistic in nature. Trait explanations, as material and efficient explanations, should be distinguished from innatist explanations, which constitute "formal" explanations, as they implicate a structural cause; for example, a gifted musician, according to innatist explanations, is not merely functionally superior to others in music, but also innately equipped with some superior neural-cognitive structures or modules dedicated to music. Blurring the distinction between material and formal explanations causes much confusion and cross-purpose communication (e.g., see Howe et al., 1998 for the "natural talent" debate).

Trait explanations of superior performance are based on interindividual differences. To predict differential development, it is not sufficient to understand interindividual differences along a few nomothetic or universal dimensions. Sometimes, it is not merely the interindividual differences in abilities but *intra-individual differences* in patterning or self-organization of abilities and dispositions that determine the developmental pathways (Ackerman, 2003; Lohman, 1994b; Lubinski & Benbow, 2006). This is a more idiographic aspect of differential development with which the next level of analysis attempts to come to grips.

Level II: Characteristic Adaptations (Design or Program Level)

The trait approach uses a reductionistic strategy, simplifying things through the isolation of basic variables and tracing the origins in terms of the most basic constituents. However, an organism as a functioning entity has a level of organizational complexity that is not captured by any trait descriptions, singly or in combination. McAdams and Pals (2006) used the term *characteristic adaptations* to describe this organism-level differentiation. Adaptations are "characteristic" because there are nonrandom, structural regularities involved in person-situation interaction, as if by design, to use Dennett's (1987) design stance. A focus on characteristic adaptations reflects an understanding that "*human lives vary with respect to a wide range of motivational, social-cognitive, and developmental adaptations, contextualized in time, place, and/or social role*" (McAdams & Pals, 2006, p. 208; emphasis added).

Characteristic adaptations include all the ways in which individuals adapt to their environments, ranging from highly general, such as a people versus object orientation, to highly specific, such as a strong interest in certain academic topics but not others, or a preference for a certain musical style but not others. In the context of the development of gifted potential and excellence, characteristic adaptations typically show leanings and preferences in a specific direction and trajectories of development that are tractable in terms of the type (performer versus producer), domain (academic, artistic, and human service), and style (creative versus proficient) of gifted expression (see Tannenbaum, 1997, discussed in Chapter 4; see also Chapter 7). This level of analysis better captures Tier 2 competencies and interests or aptitude complexes discussed in Chapter 4.

There are three main differences between traits and characteristic adaptations. First, while traits are often defined nomothetically, assuming universal functional dimensions along which all individuals from a population differ quantitatively, characteristic adaptations imply qualitative differences in how individuals make adaptations vis-à-vis an impinging environment. Second, a trait is a static, decontextualized description of the person, presumably stable over time and functional across many situations, whereas a characteristic adaptation is dynamic, functional, and contextually bound, involving real-time person-situation (and content-process) interaction, and is subject to microdevelopment (i.e., dynamic adaptation in days, weeks, and months; Granott & Parziale, 2002). Third, a trait is a relatively "pure," single-dimensional cognitive, affective, or conative quality, whereas characteristic adaptation is multifaceted and holistic, integrating cognitive, affective, and motivational functions (hence *aptitude complex*; see Ackerman, 2003). Therefore, in a characteristic adaptation, the line between the cognitive (or "intellectual") and "noncognitive" (or "nonintellective"), between ability and disposition, is blurred.

If traits are seen as biologically constitutional, characteristic adaptation reflects the higher-order principles of flexible agency and self-organization in adaptation to environmental opportunities and challenges and thus cannot be attributed solely to endogenous causes (i.e., personal factors). While acknowledging the role of personal traits, early emergence of gifted and talented competencies can be better characterized as characteristic adaptations (Feldman, 1986). Trait explanations are material and efficient in that a trait facilitates certain functions (e.g., "openness to experience" facilitates consideration of new alternatives). Elucidating differential development by resorting to the notion of characteristic adaptation represents both *formal and efficient explanations*. Such an explanation is formal in the sense that there are structural regularity and organizational principles involved to make someone this kind of person rather than other kinds, just like a construction project takes shape as a bridge, rather than a house, or as a bridge of its own kind, rather than other kinds, with its unique structural, functional, and aesthetic features. Characteristic adaptation constitutes an *efficient explanation* as well, in that there are underlying affective and motivational mechanisms that promote a certain adaptation and make it much easier than other kinds of adaptation for that individual. For example, it may be manifested as an enduring interest or *selective affinity* (see Dai & Renzulli, 2008).

To put the notion of characteristic adaptation in the larger context of psychological thinking and theorizing, a focus on characteristic adaptations in general developmental research is relatively recent, largely thanks to new conceptualizations of development as adaptive (Siegler, 1996) and an emergent emphasis on self-organization vis-à-vis contextual affordances and challenges and developmental dynamism (Fischer & Bidell, 2006). Inventive research techniques, including microgenetic methods (Siegler, 1996), which have a distinct idiographic flavor, have facilitated this kind of thinking about development, moving away from the Cartesian rationalist model of development (e.g., an increasingly rational mind is developed to cope with the complexity of the world; Piaget, 1950/2001) toward a more evolution-based model of development (e.g., structures, properties, or strategies are developmentally selected and modified because of their functional utilities in situ; see Siegler, 1996; see Fischer & Bidell, 2006, for general discussion).

Various aspects of development as characteristic adaptations have been studied, such as how children approach mathematical problem-solving tasks, explain causal connections (Siegler, 1996, 2002), and coordinate theory and evidence in the development of scientific thinking (Kuhn, 2002). This line of thinking about development as adaptation and self-organization has also forged a new union with the personality research, which has long been wrestling with the issue of trait versus state of personality functioning, and now seems to have come to terms with itself (see Mischel & Shoda, 1995) by using concepts similar to characteristic adaptations, such as situation-behavior profiles (p. 249) and personality dispositions as "a characteristic cognitive-affective processing structure" that generate distinct processing dynamics (p. 257).

Moving away from a focus on traits to a focus on characteristic adaptation as a principle for analyzing and explaining differential development indicates a shift to a higher level of organizational complexity based on the functional hierarchy represented in Figure 9.2. Although traits may contribute to characteristic adaptation, effect sizes of the correlations between a particular trait or a set of traits and dynamically observed or measured characteristic adaptation are moderate (see Ackerman, 1988). This suggests that characteristic adaptations are an emergent property of person-situation interaction that creates a mesh or union of person, content, process, and context (Snow, 1992), which cannot be reduced to traits. In other words, eliminative reductionism is not empirically supported for differential development in general and the making of giftedness in particular.

Temporal and contextual emergence of competence as a result of characteristic adaptation is a shared vision of both developmental and gifted researchers (see Dweck, 2009; Horowitz, Subotnik, & Matthews, 2009). Dai and Renzulli (2008) proposed selective affinity, maximal grip, and being at the edge of chaos as three forms of characteristic adaptation that are situated in specific task environments and sensitive to stages of talent development and contextual feedback. Ericsson (1996, 2006) proposed extended deliberate practice (another form of characteristic adaptation) as a mechanism critical to the development of expertise. Instead of looking only at self-selection effects (endogenous efficient explanations) in person-situation interaction, the significant role of socialization (exogenous efficient explanations, such as formal and informal mentorship) should also be considered in the formation of characteristic adaptation (see the later discussion of the differentiating role of sociocultural forces). In this sense, education should not only be *reactively* responsive to characteristic adaptations displayed by students, but also *proactively* contribute to characteristic adaptations deem appropriate and desirable for individuals' optimal development.

Level III: Construction of Self and Future (Intentional Level)

To make any kind of advanced development sustainable, there must be some kind of inner control mechanisms that facilitate identity, continuity, and personal meaningfulness. I suggest that this is largely achieved through what McAdam and Pals (2006) called "integrative life narratives" (p. 209). McAdams and Pals treated this level of analysis as mainly concerned with identity development ("who I am"). In the context of talent development, the construction of self and future has broader implications for knowledge building and transformation (Gruber, 1986; Shavinina & Seeratan, 2004). It involves forming enduring interests, purposes, and commitments, creating what Ziegler (2005) called "subjective action space" (p. 417), and following through with personal initiatives. From this point of view, characteristic adaptations cannot be a purely spontaneous, blind process of self-organization and adaptation. For example, individuals who are engaged in deliberate practice typically have specific future goals in mind. Explanations of differential development that involves deliberate acquisition of Tier 2 and Tier 3 competencies discussed in Chapter 4 have to resort to this level of analysis.

Dweck (1999, 2006) provides a compelling argument for the role of intentional self when she demonstrates that how people view themselves and their future directly influences what they pay attention to, what kind of goals they espouse, how much effort they are willing to expend, and how persistent they are in the face of setbacks. It is safe to assume, based on the preponderance of evidence, that individuals vary in the ways their selfhood is constructed and in the extent to which they develop enduring interests, purposes, and commitments that advance their talent development and creative productivity. *This aspect of differential development becomes increasingly decisive given the prolonged nature of development of talent and excellence.* It does not mean, of course, that a person has to set up long-term goals and stick to them no matter the changing life circumstances. It does mean, however, that he or she has to periodically reflect on and envision the kind of developmental niches, social roles, and domain contributions that are most promising for him- or herself given the available opportunities and challenges.

Although this level of description may involve traits, such as capacity, zeal, and willingness to work (Galton, 1869), as well as characteristic adaptations, such as maximal grip or organized persistence (Dai & Renzulli, 2008), the intentional-level explanation argues for the contextual, evolving nature of various forms of self-directedness such as enduring interests, purposes, and commitments (Csikszentmihalyi et al., 1993; Gruber, 1986) and specificity of social and cultural contents and contexts in which the self-construction is embedded or situated (Freeman, 2005). Edelman (1995), a neuroscientist and the 1972 Nobel Prize winner for physiology and medicine, argued that a unique characteristic of human beings is their ability to model the past and the future. He particularly stressed the role of emergence of selfhood, or *organization of purpose*, a term used by Gruber (1986), to explain the genesis of many eminent creative contributions. "By selfhood, I mean not just the individuality that emerges from genetics or immunology, but the personal individuality that emerges from developmental and social interactions" (Edelman, 1995, p. 201). This selfhood, with its remembered past and envisioned future, sets humans apart from "nonintentional objects" (p. 205).

Education, as one of the most important contextual factors, has much to do in shaping the way people view themselves and their future. It can be argued, indeed, that one of the main goals of education is to develop one's self-identity and possible selves (aspiring writers, scientists, business and social leaders, etc.), or "a personal image of excellence" (Bruner, 1979, p. 119), along with knowledge, skills, and dispositions achieved over time. Clearly, an "integrative personal narrative" in education settings goes beyond maintaining a coherent account of personal experiences; it involves a process of internalizing and transforming cultural practices, meanings, and symbol systems into a personally meaningful form (e.g., coherent life themes and career paths) through sustained, dedicated, purposeful efforts (Feldman, 2003). Construction of self and future reflects the tenet of self-directedness, and so can be considered as both *efficient and formal explanations* for differential development.

Silverstein (1988) saw "functional personal history" as the only way in which a full account of human individuality can be established. It is not coincidental that many scholars take this level of idiographic complexity into consideration when exploring the development of productive creativity (Amabile, 2001; Gardner, 1993; Gruber, 1981, 1998). Gruber's (1981) account of Darwin's intellectual journey leading to the theory of evolution illustrates and exemplifies this level of analysis. It shows how the tensions and personal conflicts experienced through confronting new information and knowledge led to the creation of an epoch-making theory. At this level, cultural contents of knowledge and beliefs are so inextricably connected with one's desires, thoughts, and feelings that without delving into this level of subjectivity, one cannot fully explain how specific advances in scientific and artistic domains were achieved (see Gruber, 1981; Fischer & Yan, 2002, for analyses of Darwin's theory development). As postulated by McAdams and Pals (2006), the integrative personal narrative or construction of self further refines the development of psychological individuality beyond characteristic adaptation. This holds true as well for the highly refined minds of eminent contributors to human civilization and culture.

Level IV: The Differentiating Role of Sociocultural Environments (Activity Level)

From a social-cultural point of view, all human activities, including academic ones, are embedded in larger social-cultural contexts that give meanings and purposes to these activities (Gee, 2003). Any competence, even as basic as an infant's language skills, can be seen as constructed through social communication with caregivers who tend to structure it in a way that facilitates the emergence of language competence (Snow, 1999). Therefore, there is always a "hidden hand" in developing human competencies: social-cultural structuring and mediation, which is often seamless and inconspicuous but powerful. This structuring and mediation does not merely serve as a catalyst to "facilitate" the development and expression of abilities and talents, but also helps shape the way we feel, think, and perform in a fundamental way (Vygotsky, 1978). The prevailing views and theories in the field of gifted studies reflect a deep individualistic bias in explaining gifted and talented competences: Etiologies of such competence are typically seen as residing within the person in question; therefore, giftedness is always possessed, or in the head. Rarely did people see gifted and talented competence as *enabled*, not merely facilitated, by technology and culture, or as distributed between the person and an interacting environment (including other people), until very recently (e.g., Barab & Plucker, 2002; Moran & John-Steiner, 2003; Sawyer, 2003; Ericsson, 2006). The recent analysis of three ethnic groups, Asian Americans, Jews, and West Indian Blacks, by Nisbett (2009) provides compelling evidence of how culture makes a difference in enhancing intellectual performance and promoting intellectual development. Multicultural experiences can also lead to creativity (Leung, Maddux, Galinsky, & Chiu, 2008). Thus the emergence of excellence at the social-contextual level is attributed to the synergistic power, as a result of reciprocation of domain and social-cultural affordances and individual and collective abilities (effectivities).

The activity level of analysis constitutes the most inclusive category, treating the other three levels of analysis as nested in functional contexts, but with new organizational principles, such as those revealed in the distinction Csikszentmihalyi (1996) makes between a *domain*, which is a body of culturally created knowledge and practices, and a *field*, which provides social organization of the domain (institutions, associations, gatekeepers, performance venues or publication outlets, commonly accepted professional standards, etc.). Defined this way, domain reflects an internal structure (subjective culture) and field reflects an external structure (social organization) that acts to maintain the internal structure. To be sure, culture is not uniform but works like a menu of items from which to choose or sample, as it were, knowingly or unknowingly (McAdams & Pals, 2006; Triandis, 1989). Explicit culture consists of "contested representations situated in public domains or institutions in which power is both exercised and resisted" (Gjerde, 2004). Implicit culture comprises more tacit and nuanced aspects of a culture, and can only be made aware of when contrasted with other cultures (e.g., how people from different cultures make ability and effort attributions; Holloway, 1988). Rather than seeing culture and person as two separate entities, they mutually constitute each other: individuals live through culture with the facilitation of socializing agents, at the same time as collaborating with others in creating (or revitalizing) and contributing to the culture in which they live (Rogoff, 2003).

At this level, talent development can be seen as fundamentally a process of enculturation, hence the significant role of education and mentorship. This is the case for child prodigies (Feldman, 1986) as well as for Nobel laureates (Zuckerman, 1983). Through the enculturation process, a host of personal competencies, beliefs, and values are developed, including technical proficiency (Bloom, 1985; Ericsson, 2006), modus operandi in the field (Dunbar, 1997; Zuckerman, 1983), personal epistemologies and worldviews (e.g., C. P. Snow, 1967; Kimble, 1984), broad intellectual dispositions (Perkins & Ritchart, 2004), and a set of core values that sustain one's work and purposes (Kuhn, 2002). Thus, sociocultural mediation, particularly education and special training, plays a crucial role in differential development, particularly in development of the kinds of knowledge and skills that are nonuniversal (Feldman, 2003, 2009).

INTEGRATION OF THE FOUR LEVELS OF ANALYSIS

As Snow (1995) pointed out, "The question is how to integrate variables defined in quite different grain size problems into a coherent biosocial model of person-situation interaction" (p. xiii). It is clear that the different levels of analysis discussed above involve qualitatively different concepts, principles, methodologies, theories, and explanatory devices, creating some degree of incommensurability (i.e., no common basis for comparison). Moreover, every time we raise the analysis up a level, a new level of complexity will be introduced, which necessarily complicates research design and interpretation. Therefore, the careful mapping of relationships between these levels of analysis becomes crucial if we are to achieve some measure of success with integration efforts. Figure 9.3 represents a framework that helps us see any differential development as a multilevel phenomenon. It also shows that what gets observed and how it is interpreted and explained depend on one's methodology and theoretical lens.

In this integrated framework, the person is seen as an open, adaptive, self-organizing, self-directed living system, constantly engaged in transactional experience with sociocultural environments, through which (and with maturation) differential development occurs. Methodologically, one can take a relatively objectivist stance, starting with nomothetic (universal) assumptions about parameters of human functioning and development and related individual differences, as differential psychology does, or one can take a relatively idiographic, subjectivist stance, looking into unique patterns of individual development and how individuals build meanings and purposes into their lives. Although differential development at the design (program), intentional, and activity levels are more amenable to idiographic approaches, using immediate observations of behavioral patterns and pattern changes, biological theories can also be developed based on clinical cases, such as the theory of hemispheric asymmetry as a cause for the development of brain abnormality and "the pathology of superiority" (Gershwind & Galaburda, 1987) or savant syndromes (Miller, 2005). The four interlocked ovals represent the nested and embedded nature of four levels of analysis. That is, properties and processes at each higher level might include, but cannot be reduced to, lower-level components. Empirically, the figure shows two important interfaces: The person-context interface is the observed interface or unit of analysis used for a study, and the observer–the observed interface indicates specific instruments of observation

Figure 9.3. Schematic representation of differential development as a multilevel developmental system, observed by different methodologies and interpreted through different theoretical lens.

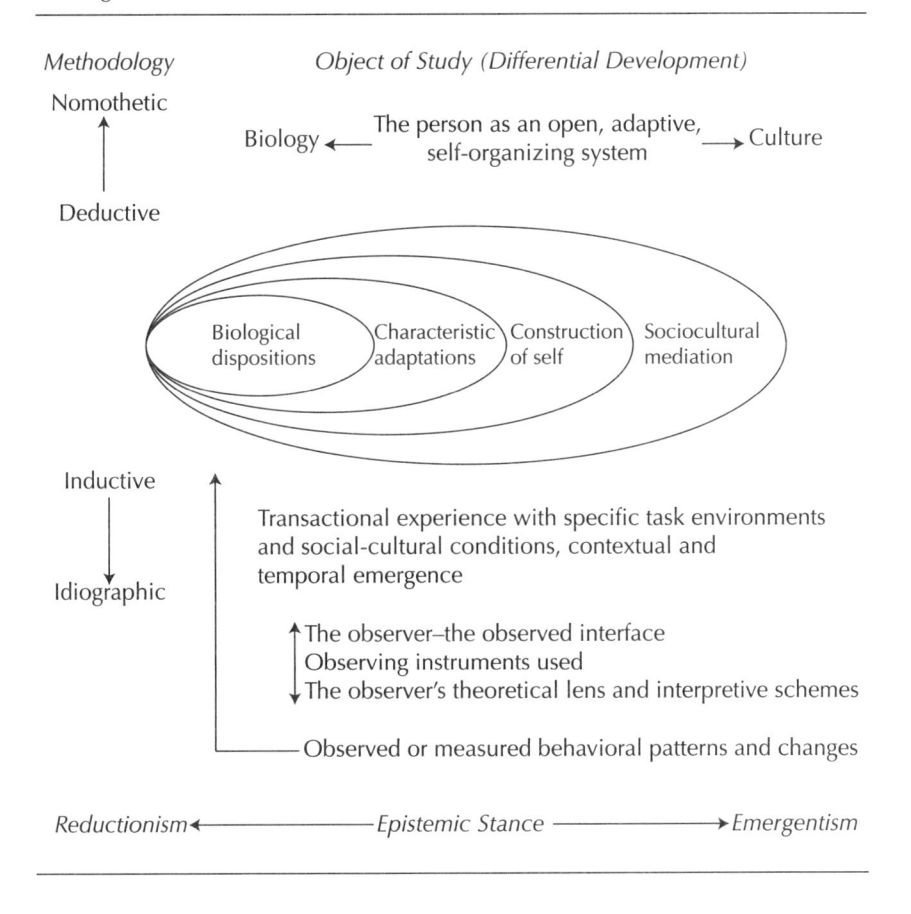

employed, interpretive scheme, and theoretical lens adopted. Taken together, they show how researchers, when observing, analyzing, and explaining differential development, position themselves in a continuum, from reductionism and atomism at the biological end and emergentism and constructivism at the social-cultural end. Finally, observed or measured behavioral patterns and changes (empirical findings) generated from a specific approach would feed back to the theory building, as indicated in the arrow pointing back upward to the ovals.

The four-level hierarchy helps raise meta-awareness of the epistemic positioning of researchers, but is in and of itself still too broad and abstract. To make it concrete, the following quote illustrates the contextual and temporal emergence of human actions and goals in a developmental context:

When small children begin to play with building blocks, they rarely have a plan or a goal to guide their actions. They will place the blocks more or less randomly next to or on top of each other until some combination of shapes suggests a particular form that the children will then seek to approximate—at this point we might say that they have a "goal" or plan to direct their actions. This goal will typically change with every new block they place along the others, as new possibilities are suggested by the developing structure. The reward that keeps the children going is the feedback that tells how closely they are able to match what they do with what they want to do.... Neither the goal nor the rewards could be specified in advance, because both emerge out of the interaction. (Csikszentmihalyi, 1978, p. 207)

We can see differential development working in the analogous way. In a child's early development, there is no clear "plan" or "blueprint" for the development of competence. Dispositions/aptitudes and characteristic adaptations are initially contextually emergent and taking shape (like block building) through experience and in response to specific environmental opportunities and challenges and gradually recognized by significant others and crystallized and solidified in oneself in the form of intentions, desires, and commitments, based on feedback, reward, and feedforward (e.g., possible selves).

Now, how do researchers position themselves in their research programs when looking at these building blocks? They typically encompass two or three levels of analysis, using a particular theoretical lens and interpretive scheme of either the reductionist or emergentist (or constructivist) nature. Table 9.1 shows a list of leading researchers in the field and how they position themselves in the human functional hierarchy discussed here.

To illustrate how particular research is conducted using different levels of analysis and how these levels can be bridged, I use existing research programs as examples. The discussion is thus mainly for illustrative purposes and cannot do full justice to the richness of the studies involved.

Integrating Dispositions/Aptitudes (Level I)
and Characteristic Adaptations (Level II)

In a typical descriptive-comparative study, gifted students are compared with "nongifted" or unidentified students on certain criterion measures to identify possible differences in cognitive or "noncognitive" processes (see Robinson & Clinkenbeard, 1998). If the criterion measures are derived from observations of real-time or long-term patterns of behavior vis-à-vis specific task environments or educational and career paths, they will be capable of capturing characteristic adaptations as they emerge over time.

Kanevsky's (1990, 1994; Kanevsky & Geake, 2004) research program serves as a good example. It involves microlevel observation of children solving problems and emergent patterns of different strategies, error rates, and help-seeking behavior. In this way, we might say that *contextual and temporal emergence*

Table 9.1. Selected works of leading researchers and theorists mapped on the human functioning hierarchy.

Level	Publication	Topic
Activity	Csikszentmihalyi et al., 1993	Experiences of talented adolescents
	Barab & Plucker, 2002	Giftedness as contextually situated
	Sawyer, 2002	Emergence of creativity through collaboration
	Bloom, 1985	Talent development from childhood to adulthood
	Feldman, 1986	Talent as confluence of factors
Intentional	Gruber, 1981	Organization of purpose
	Ziegler, 2005	Actiotope theory
	Ericsson, 2006	Deliberate practice as a main mechanism
Design or Program	Kanevsky, 1995	Theory of learning potential
	Simonton, 2005	Emergenic-epigenetic theory
	Lohman, 2005a	Aptitude theory
	Lubinski & Benbow, 2006	Emergent patterns of talent development
Biological	Feldman, 2003	Evolutionary basis of human abilities
	Heller, Perleth, & Lim, 2005	From potential to talents (expertise)
	Gagné, 2004	From natural "giftedness" to developed talents

of characteristic adaptations at Level II was captured. What Kanevsky found is that high-IQ children, compared with average-IQ children (controlling for age differences), show a distinct pattern of solving problems both in terms of effectiveness and stylistic preferences. From the perspective of multilevel analysis, metric-based IQ differences constitute Level I description of traits, and dynamic patterns of problem solving constitute Level II description of behavioral patterns and changes. Although the identified gifted children performed better on problem-solving tasks in general and tended to "turn inward" for puzzling out the problems rather than seeking external help, Kanevsky (1990) asked for caution when trying to explain differential characteristic adaptation in terms of IQ differences, as doing so is in effect reducing a complex pattern of behavior in situ to a relatively simple metric-based trait. In fact, explanation in the reversed order might work just as well; that is, differential patterns of problem solving behavior might partially explain IQ differences. Kanevsky (1990) suggested that IQ differences between the two groups of children provided a unique occasion for in-depth understanding of underlying process differences.

As another example of encompassing Levels I and II analysis, Lubinski and Benbow's (2006) longitudinal program on mathematically, verbally, and spatially gifted children demonstrates how intra-individual patterns (i.e., within-person relative strengths and weaknesses) of abilities and dispositions predict characteristic adaptations in terms of differential interests, career trajectories, and creative accomplishments over a prolonged period of time, thus bridging the trait-level description with context-sensitive patterns of characteristic adaptation. Ackerman and Heggestad (1997) accomplished the same in a cross-sectional study of college students by identify different patterns or clusters of abilities, knowledge, and interests among college students as emergent in college years (see also Ackerman, 2003). Compared to Kanevsky's (1990, 1994; Kanevsky & Geake, 2004) program, these studies can be seen as macrolevel studies of characteristic adaptation over time, which include both distal and proximal measures of aptitude, achievement, and disposition. An important insight generated from this body of research is that intra-individual differences (i.e., within-person, internally relative strengths and weaknesses) are related to characteristic adaptation in a meaningful way (Lohman, 1994b; Lupart & Toy, 2009). It speaks to the importance of integrating idiographic analysis into the traditional monothetic scheme of inter-individual dimensional differences (between-person, social-comparative strengths and weaknesses).

From an educational point of view, this type of research provides some theoretical justification of using certain aptitude tests as instruments of identification based on their short-term and long-term predictive validity of characteristic adaptation. However, as is often the case, characteristic adaptation is so fined-tuned to contextual or task constraints that the more general the predictor measures, the less its predictive efficacy. Manifest characteristic adaptations can be directly observed by teachers through instructional interaction and should also be the basis for curricular and instructional differentiation, as they carry the level of idiographic richness and complexity not captured by any nomothetic variables.

Integrating Characteristic Adaptations (Level II) and Construction of Self and Future (Level III)

As I pointed out earlier, characteristic adaptation is a more or less spontaneous emergence of a behavioral pattern in interacting with a particular environment over time, reflecting the tenet of self-organization, while construction of self and future is a more deliberate act aiming at achieving a desirable future state, reflecting the tenet of self-directedness. What bridges the two is self-awareness and self-affect (Damasio, 1999). A highly distinct example of bridging Levels II and III of analysis is what Walters and Gardner (1986) called "*crystallizing experience*" (p. 306), based on a large sample of autobiographical reports and interviews of eminent artists, musicians, mathematicians, and scientists (see also Bloom, 1985; Freeman, 1999). Crystallizing experiences are those critical, sometimes life-changing moments when individuals find their lifelong passions, or hear their calling, so to speak. Less dramatic examples of bridging these two levels of analysis include Alexander's (2004) research programs on the development of knowledge, processing strategies, and interest. Alexander shows how individuals' academic interests develop and deepen as a result of knowledge growth and deep engagement. In other words, early characteristic adaptation indicated in processing characteristics predict development of enduring life interests and commitments later on. Another example is Marsh and colleagues' (e.g., Marsh & Yeung, 1997) research program on the long-term reciprocal relationship between academic achievement and academic self-concept. They show that academic self-concept, derived from actual achievement through external (social-comparative strengths) and internal (intrapersonal, relative strengths) frames of reference, further influence achievement behaviors, such as courses students take and efforts they make. An analogous example is Richard Feynman (1999), who recalled that his interest in natural science grew to the exclusion of interest in the social sciences and humanities in his early years of development. In a way, *deliberate practice* (Ericsson, 2006) is also a construct sitting across these two levels of analysis. According to Ericsson, deliberate practice is qualitatively different from "ordinary practice" in its intensity, focus, and feedback control. Engagement in deliberate practice, then, often involves high-stakes situations (e.g., efforts to be on Olympic teams) and must have something to do with one's identity and future. It is not accidental that most of those engaged in deliberate practice studied by Ericsson and his colleagues are either established or aspiring artists, athletes, and scientists (see Ericsson et al., 1993).

What matters in crystallizing experiences is the clarity of purpose and level of determination that give one's life a clear direction and a new level of energy and momentum, which cannot be explained by Level II characteristic adaptation or Level I cognitive and affective aptitudes, hence, its additional explanatory power. Higher-level explanations must be invoked to fully explain the differential development involved. As a rule of thumb, with the onset of adolescence and increasing autonomy and the cognitive ability to envision future possibilities, self-directedness plays an increasing role in differential development. From an educational point of view, how to inspire youths in envisioning their possible selves and personal images of excellence is a main educational leverage point and challenge.

Integrating Construction of Self and Future (Level III) and Sociocultural Influences (Level IV)

Level III analysis and Level IV analysis are almost inseparable, as it is difficult to conceptualize self without some social-cultural structuring and mediation. To a large extent, characteristic adaptations (Level II analysis) are also shaped by the differential role of social-cultural influences through their affordances and constraints. However, we still can discern studies in which sociocultural influences are only alluded to or implicitly assumed, and studies in which social-cultural components are explicitly articulated and empirically defined. One type of the latter studies is fully situated observation and investigation of people at work. Dunbar (1997), for example, studied a group of scientists working in a lab through ethnography (i.e., intensive field observation). He found not only cognitive diversity and critical mass engendered by the group that are conducive to self-correction and new discovery, but also an intellectual climate conducive to identity development (see also Sawyer, 2002). Another type of social-contextual studies focus on one aspect of social-cultural influences, such as mentorship. Zuckerman (1983), for instance, recounted cases of how some Nobel laureates learned early in their careers from their Nobel laureate mentors in developing their deep insights and identity as cutting-edge researchers (see also Bloom, 1985). Walters and Gardner (1986) used the case of G. H. Hardy, a renowned English mathematician, as an example of how crystallizing experiences are often engendered through mentorship. Hardy did not develop any passion for mathematics until he met his mentor, a university professor. He recalled, "I learned for the first time what mathematics really meant. From that time on, I was on my way to becoming a real mathematician with sound mathematical ambitions and a genuine passion for mathematics" (quoted in Walters & Gardner, 1986, p. 317).

In the field of gifted education, researchers have looked at a variety of social-cultural factors, such as the role of parental "task endogeny" in their children's development of intrinsic academic interests (Gottfried, Gottfried, Bathurst, & Guerin, 1994; Gottfried et al., 2005, 2006). But more pertinent to the identity issues are those studies that looked at the social-cultural influences on gifted girls' achievement. Freeman (2004), for example, observed that in Britain as well as in other countries, the academic achievements of gifted girls in school are surpassing those of gifted boys in most school subjects and at all ages. Freeman took a more macrolevel look at the social-cultural influences, including national policies that encourage gender equity as well as learning opportunities, curriculum provisions, and social support. She argued that the main mediator of this change is the increased confidence gifted girls have in their ability to excel in their chosen endeavors. In contrast with Freeman's macrolevel approach, Hébert (2001; Hébert & Beardsley, 2001) and Worrell (2007) conducted more microlevel investigation of African American students' self-identity development in the context of various social-cultural influences. The methods they used include interview and observation as well as structured self-reports. In general, microlevel, idiographic (e.g., ethnographic and phenomenological methods) approaches help researchers get deeper into the subjective lived experiences of those who are at the center of the influx of social and cultural forces. For example, Hébert (2001) described a group of Black underachieving gifted students in an inner-city high school and how their underachievement can be understood in the context of school, neighborhood, and home environments. Hébert and Beardsley described a rural Black gifted boy who struggled and succeeded in coping and developing a strong self-identity despite poverty and environmental adversity. Without situating the study in the rich texture of the living conditions for these students, it would be hard to fathom the struggles, triumphs, and perils these youngsters experienced in managing their academic life and their social relations and keeping their youthful dreams and aspirations alive.

As indicated in Figure 9.3, each higher level of analysis may include lower-level description but has its own emergent properties, a new level of organized complexity, and higher-order explanatory principles. Levels of analysis also indicate how closely characteristics at different levels of analysis are related. Social-cultural forces have a direct bearing on intentional-level characteristics and on characteristic adaptations, but arguably do not change biological traits in a drastic way, despite their strong influence on how traits are culturally shaped and expressed. Also, as one moves up the level of analysis, simple one-to-one mapping of linear causal relationships is unlikely to succeed, as emergence is multiply determined and nonlinear (Clark, 1997; Kelso, 2000). The developmental process is better characterized as a biocultural orchestration than as a linear mechanical relationship (Li, 2003). In other words, as we move up the level of analysis, differential development and psychological individuality become more "nonuniversal," to use Feldman's (1994) term, and consequently, idiographic or case-based methods need to be employed to capture particular forms of development. The analysis comes full circle when a biopsychosocial model is constructed, involving all four explanatory factors posited by Aristotle (see Chapter 6), to explain a particular pattern of differential development, be it staged artistry or the generation of novel ideas in scientific endeavors (Tannenbaum, 1997).

RECONCEPTUALIZATION OF KEY ONTOLOGICAL ISSUES IN LIGHT OF THE FRAMEWORK

About 25 years ago, Renzulli (1986) asked a set of related questions that still have relevance to the way we conduct gifted education:

> Is giftedness an absolute or a relative concept? That is, is a person either gifted or not gifted (the absolute view) or can varying kinds and degrees of gifted behaviors be displayed in certain people, at certain times, and under certain circumstances (the relative view)? Is gifted a static concept (i.e., you have it or you don't have it) or is it a dynamic concept (i.e., it varies both within persons and within learning-performance situations)? (p. 62)

As Lohman (2001) points out, "early theories of human intelligence were not able to move beyond a belief in innateness because they lacked a cognitive theory of learning and development" (p. 92). Early theories of human intelligence were inadequate as well where developmental changes were concerned. While retaining the premise of individual differences and differential development, the Contextual, Emergent, and Dynamic (CED) framework I propose here emphasizes the irreducibility of the emergent organization of complexity and novelty in gifted and talent development. It addresses in its own way the state-trait issue, as well as the three key issues in the psychology of giftedness and talent development I discuss in Chapters 3–5, the issues of nature-nurture, domain specificity versus domain generality, and qualitative-quantitative differences.

The Trait-State Issue Regarding Gifted Competence

A distinct feature of the CED framework is that it is a process or state model, not a trait model. It should be noted that trait and state differences are not necessarily the inherent qualities of the realities under investigation but reflect how we observe the phenomenon in question. Indeed, any traits under microscopic scrutiny will reveal dynamic state qualities (Tannenbaum, 1997). Developmentally, one may observe a stable trait on a scale of macrolevel development (e.g., correlations of IQ performance at the ages of 6 and 16); in this sense, trait is nothing other than stability of a state. However, put on a scale of microlevel development, it may still reveal fluctuations. More important, trait approaches are not sensitive to qualitative, intra-personal developmental changes (or phase transitions, using the language of systems theory) both at the conceptual and technical levels (Molenaar, 2004).

Trait and state perspectives differ in another important way. Traits are decontextualized, with a tacit assumption that a trait is pervasive in its impact in whatever situation a person finds him- or herself in. Functional states are by nature sensitive to contexts. Characteristic adaptation, for example, is always sensitive to specific functional or developmental niche, rather than blind to contexts. Aptitudes and dispositions are also sensitive to particular types of situations and tasks. Therefore, the assumption of giftedness as an invariant or fixed quality across tests, domains, situations, and time is untenable and unwarranted. This said, the framework, guided by the tenet of flexible agency, also suggests that some cognitive abilities are more pervasive in influence than others and therefore may have more general and enduring impact across tasks and over time.

Dynamic systems theory views any dynamic system as a state-determined system in that it is the current state of the system that determines its future behavior (van Gelder & Port, 1995). In other words, any process (e.g., characteristic adaptation) or product (e.g., newly developed interests and identities) that occurs in *real time* has the power to influence future developmental trajectory. A specific manifestation of gifted potential or competence, then, can be seen as a functional state engendered or materialized in a specific context that has direct consequences for its future development. Changing the context, this potential may be obscured or expressed differently. In short, the CED framework is more concerned with explicating developmental processes than with individual trait descriptions; the two may have differing theoretical interests and practical utilities. Traits are broad in their conceptions, and trait theories (e.g., Gagné's DMGT theory; Gagné, 2004) are typically designed for descriptive and predictive purposes and useful for selection and identification. Process theories are intended to explain how State A gets to State B. Arguably, educators, unlike statisticians and sociologists, have a staked interest in this transition rather than predictive relations between variables, since what matters to educators is how to help students move up a notch at a given point in their zone of proximal development (Vygotsky, 1978).

The Nature-Nurture Issue

Instead of considering nature and nurture as separate, independent forces, the CED framework regards relatively endogenous and exogenous forces as jointly producing differential developmental trajectories and outcomes, which feed into further development. It stresses self-organization of competence via interaction with the environment (including cultural provisions), resulting in emergent characteristic adaptations, and development of self and future identity. It also attaches fundamental importance to the timing of certain experience and exposure as crucial for developmental pathways and trajectories. Indeed, it entertains the possibility of *sensitive periods*, depending on domains involved, during which certain environmental experiences and inputs tend to have the most instigative impact. By including biologically constituted aptitudes and dispositions in the model, the framework takes into account the role of natural endowment. However, it does not make any commitment to the notion of certain kinds of natural endowment as necessary preconditions or capacity limits for excellence, as emergence is multiply determined and there are multiple pathways to giftedness and excellence (see Papierno et al., 2005, for a similar argument for equifinality). Potential limits of one's potential (asymptotic competence) are theoretically conceivable and likely domain specific, but are difficult to gauge unless in competitive sports, where best records can be tracked over time to display upward, downward, or flat trajectories. The framework is more concerned with the nature of domain activities in terms of affordances and constraints and how they play out to make a domain a better developmental niche for some individuals but not for others. Therefore, a theory of nature-nurture relationships is by necessity domain specific.

The Domain Specificity Versus Domain Generality Issue

Whether intelligence and creativity are domain specific or domain general is a lingering issue that affects how we define giftedness. The CED framework refutes any notion of the preordained or innate basis of manifest talents, though it allows for a major role of one's inclinations or propensities vis-à-vis environmental opportunities and choices (hence, *selective affinity*) and possible dedicated learning and functioning mechanisms that help human beings cope with specific types of information. However, the framework, in light of the tenet of flexible agency, stresses the human ability to acquire novel, complex skills through adaptive learning and extended periods of special training and development and thus does not postulate specific types or domains of giftedness as "natural kinds" (cf. Gagné, 2004; Gardner, 1983). Rather, it argues that any manifest exceptional competence or talent is an acquired system by turning domain-relevant components into domain-specific units through self-organization. This process also likely reflects a flexible, adaptive, goal-directed agency and thus has a distinct domain-general component; that is, this kind of agency (arguably only equipped by human beings) is particularly designed to cope with novelty and complexity that one has never encountered, or with cultural artifacts and symbolic systems or semiotic domains, to which a person cannot form proper responses without extended learning experiences. Ease of learning, given the preponderance of evidence, has both domain-general and domain-specific explanations. The contextual, emergent, dynamic view of human development does not endorse a deterministic account of talent development that implies a fixed, predetermined developmental path, as if knowing the initial condition will permit prediction of long-term outcomes. Rather, it favors an account of differential development that has some degree of indeterminacy; whether one will be a superior performer or producer, in academic, artistic, or other social and practical enterprises, in creative or proficient fashion (Tannenbaum, 1997), depends on personal abilities, inclinations, decisions, and life circumstances and the availability of social and technical support at many critical junctures of one's development. This is why it occurs, in Renzulli's words, only "in certain people, at certain times, and under certain circumstances" (see Renzulli, 1986, p. 62). In general, the CED framework predicts a trajectory of increasing differentiation in terms of an increasingly distinct personal profile of strengths and weaknesses (domain knowledge, skills, and dispositions) and interests and dislikes (affect and conation), accompanied by a natural tendency for integration through self-organization and self-direction.

The Issue of Qualitative-Quantitative Differences

The CED framework shows many qualitative changes as indicated in different levels of analysis; these discontinuous changes or phase transitions in one's life set people apart from one another (thus, qualitative differences in differential development). The CED framework also predicts that initial differences between individuals could be small (and quantitative, if you will), but differential development tends to branch out quickly, for both endogenous and exogenous reasons, producing large differences, sometimes in the form of qualitatively different pathways, and sometimes in the form of large achievement gaps (exceptionally advanced levels of development). To the extent that the analysis taps into the idiographic depth of an individual's life (incorporating characteristic adaptations, unique construction of self, and particular sociocultural influences), exceptionality of the development is likely to reveal itself.

RESEARCH AND PRACTICAL IMPLICATIONS OF THE FRAMEWORK

The "gifted" and "nongifted" descriptive research paradigm has dominated the field for decades (see Robinson & Clinkenbeard, 1998, for a review). This paradigm is predicated on an understanding of giftedness as traits or a constellation of traits, because who are "gifted" and who are not has been already determined. It is also intended to generate a generalizable, "standard" or "modal" image of the gifted child (intellectually or otherwise). The CED model provides an alternative, more dynamic, pluralistic vision of talent development for research. The dynamic and contextual view of the emergence of gifts and talents calls for innovative research methodology that can (a) identify a relational property of person-task interaction in all its richness of meaning and cognitive and affective underpinnings, (b) track temporal trajectories at a micro- or macrolevel to show how and when development occurs, (c) identify emergent properties and how they feed into further development, and (d) show differential developmental pathways and trajectories. In short, it takes a developmental approach. To track developmental processes and changes, duration of engagement in a specific task or domain, and timing of developmental events, there is a host of methods and analytic techniques that can be used (e.g., Siegler, 2002; Singer & Willett, 2003). Two methods are particularly useful for revealing the emergence and development of exceptional competence. *Growth curve modeling* is a more nomothetic approach that draws intra-individual growth functions with a relatively large, heterogeneous sample of individuals and then compares the observed growth curves (some steep, and others flat) across individuals (Willett & Sayer, 1994). *The microgenetic method* is a more idiographic approach that intensively observes and records the behavioral and cognitive changes of a relatively small number of individuals within a short period of time and identifies specific patterns of changes (Steiner, 2003). The main purpose is to capture giftedness in the making (i.e., a dynamic view of giftedness), rather than in what ways a predetermined group of gifted individuals differ from the "nongifted," as suggested by the gifted–nongifted research paradigm (i.e., a static view of giftedness).

An educator assuming the role of scientist-practitioner could start with a general assumption about differential development. Although the infrastructure of the human mind is not fully programmed or developed in the formative years of childhood, biological dispositions and aptitudes can be detected in everyday or formal observations of children. In the process of children's growing into adolescence, a variety of characteristic adaptations, in terms of distinct achievement patterns, interests, and self-conceptions, become manifest and subject to empirical observation and assessment. As adolescents grow into adulthood, their unique personhood emerges as an important force in career and life decisions and trajectories and for ultimate accomplishments. Thus, *the roads to excellence can be described as a process of internalizing and transforming existing cultural practices, meanings, symbol systems, and values into a form useful for the society and meaningful to the individual.* This developmental process is not "universal" but involves self-selection, socialization, characteristic adaptation, sustained self-directed development, and the management of stability and instability. These developmental constraints and opportunities should be taken into consideration in designing gifted education and interventions. *Curriculum and instruction in this developmental context is nothing but an appropriate course of action to move individual learners along on a path to personal excellence.* Thus, for educators, particularly educators of precocious and advanced learners, these four levels of analysis can be easily translated into curricular goals and agendas.

CONCLUSION: CONTEXTUAL-TEMPORAL EMERGENCE OF GIFTEDNESS AND EXCELLENCE

The mainstream research on giftedness (particularly intellectual giftedness) can be characterized as attempts to pinpoint essential characteristics of the gifted child once and for all so that we could identify them with certainty and reliability, and serve their unique educational needs. This tradition has been increasingly challenged for scientific as well as social and political reasons. Developmental approaches have gained momentum in recent years (see Feldman, 2009; Horowitz, Subotnik, & Matthews, 2009). As the persistent reductionistic search for the holy grail of giftedness in the past century seems to have met with serious difficulties, the Contextual, Emergent, and Dynamic (CED) framework, with its organismic and contextualist view of individual development, offers a viable alternative. It provides a new way of understanding giftedness and excellence as a result of differential development. By arguing the applicability of basic developmental tenets to the emergence of gifted competence, it alleviates the need to develop a theory of giftedness and talent development that is insulated from the general developmental literature and theories. By putting the person squarely in the functional context and using *person-in-context* as a unit of analysis, it holds out the hope of resolving or easing the ontological tensions discussed in length in Chapters 3–5 and balancing various epistemic stances and worldviews discussed in Chapter 6. By laying out different levels of analysis, it has the potential to integrate various kinds of research that tend to focus on some, but not other, aspects of the differential development. From a practical point of view, its emphasis on developmental processes of doing/becoming in terms of characteristic adaptation and construction of self and future can potentially facilitate educational programming and curricular differentiation. Its distinct idiographic orientation in understanding differential and exceptional development is more conducive to educational and counseling or clinical applications.

Toward a Developmentally Responsive, Socially Responsible Gifted Education

The general objects—are to provide an education adapted to the years, the capacity, and the condition of everyone, and directed to their freedom and happiness—We hope to avail the state of those talents which nature has sown as liberally among the poor as the rich, but which perish without use, if not sought for and cultivated.

—Thomas Jefferson, *Notes on the State of Virginia*

Americans have shown ambivalence about high academic and artistic performance and interest. We prize creativity and academic success, particularly if it leads to a practical accomplishment. But some also pin negative names such as nerd or dweeb on students who excel academically, and high-achieving minority students are sometimes accused of "acting white."

—Pat O'Connell Ross, *National Excellence*

ABOUT TWENTY YEARS AGO, Renzulli and Reis (1991) wrote on a quiet crisis in gifted education, addressing the urgent issue of how to ensure equity while pursuing excellence and about the issue of why some of the well-entrenched theoretical assumptions stand in the way of making necessary changes in serving the most promising youths for the sake of these individuals as well as society at large. Since then, many scholars and educators have seriously reflected on the state of gifted education and reexamined deeply held underlying assumptions. The collective consciousness of the field is embodied in numerous publications and presentations, but manifests itself most clearly in a couple of special issues of the *Journal for the Education of the Gifted* and the *Roeper Review* and an edited volume in 2003 (Borland, 2003).

CHANGING THEORETICAL, EDUCATIONAL, AND SOCIAL CONTEXTS

Even though scholars and educators in the field still disagree on many issues, there is an emergent consensus that some major changes or even a "paradigm shift" is needed for the viability and vitality of gifted education in the 21st century (e.g., Borland, 2003; Feldman, 2003; Gallagher, 2000a, 2000b). To provide a backdrop for this "crisis" or opportunity for change, Feldman (2003) listed, among others, the following observations:

- The scholarly foundations for gifted education, including conceptions of giftedness and related measurement technologies, have been challenged in fundamental ways.
- Research and theory in the field of gifted education have become somewhat stagnant. The paradigm that has guided the field may have exhausted its most valuable resources.
- Ideas and theories developed outside the field of gifted studies and education pose some serious challenges to its central assumptions.
- Different conceptions of giftedness across cultures and contextualization of the very notion of giftedness makes it increasingly harder to defend IQ-based conception of giftedness.
- The resources dedicated to gifted studies and education have been diminishing and likely will diminish further, partly because the alleged "special needs" of the gifted and talented are less compelling compared with those of their disabled peers.
- The population of the United States is changing dramatically, with increasing racial and ethnic diversity; the call for equitable representation in gifted education becomes ever louder.
- There are growing resentments among those outside the field toward those passionate advocates inside the circle, particularly at a time when educational reformers in the United States are calling for detracking and full inclusion. The resentments often take the form of antielitism.
- The landscape of jobs and careers is changing dramatically. Abilities and skills crucial for effective functioning in the 21st century may be quite different from those needed in the past century.

As can been seen, the first four points are mainly theoretical and conceptual, and the last four are related to changes in society and education systems. As I pointed out in Chapter 1, the internal (conceptual) tension has been building up from within, and with external (societal) pressures, will eventually cause the eruption of a seemingly dormant volcano (a crisis in gifted education). As I reiterated many times in preceding chapters, gifted education, as an institutionalized social practice, is part of a larger culture that values excellence and believes in the importance of nurturing exceptional competence and excellence in sciences and arts and other domains of human endeavor. Thus, there is a distinct normative side of how we view human potential and its development and related individual differences, how we define the purposes of gifted education and conduct gifted education accordingly. Solutions for the three main issues are still outstanding.

The first is using an IQ-based definition of giftedness started by Terman (1925). In historical hindsight, in effect it used a strategy of putting all the eggs in one basket (high IQ scores) with the assumption that children identified this way represent a gene pool that is likely to yield the greatest payoff in terms of excellence in adulthood. This strategy, along with its natural endowment and domain-general assumption of human potential, is challenged empirically as well as theoretically (e.g., Lohman, 2005a; Subotnik, Kassan, Summers, & Wasser, 1993). For the champions of the tradition of the categorical approach to gifted identification and education (the gifted child canonically defined as possessing certain psychological traits, such as high IQ), the challenge is how to open up the system to allow for more diverse ways of defining and expressing excellence rather than sticking to the IQ or *g* doctrine. The field of gifted education is clearly moving toward a developmental view of giftedness as contextually and temporally emergent and evolving. For the advocates of talent developmental approaches, however, how to reinterpret IQ scores and incorporate IQ tests in a broader assessment system remains to be clarified.

The second issue is the tension between equity and excellence, which is felt not just in the United States, but also in Europe, Asia, and any other place where equal rights to education are advocated (see Persson, Joswig, & Balogh, 2000, for a survey of gifted education in Europe). For the advocates of gifted education, the question is, How do they respond to outside criticism that gifted education is privileging the socially privileged? If they continue to use vaguely defined "unique needs" of the gifted, its effectiveness as well as its ethical and educational justification will continue to be problematic. For the educational reformers and social critics who blame gifted education for not coming along with efforts to undo tracking practice, the question is, How do they deal with the Matthew Effect, which inevitably creates disparity in educational achievement (Ceci & Papierno, 2005), a rude awakening that equal opportunity for all would unlikely bring equal outcomes? Should education lift those at the bottom up at the expense of neglecting those at the top? Would that be equitable educational practice? What would be the practical consequences of such practice for the nation?

The third issue is the changing world (Friedman, 2006) that new generations will have to adapt to; globalization (the world is flat now) makes nations' economic and technological competitiveness more distinct and urgent. The skill sets expected for success in the 21st century may be fundamentally different from those for the past century; skills traditionally reserved for "the gifted" are now expected of all high school graduates. The Partnership for 21st Century Skills (2009), a U.S.-based education advocacy group, for example, lists problem solving, critical thinking, innovation, communication skills, lifelong learning, and knowledge and technology literacy as being crucial for effectively functioning in the 21st century, a far cry from the beginning of the 20th century, when basic education merely meant mastery of a limited vocabulary and numerical skills (see Bransford et al., 1999). The tide of education is rising in terms of higher standards and expectations for all. Yet the reality is that top students in the United States compare unfavorably in international rankings of academic achievement

(Benbow & Stanley, 1996; Ceci & Papierno, 2005); precocious and advanced students are chronically left unchallenged in regular classrooms, as was reported in the U.S. Department of Education report in the early 1990s (Ross, 1993; see also Benbow & Stanley, 1996). There is a general problem in schools nationwide of providing for excellence in terms of personnel training, curriculum provision, and available services. Relatively few teachers know how to differentiate curriculum and instruction for the most advanced students in regular classrooms. Strategies, such as grouping and acceleration, to deal with such educational deficiencies are either not familiar to teachers or simply prohibited for administrative convenience. The more recent Fordham Foundation report (Loveless et al., 2008) found that achievement of the academically most advanced students suffered as a result of the federal educational initiative No Child Left Behind (NCLB), which was intended to bring all students (from third to eighth grades) up to a minimum proficiency level in math, reading, and other core school subjects. Indeed, many advocates of gifted education have argued that gifted children were left behind by NCLB (e.g., Goodkin & Gold, 2007).

GIFTED EDUCATION AT THE CROSSROADS: DEFINITIONS, AIMS, AND GUIDING PRINCIPLES

Responses to the call for fundamental changes or a paradigm shift in gifted education vary. Some scholars and educators lean toward the conservative side, others tend toward the liberal side, and still others sit in the middle (i.e., moderates). The hallmark of conservatism (in the exact sense of the word) is its insistence on the existence of a definable and identifiable category of school children as "gifted" and this being the raison d'être of gifted education (Gallagher, 2000a). Within these confines, modifications and adaptations should be made in response to theoretical advances and changing environments (Gallagher, 2006a, 2000b). Those who lean toward the liberal side argue for more pluralistic and dynamic conceptions of giftedness and more flexible, inclusive identification and educational programming, although IQ or similar aptitude tests can still be part of how gifted children are identified (e.g., Renzulli, 1986, 1999). The more radical departure from the tradition of gifted education is demonstrated by those education scholars who call for eradicating the IQ-based "gifted child" approach and moving toward a completely new paradigm, in the form of talent development for all (e.g., Treffiger & Feldhusen, 1996), achievement-based conceptions, identification, provisions for exceptionally advanced students (Matthews & Foster, 2006), or gifted education without (the identification and labeling of) gifted children (or gifted programs) (Borland, 2003, 2005). Incidentally, clarification is needed for the phrase "gifted education without gifted children (or gifted programs)." Gifted education without gifted programs means that gifted-education services can be seamlessly distributed and woven into the fabric of the education system so that curricular differentiation and instructional adaptation are made on a regular basis in response to individual students' demonstrated advancing needs rather than because they are "gifted"; consequently, there is no need to designate a particular group of children as "gifted" and by default all the rest as "nongifted" (see Borland, 2003).

There are epistemic and normative reasons why scholars and educators differ in their positions and perspectives. Despite their differences, all have come to the consensus that changes are needed and that we, the educators of our children, talented and not so talented, are in the same boat. After all, the ultimate goals of gifted education are not that different from those for "general education," and gifted education as a frontier of educational excellence has much to offer education in general (Renzulli, 1998; Tomlinson & Callahan, 1992). As I argue elsewhere (Dai, 2009), how to define the role of gifted education and find its proper niche in the larger context of education and educational reform, and how to manage its relationship with regular education, will determine the relevance and viability of gifted education within the education system in the long run.

Given the framework I presented in the previous chapter, what can we say about the future of gifted education? In the following section, I will discuss principles that we can derive from the review of the ontological, epistemological, and normative tensions and the contextual, emergent, dynamic (CED) framework I present in Chapter 9. These principles have to do with (1) how we define giftedness, (2) how we identify gifted and talented children or assess their readiness for advanced challenges, (3) how we define the rationale or purposes of gifted education, (4) how we set up curriculum experiences and make instructional adaptations with particular purposes and goals of gifted education in mind and particular groups of children in our hands, and (5) how we conceptualize the counseling needs of these children and psychological interventions. I will attempt to show that when the principles I delineate are observed in practice; we will get closer to what I identify as a developmentally responsive, socially responsible gifted education. My discussion, for obvious reasons, remains conceptual and programmatic, rather than dealing with the nitty-gritty of practical know-how.

Definition of Giftedness and Gifted Students

The field of gifted education has long been plagued by the issue of how to define giftedness and gifted students. Those who insist on searching for a clear definition (e.g., Gagné, 1999b) argue that without such a consensus definition, there is no common conceptual and empirical basis for comparing research studies, as each study may define giftedness in its own idiosyncratic way (Ziegler & Raul, 2000). Practically, there will be no consistent or coherent set of criteria for identification based on a common definition of giftedness (Gagné, 1999b). Those who are skeptical about whether we can get even close to such a consensus definition argue that if the gifted and talented "come in a tremendous variety of shapes, forms, and sizes," as Passow (1981, p. 8) put it, it would be futile, even harmful, to create a cookie-cutter definition or Procrustean bed of giftedness that is presumed to fit all descriptions and observations of behaviors that we deem "gifted," or "superior," or "exceptional." In other words, giftedness as an abstraction has no unitary identity or essence and thus fundamentally defies any essentialist definition.

The pragmatics of using "giftedness" or "gifted children." The difficulty in developing a consensus definition also has to do with the unsettled issues or tensions of potential versus achievement, one versus many, and qualitative versus quantitative differences discussed in length in Chapters 3–5. For example, Borland (1999) took issue with Gagné's (1999b, 2004) differentiation of natural abilities (i.e., giftedness or natural endowment) from systematically developed skills and expertise (i.e., talent) by arguing that the distinction or dichotomy is empirically moot (e.g., how to distinguish abilities that are "spontaneously" developed and those that take "systematic" learning, training and practice; see also Lohman, 2006, for a similar argument) and practically not useful (e.g., should we select a person based on "giftedness" criteria or based on "talent" criteria?). Borland's major argument is that human abilities are so multifaceted and their etiologies so idiosyncratic that any universal or nomothetic system of classification does a disservice to the understanding of how abilities and talents come about. The difference between Gagné and Borland reveals both ontological commitments (e.g., one or many) as well as epistemological differences between nomothetic and idiographic orientations, which I discuss in Chapter 6. From the vantage point of the CED framework, a major problem of using any single analytic conceptual structure such as "natural ability" or "general intelligence" in defining giftedness is *reification*, which is also Borland's main concern (see Borland, 1997a, 2003); namely, creating something as explanatory that is not real and treating something abstract as having material existence. It further perpetuates a fixed concept of human potential in which you have to *possess* this precious natural endowment in the first place before you can rise to developmental challenges, or somehow your potential is determined by the presence and degree of psychometrically defined giftedness. The CED framework refutes such a static view of giftedness, although we still can use the term *gifted* descriptively, as in our natural language, equivalent to adjectives such as *exceptional, superior, outstanding*, and *extraordinary* to describe a person (a gifted artist, a gifted scientist, etc.) and infer a superior quality or competence in that person. However, the term in and of itself does not denote anything theoretical concerning nature or nurture, domain specificity or domain generality, or qualitative or quantitative differences. Precisely because "gifted" is not an analytic or objectively definable concept, most theories of giftedness are what Sternberg and Davidson (1986) called "implicit theories" (p. 3), whether they prescribe three, four, or five factors or components; there is no way to verify which theory is more viable than others.

Should we discard the term *gifted* altogether if *gifted* or *giftedness* does not represent a scientifically and objectively definable concept? In her 1993 Department of Education report, Ross (1993) suggested that "the term 'gifted' connotes a mature power rather than a developing ability and, therefore, is antithetical to recent research findings about children" (p. 26). Because of the miscommunication and confusion engendered by the ambiguity of the concept of giftedness or "gifted children" and its possible negative social impact, some scholars suggest that we abandon the terms *general giftedness* (based on the notion of general intelligence), *gifted children*, and *gifted education* (e.g., Feldhusen & Jarwan, 2000, p. 279; Feldhusen, 2003, p. 34) and instead use more specific talent-based definitions and concepts, which are definable and amenable to assessment and identification. I personally would prefer to use more neutral and less ambiguous terms such as *children of high ability* or *children of high promise*. These terms are less ambiguous and thus less likely to be associated with surplus meanings. However, given the fact that *giftedness*, *gifted children*, and *gifted education* are deeply entrenched in our practical communication and scholarly discourse, it is unlikely they will disappear from our lexicon any time soon.

A developmental solution. My review of the literature and the CED developmental framework I discuss in Chapter 9 does suggest ways to define those high qualities we value more precisely and further nurture them in a developmentally meaningful manner.

Numerous definitions of "the gifted and talented" tend to fall into two main categories: *developmental precocity* and *achievement at an advanced level*. In the preschool and early elementary school years, *precocious children* can be used; for later developmental stages, particularly when academic experience and knowledge are involved, *academically advanced students* can be used. Precocity, meaning exceptionally early in development or occurrence, is typically defined along developmental dimensions, such as cognitive, social-emotional, and physical and thus can be cognitive, emotional, and motivational or a combination of these dimensions. High IQ, particularly in the early years, can be seen as a form of intellectual precocity. The recent child development literature has suggested much domain specificity of child development, such as rudimentary senses of numbers, force, living things, and theory of mind; therefore, precocity can also be highly domain specific in the sense of sensitivities and deep intuitions regarding a particular type or domain of information (e.g., mathematically precocious children in the SMPY program; Stanley, 1996). Neo-Piagetian researchers also identified mathematical, narrative, and spatial-artistic precocity in childhood (Porath, 2006a; see also Feist, 2004). As for the second category, advanced levels of achievement in a particular domain, they are more easily recognizable by age-appropriate criteria and standards. For precocious children, what we are interested in is their "potential" as manifest in demonstrated developing competencies and dispositions, typically in informal learning settings. For advanced learners, what we observe is manifest emergent excellence, typically occurring in more formal educational and training conditions. Of course, overlapping cases can occur. For instance, child prodigies and some precocious children (Feldman, 1986; Stanley, 1996) are both highly precocious and able to achieve domain excellence at a much faster rate and much earlier age. Nevertheless, for conceptual clarity, precocity and advanced achievement are two distinct, defining characteristics of gifted and talented children. Both indicate human potential for further development, but differ in terms of actualization and developmental complexity (differentiation and integration). The former describes behavioral and psychological characteristics that are developmentally advanced compared with those of most age peers with similar experiences; and the latter describes domain achievement that are advanced by age-appropriate professional standards and are likely as a result of both abilities being channeled into the domain activities and dedicated efforts. The distinction is consistent with Mayer's (2005) suggestion that giftedness be used "as an age-specific term that refers to potential for beginning stage, achievement for the intermediate stage, and eminence for the advantage stage" (p. 439).

A major difference between the differentiation of precocity and advanced achievement I make here and Gagné's differentiation of giftedness and talent is that in the CED framework, talent development is not necessarily contingent on a specific pattern of precocity (e.g., high IQ), although the two can be correlated, while in Gagné's (2004) DMGT model, systematically developed talents entail natural endowment (giftedness); in other words, exceptional natural endowment is a *necessary* precondition for advanced talent development. In comparison, the CED framework does not set any a priori limits to human potential in that regard. More important, based on the state-determined rather than trait-determined view of talent development, proximal measures of real-time performance and competence at a particular point in time are more predictive of future trajectories than distal ones. Evidence shows that the best predictor of future achievement in a domain is the current level of performance and achievement in that domain, not some traitlike aptitudes (see Lohman, 2005a).

Potential versus achievement. Should we discard the notion of precocity and high potential, if manifest advanced talent development provides a more solid grounding for a conception of development of excellence? The answer is no. There are developmental as well as social reasons why we still need to preserve the notion of high potential. Nurturing of excellence is always socially and educationally mediated. Therefore, when individuals fail to develop their talents at a level they are capable of, there may be environmental causes. Educational and culturally enriching opportunities and resources vary greatly, leading to different levels of manifestation of competencies and talents. Thus, for those who have yet to develop an advanced level of mastery or achievement, the notion of precocity, high potential, or aptitude becomes a good alternative to identify children of promise, given our knowledge of the predictive efficacy of related measures of high potential, such as IQ tests. Lohman (2005a), for instance, distinguished between two groups of gifted students: "high-accomplishment students," who currently display academic excellence in a particular domain, and "high-potential students" who "display the aptitude to develop high levels of accomplishment offered by a particular class of instructional treatment" (p. 334). The policy implications of the distinction are clear for the inclusion of more underrepresented minority students for gifted education. Likewise, Robinson (2005) suggested that in addition to identifying "those with rapidly developing talents who are markedly different from their age-peers—perhaps the top 1 or 3 percent of their age cohorts," we must identify "children of promise," "children whose talents are well above average (perhaps in the top 10 percent) and who come from backgrounds that have not afforded them the resources that might have optimized their development" (pp. 290–291). More generally, underachievement among highly able students is quite prevalent, for both endogenous and exogenous reasons. Characteristic adaptations of the gifted and talented not in line with traditional academic paths may be quite common (see Subotnik & Olszewski-Kubilius, 1997). For example, Bill Gates was an underachiever in school in a conventional sense, given his ability. Therefore, a definition of gifted and talent development should go beyond the conventional routes of achievement to capture a variety of excellence and pathways to excellence.

Defining emergent excellence as characteristic adaptation. Along with precocity and advanced knowledge and skills, I suggest that *emergent excellence* in a line of human endeavor be used as a characteristic adaptation and central concern of gifted education. Recall that *characteristic adaptation* indicates the contextual and temporal emergence of a unique pattern of behavior (the performer or producer breed; the academic, artistic, vocational-technical, or service orientation; the proficient or creative kind) that is more complex than any measure of aptitude and disposition can predict and more personal and unique than the norm-referenced notion of high academic (or artistic) accomplishment can capture. For emergent excellence, the criteria of "demonstrability," "productivity," "rarity," and "value" (Sternberg, 1995) can readily be applied to a performance; yet it affords much flexibility and diversity in terms of what kind of excellence is evident and how excellence is expressed; thus Bill Gates's unique penchant for and fascination with building and cracking codes or the passion of a group of high school students in West Virginia (the "rocket boys") to build rockets, inspired by Sputnik (Hickam, 1998), can be validated and nurtured. The qualifier *emergent* has two meanings. First, it stresses the contextual and temporal unfolding of manifestation of excellence; second, it highlights the developing and evolving nature of excellence we have observed. That is, what we hail as "gifted" in children rarely takes the form of mature, consummated performance, but rather a developing one showing a promising trajectory (Feldhusen, 2003), and what is touted as "high accomplishment" in children, by the standard of eminent scholarly productivity or artistry beyond mere mastery and expertise, can at best be characterized as high potential (Lohman, 2005a). Defined this way, the role of gifted education becomes clear: How do we further encourage and nurture this emergent quality, given what we know about the development of talents and creative productivity? In essence, it is consistent with Renzulli's (1986) view of the emergence of gifted behavior in some individuals (not others) at certain points in time (not other points) and in some places (not others), and his argument that the main task of gifted education is not merely to identify the gifted, but also to nurture and develop this quality (Renzulli, 1999).

Emergent excellence by nature is domain specific, broad or narrowly defined, and therefore consistent with the recent call for a domain-specific definition of gifted children, which facilitates corresponding and commensurate educational provisions (VanTassel-Baska, 2005). It is in keeping with a talent-development-for-all approach to gifted education (Renzulli & Reis, 1997; Treffinger & Feldhusen, 1996). It should be pointed out that talent development for all means the system is open to all and offers equal and fair opportunity to develop talents in academic, artistic, vocational, social, and other domains, though how far individuals can go is constrained by their ability and commitment; there must be some checks and balances to ensure the effectiveness of specific programs or services and the success of the willing. Talent development for all does not mean that "everyone is gifted," as some people might characterize this approach. Defining giftedness as emergent excellence is also consistent with Matthews and Foster's (2006) mastery model of gifted performance, which is a state theory (advanced development observed at a particular point in time) in contrast to general aptitude-based models of giftedness.

Identification of Gifted Children

There are two kinds of situations that call for formal or informal identification of gifted children in educational settings. One is classroom based, involving identifying individual-based, specific educational needs for curricular differentiation in regular classrooms, or proper placement such as subject- or grade-based acceleration. The other is program based, involving eligibility and qualification for a particular gifted program. In either case, there is no need to make the assumption of gifted children as a homogeneous group (i.e., a categorical approach). Labeling children as "gifted" is unnecessary in both situations and should be avoided whenever possible. The process of identification is not to determine whether a person is "gifted" or not, but to "identify how subsequent opportunities, resources, and encouragement can be provided to support continuous escalations of student involvement in both required and self-selected activities" (Renzulli & Dai, 2003; p. 935). Although situations calling for identification vary and may require different strategies and systems of identification, the CED framework suggests the following guiding principles in identification:

The principle of authenticity and demonstrability. A claim for potential or advanced level of academic, artistic, or other development can be seen as authentic to the extent that behavioral or performance evidence bears it out in an unequivocal manner with minimal inference. The principle also means that measures of performance in relevant authentic settings are favored over contrived tests, as the former better represents the necessary ingredients for future success in a given line of development.

The principle of unfolding over time. This principle suggests that the earlier the identification, the less certain we are as to whether a child identified as precocious or gifted and talented will live up to our expectations. As a corollary of this principle, assessment and identification for the purposes of curricular differentiation and proper educational placement should be diagnostic and ongoing in nature and conducted on an individual-by-individual basis. It does not make sense, for instance, to base a medical diagnosis and prognosis on a medical record documented 5 years ago. By the same token, it is highly problematic to label a child "gifted" in a once-and-for-all fashion: once gifted, always gifted. Repeated and continual assessment and evaluation are needed to ensure proper assessment of progress, emergent problems, educational needs, and solutions (Feldhusen & Jarwan, 2000). More formal identification is often called for, as required by state laws, for eligibility or qualification for designated program services. Under such circumstances, proper checks and balances (e.g., admission and evaluation policies; Subotnik & Coleman, 1996) need to be put in place to ensure that the progress of students is monitored and evaluated and that proper intervention measures are taken to ensure the effectiveness of a program. This principle does not necessarily mean that educators can act only reactively, waiting until valuable qualities emerge, as the two-stage identification-differentiation strategy prescribes. Proactive provisions of curriculum experiences can be used to facilitate the emergence of interest, task commitment, and creative expression (Passow, 1981; Renzulli, 1986) or any form of characteristic adaptation as an integral part of promoting and identifying the emergence and development of gifted and talented competencies. This way of using curriculum experiences as an occasion for identification is akin to the Response to Intervention (RTI) strategy used with students with learning disabilities (Vellutino et al., 2006). Thus, unfolding of talents over time occurs, dynamically, in the reciprocal interaction of programming, instruction, and identification.

The principle of increasing differentiation. As the child moves to the later stages of development, particularly with the onset of adolescence (around 11–12 years of age), we should look into patterns and trajectories of development in terms of characteristic adaptation, using mode of functioning, domain, and style, delineated by Tannenbaum (1997), as a framework. That is, a person can gear toward being a producer rather than a performer (mode of functioning) in an academic discipline rather than staged artistry (domain) and eventually demonstrate a proficient rather than creative style of thinking and expression. We should expect developmental precocity, if any, to further manifest itself in domain-specific excellence given a particular provision of instruction, training, and deliberate practice (Coleman & Cross, 2005; Porath, 2006b). In other words, some evidence of productivity needs to be in place. Moreover, increasing differentiation also means that specific targeted interventions become more viable over time, as patterns of characteristic adaptation become clearer and interests become more enduring and life themes and passions, and even self-identity, become more distinct.

The principle of optimal match. From a developmental point of view, it does not make sense to identify the gifted and talented for the sake of identification. Merely identifying "the gifted" is no longer meaningful without asking the following question: What is the identification for? Reactively or proactively, the educational purposes of identification are to find an optimal match between a person with a specific cognitive-affective profile and pattern of strengths and interests and, on the one hand, the level of knowledge and skills, and, on the other, an educational provision particularly suited for further developing these strengths and interests. Identification and proper educational provisions should be considered an integrated system rather than separate entities. Just as a generic definition of the gifted does not offer a clear justification for specialized education provisions, a generic gifted program that offers only vaguely defined "enrichment" experiences can also be problematic and lacking in substance.

The principle of balancing objective measures and expert judgments. This is based on the fallibility of both objective measures and human judgments and the fact that idiographic complexity of individual functioning often defies nomothetic prescription, as discussed in Chapter 6. As Stanley (1997) pointed out, "Approaches that are too quantitative may miss the mark, as also may those that are too qualitative and unrestrained by need for precision. A nice balance of objectivity and subjectivity seems desirable" (p. 105). Consequently, a two-phase, clinical model of diagnostic assessment, in which testing is considered an information-gathering device along with other assessment vehicles such as observation (see Beutler & Rosner, 1995), is preferred to a metric-based identification scheme as used in identifying the individuals with intellectual disabilities (American Association on Mental Retardation, 1992).

Aims of Gifted Education

What do we try to accomplish by identifying gifted and talented students? A traditional response to this question is that gifted education is set up to educate the gifted. More specifically, the argument about "unique needs" is used to defend gifted education, with the assumption that somehow "being gifted" engenders a set of unique needs. As a corollary, a generic group or category of gifted children (or, more narrowly, "intellectually gifted") becomes the very rationale or raison d'être for the existence of gifted education. However, if the homogeneity of children we identify as "gifted" does not hold, then the broadly defined "unique needs" born out of alleged giftedness become problematic, as these children's "needs" might well be quite different (e.g., some have the right makeup and penchant for astronauts, others for historians, and still others creative writers or filmmakers). As I pointed out earlier, a generic conception of "giftedness" runs the risk of reification, as if giftedness or being gifted had its own essence or substance and maintained its own unity, identity, and continuity, what I call an essentialist construal of giftedness (see also Borland, 1997a, 2003). By the same token, a conception of generic gifted education runs the risk of chasing a phantom. To be sure, when we see an intellectually precocious or academically advanced child who is not sufficiently challenged and feel bored in school, we as educators naturally feel obligated to do something about it; thus there is nothing wrong with "serving the gifted." Actually, the whole SMPY program at Johns Hopkins was an offshoot of Julian Stanley's efforts to help Joseph Bates, an extremely bright eighth grader, to find an appropriate educational placement (see Stanley, 1996). However, the notion of "serving the gifted" in a wholesale fashion is not articulated enough about why a child like Joseph Bates needs more challenge in his or her education. It has to do with the principle of optimal match discussed earlier: What is the best thing we can offer educationally to an individual child at a particular point in her education?

For social, scientific, as well as pragmatic reasons, the purpose of gifted education should no longer be that of serving a fixed category or group of children based on some unwarranted assumption of homogeneity and "unique needs." Instead, it is to promote and nurture, as other sectors of education do, the highest level of excellence that is humanly possible in a variety of culturally valuable endeavors through learning and development. As I argued in Chapter 8, gifted education should not be about giftedness; it should be about excellence. *The special role or niche of gifted education within the larger education system lies in its focus on the precocious and most advanced learners; accordingly, the level of excellence gifted education is aimed at, and the curriculum paths tailored to the precocious and advanced, are distinctive.* Although excellence, particularly academic excellence, is the main goal of gifted education, the issues of choice, equity, diversity, and efficiency are not trivial and deserve their due attention (see Chapter 8). Talents in artistic, vocational-technological, and social and human service areas should also feature prominently whenever resources and expertise in school permit. Here, I confine my discussion to academic and vocational excellence and define it as a kind of excellence that potentially leads to a productive career, which can be manifested as either high proficiency and expertise or creative productivity. This kind of excellence is to be distinguished from excellence manifested as *avocational* talents pursued mainly for leisure and enjoyment. In Chapter 7, I discuss in some detail the distinction and relationship between expertise and creativity and their curricular and instructional implications. Below I delineate some overarching principles for curriculum and instruction based on what we know about the development of high-level expertise and creativity.

Curriculum Differentiation and Instructional Adaptation

If precocity, advanced achievement, or various forms of emergent excellence all has a trajectory of *contextual-temporal emergence*, as delineated in the CED framework (see Figure 9.1), then a curriculum for a particular child is nothing but a curriculum of emergent and evolving excellence; in that sense, an effective curriculum is an integral part of the development of high-level excellence. In Latin, *curriculum* means a "course" or "pathway." In school, this course is set up as sequence and scope of learning materials and experiences in terms of content, process, and product articulated as curriculum standards, typically age graded. The tension between the standard curriculum set up for all and unique developmental trajectories and pathways of individual children has long been recognized by Dewey (1902/1990) and Whitehead (1929), among others. From the viewpoint of precocious and advanced learners, the school system is too rigid; from the viewpoint of the school system, these children sometimes raise the school's reputation and are a "selling point" for the school, but when curriculum matters are concerned, they are a distinct inconvenience. It is very much for this reason that curriculum differentiation and instructional adaptation are called for, and curriculum specialists are needed to facilitate the process. However, based on contextual and temporal emergence, the curriculum cannot be preplanned or -engineered; rather, it consists of a chain of educational opportunities, choices, and experiences that help precocious and advanced learners to internalize and transform knowledge and skills in a personally meaningful and productive way and chart their own course of development, ultimately leading to careers of high-level expertise and creativity.

Consequently, whether in specialized schools (e.g., academies of arts and sciences) or regular schools, the mode of curriculum delivery for the precocious and advanced should be focused and disciplined, yet diverse and flexible, allowing for much freedom to explore students' own niche potential. This arrangement is what I call *developmentally responsive practice*. It can take both reactive and proactive forms. Reactively, curriculum differentiation should be responsive to forms of emergent excellence within the regular classroom or beyond. Proactively, curriculum differentiation should promote talent development by introducing novelty, new excitement, and intellectual challenges into the learning materials, encourage self-direction, and facilitate crystallizing experiences. Curriculum differentiation and instructional adaptation as ways of enhancing differentiation and integration in developing excellence should follow the principles discussed below. As can be seen, none of these principles are unique to precocious and advanced learners; yet, depending on the nature of precocity or specific patterns of advanced achievement, appropriate curricular provisions and instructional adaptations may be quite different.

The principle of optimal challenge. Optimal challenge has both cognitive and motivational underpinnings. Cognitively, optimal challenge is within a zone of proximal development, wherein a child can perform a challenging task with the assistance of more competent others, such as a teacher, a coach, or a mentor (Vygostky, 1978). Motivationally, the task is within an optimal zone when is challenging enough to keep a learner alert, engaged, and active in thinking, reasoning, and problem solving, but not to the extent of overwhelming the learner with its difficulty level (Csikszentmihalyi, 1990). Curriculum differentiation, such as curriculum compacting or subject-based acceleration, is called for when optimal challenge is absent and the student in question is apparently bored.

The principle of deep intellectual engagement. This principle should be reflected in both content and process and ultimately in the evaluation of learning outcomes. For content learning, it means deep disciplinary or cross-disciplinary inquiry beyond factual information into the conceptual and epistemological foundations of knowledge. For processing or thinking skills, it means frequent use of inquiry-based pedagogy and project-based learning dealing with authentic issues that engage reasoning and problem solving (Aulls & Shore, 2008). If precocious and advanced learners tend to generalize and transfer learning (e.g., see single problems as instances of a class of problems), then it should be capitalized upon to further their metalevel inquiry into the nature of doing science or history or the interdisciplinary differences. If they tend to self-scaffold their problem solving (Kanevsky, 1990), then more open-ended questions and problems will pique their intellectual curiosity and activate the need for cognition and logical coherence. If they have a tendency to extrapolate, teachers should sow the seeds of creativity by triggering their imagination in envisioning new possibilities of interpretation, explanation, and application.

The principle of continuity of curriculum experiences. Just as the contextual-temporal emergence of excellence takes time and entails a continuity of experience, curriculum offerings should not be fragmented, disconnected, or compartmentalized. This does not mean that one should engineer the process of differentiation and integration, except for some highly technical and specialized disciplines; rather, the pieces will fall into place to form the whole when experiences are meaningful to individuals and pursued in a serious manner. It does mean, however, that what is going on between regular classrooms and pullout programs, or between domain or discipline experiences and intellectual, social, and practical experiences outside the classroom should be in sync rather than disjointed, and whatever a student gets started with, there should be an opportunity to follow through. Otherwise, students may turn from one thing to another merely as busy "school work" without any personal meaning attached to the activities and experiences.

    The principle of relevance. Relevance of curricular experiences has both personal and social ramifications (Gagné, 2007). A curricular experience is personally relevant if it is connected to the learner's past experience and knowledge and demonstrates its meaningfulness in the larger scheme of things and if it stirs up interest and capitalizes on the strengths and inclinations of the learner. A curricular experience is socially relevant if it connects schooling and society in a meaningful way. For example, the 21st Century Skill Partnership advocates teaching core subjects (e.g., language arts, math, science, history) in the context of 21st-century themes (e.g., global awareness; financial, economic, business, and entrepreneurial literacy; civic literacy), aimed at developing creativity, critical thinking, and communication skills, among others (Partnership for 21st Century Skills, 2009). For precocious and advanced learners, curriculum options can include those that enhance a skill set crucial for making major contributions to the economic, social, and cultural development in a nation or beyond in the 21st century.

    The principle of balancing breadth and depth. In a high-tech age, specialized, technical mastery of instruments and equipments will prove essential even for scientists who used to rely on their minds rather than tools for cutting-edge research (Ziegler, 2005). On the other hand, many creative and innovative ideas come from the cross-fertilization of disciplinary knowledge and the application of advances in one domain to another; a person who has multiple skills and talents stands the best chance of combining them and turning them into an innovative application. Moreover, we know that the development of artistic sensitivities and modes of thinking have an unintended positive effect on scientific and technical endeavors, presumably because of their activation of the intuitive mind and imagination (Root-Bernstein, 2009). Therefore, learning experiences designed by the instructor should have a sufficient depth of disciplinary knowledge and domain practices while maintaining the broad scope of liberal education. Both discipline-based content and integrated thematic units can be used for balancing depth and breath (Subotnik & Coleman, 1996). It is unrealistic, of course, to expect our students, upon their graduation from high school, to have a strong command of disciplinary knowledge; much remains to be learned in their undergraduate years and beyond. In a time of rapid growth in knowledge base, learning how to learn becomes more critical than absorbing large amounts of information. Deep intellectual engagement means going beyond technical mastery to develop a deep understanding of advances and trends of knowledge and technology in the 21st century and what they mean to one's personal future.

The principle of integrating cognitive and affective experiences. There is a cognitivist bias in existing psychological and educational theories of the acquisition of knowledge and skills, as if knowledge and skills can be cognitively acquired and meaningfully stored (and later retrieved) without the participation of emotion and motivation. In my efforts, in collaboration with Robert Sternberg, to reconceptualize intellectual functioning and development (Dai & Sternberg, 2004), I squarely put learning, thinking, and reasoning in situ, comprising (a) the individual person, who is capable of feeling, thinking, and acting (and experiences oneself as such); (b) a world of immediate or cognitively mediated (represented) objects, tools, and systems, with distinct meanings and valences to the person; and (c) a community of learners, who have their shared and unique dispositions and positional identities. Defined this way, a sheer technical orientation to learning becomes problematic (Dai & Renzulli, 2000). A curriculum that treats knowledge acquisition and emotional learning or intellectual character or identity building as parallel goals (e.g., Folsom, 2006; Perkins & Ritchhart, 2004) would enhance the personal relevance and meaningfulness of the curriculum, hence deep intellectual engagement and personal growth.

Counseling and Psychological Interventions for Excellence

If curriculum is one wing of gifted education aimed at nurturing excellence, psychological counseling and academic and career guidance can be seen as another. Conceptions and models of counseling gifted children, adolescents, and young adults have been developed (Mendaglio & Peterson, 2007), including psychotherapy models, dealing with psychological precocity- (developmental asynchrony) and personality-related issues (including underachievement); educational and career guidance models, dealing with educational planning and career-related issues; and psychoeducation models, dealing with self-development, and achievement- and identity-related issues (see Moon, 2007). In principle, developmental approaches to counseling and guidance is most consistent with the CED framework; that is, the focus of counseling and psychological interventions is not on fixing "problems," but on promoting personal growth, self-development, and talent development (Colangelo & Assouline, 2000; Silverman, 1993).

Just as gifted education is not about giftedness but excellence, as I argued above, counseling and psychological interventions should not be fixated on issues such as how to normalize gifted children or the opposite, how to develop their unique "gifted" identity. So, what are counseling and psychological interventions for if "giftedness" is not the focus? The reasons for counseling and guidance have to do with the inherent social and emotional costs of pursuing excellence.

Granted, gifted individuals may have psychological issues unique to their personalities, but the fact that they are not a homogeneous group in terms of personality defies any sweeping generalization about what their psychological and counseling needs are. However, I submit that individuals in the process of pursuing excellence will encounter problems and feel frustrated, confused, discouraged, alienated, or otherwise uncertain about whether they are on the right track in their pursuit of interests, dreams, and passions. High aspirations and self-expectations, sometimes along with high social expectations, add stress to their lives in a way typically not felt by others. Besides, the process of *becoming* from the current state to a future, desired state has many uncertainties. Helping individuals deal with uncertainties about themselves and their future becomes a counselor's main task. The following are among the most important purposes of counseling: counseling for educational planning, for self-development, for developing coping skills, and for managing developmental instability.

Identifying patterns of strengths and propensities, not giftedness. Counselors are often called upon to diagnose whether a child is "gifted" or not. In light of the CED argument that the quality we deem "gifted" is not static and absolute but dynamic and contextual in nature, the diagnostic function in the counseling process is not to confirm or disconfirm the "giftedness" of a child. Instead, school counselors can help, along with teachers and parents, to (1) diagnostically *identify* strengths and propensities as well as possible weaknesses of a child at a particular point in time, (2) *conceptualize* possible developmental trajectories and pathways, and (3) *suggest* educational options and parental actions.

Envisioning possible selves and encouraging self-initiative. Developing a personal identity conducive to focused efforts and sustained strivings is a crucial step in pursuit of excellence, according to the CED framework. Therefore, it is more productive to focus on *possible selves* (Markus & Nurius, 1986) that precocious and advanced learners come to envision and articulate: what they are aspiring to be, where their interests and passions lie, and what kind of life they would find most rewarding. Role models can be identified for these purposes. This kind of counseling and guidance can be tailored to specific subpopulations. For example, it may be used for academically advanced girls who are struggling with meeting gender-stereotypical expectations on the one hand and personal interests and strivings on the other, or disadvantaged minority students whose aspirations may be thwarted by stereotype threat (Ambrose, 2003a; Steele, 1997). For these groups of adolescents, the development of an identity that is true to themselves and conducive to the pursuit of excellence may be particularly important (Hébert & Beardsley, 2001; Worrell, 2007). Envisioning possible selves is not enough. Counselors should encourage their clients to take personal initiative and actively explore themselves through action. Only then will crystallizing experiences likely follow.

Developing coping skills and resilience. One of the reasons why counseling should be aimed at promoting growth rather than fixing problems is that the ultimate agent for change is oneself, not the helping others. Learning to cope with a variety of stresses and setbacks is essential for maintaining psychological health and resilience while pursuing one's goals. Situations that call for coping skills include facing setbacks and having self-doubts (Dweck, 1999), social comparison and competition (the big fish turns small in a big pond; see Dai & Rinn, 2008), procrastination because of undue concerns about imperfection (Schuler, 2002), and alienation from peers (Kerr, 1997). Ironically, negative experiences are not necessarily negative at all; they are opportunities for growth. For instance, the solitude of some gifted girls may help them turn inward and contemplate the self and the world, and as a result their inner experiences and intellectual life be enriched (Kerr, 1997). Likewise, experiences of overcoming obstacles and setbacks are an opportunity for a reality check and the realization that one should not expect smooth sailing in pursuing one's dreams and that persistence and perseverance ultimately will pay off.

Coping skills and resilience are particularly important for high-achieving minority students who are likely to experience extra stress in their academic and social life. Kitano (2003) recommended a range of research-based positive coping strategies that were proved to be effective for high-achieving ethnic-minority women, such as active ignoring, reframing in a positive way, and thinking through problems.

Managing instability. Several models of counseling the gifted allude to the fragility of an unstable developing system (see Mendaglio & Peterson, 2007). From the dynamic system's point of view, such instability is a good thing, indicating the vitality of its growth potential. Talent development means continually trying something new or entering uncharted territory. The feeling of losing direction or of reaching a plateau (i.e., asymptote) is quite common. Self-doubt about whether the person is overreaching him- or herself can also dawn on the individual. The counselor should "normalize" these feelings and suggest ways to balance the stability and instability of development. In *The Lost World*, Michael Crichton (1996) has this to say about managing instability: "Complex systems tend to locate themselves at a place we called 'the edge of chaos.' We imagine the edge of chaos as a place where there is enough innovation to keep a living system vibrant, and enough stability to keep it from collapsing into anarchy" (p. 4). Novelty seeking is quite common among children; for precocious children and adolescents, their overexcitability, to use Dabrowski's word, is a catalyst for expanding their world. We can consider bipolar dimensions of personality characteristics that are either *experience producing* (i.e., differentiation) or *experience integrating* (i.e., integration) (Dai & Renzulli, 2008). For example, excitability is experience producing, while independent judgment is experience integrating; imagination is experience producing, and reflection is experience integrating.

Successful development transitions would ensure continuity of one's talent development and personal growth (Horowitz et al., 2009). The counselor's job is to identify balancing issues and suggest proper actions.

THE PROSPECTS OF GIFTED EDUCATION: FROM RESEARCH TO PRACTICE

The preceding delineation of goals and principles are normative, suggesting what ought to be (ideal conditions), but there are empirical (research) and pragmatic (institutional and pedagogical) aspects of making them a reality.

Evidence-Based Practice in a Time of Accountability

Education in the United States has a long tradition of resorting to empiricism for solutions to some of its problems. Research- or evidence-based decision making and practice is considered the norm for the conduct of education (Shavelson & Towne, 2002). The accountability movement in the past decade or so has furthered this "show me the results" trend. Gifted education is often criticized for operating under vague assumptions rather than solid empirical evidence of the effectiveness of its programs (e.g., Berliner & Biddle, 1995). Evaluating the effectiveness of provisions of gifted education turns out to be more difficult than, say, evaluating a regular class, largely because of its diversity in curricular contents, modes of delivery, and the restricted nature of the samples involved (see Borland, 1997b for a review). To make gifted education developmentally responsive and socially responsible, it is not very meaningful to ask generically whether a gifted program or provision works; rather, it is important to be specific about what works, for whom, and why (theory). Functions and purposes of research in gifted education include at least the following:

Understanding the nature, goals, and effectiveness of a specific education provision or practice. Such research goes beyond the question of whether a program is effective in achieving its set goals and objectives to seek fundamental understanding of how precocious and advanced learners interact with an educational provision and what kind of impact a program exerts on them. It is sometimes called use-inspired research (Stokes, 1997). An example of such research is VanTassel-Baska and colleagues' research program on curriculum development for gifted learners (e.g., VanTassel-Baska, Johnson, Hughes, & Boyce, 1996; VanTassel-Baska, Zuo, Avery, & Little, 2002). In the context of the CED framework, it is particularly important to see how specific education provisions and practices engender particular patterns of characteristic adaptation in students, what indicates the emergent excellence, and how educational practices can be made more responsive to emergent excellence.

Supporting effectiveness claims. The accountability movement tends to focus on minimum standards for all, rather than the possible heights of excellence some students can rise to. In general, it is easier to show how an educational intervention brings a group of low-performing students up to a satisfactory level than what brings a group of high-achieving students to reach new heights (e.g., Loveless et al., 2008) if the ceiling effects are present. Also, the growth of higher-order skills is more difficult to measure than that of basic skills. However, gifted education, if it is to survive the scrutiny of outside critics, has to provide convincing evidence that it does produce excellence or trajectories leading to excellence, even though designing such research can be difficult, as proper control or comparison groups are hard to find. "Report cards" issued in 2006 by several leading scholars on the state of gifted-education research were not very impressive (see VanTassel-Baska, Robinson, Coleman, Shore, & Subotnik, 2006); as VanTassel-Baksa (2006) stated, except for acceleration and grouping, "few other topics have elicited consistent research over time that coalesces around key ideas to promote effective policy formation or practice" (p. 339). Effectiveness of a provision should be based on articulated objectives and standards rather than vaguely framed ideas, evidenced by authentic performance, rather than self-reports of participants that are equivalent to "customer satisfaction."

Supporting generalizability and scalability of particular approaches. A common purpose of research is to produce generalizable knowledge. One of the purposes of educational research is to see how a particular approach that works for some individuals would work for similar others. In fact, some of the innovative educational practices were tried and researched initially in gifted education and then migrated to general classrooms (see Renzulli & Dai, 2003; Tomlinson & Callahan, 1992). The research and development (R&D) efforts are warranted to discover generalizable models of curriculum differentiation and instructional adaptation that support a particular line of academic and career development or integration of cross-disciplinary knowledge. A distinct advantage of the CED framework is that it is a general model for differential development, potentially covering a wide range of divergent developmental paths that have generality.

Supporting socially responsible practices. Socially responsible practices should be broadly defined, including, but not restricted to, the issue of equity. In fact, all public values, equity, excellence, choice, diversity, and efficiency can be considered part of how the social responsibility of education is defined. The role of research is to empirically demonstrate how these values are honored and balanced in particular educational provisions through objectively verifiable evidence and the subjective accounts of stakeholders. For example, Reis (see Reis & Renzulli, 1982) conducted a study of the Revolving Door Identification Model, which shows that using more inclusive or liberal cutoffs for an enrichment program not only gave more students access to enrichment experiences but also produced equally beneficial effects for the participating students. More research is needed to show how educational provisions can benefit those minority students who are underrepresented in gifted education and, more important, how diversity in identification criteria leads to varied forms of excellence and how the standards of excellence are maintained in efforts to ensure equal rights.

Institutional and Instructional Leadership for Excellence

No matter how strong the research base is, without commitment on the part of school leaders and classroom teachers, it is unlikely that gifted education can succeed, or even survive. With the changing landscape of gifted education, how may schools take on this new challenge of developing talents in various academic areas and pursuing forms of excellence as a major priority? To meet this challenge, I reiterate what should transpire in the practice of gifted education as follows: (a) Gifted education should no longer be set up to serve only the top 3 to 5% of students designated as "gifted" but should instead be open to all who demonstrate emergent talents valued by the culture and show interest and commitment to further developing their talents and pursuing excellence; (b) consequently, gifted education should no longer take exclusively the form of special pullout or self-contained programs, but offer a broad range of advanced-level educational services to interested students in the hope that these experiences will become a stepping-stone for follow-up on either a group or an individual basis. (c) The key question should no longer be whether the putatively "unique needs" of the gifted are served, but whether the most able and advanced are sufficiently challenged in school, whether curriculum differentiation and instructional adaptations are properly made for them, and what advanced learning opportunities are available to them (see Renzulli, 2005; Renzulli & Dai, 2003; Rogers, 2007; Shore & Delcourt, 1996; Tomlinson, 1996, for detailed recommendations). What kind of institutional and instructional leadership is needed to make this new paradigm effectively grounded in their practice? I suggest that it takes at least three elements or ingredients for successful implementation of this approach.

The first element is an institutional commitment to developing a culture of excellence in school. Although the range of talents each school decides to focus on may vary, depending on available resources and expertise (e.g., some may focus exclusively on academics, others include artistic and vocational-technical, and still others use integrated curriculum), excellence in academics, arts, vocational, and social or human service areas has to be valued, revered, and celebrated as part of their school identity (surely they can add their outstanding sports programs to the list).

The second element is administrative and logistic in nature: The school policy regarding grouping, educational placement, and class scheduling should be flexible enough to allow the many and varied demonstrated potentials and emergent excellence to be properly nurtured. Furthermore, there should be an infrastructure providing platforms, resources, and technical support and expert coaching for advanced learning activities. Information technology shows great promise in this regard.

The third element is a strong, committed, well-prepared teaching staff. Ultimately, it is teachers who make a difference in students' lives. No matter how great existing curriculum models and pedagogical practices are, there is always an active role of the teacher to interpret the instructional approaches and creatively adapt them to local situations and particular groups of students. What does it mean to become a reflective practitioner (Schön, 1983) in the context of the changing philosophy and practice of gifted education? My suggestion is that all gifted educators seriously reflect on two questions: Are our existing practices sufficiently responsive to developmental changes and opportunities (e.g., emergent excellence)? and, Are our existing practices socially responsible, particularly in terms of excellence and equity? Reflection on these two questions will hopefully help us develop a new vision of gifted education that not only is socially defensible, but also will serve the best interest of all students.

CONCLUSION: CAN GIFTED EDUCATION WORK WITHOUT GIFTED PROGRAMS?

Renzulli (1998) called for developing the gifts and talents of all students, not just the "gifted." Several years later, Borland (2003) announced "the death of giftedness" and articulated a bold vision: "gifted education without gifted children" (p. 105). The essence of his argument is that we can do everything that gifted education is meant to do, not in the name, however, of alleged "giftedness," which is an empty abstraction, but for addressing the manifest educational needs of particular individuals at a particular point in time.

> Teachers, administrators, students, and parents would have to expect differentiation of curriculum and instruction to take place as a matter of course. . . . Our system of education would have to give up the notions of "the normal," "the disabled," and "the gifted" as they are typically applied in schools, especially for purposes of classification and grouping, and simply accept difference as the rule. (Borland, 2003, p. 121)

Here is a hypothetical scenario: If curriculum differentiation and instructional adaptation are so prevalent that almost every child's potential is properly nurtured to the best of our ability, do we still need a separate "gifted program"? The answer is probably no, as the essence of gifted education—helping precocious and advanced learners to reach new heights of excellence—should be part of the educational agenda in all classrooms. This scenario is, of course, idealistic, as it hinges on a school condition that is maximally flexible in administration, fully individualized in teaching, abundant in resources, and equipped with highly versatile teachers (one may further add, without rigidly imposed constraints such as a fixed, mandated curriculum for all; see Schank & Cleary, 1995). As I point out in Chapter 8, many problems we have encountered originated in the age-graded schooling system. It is a convenient and efficient way to run schools but educationally and developmentally inconvenient to many students because of individual and group differences. The realities of the current school system suggest that gifted programs still have reasons for existence. Archambault et al. (1993), for example, conducted a national study of how regular classroom teachers deal with high-ability students. Only about 5% of the teachers in the study knew how to make instructional differentiation for these students. The situation did not change much a decade later (see Westberg & Archambault, 2004). It is clear that gifted programs will not die out anytime soon in the scene of gifted education. Even special schools for the gifted and talented, such as many governor's academies in the United States, New York's Bronx High School of Science, and Israel's Arts and Science Academy, still have a role to play. Until modern schooling gives up its one-size-fits-all curriculum and instruction and is restructured to be fully responsive to emergent learning and achievement differences, qualitative as well as qualitative, gifted programs will still prove a valuable addition to regular classroom teaching. In many ways, special programs for the gifted and talented are just a more efficient way to provide advanced educational activities, given the structure of regular schools.

However, looking into the future, changes in the direction of "gifted education without gifted programs" are not impossible. Baker (2007), for example, argued that the current system of educational evaluation is too uniform to allow a variety of talents to flourish. She suggested the establishment of a certification system, which recognizes a variety of talent accomplishments and excellence in high school as part of credentials of high school graduates. Sufficient flexibility and choice (e.g., varied advanced course offerings) afforded by such a system would provide a new outlet for expression and development of talents, a new form of providing for the diverse educational needs of advanced students. The advantages of a distributed gifted education include flexibility, choice, diversity, and equitable and maximal participation. The advantages of special programs (particularly self-contained ones) and schools have to do with easy management, quality control, and efficient use of resources and expertise.

Although gifted programs (or schools) are likely to stay as long as advanced students' needs are not met in regular schools or classrooms, we should bear in mind that education for excellence has existed for thousands of years, compared with less than 100 years of "gifted education" in United States (since the 1920s). Therefore, a more critical question for us is, Can the value of excellence prevail in the midst of an equalitarian, or even populist, sentiment? If the answer is yes, more advanced learners will get the kind of education they need, whether in the form of gifted programs or of curriculum differentiation and acceleration. Another equally important question is, Are we ready to embrace the many and varied forms of excellence beyond the IQ doctrine? If the answer is yes, the field of gifted education will move on to a new phase. It should be noted that many countries don't have explicit gifted programs or mandated gifted education, and, for better or worse, they don't even have IQ testing; this does not mean, though, that in these countries, excellence is not promoted, identified, nurtured, and rewarded. If, on the other hand, excellence, academic or otherwise, is not valued in its own right, we will likely see it shortchanged whenever budgets get tight or other priorities seem more compelling. Ultimately, a social utilitarian approach to gifted education will prove myopic and unsustainable. Surely a strong talent pool prepared through education is invaluable social capital that serves the national interest in a fundamental way, socially and economically. But it is more important that we value excellence in its own right and make it part of our cultural identity.

Glossary

Affordances and constraints. Basic concepts of ecological psychology, affordances are environmental and social circumstances that allow or invite living organisms to achieve certain goals and satisfy certain needs; constraints are conditions and requirements that need to be satisfied in order to achieve the desired goals. For example, an apple is there for grabbing for an infant, but achievement of this goal is constrained by the infant's ability to perform the act of grabbing; developmentally, the ability of grabbing itself is environmentally shaped by the affordances and constraints of the infant-apple interaction.

Aptitude. This term connotes being "apt to" to do something. Aptitude in educational and psychological research is associated with aptitude tests, such as IQ tests, SAT, ACT, or GRE, typically used for selection and placement purposes. Technically, what makes a test a good aptitude test is its predictive validity vis-à-vis a particular outcome criterion; that is, the test can predict how well a person will learn and achieve in a particular context (e.g., whether a person with high GRE scores will do well in graduate school). In other words, aptitude tests estimate one's *potential*. Aptitude is also used in another way, in terms of whether one is prone or fit to benefit from an instructional situation. The match and mismatch of the learner and instructional provision is called aptitude-treatment interaction (ATI; see Cronbach & Snow, 1977; Snow 1992). When mismatch occurs, the term *inaptitude* is used.

Behavioral genetics. This is a branch of the behavioral sciences concerned with genetic contributions to behavioral variations in populations. Since identical twins share 100% of their genes, various quasi-experimental designs have been employed using twins reared together versus apart and comparing identical and fraternal twins, among other features. Findings of behavioral genetics research are often used as supporting evidence for the genetic contribution to human traits such as intelligence differences.

Brain and mind. Brain is physical; mind is mental. Without the brain, mental events (e.g., perceiving, feeling, thinking, and reasoning) will not occur. Thus the brain works as an infrastructure that supports various mental functions. At the risk of oversimplification, the brain is like hardware and the mind is like software. Software design is constrained by hardware properties; however, how the mind is "programmed" heavily depends on social-cultural experiences and education. The brain-mind problem is a variant of the age-old mind-body problem and is at the core of the nature-nurture debate.

Child prodigy. Child prodigies, an extreme case of precocity, demonstrate unusual talents and competencies at very young ages. They are typically found in the fields of music, mathematics, the visual arts, and certain intellectual games, such as chess (see Feldman, 1986). The existence of child prodigies suggests the role of natural endowment, or "natural talent," in that there is an assumption that most of their age peers with similar exposure and experience will not perform even close to the levels they have reached. See also *Precocity.*

Competence versus performance. The distinction between competence and performance is an important one in the discussion of children's superior performance. When we focus on performance, we look at task constraints and what cognitive or motivational processes are involved in satisfying these constraints to get the job done. When competence is the focus, we infer an enduring quality that distinguishes a person from others. Researchers on gifted and talented children are typically biased in favor of individual differences in competence as an explanation of superior performance, whereas researchers on expertise are typically biased in favor of how the performer overcomes performance constraints through developing cognitive skills and proficiency.

Creativity. The concept of creativity is subject to many definitions and perspectives. Research on creativity typically focuses on three dimensions: person, process, and product. A person may be prone to generating creative ideation or expression. Various cognitive and affective characteristics are identified as facilitative of creativity. Creativity involves perceptual and thinking processes that usually take a considerable amount of time from the inception of an idea to its full fruition; from incubation, moments of "sudden insights," to laborious verification or implementation. A product is creative to the extent that it is novel and is valuable for intellectual, artistic, practical, and social purposes. Some scholars distinguish between big-*C* creativity, that is epoch-making, groundbreaking creativity, and small-*c*, everyday creativity. This distinction highlights the importance of judging creativity by the merits and impact of products. In gifted-education contexts, the focus is on the person (how to identify the creatively gifted) and the process (e.g., how to promote creative thinking and inclinations). Recently, the issue of whether creativity has domain specificity has become more prominent (see Sternberg et al., 2004). See also *Domain specificity.*

Curriculum differentiation. This is a broad term referring to any teaching practice that attempts to tailor educational provisions to the current needs of students. The basic assumption underlying curriculum differentiation is that an educational provision appropriate for one child may not be so for another at a given point in time. Typically, a child's history of learning, prior knowledge, motivation, and ability to handle a particular learning task are all considerations for curriculum differentiation. For gifted and talented children, curriculum differentiation often takes the form of curriculum compacting, enrichment, and acceleration. Curriculum differentiation in elementary school is typically done in the regular classroom. At the high school level, special programs and AP classes are ways to deal with diverse student needs.

Developmental complexity. This phrase denotes a tendency of a developing organism to construct an increasingly complex skill set to meet environmental challenges mainly through the differentiation and integration of cognitive responses and performance components. More specifically, it assumes that in the early years, one's response repertoire is relatively simple, consisting of many spontaneous responses, learned or native. Over time, more sophisticated and well-coordinated responses are orchestrated to deal with a particular challenge for which simple response is no longer adequate. At the very high level of proficiency or expertise, responses are fine-tuned to task situations to such a level that any regularities and anomalies are quickly detected. In principle, superior competencies displayed by children are developmentally less complex than those displayed at later stages of development. This principle has implications for the nature-nurture debate: Teasing apart the contributions of nature and nurture become almost impossible with high developmental complexity of a particular talent or expertise.

Distributed intelligence and creativity. Intelligence in a psychometric sense refers to individual difference in some basic cognitive functions. To view intelligence as distributed means to switch to a more contextual view of intellectual functioning. To the extent that an intelligent performance hinges on environmental stimulation, resources, and technical support, intelligence is not something residing in the head but *distributed* between the person and the environment (situations, symbols, tools, etc.). When other people's minds are involved in learning and solving a particular problem, intelligence is socially distributed, and it might be more appropriately called collective intelligence. Similarly, the case can be made about creativity, which is traditionally seen as *possessed* by individuals. The notion of distributed intelligence or creativity emphasizes the contextual and emergent nature of intelligent acts and thus downplays the role of superior individual minds as indispensable for high-level performance.

Domain specificity. This phrase is typically used in two senses. In the first sense, the human brain is evolutionarily equipped with different human capacities to deal with different challenges, some physical (e.g., visual acuity and spatial reasoning) and others social (e.g., recognizing faces or reading emotions). In the second sense, any human competence is a circumscribed one, confined to a particular functional context, and thus is not an all-purpose and omnipotent mechanism. The evolution-based argument can be seen as a strong version of the domain-specificity argument, as it implies that the mind is innately programmed in a domain-specific way. The functional-boundedness argument can be seen as a weak version, as domain specificity in this sense does not preclude the possibility that a particular domain-specific competence is developed through applying domain-general but relevant capabilities and mechanisms. Domain specificity of exceptional competence in domains of cultural importance means that each domain should be treated as having a unique set of requirements. Social and practical domains involve real-time decision making, and intellectual domains involve mastery of special symbol systems and significant verbal mediation. Consequently, the centrality of a human ability (e.g., spatial, mathematical, or verbal ability) vis-à-vis a domain can be determined by detailed analysis of the task constraints in that domain.

Dynamic versus static assessment. Tools afford dynamic assessment if they are capable of capturing a change of interest from State A to State B. In contrast, static assessment only provides information about a state of performance or behavior at a time. Static assessment is like a series of snapshots, and dynamic assessment provides a motion picture. Dynamic assessment has the potential to capture the progress made in goal-directed learning and problem-solving activities and discerning *how* people differ in tackling a particular class of tasks. Static assessment typically gives a summary of *how well* a person performed compared with others without information about how he or she did it.

Dynamic systems. The term *system* implies that a whole consists of several parts or components in such an organized manner that changes in one part affects other parts. A system is dynamic if it is a changing system from one state to another over time. Thus a developing child is a dynamic system, and a person attempting to solve a problem represents the changing state of a dynamic system interacting with the environment. Treating human beings as dynamic systems means that we can theoretically view any superior human performance and competence as progressing through a developmental trajectory from a relatively simple state to an increasingly more complex one.

Epigenesis. Physical, behavioral, and psychological traits are epigenetic if they are not genetically determined but are acquired through genetic, behavioral, and environmental interactions, which are mediated by developmental changes and are sensitive to environmental variations and developmental timing. Some aspects of human development are genetically determined, such as eye color and height, but most psychological traits are epigenetically developed and probabilistic in nature (hence *probabilistic epigenesis*; see Gottlieb, 1998).

Epistemic stance. This term was used by Daniel Dennett to characterize how people cognitively position themselves when looking at a particular phenomenon. They can take a physical stance, in which they see things as physical materials that are predictable according to physical laws (e.g., Newtonian physics). They can also take a design stance, which assumes the existence of a particular relationship between a structure and the function(s) it serves. Biologists and engineers typically take this latter stance. Alternatively, they can take an intentional stance, treating an organism (e.g., a cat) or object (e.g., a robot) as having goals, purposes, and intentions, in some way capable of self-direction and self-initiated, goal-directed behavior.

Equifinality. This refers to a situation in which two systems may not have all components in common or have started in the same place, yet reach the same end state. Factors leading to the emergence of the same form or properties do not need to be the same for different individuals. Equifinality of human potential means we should not trace ultimate human accomplishments back to their origins as if their origins must be the same. For example, Nobel laureates have all achieved the same level of eminence, but their individuality and the life circumstances that led to their outstanding accomplishments were quite different.

Essentialism or realism. Essentialism is the belief that for every discernable phenomenon or object, there is an underlying essence or deep structure that maintains its unity, identity, and continuity. Uncovering this essence helps to explain the phenomenon or object in question. Essentialist thinking has played a predominant role in the history of conceptions of giftedness, particularly in the concept of general intelligence as a quintessential part of giftedness. See also *Ontological commitments, worldviews, epistemic stances*; *Reification*.

Expertise. Expertise is high-level proficiency in a particular human endeavor to professional standards. It is characterized by keen insight into the problems at hand, usually through pattern recognition, facility in finding promising ways to tackle problems, and deep understanding of the inner workings of things in a domain of expertise. Typically it takes 10 or more years of serious study and practice to reach the level of expertise. It is argued that expertise may be necessary for creativity, but is usually not sufficient for creativity. Exceptions can be found in domains or a productive mode of functioning where expertise involves creative problem solving, such as in the games of chess or go, or in architecture or music composition.

Heritability. A technical term, this indicates the extent to which certain physical, behavioral, and psychological characteristics have genetic origins. As used in quantitative genetics research, heritability (h^2) is mathematically estimated, indicating the proportion of phenotypic variance (eye color, height, introversion, IQ, or other traits) in a population that can be attributed to genetic variance (i.e., differences in inherited genes) in that population.

Innatism. Innatism is used in psychology to suggest that certain mental capacities and structures are innately determined or genetically preordained, regardless of what kinds of environment people find themselves in. The most famous innatist argument is *universal grammar*, postulated by Noam Chomsky to explain children's language development without apparent direct instruction. Strong innatists often argue for modular devices in the brain in tackling specific types of information or stimuli. Innatist arguments should be distinguished from genetic-endowment arguments. A general genetic advantage in cognitive functioning can be simply higher efficiency of the system as a whole and does not necessarily imply superior innate or inborn structures.

Microdevelopment and macrodevelopment. Developmental changes that can be observed or measured within a short period such as weeks or months are microdevelopmental. Macrodevelopmental changes occur over a much longer time, such as years. Traditionally, developmental researchers have been concerned mainly with macrodevelopment, assuming that order by changes over time can be observed for all. More recently, micro-level developmental processes and developmental variability or diversity have been brought to wider attention largely because of an understanding that development involves real-time organization and modification of behavior vis-à-vis developmental challenges. Intensive observation and follow-up on microdevelopment are done through microgenetic methods (see Granott & Parziale, 2002).

Modularity. This term refers to the unique properties of relatively independent functional units or devices in the brain that are specialized in processing particular kinds of information. Some identified characteristics include domain specificity, mandatoriness (i.e., automatic, not subject to conscious control), limited central access (e.g., its workings are impervious to cognition), speed, information encapsulation, fixed neural architecture or mechanisms, specific breakdown patterns, and specific ontogeny (i.e., a characteristic course of development). There is no consensus on the identification of defining characteristics of a modular device (see Seok, 2006; Barrett & Kurzban, 2006).

Neural efficiency hypothesis. This hypothesis postulates that superior cognitive performance on certain ability tests is largely the result of cognitive efficiency, such as processing speed, reaction time, fast information uptake, working-memory capacity that affords simultaneous processing of more information, and effective cognitive inhibition of irrelevant information, all of which can be traced to neural substrates. According to this view, gifted children's ease of learning and superior performance largely results from a neural advantage. The neural efficiency hypothesis reflects a reductionist view of giftedness.

Nomothetic versus idiographic approach. The term *nomothetic* pertains to universal laws, and the term *idiographic* pertains to particular individual cases. The terms were initially used in personality research to describe two differing approaches: nomothetic approaches try to identify dimensions and typologies so that individuals can be compared on some common scales or measures; idiographic approaches, by contrast, focus on unique individuality, in all its richness, complexity, and dynamism. Allport (1937) alternatively calls these two approaches dimensional and morphogenic approaches to personality research. The methodological differences are sometimes seen as reflecting differences between rationalist and naturalistic epistemologies. In the field of gifted studies and education, IQ-based definitions and theories of giftedness in effect use an nomothetic or dimensional approach, and case studies of child prodigies and eminent individuals can be seen as examples of idiographic approaches.

Ontological commitments, worldviews, epistemic stances. Ontological commitments are deep convictions about reality that are held by researchers or scientists and that lay the foundation for their work. Unlike specific theories or theoretical predictions, ontological commitments are "philosophical" and typically not falsifiable (i.e., cannot be proved wrong; Lakatos, 1978). Similar to ontological commitments, worldviews are general outlooks that frame one's perspectives on specific issues in a profound way, including how facts and data are interpreted (Pepper, 1942). Overtone (1984) identified three basic worldviews regarding human psychology: mechanistic, organismic, and contextual. In comparison, epistemic stances, at least as used by Dennett (1987), are more strategic; they concern how a particular stance helps us make right predictions about the behavior of an object. Epistemic stances include physical, design, and intentional stances.

Precocity. When an ability occurs exceptionally early in development, it is a sign of precocity. Child prodigies are a distinct case of precocity. In the field of gifted studies and education, some scholars believe that precocity captures the essence of being gifted, but others feel that gifted children are more than precocious, since precocity implies a developmental advantage (early bloomers) that can dissipate over time, whereas the gifted and nongifted reflect individual differences that cannot be explained by mere early occurrences of certain mental properties or qualities. The question was raised by Halbert Robinson in the 1970s and remains to be addressed (see Shore, 2000).

Producers versus performers. The distinction suggests important functional differences between those who excel at producing new products (theories, gadgets, music pieces, etc.) and those who excel at performing skilled routines (air traffic control operators, performing soloists, athletes, cardiovascular surgeons, etc.). The distinction should not be confused with that between proficiency and creativity, as both producers and performers can be of the proficient or creative type (see Tannenbaum, 1997).

Proximal versus distal variables and measurements. With proximal variables and related measurements, the measurement is situationally tied to task constraints at hand and are indicative of the current state of knowledge or competence. Distal measurements are less sensitive to time and situation and imply a more enduring nature of the quality being measured. This technical aspect of measurement and assessment is important when deciding how much weight a particular piece of information should carry for selection and educational placement purposes.

Rate of learning versus asymptote of performance. These are two main criteria or parameters we use to gauge whether one is gifted, precocious, or advanced. The rate of learning is how fast one can learn a particular task or class of tasks. The asymptote of performance is the point at which performance reaches its bottleneck or hits its ceiling, and no meaningful gains are visible despite more trials and more improvement efforts. It is important to note that although apparent variations in rates of learning and asymptotes of performance can be observed in the classroom, only in a strictly controlled laboratory environment can we get a relatively "pure" measure of rates of learning or asymptotes of performance, not "contaminated" or "confounded" by extraneous variables such as resources, support, performance conditions, and motivation.

Reductionism versus emergentism. A tendency to explain complex matters in simple terms and to see a multitude of phenomena as following the same set of laws and principles is reductionism. From a systems perspective, reductionism is a belief that any matter of seemingly higher-level complexity can be decomposed to lower-level components or regularities. Thus cellular-level phenomena can be explained in molecular terms. The most successful story of reductionism is physics, wherein a small but universally applicable set of mathematically expressed laws and theorems is formulated and repeatedly validated. Emergentism, like holism (the whole is more than the sum of all parts), is nonreductionistic, if not antireductionistic, but it is more than what holism implies. Emergentism is concerned with emergent properties that cannot be accounted for by any single element working alone and do not resemble any of the elements that give rise to these properties. Emergentism also argues that there are higher-order organizational principles and regularities commensurate with the complexity of the matter in question. Thus social interaction reveals emergent properties and regularities that cannot be explained by characteristics of individuals involved. Highly intelligent and creative behavior can emerge from the social interaction of apparently regular folks (see Dai, 2005; Sawyer, 2002).

Reification. When something abstract is treated as having material existence, reification is occurring. In psychology, psychological constructs such as intelligence, motivation, and self-concept are conceptual tools that help us organize and make meaningful a set of observations. Reification is a real danger in discussing gifted and talented children, since the elusive quality of "being gifted or talented" can be reified as an entity without there being a clear understanding of the specific nature of varied gifted and talented manifestations. See also *Essentialism or realism.*

Savants. Sometimes called "idiot savants" or "mono-savants," savants are individuals who demonstrate unusual talents in certain domains (e.g., mental calculation, painting) but otherwise are mentally disabled or challenged. Often, developmental abnormality is involved (e.g., autism) in the savant syndrome. Savants provide a special window through which many lessons can be learned about nature-nurture and domain specificity–domain generality issues (see Miller, 2005).

Situated cognition. This phrase indicates that cognition is not just representing the world in the mind through symbols, but is fine-tuned to situational affordances and constraints, so much so that changing the context will impair cognitive performance. An instructive example is Brazilian children who are highly capable of doing street math because of their experiences and practices in street peddling, but are "disabled" when the same problems they encounter in the street are presented in the form of school math. The situative perspective has implications for the contextual boundedness of gifted competence or potential.

Talent. As used colloquially, this word has two connotations: First, it is an attribution people make that implies a superior quality in the person involved, thus implicating "natural endowment"; second, the term implies domain specificity or a special flair for a certain activity but not for others. In contrast, the term *gifted* can be used to either describe domain-specific talents ("He is gifted musician") or infer a general intellectual quality in the person ("She is brilliant and gifted"). In practice, the term *gifted* implies a more general advantage or pervasive personal characteristic than does the term *talented*.

References

Ackerman, C. M. (2009). The essential elements of Dabrowski's theory of positive disintegration and how they are connected. *Roeper Review, 31*, 81–95.

Ackerman, P. L. (1988). Determinants of individual differences during skill acquisition: Cognitive abilities and information processing. *Journal of Experimental Psychology: General, 117*, 288–318.

Ackerman, P. L. (1999). Traits and knowledge as determinants of learning and individual differences: Putting it all together. In P. L. Ackerman, P. C. Kyllonen, & R. D. Roberts (Eds.), *Learning and individual differences: Process, traits, and content determinants* (pp. 437–460). Washington, DC: American Psychological Association.

Ackerman, P. L. (2003). Aptitude complexes and trait complexes. *Educational Psychologist, 38*, 85–93.

Ackerman, P. L., & Heggestad, E. D. (1997). Intelligence, personality, and interest: Evidence for overlapping traits. *Psychological Bulletin, 121*, 219–245.

Ackerman, P. L., & Kanfer, R. (2004). Cognitive, affective, and conative aspects of adult intellect within a typical and maximal performance framework. In D. Y. Dai & R. J. Sternberg (Eds.), *Motivation, emotion, and cognition: Integrative perspectives on intellectual functioning and development* (pp. 119–141). Mahwah, NJ: Lawrence Erlbaum.

Alexander, J. M., Carr, M., & Schwanenflugel, P. J. (1995). Development of metacognition in gifted children: Directions for future research. *Developmental Review, 15*, 1–37.

Alexander, P. A. (2004). A model of domain learning: Reinterpreting expertise as a multidimensional, multistage process. In D. Y. Dai & R. J. Sternberg (Eds.), *Motivation, emotion, and cognition: Integrative perspectives on intellectual functioning and development* (pp. 273–298). Mahwah, NJ: Lawrence Erlbaum.

Allman, J. M., Hakeem, A., Erwin, J. M., Nimchinsky, E., & Hof, P. (2001). The anterior cingulate cortex: The evolution of an interface between emotion and cognition. In A. R. Damasio, A. Harrington, J. Kagan, B. S. McEwen, H. Moss, & R. Shaikh (Eds.), *Unity of knowledge: The convergence of natural and human science* (pp. 107–117). New York: New York Academy of Sciences.

Allport, G. W. (1937). *Patterns and growth in personality*. New York: Holt, Rinehart & Winston.

Amabile, T. M. (2001). Beyond talent: John Irving and the passionate craft of creativity. *American Psychologist, 56*, 333–336.

Ambrose, D. (2000). World-view entrapment: Moral-ethical implications for gifted education. *Journal for the Education of the Gifted, 23*, 159–186.

Ambrose, D. (2003a). Barriers to aspiration development and self-fulfillment: Interdisciplinary insights for talent discovery. *Gifted Child Quarterly, 47*, 282–294.

Ambrose, D. (2003b). Theoretical scope, dynamic tensions, and dialectical processes: A model for discovery of creative intelligence. In D. Ambrose, L. M. Cohen, & A. J.

Tannenbaum (Eds.), *Creative intelligence: Toward theoretical integration*. Cresskill, NJ: Hampton Press.

Ambrose, D. (2005). Interdisciplinary expansion of conceptual foundations: Insights from beyond our field. *Roeper Review, 27,* 137–143.

American Association on Mental Retardation (1992). *Mental retardation: Definition, classification, and systems of support* (9th ed.). Washington, DC: Author.

American Educational Research Association, American Psychological Association, & National Council on Measurement in Education. (1999). *Standards for educational and psychological testing.* Washington, DC: National Council on Measurement in Education.

Anderson, J. R. (1987). Skill acquisition: Compilation of weak-method problem situations. *Psychological Review, 94,* 192–210.

Angoff, W. H. (1988). The nature-nurture debate, aptitudes, and group differences. *American Psychologist, 43,* 713–720.

Archambault, F. X. J., Westberg, K. L., Brown, S. W., Hallmark, B. W., Emmons, C. L., & Zhang, W. (1993). *Regular classroom practices with gifted students: Results of a national survey of classroom teachers* (Research Report No. 93101). Storrs: University of Connecticut, National Research Center on the Gifted and Talented.

Ashby, F. G., Isen, A. M., & Turken, A. U. (1999). A neuropsychological theory of positive affect and its influence on cognition. *Psychological Review, 106,* 529–550.

Aulls, M. W., & Shore, B. M. (2008). *Inquiry in education: The conceptual foundations for research as a curricular imperative.* New York: Erlbaum.

Baker, E. L. (2007). The end(s) of testing. *Educational Researcher, 36,* 309–317.

Balchin, T., Hymer, B. J., & Matthews, D. J. (Eds.) (2009). *The Routledge international companion to gifted education.* Abingdon, UK: Routledge.

Baltes, P. B. (1998). Testing the limits of the ontogenetic sources of talent and excellence. *Behavioral and Brain Sciences, 21,* 407–408.

Baltes, P. B., Lindenberger, U., & Staudinger, U. M. (1998). Life-span theory in developmental psychology. In W. Damon & R. M. Lerner (Eds.), *Handbook of child development: Vol. 1: Theoretical models of human development* (pp. 1029–1041). New York: Wiley.

Bamberger, J. (1986). Cognitive issues in the development of musically gifted children. In R. J. Sternberg & J. E. Davidson (Eds.), *Conceptions of giftedness* (pp. 388–413). Cambridge, UK: Cambridge University Press.

Bandura, A. (1986). *Social foundations of thought and action: A social cognitive theory.* Englewood Cliffs, NJ: Prentice Hall.

Bandura, A. (1997). *Self-efficacy: The exercise of control.* New York: W. H. Freeman.

Bangert, M., & Schlaug, G. (2006). Specialization of the specialized in features of external human brain morphology. *European Journal of Neuroscience, 24,* 1832–1834.

Barab, S. A., & Plucker, J. A. (2002). Smart people or smart context? Cognition, ability, and talent development in an age of situated approaches to knowing and learning. *Educational Psychologist, 37,* 165–182.

Barrett, H. C., & Kurzban, R. (2006). Modularity in cognition: Framing the debate. *Psychological Review, 113,* 628–647.

Bates, E., & Carnevale, G. F. (1993). New directions in research on language development. *Developmental Review, 13,* 436–470.

Benbow, C. P., & Stanley, J. C. (1996). Inequity in equity: How "equity" can lead to inequity for high-potential students. *Psychology, Public Policy, and Law, 2,* 249–292.

Bereiter, C. (2002). *Education and mind in the knowledge age*. Mahwah, NJ: Lawrence Erlbaum Associates.

Berg, C. A. (2000). Intellectual development in adulthood. In R. J. Sternberg (Ed.), *Handbook of intelligence* (pp. 117–137). Cambridge, UK: Cambridge University Press.

Berliner, D. C., & Biddle, R. J. (1995). *The manufactured crisis: Myths, fraud, and the attack on America's public schools*. Reading, MA: Addison-Wesley.

Bernal, E. M. (2003). To no longer educate the gifted: Programming for gifted students beyond the era of inclusionism. *Gifted Child Quarterly, 47*, 183–191.

Beutler, L. E., & Rosner, R. (1995). Introduction to psychological assessment. In L. E. Beutler & R. Rosner (Eds.), *Integrative assessment of adult personality* (pp. 1–24). New York: Guilford Press.

Bidell, T. R., & Fischer, K. W. (1997). Between nature and nurture: The role of human agency in the epigenesis of intelligence. In R. J. Sternberg & E. Grigorenko (Eds.), *Intelligence, heredity, and environment* (pp. 193–242). New York: Cambridge University Press.

Binet, A., & Simon, T. (1916). *The development of intelligence in children* (E. S. Kite, Trans.). Baltimore: Williams & Wilkins.

Block, N. J., & Dworkin, G. (1976). *The IQ controversy*. New York: Pantheon.

Bloom, B. S. (1985). *Developing talent in young people*. New York: Ballantine Books.

Bonsangue, M. V., & Drew, D. E. (1995). Increasing minority students' success in calculus. *New Directions for Teaching and Learning, 11*, 501–518.

Borkowski, J. G., & Peck, V. A. (1986). Causes and consequences of metamemory in gifted children. In R. J. Sternberg & J. E. Davidson (Eds.), *Conceptions of giftedness* (pp. 182–200). Cambridge, UK: Cambridge University Press.

Borland, J. H. (1996). Gifted education and threat of irrelevance. *Journal for the Education of the Gifted, 19*, 129–147.

Borland, J. H. (1997a). The construct of giftedness. *Peabody Journal of Education, 72*(3 & 4), 6–20.

Borland, J. H. (1997b). Evaluating gifted programs. In N. Colangelo & G. A. Davis (Eds.), *Handbook of gifted education* (2nd ed., pp. 253–266). Boston: Allyn & Bacon.

Borland, J. H. (1999). The limits of consilience: A reaction to Françoys Gagné's "My convictions about the nature of abilities, gifts, and talents." *Journal for the Education of the Gifted, 22*, 137–147.

Borland, J. H. (2003). The death of giftedness. In J. H. Borland (Ed.), *Rethinking gifted education* (pp. 105–124). New York: Teachers College Press.

Borland, J. H. (2005). Gifted education without gifted children: The case for no conception of giftedness. In R. J. Sternberg & J. E. Davidson (Eds.), *Conceptions of giftedness* (2nd ed., pp. 1–19). Cambridge, UK: Cambridge University Press.

Borland, J. H. (2008). Identification. In J. A. Plucker & C. M. Callahan (Eds.), *Critical issues and practices in gifted education: What the research says* (pp. 261–280). Austin, TX: Prufrock Press.

Bouffard-Bouchard, T., Parent, S., & Larivée, S. (1993). Self-regulation on a concept-formation task among average and gifted students. *Journal of Experimental Child Psychology, 56*, 115–134.

Bransford, J. D., Brown, A. L., & Cocking, R. R. (1999). *How people learn: Brain, mind, experience, and school*. Washington, DC: National Academy Press.

Bredo, E. (2009). Getting over the methodology wars. *Educational Researcher, 38*, 441–448.

Brody, N. (2000). History of theories and measurements of intelligence. In R. J. Sternberg (Ed.), *Handbook of intelligence* (pp. 16–33). Cambridge, UK: Cambridge University Press.

Bronfenbrenner, U. (1989). Ecological systems theory. In R. Vasta (Ed.), *Annals of child development, Vol. 6: Six theories of child development*. Greenwich, CT: JAI Press.

Bronfenbrenner, U., & Ceci, S. J. (1994). Nature-nurture reconceptualized in developmental perspective: A bio-ecological model. *Psychological Review, 101*, 568–586.

Bruner, J. (1979). *On knowing: Essays for the left hand*. Cambridge, MA: Belknap Press of Harvard University Press.

Callahan, C. M., & Miller, E. M. (2005). A child-responsive model of giftedness. In R. J. Sternberg & J. E. Davidson (Eds.), *Conceptions of giftedness* (2nd ed., pp. 38–51). Cambridge, UK: Cambridge University Press.

Campione, J. C., & Brown, A. L. (1978). Toward a theory of intelligence: Contributions from research with retarded children. *Intelligence, 2*, 279–304.

Cantor, N. (1990). From thought to behavior: "Having" and "doing" in the study of personality and cognition. *American Psychologist, 45*, 735–750.

Carpenter, P. A., Just, M. A., & Shell, P. (1990). What one intelligence test measures: A theoretical account of the processing in the Raven Progressive Matrices Test. *Psychological Review, 97*, 404–431.

Carraher, T. N., Carraher, D. W., & Schliemann, A. D. (1985). Mathematics in the streets and in schools. *British Journal of Developmental Psychology, 3*, 21–29.

Carroll, J. B. (1993). *Human cognitive abilities: A survey of factor-analytic studies*. Cambridge: Cambridge University Press.

Carroll, J. B. (1997). Psychometrics, intelligence, and public perception. *Intelligence, 24*, 25–52.

Case, R. (1992). *The mind's staircase: Exploring the conceptual underpinnings of children's thought and knowledge*. Hillsdale, NJ: Lawrence Erlbaum.

Casey, M. B., Winner, E., Benbow, C., Hayes, R., et al. (1993). Skill at image generation: Handedness interacts with strategy preference for individuals majoring in spatial fields. *Cognitive Neuropsychology, 10*, 57–77.

Cattell, R. B. (1971). *Abilities: Their structure, growth, and action*. Boston: Houghton Mifflin.

Ceci, S. J. (1996). *On intelligence: A bio-ecological treatise on intellectual development* (2nd ed.). Cambridge, MA: Harvard University Press.

Ceci, S. J. (2003). Cast in six ponds and you'll reel in something: Looking back on 25 years of research. *American Psychologist, 58*, 855–864.

Ceci, S. J., & Liker, J. (1986). A day at the races: A study of IQ, expertise, and cognitive complexity. *Journal of Experimental Psychology: General, 115*, 255–266.

Ceci, S. J., & Papierno, P. B. (2005). The rhetoric and reality of gap closing: When the "have-nots" gain but the "haves" gain even more. *American Psychologist, 60*, 149–160.

Ceci, S. J., & Ruiz, A. (1993). Transfer, abstractness, and intelligence. In D. K. Detterman & R. J. Sternberg (Eds.), *Transfer on trial: Intelligence, cognition, and instruction* (pp. 168–191). Norwood, NJ: Ablex.

Ceci, S. J., & Williams, W. M. (1997). Schooling, intelligence, and income. *American Psychologist, 52*, 1051–1058.

Ceci, S. J., Williams, W. M., & Barnett, S. M. (2009). Women's underrepresentation in science: Sociocultural and biological considerations. *Psychological Bulletin, 135,* 218–261.

Chess, S., & Thomas, A. (1996). *Temperament: Theory and practice.* New York: Brunner/ Mazel.

Chi, M. T. H. (1978). Knowledge structures and memory development. In R. S. Siegler (Ed.), *Children's thinking: What develops?* (pp. 73–96). Hillsdale, NJ: Lawrence Erlbaum.

Chi, M. T. H., Feltovich, P. J., & Glaser, R. (1981). Categorization and representation of physics problems by experts and novices. *Cognitive Science, 5,* 121–152.

Clark, A. (1997). *Being there: Putting brain, body, and world together again.* Cambridge, MA: MIT Press.

Cleary, T. A., Humphreys, L. G., Kendrick, S. A., & Wesman, A. (1975). Educational uses of tests with disadvantaged students. *American Psychologist, 30,* 15–41.

Cohen, S. M. (2006). Lecture on the four causes. Retrieved on June 10, 2009, from http:// faculty.washington.edu/smcohen/320/4causes.htm.

Colangelo, N., & Assouline, S. G. (2000). Counseling gifted students. In K. A. Heller, F. J. Monk, R. J. Sternberg, & R. F. Subotnik (Eds.), *International handbook of giftedness and talent* (2nd ed., pp. 595–607). Amsterdam: Elsevier Science.

Colangelo, N., Assouline, S. G., & Gross, M. U. M. (2004). *A nation received: How schools hold back America's brightest students* (Vol. 1). Iowa City, IA: Belin-Blank International Center for Gifted Education and Talent Development.

Coleman, L. J. (2003). Gifted-child pedagogy: Meaningful chimera? *Roeper Review, 25,* 163–164.

Coleman, L. J., & Cross, T. L. (2005). *Being gifted in school: An introduction to development, guidance, and teaching.* Waco, TX: Prufrock Press.

Coleman, L. J., Sanders, M. D., & Cross, T. L. (1997). Perennial debates and tacit assumptions in the education of gifted children. *Gifted Child Quarterly, 41,* 105–111.

Cosmides, L., & Tooby, J. (2003). *Universal minds: Explaining the new science of evolutionary psychology.* London: Weidenfeld & Nicolson.

Cramond, B., Matthews-Morgan, J., Bandalos, D., & Zuo, L. (2005). A report on the 40-year follow-up of the Torrance Tests of Creative Thinking: Alive and well in the new millennium. *Gifted Child Quarterly, 49,* 283–291.

Crichton, M. (1996). *The lost world.* New York: Ballantine Books.

Cronbach, L. J. (1957). The two disciplines of scientific psychology. *American Psychologist, 12,* 671–684.

Cronbach, L. J. (1975). Beyond the two disciplines of scientific psychology. *American Psychologist, 30,* 116–127.

Cronbach, L. J. E. (Ed.) (2002). *Remaking the concept of aptitude: Extending the legacy of Richard E. Snow.* Mahwah, NJ: Lawrence Erlbaum.

Cronbach, L. J., & Snow, R. E. (1977). *Aptitudes and instructional methods: A handbook for research on interactions.* New York: Irvington.

Cross, T. L. (2003). Rethinking gifted education: A phenomenological critique of the politics and assumptions of the empirical-analytic mode of inquiry. In J. H. Borland (Ed.), *Rethinking gifted education* (pp. 72–79). New York: Teachers College, Columbia University.

Csikszentmihalyi, M. (1978). Intrinsic reward and emergent motivation. In M. R. Lepper & D. Greene (Eds.), *The hidden costs of reward: New perspectives on the psychology of human motivation.* Hillsdale, NJ: Erlbaum.

Csikszentmihalyi, M. (1990). *Flow: The psychology of optimal experience*. New York: Harper & Row.

Csikszentmihalyi, M. (1996). *Creativity: Flow and the psychology of discovery and invention*. New York: HarperCollins.

Csikszentmihalyi, M., Rathunde, K., & Whalen, S. (1993). *Talented teenager*. New York: Cambridge University Press.

Csikszentmihalyi, M., & Robinson, R. E. (1986). Culture, time, and the development of talent. In R. J. Sternberg & J. E. Davidson (Eds.), *Conceptions of giftedness* (pp. 264–284). Cambridge, UK: Cambridge University Press.

Dai, D. Y. (2002). Are gifted girls motivationally disadvantaged? Review, reflection, and redirection. *Journal for the Education of the Gifted*, *25*, 315–358.

Dai, D. Y. (2004a). Putting it all together: Some concluding thoughts. In D. Y. Dai & R. J. Sternberg (Eds.), *Motivation, emotion, and cognition: Integrative perspectives on intellectual functioning and development* (pp. 419–431). Mahwah, NJ: Lawrence Erlbaum.

Dai, D. Y. (2004b). Why the transformation metaphor doesn't work well: A comment on Gagne's DMGT model. *High Ability Studies*, *15*, 157–159.

Dai, D. Y. (2005). Reductionism versus emergentism: A framework for understanding conceptions of giftedness. *Roeper Review*, *27*, 144–151.

Dai, D. Y. (2006). There is more to aptitude than cognitive capacities. *American Psychologist*, *61*, 723–724.

Dai, D. Y. (2009). Essential tensions surrounding the concept of giftedness. In L. Shavinina (Ed.), *International handbook on giftedness* (pp. 39–80). New York: Springer.

Dai, D. Y., & Coleman, L. J. (2005). Introduction to the special issue on nature, nurture, and development of exceptional competence. *Journal for the Education of the Gifted*, *28*, 254–269.

Dai, D. Y., Moon, S. M., & Feldhusen, J. F. (1998). Achievement motivation and gifted students: A social cognitive perspective. *Educational Psychologist*, *33*, 45–63.

Dai, D. Y., & Renzulli, J. S. (2000). Dissociation and integration of talent development and personal growth: Comments and suggestions. *Gifted Child Quarterly*, *44*, 247–251.

Dai, D. Y., & Renzulli, J. S. (2008). Snowflakes, living systems, and the mystery of giftedness. *Gifted Child Quarterly*, *52*, 114–130.

Dai, D. Y., & Rinn, A. N. (2008). The big-fish-little-pond effect: What do we know and where do we go from here? *Educational Psychology Review*, *20*, 283–317.

Dai, D. Y., & Sternberg, R. J. (2004). Beyond cognitivism: Toward an integrated understanding of intellectual functioning and development. In D. Y. Dai & R. J. Sternberg (Eds.), *Motivation, emotion, and cognition: Integrative perspectives on intellectual functioning and development* (pp. 3–38). Mahwah, NJ: Lawrence Erlbaum.

Damasio, A. R. (1999). *The feeling of what happens: Body and emotion in the making of consciousness*. New York: Harcourt Brace.

Davidson, R. J. (2001). Toward a biology of personality and emotion. In A. R. Damasio, A. Harrington, J. Kagan, B. S. McEwen, H. Moss & R. Shaikh (Eds.), *Unity of knowledge: The convergence of natural and human science* (pp. 191–207). New York: New York Academy of Sciences.

Deary, I. J. (2002). *G* and cognitive elements of information processing: An agnostic view. In R. J. Sternberg & E. L. Grigorenko (Eds.), *The general factor of intelligence* (pp. 151–182). Mahwah, NJ: Erlbaum.

DeHaan, R. G., & Havighurst, R. J. (1957). *Educating the gifted.* Chicago: University of Chicago Press.

Delisle, J. (2003). To be or to do: Is a gifted child born or developed? *Roeper Review, 26,* 12–13.

Dennett, D. (1987). *The intentional stance.* Cambridge, MA: Bradford Books/MIT Press.

Detterman, D. K., & Daniel, M. H. (1989). Correlations of mental tests with each other and with cognitive variables are highest in low IQ groups. *Intelligence, 13,* 349–360.

Dewey, J. (1990). *The school and society, and the child and the curriculum.* Chicago: University of Chicago Press. (Original work published 1902)

Diamond, M. C., Scheibel, A. B., Murphy, G. M., & Harvey, T. (1985). On the brain of a scientist: Albert Einstein. *Experimental Psychology, 88,* 1998–2004.

Dickens, W. T., & Flynn, J. R. (2001). Heritability estimates versus large environmental effects: The IQ paradox resolved. *Psychological Review, 108,* 346–369.

Dmitrieva, E. S., Gel'man, V. Y., Zaitseva, K. A., & Orlov, A. M. (2006). Ontogenetic features of the psychophysiological mechanisms of perception of the emotional component of speech in musically gifted children. *Neuroscience and Behavioral Physiology, 36,* 53–62.

Donovan, M. S., & Cross, C. T. (Eds.) (2002). *Minority students in special and gifted education (Committee on Minority Representation in Special Education, Division of Behavioral and Social Sciences and Education, National Research Council).* Washington, DC: National Academy Press.

Dronkers, N. F. (1999). Neural basis of language. In R. A. Wilson & F. C. Keil (Eds.), *The MIT encyclopedia of the cognitive sciences* (pp. 448–451). Cambridge, MA: MIT Press.

Dunbar, K. (1997). How scientists think: On-line creativity and conceptual change in science. In T. B. Ward, S. M. Smith & J. Vaid (Eds.), *Creative thought: An investigation of conceptual structures and processes* (pp. 461–493). Washington, DC: American Psychological Association.

Duschl, R. A., & Duncan, R. G. (2009). Beyond the fringe: Building and evaluating scientific knowledge systems. In S. Tobias & T. M. Duffy (Eds.), *Constructivist instruction: Success or failure?* (pp. 311–332). New York: Routledge.

Dweck, C. S. (1999). *Self-theories: Their role in motivation, personality, and development.* Philadelphia: Psychology Press.

Dweck, C. S. (2006). *Mindset: The new psychology of success.* New York: Random House.

Dweck, C. S. (2009). Foreword. In F. D. Horowitz, R. F. Subotnik, & D. J. Matthews (Eds.), *The development of giftedness and talent across the lifespan* (pp. xi–xiv). Washington, DC: American Psychological Association.

Dweck, C. S., Mangels, J. A., & Good, C. (2004). Motivational effects on attention, cognition, and performance. In D. Y. Dai & R. J. Sternberg (Eds.), *Motivation, emotion, and cognition: Integrative perspectives on intellectual functioning and development* (pp. 41–55). Mahwah, NJ: Lawrence Erlbaum.

Edelman, G. M. (1989). *The remembered present: A biological theory of consciousness.* New York: Basic Books.

Edelman, G. M. (1995). Memory and the individual soul: Against silly reductionism. In J. Cornwell (Ed.), *Nature's imagination: The frontiers of scientific vision* (pp. 200–206). Oxford, UK: Oxford University Press.

Emmons, R. A. (1986). Personal strivings: An approach to personality and subjective well-being. *Journal of Personality and Social Psychology, 51,* 1058–1068.

Ercikan, K., & Roth, W.-M. (2006). What good is polarizing research into qualitative and quantitative? *Educational Researcher*, *35*, 14–23.

Ericsson, K. A. (1996). The acquisition of expert performance: An introduction to some of the issues. In K. A. Ericsson (Ed.), *The road to excellence: The acquisition of expert performance in the arts and sciences, sports, and games* (pp. 1–50). Mahwah, NJ: Lawrence Erlbaum Associates.

Ericsson, K. A. (1998). Basic capacities can be modified or circumvented by deliberate practice: A rejection of talent accounts of expert performance. *Behavioral and Brain Sciences*, *21*, 413–414.

Ericsson, K. A. (2006). The influence of experience and deliberate practice on the development of superior expert performance. In K. A. Ericsson, N. Charness, P. J. Feltovich, & R. R. Hoffman (Eds.), *The Cambridge handbook of expertise and expert performance* (pp. 683–703). New York: Cambridge University Press.

Ericsson, K. A., & Charness, N. (1993). Expert performance: Its structure and acquisition. *American Psychologist*, *49*, 725–747.

Ericsson, K. A., Charness, N., Feltovich, P. J., & Hoffman, R. R. (Eds.) (2006). *The Cambridge handbook of expertise and expert performance*. New York: Cambridge University Press.

Ericsson, K. A., Krampe, R. T., & Tesch-Römer, C. (1993). The role of deliberate practice in the acquisition of expert performance. *Psychological Review*, *100*, 363–406.

Ericsson, K. A., & Lehmann, A. C. (1996). Expert and exceptional performance: Evidence of maximal adaptation to task constraints. *Annual Review of Psychology*, *47*, 273–305.

Ericsson, K. A., Nandagopal, K., & Roring, R. W. (2005). Giftedness viewed from the expert-performance perspective. *Journal for the Education of the Gifted*, *28*, 287–311.

Ericsson, K. A., Nandagopal, K., & Roring, R. W. (2007a). Giftedness and evidence for reproducibly superior performance: An account based on the expert-performance framework. *High Ability Studies*, *18*, 3–55.

Ericsson, K. A., Nandagopal, K., & Roring, R. W. (2007b). Misunderstandings, agreements, and disagreements: Toward a cumulative science of reproducibly superior aspects of giftedness. *High Ability Studies*, *18*, 97–115.

Ericsson, K. A., & Williams, A. M. (2007). Capturing naturally occurring superior performance in the laboratory: Translational research on expert performance. *Journal of Experimental Psychology: Applied*, *13*, 115–123.

Eysenck, H. J. (1995). *Genius: The natural history of creativity*. Cambridge, UK: Cambridge University Press.

Feist, G. (1998). A meta-analysis of personality in scientific and artistic creativity. *Personality and Social Psychology Review*, *2*, 290–309.

Feist, G. J. (2004). The evolved fluid specificity of human creative talent. In R. J. Sternberg, E. L. Grigorenko, & J. L. Singer (Eds.), *Creativity: From potential to realization* (pp. 57–82). Washington, DC: American Psychological Association.

Feist, G. J. (2006). How development and personality influence scientific thought, interest, and achievement. *Review of General Psychology*, *10*, 163–182.

Feldhusen, J. F. (1986). A conception of giftedness. In R. J. Sternberg & J. E. Davidson (Eds.), *Conceptions of giftedness* (pp. 112–127). Cambridge, UK: Cambridge University Press.

Feldhusen, J. F. (1992). *TIDE: Talent identification and development in education*. Sarasota, FL: Center for Creative Learning.

Feldhusen, J. F. (2003). Lewis M. Terman: A pioneer in the development of ability tests. In B. J. Zimmerman & D. H. Schunk (Eds.), *Educational psychology: A century of contributions* (pp. 155–169). Mahwah, NJ: Lawrence Erlbaum Associates.

Feldhusen, J. F., & Jarwan, F. A. (2000). Identification of gifted and talented youth for educational programs. In K. A. Heller, F. J. Monk, R. J. Sternberg, & R. F. Subotnik (Eds.), *International handbook of giftedness and talent* (2nd ed., pp. 271–282). Amsterdam: Elsevier Science.

Feldman, D. H. (1986). *Nature's gambit: Child prodigies and the development of human potential*. New York: Basic Books.

Feldman, D. H. (1992). Has there been a paradigm shift in gifted education? Some thoughts on a changing national scene. In N. Colangelo, S. G. Assouline, & D. L. Ambrose (Eds.), *Talent development: Proceedings from 1991 Henry and Jocelyn Wallace National Research Symposium on Talent Development* (pp. 89–94). Unionville, NY: Trillium.

Feldman, D. H. (1994). *Beyond universals in cognitive development* (2nd ed.). Norwood, NJ: Ablex.

Feldman, D. H. (2003). A developmental, evolutionary perspective on giftedness. In J. H. Borland (Ed.), *Rethinking gifted education* (pp. 9–33). New York: Teachers College, Columbia University.

Feldman, D. H. (2009, August). *Giftedness and development: What kind of theory?* Paper presented at the annual meeting of American Psychological Association, Toronto, Canada.

Feynman, R. P. (1999). *The pleasure of finding things out*. Cambridge, MA: Perseus.

Fischer, K. W., & Bidell, T. R. (2006). Dynamic development of action and thought. In W. Damon & R. M. Lerner (Eds.), *Handbook of child psychology* (6th ed.): Vol. 1, *Theoretical model of human development* (pp. 313–399). Hoboken, NJ: John Wiley & Sons.

Fischer, K. W., & Pipp, S. L. (1984). Process of cognitive development: Optimal level and skill acquisition. In R. J. Sternberg (Ed.), *Mechanisms of cognitive development* (pp. 45–75). New York: Freeman.

Fischer, K. W., & Yan, Z. (2002). Darwin's construction of the theory of evolution: Microdevelopment of explanations of variation and change in species. In N. Granott & J. Parziale (Eds.), *Microdevelopment: Transition processes in development and learning* (pp. 294–318). Cambridge, UK: Cambridge University Press.

Fodor, J. A. (1983). *The modularity of mind*. Cambridge, MA: The MIT Press.

Folsom, C. (2006). Making conceptual connections between gifted and general education: Teaching for intellectual and emotional learning (TIEL). *Roeper Review, 28,* 79–87.

Ford, D. Y. (2003). Desegregating gifted education: Seeking equity for culturally diverse students. In J. H. Borland (Ed.), *Rethinking gifted education* (2nd ed., pp. 143–158). New York: Teachers College Press.

Ford, M. E. (1994). A living systems approach to the integration of personality and intelligence. In R. J. Sternberg & P. Ruzgis (Eds.), *Personality and intelligence* (pp. 188–217). Cambridge, UK: Cambridge University Press.

Frasier, M. M. (1997). Gifted minority students: Reframing approaches to their identification and education. In N. Colangelo & G. A. Davis (Eds.), *Handbook on gifted education* (pp. 498–515). Needham Heights, MA: Allyn & Bacon.

Fredrickson, B. L. (1998). What good are positive emotions? *Review of General Psychology*, *2*, 300–319.

Freeman, C. (1999). The crystallizing experience: A study of musical precocity. *Gifted Child Quarterly*, *43*, 75–84.

Freeman, J. (2004). Cultural influences on gifted gender achievement. *High Ability Studies*, *15*, 7–23.

Freeman, J. (2005). Permission to be gifted: How conceptions of giftedness can change lives. In R. J. Sternberg & J. E. Davidson (Eds.), *Conceptions of giftedness* (2nd ed., pp. 80–97). Cambridge, UK: Cambridge University Press.

Frensch, P. A., & Sternberg, R. J. (1989). Expertise and intelligent thinking: When it is worse to know better? In R. J. Sternberg (Ed.), *Advances in the psychology of human intelligence* (Vol. 5, pp. 157–188). Hillsdale, NJ: Lawrence Erlbaum.

Friedman, T. L. (2006). *The world is flat: A brief history of the 21st century*. New York: Farrar, Straus & Giroux.

Fruchter, N. & Siegle, D. (2004, November 28). Are gifted programs good? *No. New York Daily News*.

Gagné, F. (1985). Gifted and talent: Reexamining a reexamination of the definitions. *Gifted Child Quarterly*, *29*, 103–112.

Gagné, F. (1999a). Is there any light at the end of the tunnel? *Journal for the Education of the Gifted*, *22*, 191–234.

Gagné, F. (1999b). My convictions about the nature of abilities, gifts, and talents. *Journal for the Education of the Gifted*, *22*, 109–136.

Gagné, F. (2004). Transforming gifts into talents: The DMGT as a developmental model. *High Ability Studies*, *15*, 119–147.

Gagné, F. (2005a). From gifts to talents: The DMGT as a developmental model. In R. J. Sternberg & J. E. Davidson (Eds.), *Conceptions of giftedness* (2nd ed., pp. 98–119). Cambridge, UK: Cambridge University Press.

Gagné, F. (2005b). From noncompetence to exceptional talent: Exploring the range of academic achievement within and between grade levels. *Gifted Child Quarterly*, *49*, 139–153.

Gagné, F. (2007). Ten commandments for academic talent development. *Gifted Child Quarterly*, *51*, 93–118.

Gagné, F. (2009a). Building gifts into talents: Detailed overview of the DMGT 2.0. In B. MacFarlane & T. Stambaugh (Eds.), *Leading change in gifted education: The Festschrift of Dr. Joyce VanTassel-Baska* (pp. 61–80). Waco, TX: Prufrock Press.

Gagné, F. (2009b). Debating giftedness: Pronat vs. antinat. In L. Shavinina (Ed.), *International handbook on giftedness* (pp. 155–198). New York: Springer.

Gallagher, J. J. (1991). Editorial: The gifted: A term with surplus meaning. *Journal for the Education of the Gifted*, *14*, 353–365.

Gallagher, J. J. (1996). A critique of critiques of gifted education. *Journal for the Education of the Gifted*, *19*, 234–249.

Gallagher, J. J. (2000a). Changing paradigms for gifted education in the United States. In K. A. Heller, F. J. Monk, R. J. Sternberg, & R. F. Subotnik (Eds.), *International handbook of giftedness and talent* (2nd ed., pp. 681–693). Amsterdam: Elsevier Science.

Gallagher, J. J. (2000b). Unthinkable thoughts: Education of gifted students. *Gifted Child Quarterly*, *44*, 5–12.

Gallagher, J. J., & Courtright, R. D. (1986). The educational definition of giftedness and its policy implications. In R. J. Sternberg & J. E. Davidson (Eds.), *Conceptions of giftedness* (pp. 93–111). Cambridge, UK: Cambridge University Press.

Galton, F. (1869). *Hereditary genius: An inquiry into its laws and consequences.* London: Macmillan.

Galton, F. (1874). *English men of science: Their nature and nurture.* London: Macmillan.

Galton, F. (1883). *Inquiries into human faculty and its development.* London: Macmillan.

Gardner, H. (1983). *Frames of mind.* New York: Basic Books.

Gardner, H. (1993). *Creating minds.* New York: Basic Books.

Gardner, H. (1997). *Extraordinary minds: Portraits of 4 exceptional individuals and an examination of our extraordinariness.* New York: Basic Books.

Gardner, H. (1998). Are there additional intelligences? The case for naturalist, spiritual, and existential intelligences. In J. Kane (Ed.), *Education, information, and transformation.* Englewood Cliffs, NJ: Prentice-Hall.

Gardner, H. (2003). Three distinct meanings of intelligence. In R. J. Sternberg, J. Lautrey, & T. I. Lubert (Eds.), *Models of intelligence: International perspectives* (pp. 43–54). Washington, DC: American Psychological Association.

Gardner, H., Csikszentmihalyi, M., & Damon, W. (2001). *Good work: When excellence and ethics meet.* New York: Basic Books.

Gaser, C., & Schlaug, G. (2003). Brain structures differ between musicians and non-musicians. *The Journal of Neuroscience, 23,* 9240–9245.

Gaztambide-Fernández, R. (2009). What is an elite boarding school? *Review of Educational Research, 79,* 1090–1128.

Gazzaniga, M. S. (2000). Cerebral specialization and interhemispheric communication: Does the corpus callosum enable the human condition? *Brain, 123,* 1293–1326.

Geake, J. G. (2008). High abilities at fluid analogizing: A cognitive neuroscience construct of giftedness. *Roeper Review, 30,* 187–195.

Geake, J. (2009). Neuropsychological characteristics of academic and creative giftedness. In L. Shavinina (Ed.), *International handbook on giftedness.* New York: Springer Science.

Geary, D. C. (1995). Reflections of evolution and culture in children's cognition. *American Psychologist, 50,* 24–37.

Geary, D. C. (2005). *The origin of mind: Evolution of brain, cognition, and general intelligence.* Washington, DC: American Psychological Association.

Gee, J. P. (2003). Opportunity to learn: A language-based perspective on assessment. *Assessment in Education, 10,* 27–46.

Gershwind, N., & Galaburda, A. M. (1987). *Cerebral lateralization: Biological mechanism, associations, and pathology.* Cambridge, MA: MIT Press.

Getzels, J. W., & Jackson, P. W. (1962). *Creativity and intelligence: Explorations with gifted students.* New York: Wiley.

Gjerde, P. F. (2004). Culture, power, and experience: Toward a person-centered cultural psychology. *Human Development, 47,* 138–157.

Gladwell, M. (2008). *Outliers: The story of success.* New York: Little Brown.

Glaser, R., & Chi, M. T. H. (1988). Overview. In R. Glaser, M. T. H. Chi, & M. J. Farr (Eds.), *The nature of expertise* (pp. xv–xxviii). Hillsdale, NJ: Lawrence Erlbaum.

Goertzel, V., & Goertzel, T. G. (2004). Cradle of eminence (2nd ed.). Scottsdale, AZ: Great Potential Press.

Goldberg, E. (2001). *The executive brain: Frontal lobes and the civilized mind.* Oxford: Oxford University Press.

Goodkin, S., & Gold, D. G. (2007, August 27). The gifted children left behind. *The Washington Post.*

Gottfredson, L. S. (1997). Editorial: Mainstream science on intelligence: An editorial with 52 signatories, history, and bibliography. *Intelligence, 24,* 13–23.

Gottfried, A. E., & Gottfried, A. W. (2004). Toward the development of a conceptualization of gifted motivation. *Gifted Child Quarterly, 48,* 121–132.

Gottfried, A. W., Gottfried, A. E., Bathurst, K., & Guerin, D. W. (1994). *Gifted IQ: Early developmental aspects: The Fullerton longitudinal study.* New York: Plenum.

Gottfried, A. W., Gottfried, A. E., Cook, C. R., & Morris, P. E. (2005). Educational characteristics of adolescents with gifted academic intrinsic motivation: A longitudinal investigation from school entry through early adulthood. *Gifted Child Quarterly, 49,* 172–186.

Gottfried, A. W., Gottfried, A. E., & Guerin, D. W. (2006). The Fullerton Longitudinal Study: A long-term investigation of intellectual and motivational giftedness. *Journal for the Education of the Gifted, 29,* 430–450.

Gottfried, A.W., Gottfried, A. E., & Guerin, D. W. (2009). Issues in early prediction and identification of intellectual giftedness. In F. D. Horowitz, R. F. Subotnik, & D. J. Matthews (Eds.), *The development of giftedness and talent across the life span* (pp. 43–56). Washington, DC: American Psychological Association.

Gottlieb, G. (1998). Normally occurring environmental and behavioral influences on gene activity: From central dogma to probabilistic epigenesis. *Psychological Review, 105,* 792–802.

Gould, S. J. (1981). *The mismeasure of man.* New York: W. W. Norton.

Graham, S. (2009). Giftedness in adolescence: African American gifted youth and their challenges from a motivational perspective. In F. Horowitz, R. F. Subotnik, & D. Matthews (Eds.), *The development of giftedness and talent across the lifespan* (pp. 109–129). Washington, DC: American Psychological Association.

Granott, N., & Parziale, J. (2002). Microdevelopment: A process-oriented perspective for studying development and learning. In N. Granott & J. Parziale (Eds.), *Microdevelopment: Transition processes in development and learning* (pp. 1–28). Cambridge, UK: Cambridge University Press.

Grant, B. A. (2002). Justifying gifted education: A critique of needs claims and a proposal. *Journal for the Education of the Gifted, 25,* 359–374.

Grant, B. A., & Piechowski, M. M. (1999). Theories and the good: Toward child-centered gifted education. *Gifted Child Quarterly, 43,* 4–12.

Gratz v. Bollinger, 539 U.S. 244 (2003).

Greenough, W. T. (1976). Enduring brain effects of differential experience and training. In M. R. Rosenzweig & E. L. Bennett (Eds.), *Neural mechanisms of learning and memory* (pp. 255–278). Cambridge, MA: MIT Press.

Grinder, R. E. (1985). The gifted in our midst: By their divine deeds, neuroses, and mental test scores we have known them. In F. D. Horowitz & M. O'Brien (Eds.), *The gifted and talented: Developmental perspectives* (pp. 5–35). Washington, DC: American Psychological Association.

Gross, M. U. M. (1993). *Exceptionally gifted children.* London: Routledge.

Gruber, H. E. (1981). *Darwin on man: A psychological study of scientific creativity* (Rev. ed.). Chicago: University of Chicago Press.

Gruber, H. E. (1986). The self-construction of the extraordinary. In R. J. Sternberg & J. E. Davidson (Eds.), *Conceptions of giftedness* (pp. 247–263). Cambridge: Cambridge University Press.

Gruber, H. E. (1995). Insight and affect in the history of science. In R. J. Sternberg & J. E. Davidson (Eds.), *The nature of insight* (pp. 397–431). Cambridge, MA: MIT Press.

Gruber, H. E. (1998). The social construction of extraordinary selves: Collaboration among unique creative people. In R. C. Friedman & K. B. Rogers (Eds.), *Talent in context: Historical and social perspectives on giftedness* (pp. 127–147). Washington, DC: American Psychological Association.

Grutter v. Bollinger, 539 U.S. 306 (2003).

Guilford, J. P. (1967). *The nature of human intelligence*. New York: McGraw-Hill.

Gustafsson, J.-E., & Undheim, J. O. (1996). Individual differences in cognitive functions. In D. C. Berliner & R. C. Calfee (Eds.), *Handbook of educational psychology* (pp. 186–242). New York: Simon & Schuster Macmillan.

Haensly, P., Reynolds, C. R., & Nash, W. R. (1986). Giftedness: coalescence, context, conflict, and commitment. In R. J. Sternberg & J. E. Davidson (Eds.), *Conceptions of giftedness* (pp. 128–148). New York: Cambridge University Press.

Haier, R. J. (2001). PET studies of learning and individual differences. In J. L. McClelland & R. S. Siegler (Eds.), *Mechanisms of cognitive development: Behavioral and neural perspectives* (pp. 123–145). Mahwah, NJ: Lawrence Erlbaum Associates.

Haier, R. J., & Jung, R. E. (2008). Brain imaging studies of intelligence and creativity: What is the picture for education? *Roeper Review, 30*, 171–180.

Hall, V. C. (2003). Educational psychology from 1890 to 1920. In B. J. Zimmerman & D. H. Schunk (Eds.), *Educational psychology: A century of contributions* (pp. 3–39). Mahwah, NJ: Lawrence Erlbaum Associates.

Hannah, C. L., & Shore, B. (1995). Metacognition and high intellectual ability: Insights from the study of learning-disabled gifted students. *Gifted Child Quarterly, 39*, 95–109.

Hannah, C. L., & Shore, B. (2007). Twice-exceptional students' use of metacognitive skills on a comprehension monitoring task. *Gifted Child Quarterly, 52*, 3–18.

Hartas, D., Lindsay, G., & Muijs, D. (2008). Identifying and selecting able students for the NAGTY summer school: Emerging issues and future considerations. *High Ability Studies, 19*, 5–18.

Harter, S. (1999). *The construction of the self: A developmental perspective*. New York: Guilford Press.

Hatano, G., & Inagaki, K. (1986). Two courses of expertise. In H. Stevenson, H. Azuma, & A. Hakuta (Eds.), *Child development and education in Japan*. Washington, DC: Center for Applied Linguistics.

Hébert, T. P. (2001). "If I had a new notebook, I know things would change": Bright underachieving young men in urban classrooms. *Gifted Child Quarterly, 45*, 174–194.

Hébert, T. P., & Beardsley, T. M. (2001). Jermaine: A critical case study of a gifted Black child living in rural poverty. *Gifted Child Quarterly, 45*, 85–103.

Heller, K. A., Perleth, C., & Lim, T. K. (2005). The Munich Model of Giftedness designed to identify and promote gifted students. In R. J. Sternberg & J. E. Davidson (Eds.),

Conceptions of giftedness (2nd ed., pp. 147–170). Cambridge, UK: Cambridge University Press.

Herrnstein, R. J., & Murray, C. (1994). *The bell curve: Intelligence and class structure in American life.* New York: The Free Press.

Hertzog, N. (2009). The arbitrary nature of giftedness. In L. Shavinina (Ed.), *International handbook on giftedness* (pp. 205–214). New York: Springer.

Hickam, H. (1998). *October sky: A memoir (originally published as Rocket Boys).* New York: Dell.

Hidi, S. (1990). Interest and its contribution as a mental resource for learning. *Review of Educational Research, 60,* 549–571.

Hidi, S., Renninger, K. A., & Krapp, A. (2004). Interest, a motivational construct that combines affective and cognitive functioning. In D. Y. Dai & R. J. Sternberg (Eds.), *Motivation, emotion, and cognition: Integrative perspectives on intellectual functioning and development* (pp. 89–115). Mahwah, NJ: Lawrence Erlbaum.

Hill, L., Craig, I., Asherson, P., Ball, D., Eley, T., Ninomiya, T., et al. (1999). DNA pooling and dense marker maps: A systematic search for genes for cognitive ability. *Neuroreport: For Rapid Communication of Neuroscience Research, 10,* 843–848.

Hirschfeld, L. A., & Gelman, S. A. (1994). Toward a topography of mind: An introduction to domain specificity. In L. A. Hirschfeld & S. A. Gelman (Eds.), *Mapping the mind: Domain specificity in cognition and culture* (pp. 3–35). New York: Cambridge University Press.

Hoh, P.-S. (2008). Cognitive characteristics of the gifted. In J. A. Plucker & C. M. Callahan (Eds.), *Critical issues and practices in gifted education: What the research says* (pp. 57–83). Austin, TX: Prufrock Press.

Hollingworth, L. S. (1924). Provisions for intellectually superior children. In M. V. O'Shea (Ed.), *The child, his nature, and his needs* (pp. 277–299). New York: A Contribution of the Children's Foundation.

Hollingworth, L. S. (1942). *Children above 180 IQ.* New York: World Book.

Holloway, S. D. (1988). Concepts of ability and effort in Japan and the United States. *Review of Educational Research, 58,* 327–345.

Holton, G. (1981). Thematic presuppositions and the direction of scientific advance. In A. F. Heath (Ed.), *Scientific explanation* (pp. 1–27). Oxford: Clarendon Press.

Holyoak, K. J., & Thagard, P. (1995). *Mental leaps: Analogy in creative thought.* Cambridge: MA: MIT Press.

Horn, J. (1986). Some thoughts about intelligence. In R. J. Sternberg & D. K. Detterman (Eds.), *What is intelligence? Contemporary viewpoints on its nature and definition* (pp. 91–96). Norwood, NJ: Ablex.

Horowitz, F. D. (2000). Child development and the PITS: Simple questions, complex answers, and developmental theory. *Child Development, 71,* 1–10.

Horowitz, F. D. (2009). Introduction: A developmental understanding of giftedness and talent. In In F. D. Horowitz, R. F. Subotnik, & D. J. Matthews (Eds.), *The development of giftedness and talent across the lifespan* (pp. 3–19). Washington, DC: American Psychological Association.

Horowitz, F., & O'Brien, M. (Eds.). (1985). *The gifted and the talented: Developmental perspectives.* Washington, DC: American Psychological Association.

Horowitz, F. D., Subotnik, R. F., & Matthews, D. J. (Eds.) (2009). *The development of giftedness and talent across the life span.* Washington, DC: American Psychological Association.

Howe, K. R. (2009). Positivist dogmas, rhetoric, and the education science question. *Educational Researcher, 38,* 428–440.

Howe, M. J. A. (1997). *IQ in question: The truth about intelligence.* London: Sage.

Howe, M. J. A., Davidson, J. W., & Sloboda, J. A. (1998). Innate talents: Reality or myth? *Behavioral and Brain Sciences, 21,* 399–442.

Hunt, E. (1986). The heffalump of intelligence. In R. J. Sternberg & D. K. Detterman (Eds.), *What is intelligence? Contemporary viewpoints on its nature and definition* (pp. 101–107). Norwood, NJ: Ablex.

Hunt, E. (1999). Intelligence and human resources: Past, present, and future. In P. L. Ackerman, P. C. Kyllonen & R. D. Roberts (Eds.), *Learning and individual differences: Process, traits, and content determinants* (pp. 3–28). Washington, DC: American Psychological Association.

Hunt, E. (2006). Expertise, talent, and social encouragement. In K. A. Ericsson, N. Charness, P. J. Feltovich, & R. R. Hoffman (Eds.), *The Cambridge handbook of expertise and expert performance* (pp. 31–38). New York: Cambridge University Press.

Hutchins, E. (1995). *Cognition in the wild.* Cambridge, MA: MIT Press.

Israel Center for Excellence Through Education. (2009) Leading the journey of excellence. Retrieved on September 11, 2009, from: http://www.excellence.org.il/eng/.

Jackson, N. E., & Butterfield, E. C. (1986). The self-construction of the extraordinary. In R. J. Sternberg & J. E. Davidson (Eds.), *Conceptions of giftedness* (pp. 151–181). Cambridge, UK: Cambridge University Press.

Jaušovec, N. (1997). Differences in EEG alpha activity between gifted and non-identified individuals: Insights into problem solving. *Gifted Child Quarterly, 41,* 26–32.

Jefferson, T. (1955). *Notes on the State of Virginia.* Chapel Hill: University of North Carolina Press.

Jensen, A. R. (1993). Spearman's *g*: Links between psychometrics and biology. *Annals of the New York Academy of Sciences, 702,* 103–131.

Jensen, A. R. (2001). Spearman's hypothesis. In J. M. Collis & S. Messick (Eds.), *Intelligence and personality: Bridging the gap between theory and measurement* (pp. 3–24). Mahwah, NJ: Lawrence Erlbaum.

Jensen, A. R., Cohn, S. J., & Cohn, C. M. G. (1989). Speed of information processing in academically gifted youths and their siblings. *Personality and Individual Differences, 10,* 29–34.

Jin, S.-H., Kim, S. Y., Park, K. H., & Lee, K.-J. (2007). Differences in EEG between gifted and average students: Neural complexity and functional cluster analysis. *International Journal of Neuroscience, 117,* 1167–1184.

Jin, S.-H., Kwon, Y.-J., Jeong, J.-S., Kwon, S.-W., & Shin, D.-H. (2006). Differences in brain information transmission between gifted and normal children during scientific hypothesis generation. *Brain and Cognition, 62,* 191–197.

Just, M. A., & Carpenter, P. A. (1992). A capacity theory of comprehension: Individual differences in working memory. *Psychological Review, 99,* 122–149.

Kagan, J. (2002). *Surprise, uncertainty, and mental structures.* Cambridge, MA: Harvard University Press.

Kahneman, D. (2003). A perspective on judgment and choice: Mapping bounded rationality. *American Psychologist, 58,* 697–720.

Kalbfleisch, M. L. (2008). Getting to the heart of the brain: Using cognitive neuroscience to explore the nature of human ability and performance. *Roeper Review, 30,* 162–170.

Kalbfleisch, M. L. (2009). The neural plasticity of giftedness. In L. Shavinina (Ed.), *International handbook on giftedness* (pp. 275–293). New York: Springer.

Kandel, E. R., & Squire, L. R. (2001). Breaking down scientific barriers to the study of brain and mind. In A. R. Damasio, A. Harrington, J. Kagan, B. S. McEwen, H. Moss, & R. Shaikh (Eds.), *Unity of knowledge: The convergence of natural and human science* (pp. 118–135). New York: New York Academy of Sciences.

Kanevsky, L. (1990). Pursuing qualitative differences in the flexible use of problem-solving strategy by young children. *Journal for the Education of the Gifted, 13,* 115–140.

Kanevsky, L. S. (1994). A comparative study of children's learning in the zone of proximal development. *European Journal for High Ability, 5,* 163–175.

Kanevsky, L. (1995). Learning potentials of gifted students. *Roeper Review, 17,* 157–163.

Kanevsky, L. (2000). Dynamic assessment of gifted students. In K. A. Heller, F. J. Monk, J. Sternberg, & R. F. Subotnik (Eds.), *International handbook of giftedness and talent* (2nd ed., pp. 283–295). Amsterdam: Elsevier Science.

Kanevsky, L., & Geake, J. (2004). Inside the zone of proximal development: Validating a multifactor model of learning potential with gifted students and their peers. *Journal for the Education of the Gifted, 28,* 182–217.

Kaplan, S. N. (2003). Is there a gifted-child pedagogy? *Roeper Review, 25,* 165–166.

Karmiloff-Smith, A. (1992). *Beyond modularity: A developmental perspective on cognitive science.* Cambridge, MA: MIT Press.

Karmiloff-Smith, A. (2004). Bates' emergentist theory and its relevance to understanding genotype/phenotype relations. In M. Tomasello & D. I. Slobin (Eds.), *Beyond nature-nurture: Essays in honor of Elizabeth Bates* (pp. 219–236). Mahwah, NJ: Lawrence Erlbaum Associates.

Karnes, F. A., & Bean, S. M. (1995). *Leadership for students: A practical guide.* Waco, TX: Prufrock Press.

Keating, D. P. (2009). Developmental science and giftedness: An integrated lifespan framework. In F. D. Horowitz, R. F. Subotnik, & D. J. Matthews (Eds.), *The development of giftedness and talent across the lifespan* (pp. 189–208). Washington, DC: American Psychological Association.

Kelley, T. L. (1927). *Interpretation of educational measurement.* New York: World Book.

Kelso, J. A. S. (2000). Principles of dynamic pattern formation and change for a science of human behavior. In L. R. Bergman, R. B. Cairns, L.-G. Nilsson, & L. Nystedt (Eds.), *Developmental science and the holistic approach* (pp. 63–83). Mahwah, NJ: Lawrence Erlbaum.

Kemp, A. E. (1996). *The musical temperament.* Oxford: Oxford University Press.

Kerr, B. A. (1985). *Smart girls, gifted women.* Columbus, OH: Ohio Psychology Press.

Kerr, B. A. (1997). Developing talents in girls and young women. In N. Colangelo & G. A. Davis (Eds.), *Handbook of gifted education* (pp. 483–497). Boston, MA: Allyn & Bacon.

Kimble, G. A. (1984). Psychology's two cultures. *American Psychologist, 39,* 833–839.

Kirschenbaum, R. J. (1998). Dynamic assessment and its use with underserved gifted and talented populations. *Gifted Child Quarterly, 42,* 140–147.

Kitano, M. K. (2003). What's missing in gifted education reform. In J. H. Borland (Ed.), *Rethinking gifted education* (pp. 159–170). New York: Teachers College, Columbia University.

Kitano, M. K., & Perkins, C. O. (2000). Gifted European American women. *Journal for the Education of the Gifted, 23*, 287–313.

Koch, S., & Leary, D. E. (Eds.) (1992). *A century of psychology as science.* Washington, DC: American Psychological Association.

Kolb, D. A. (1971). *Individual learning styles and the learning process.* Cambridge, MA: MIT Press.

Kuhl, J. (1985). Volitional mediators of cognition-behavior consistency: Self-regulatory processes and action versus state orientation. In J. Kuhl & J. Beckmann (Eds.), *Action control: From cognition to behavior* (pp. 101–128). Berlin: Springer.

Kuhn, D. (1999). A developmental model of critical thinking. *Educational Researcher, 28*(2), 16–26.

Kuhn, D. (2002). A multi-component system that constructs knowledge: Insights from microgenetic study. In N. Granott & J. Parziale (Eds.), *Microdevelopment: Transition processes in development and learning* (pp. 109–130). Cambridge, UK: Cambridge University Press.

Kuhn, T. S. (1962). *The structure of scientific revolution.* Chicago: University of Chicago Press.

Kuhn, T. S. (1977). *The essential tension: Selected studies in scientific tradition and change.* Chicago: University of Chicago Press.

Kunda, Z. (1990). The case for motivated reasoning. *Psychological Bulletin, 108*, 480–498.

Kyllonen, P. C., & Christal, R. (1990). Reasoning ability is (little more than) working-memory capacity? *Intelligence, 14*, 389–433.

Lajoie, S. P., & Shore, B. (1986). Intelligence: Speed and accuracy tradeoff in high aptitude individuals. *Journal for the Education of the Gifted, 9*, 85–104.

Lakatos, I. (1978). *The methodology of scientific research programs.* Cambridge, UK: Cambridge University Press.

Langley, P., Simon, H. A., Bradshaw, G. L., & Zytkow, J. M. (1987). *Scientific discovery: Computational explorations of the creative process.* Cambridge, MA: MIT Press.

Laycraft, K. (2009). Positive maladjustment as a transition from chaos to order. *Roeper Review, 31*, 113–122.

Lehman, H. C. (1953). *Age and achievement.* Princeton, NJ: Princeton University Press.

Lehmann, A. C., & Ericsson, K. A. (1998). The historical development of domains of expertise: Performance standards and innovations in music. In A. Steptoe (Ed.), *Genius and mind* (pp. 67–94). Oxford: Oxford University Press.

Lerner, R. M. (2004). Genes and the promotion of positive human development: Hereditarian versus developmental systems perspectives. In C. G. Coll, E. L. Bearer, & R. M. Lerner (Eds.), *Nature and nurture: The complex interplay of genetic and environmental influences on human behavior and development* (pp. 1–33). Mahwah, NJ: Lawrence Erlbaum Associates.

Lerner, R. M., & Busch-Rossnagel, N. A. E. (1981). *Individuals as producers of their development: A life-span perspective.* New York: Academic Press.

Leung, A. K., Maddux, W. W., Galinsky, A. D., & Chiu, C. (2008). Multicultural experience enhances creativity: The when and how. *American Psychologist, 63*, 169–181.

Li, S.-C. (2003). Biocultural orchestration of developmental plasticity across levels: The interplay of biology and culture in shaping the mind and behavior across the life span. *Psychological Bulletin, 129,* 171–194.

Li, S.-C., Lindenberger, U., Hommel, B., Aschersleben, G., Prinz, W., & Baltes, P. B. (2004). Transformations in the couplings among intellectual abilities and constituent cognitive processes across the life span. *Psychological Science, 15,* 155–163.

Lippmann, W. (1976). The abuse of the tests. In N. J. Block & G. Dworkin (Eds.), *The IQ controversy* (pp. 18–20). New York: Pantheon.

Liu, T., Shi, J., Zhao, D., & Yang, J. (2008). The event-related low-frequency activity of highly and average intelligent children. *High Ability Studies, 19,* 131–139.

Loewen, S. (2006). Exceptional intellectual performance: A neo-Piagetian perspective. *High Ability Studies, 17,* 159–181.

Lohman, D. F. (1993). Teaching and testing to develop fluid abilities. *Educational Researcher, 22*(7), 12–23.

Lohman, D. F. (1994a). Component scores as residual variation (or why the intercept correlates better). *Intelligence, 19,* 1–11.

Lohman, D. F. (1994b). Spatially gifted, verbally inconvenienced. In N. Colangelo, S. G. Assouline, & D. L. Ambroson (Eds.), *Talent development* (Vol. 2, pp. 251–263). Dayton, OH: Ohio Psychology Press.

Lohman, D. F. (2001). Issues in the definition and measurement of abilities. In J. M. Collis & S. Messick (Eds.), *Intelligence and personality: Bridging the gap between theory and measurement* (pp. 79–98). Mahwah, NJ: Lawrence Erlbaum.

Lohman, D. F. (2005a). An aptitude perspective on talent identification: Implications for identification of academically gifted minority students. *Journal for the Education of the Gifted, 28,* 333–360.

Lohman, D. F. (2005b). Review of Naglieri and Ford (2003): Does the Naglieri Nonverbal Ability Test identify equal proportions of high-scoring White, Black, and Hispanic students? *Gifted Child Quarterly, 49,* 19–28.

Lohman, D. F. (2006). Beliefs about differences between ability and accomplishment: From folk theories to cognitive science. *Roeper Review, 29,* 32–40.

Lohman, D. F., & Korb, K. A. (2006). Gifted today but not tomorrow? Longitudinal changes in ability and achievement during elementary school. *Journal for the Education of the Gifted 29,* 451–484.

Lohman, D. F., & Rocklin, T. (1995). Current and recurrent issues in the assessment of intelligence and personality. In D. H. Saklofske & M. Zeidner (Eds.), *International handbook of personality and intelligence* (pp. 447–474). New York: Plenum.

Loveless, T., Farkas, S., & Duffett, A. (2008). *High-achieving students in the era of NCLB: A Fordham Foundation report.* Issued on June 18, 2008, by the Fordham Foundation. Retrieved on July 24, 2009, from http://www.edexcellence.net/doc/20080618_high_achievers.pdf.

Lubinski, D. (2004). Introduction to the special section on cognitive abilities: 100 years after Spearman's (1904) "'General intelligence,' objectively determined and measured." *Journal of Personality and Social Psychology, 86,* 96–111.

Lubinski, D., & Benbow, C. P. (1992). Gender differences in abilities and preferences among the gifted. *Current Directions in Psychological Science, 1,* 61–66.

Lubinski, D., & Benbow, C. P. (2000). States of excellence. *American Psychologist, 55,* 137–150.

Lubinski, D., & Benbow, C. P. (2006). Study of mathematically precious youth after 35 years. *Perspectives on Psychological Science, 1,* 316–345.

Lubinski, D., & Dawis, R. V. (1992). Aptitudes, skills, and proficiencies. In M. D. Dunnette & L. M. Hough (Eds.), *Handbook of industrial/organizational psychology* (2nd ed., Vol. 3, pp. 1–59). Palo Alto, CA: Consulting Psychologists Press.

Lubinski, D., Webb, R. M., Morelock, M. J., & Benbow, C. P. (2001). Top 1 in 10,000: A 10-year follow-up of the profoundly gifted. *Journal of Applied Psychology, 86,* 718–729.

Luchins, A. S., & Luchins, E. H. (1970). *Wertheimer's seminar revisited: Problem solving and thinking* (Vol. 1). Albany: State University of New York Press.

Lupart, J., & Toy, R. (2009). Twice-exceptional: Multiple pathways to success. In L. Shavinina (Ed.), *International handbook on giftedness* (pp. 507–525). New York: Springer.

Maker, C. J. (1996). Identification of gifted minority students: A national problem, needed changes, and a promising solution. *Gifted Child Quarterly, 40,* 41–50.

Margolin, L. (1994). *Goodness personified: The emergence of gifted children.* Hawthorne, NY: Aldine De Gruyer.

Margolin, L. (1996). A pedagogy of privilege. *Journal for the Education of the Gifted, 19,* 164–180.

Markus, H., & Nurius, P. (1986). Possible selves. *American Psychologist, 41,* 954–969.

Marland, S. P. (1972). *Education of the gifted and talented: Report to the Congress of the United States by the U.S. Commissioner of Education.* Washington, DC: Government Printing Office.

Marsh, H. W., Trautwein, U., Ludtke, O., Baumert, J., & Köller, O. (2007). The big fish little pond effect: Persistent negative effects of selective high schools on self-concept after graduation. *American Educational Research Journal, 44,* 631–669.

Marsh, H. W., & Yeung, A. S. (1997). Causal effects of academic self-concept on academic achievement: Structural equation models of longitudinal data. *Journal of Educational Psychology, 89,* 41–54.

Maslow, A. H. (1970). *Motivation and personality.* New York: Harper & Row.

Masunaga, H., & Horn, J. (2001). Expertise and age-related changes in components of intelligence. *Psychology and Aging, 16,* 293–311.

Matthews, D. J., & Foster, J. F. (2006). Mystery to mastery: Shifting paradigms in gifted education. *Roeper Review, 28,* 64–69.

Mayer, R. E. (2003). E. L. Thorndike's enduring contributions to educational psychology. In B. J. Zimmerman & D. H. Schunk (Eds.), *Educational psychology: A century of contributions* (pp. 113–154). Mahwah, NJ: Lawrence Erlbaum Associates.

Mayer, R. E. (2005). The scientific study of giftedness. In R. J. Sternberg & J. E. Davidson (Eds.), *Conceptions of giftedness* (2nd ed., pp. 437–447). Cambridge, UK: Cambridge University Press.

McAdams, D. P., & Pals, J. L. (2006). A new big five: Fundamental principles for an integrative science of personality. *American Psychologist, 61,* 204–217.

McCall, R. B. (1981). Nature-nurture and the two realms of development: A proposed integration with respect to mental development. *Child Development, 52,* 1–12.

McCrae, R. R., Costa, P. T. (1987). Validation of the five-factor model of personality across instruments and observers. *Journal of Personality and Social Psychology, 52,* 81–90.

McKeough, A., Genereux, R., & Jeary, J. (2006). Structure, content, and language usage: How do exceptional and average storywriters differ? *High Ability Studies, 17,* 203–223.

Mendaglio, S. (Ed.) (2008). *Dabrowski's theory of positive disintegration.* Scottsdale, AZ: Great Potential Press.

Mendaglio, S., & Peterson, J. S. (Eds.) (2007). *Models of counseling gifted children, adolescents, and young adults*. Waco, TX: Prufrock Press.

Merton, R. K. (1973). *The sociology of science*. Chicago: University of Chicago Press.

Messick, S. (1992). Multiple intelligences or multilevel intelligence? Selective emphasis on distinctive properties of hierarchy: On Gardner's *Frames of Mind* and Sternberg's *Beyond IQ* in the context of theory and research on the structure of human abilities. *Psychological Inquiry, 3*, 365–384.

Messick, S. (1995). Validity of psychological assessment: Validation of inferences from persons' responses as scientific inquiry into score meaning. *American Psychologist, 50*, 741–749.

Miller, A. I. (1996). *Insights of genius: Imagery and creativity in science and art*. New York: Springer-Verlag.

Miller, L. K. (2005). What the savant syndrome can tell us about the nature and nurture of talent. *Journal for the Education of the Gifted, 28*, 361–373.

Mischel, W., & Shoda, Y. (1995). A cognitive-affective system theory of personality: Reconceptualizing situations, dispositions, dynamics, and invariance in personality structure. *Psychological Review, 102*, 246–268.

Molenaar, P. C. M. (2004). A manifesto on psychology as idiographic science: Bringing the person back into scientific psychology, this time forever. *Measurement, 2*, 201–218.

Mönks, F. J., & Mason, E. J. (1993). Developmental theories and giftedness. In K. A. Heller, F. J. Mönk, & A. H. Passow (Eds.), *International handbook of research and development of giftedness and talent* (pp. 89–101). Oxford, UK: Pergamon.

Mönks, F. J., & Mason, E. J. (2000). Developmental psychology and giftedness: Theories and research. In K. A. Heller, F. J. Monk, R. J. Sternberg, & R. F. Subotnik (Eds.), *International handbook of giftedness and talent* (2nd ed., pp. 141–155). Amsterdam: Elsevier Science.

Moon, S. M. (2007). Counseling issues and research. In S. Mendaglio & J. S. Peterson (Eds.), *Models of counseling gifted children, adolescents, and young adults* (pp. 7–32). Waco, TX: Prufrock Press.

Moran, S., & John-Steiner, V. (2003). Creativity in the making: Vygotsky's contemporary contribution to the dialectic of development and creativity. In R. K. Sawyer, V. John-Steiner, S. Moran, R. J. Sternberg, D. H. Feldman, J. Nakamura, & M. Csikszentmihayi (Eds.), *Creativity and development* (pp. 61–90). Oxford: Oxford University Press.

Morelock, M. J. (1996). On the nature of giftedness and talent: Imposing order on chaos. *Roeper Review, 19*, 4–12.

Muthén, B., & Muthén, L. K. (2000). Integrating person-centered and variable-centered analyses: Growth mixture modeling with latent trajectory classes. *Alcoholism: Clinical & Experimental Research, 24*, 882–891.

NAGC. (2009). *Javits program description: Jacob Javits Gifted and Talented Students Education Act*. Retrieved on July 24, 2009, from http://www.nagc.org/index.aspx?id=572.

Naglieri, J. A. (2008). Traditional IQ: 100 years of misconception and its relationship to minority representation in gifted programs. In J. L. VanTassel-Baska (Ed.), *Alternative assessments with gifted and talented students* (pp. 67–88). Waco, TX: Prufrock.

Naglieri, J. A., & Ford, D. Y. (2003). Addressing under-representation of gifted minority children using the Naglieri Nonverbal Ability Test (NNAT). *Gifted Child Quarterly, 47*, 155–160.

Naglieri, J. A., & Ford, D. Y. (2005). Increasing minority children's participation in gifted classes using the NNAT: A response to Lohman. *Gifted Child Quarterly, 49*, 29–36.

National Commission on Excellence in Education. (1983). *A nation at risk: The imperative for educational reform.* Retrieved on September 11, 2009, from http://www.ed.gov/pubs/NatAtRisk/index.html.

Neisser, U. (1979). The concept of intelligence. *Intelligence, 3*, 217–227.

Neisser, U., Boodoo, G., Bouchard, T. J., Boykin, A. W., Brody, N., Ceci, S. J., et al. (1996). Intelligence: Knowns and unknowns. *American Psychologist, 51*, 77–101.

Newell, A. (1990). *Unified theories of cognition.* Cambridge, MA: Harvard University Press.

Newman, S. D., Carpenter, P. A., Varma, S., & Just, M. A. (2003). Frontal and parietal participation in problem solving in the Tower of London: fMRI and computational modeling of planning, and high-level perception. *Neuropsychologia, 41*, 1668–1682.

Nisbett, R. E. (2009). *Intelligence and how to get it: Why schools and culture count.* New York: W. W. Norton.

Norton, A., Winner, E., Cronin, K., Overy, K., Lee, D. J., & Schlaug, G. (2005). Are there pre-existing neural, cognitive, or motoric markers for musical ability? *Brain and Cognition, 59*, 124–134.

Novick, M. R. (1982). Educational testing: Inferences in relevant subpopulations. *Educational Researcher, 11*, 4–10.

Oaks, J., & Well, A. S. (1998). Detracking for high student achievement. *Educational Leadership, 55*(6), 38–41.

O'Boyle, M. W. (2008). Mathematically gifted children: Developmental brain characteristics and their prognosis for well-being. *Roeper Review, 30*, 181–186.

Obler, L. K., & Fein, D. (1988). *The exceptional brain: Neuropsychology of talent and special abilities.* New York: Guilford Press.

Okamoto, Y., Curtis, R., Jabagchourian, J. J., & Weckbacher, L. M. (2006). Mathematical precocity in young children: A neo-Piagetian perspective. *High Ability Studies, 17*, 183–202.

Overtone, W. F. (1984). World views and their influence on psychological theory and research: Kuhn-Lakatos-Laudan. In H. W. Reese (Ed.), *Advances in child development and behavior* (Vol. 18, pp. 191–226). Orlando, FL: Academic Press.

Page, S. E. (2008). *The difference: How the power of diversity creates better groups, firms, schools, and societies.* Princeton, NJ: Princeton University Press.

Pajares, F. (1996). Self-efficacy beliefs and mathematical problem-solving of gifted students. *Contemporary Educational Psychology, 21*, 325–344.

Panksepp, J. (1998). *Affective neuroscience: The foundations of human and animal emotions.* New York: Oxford University Press.

Papierno, P. B., Ceci, S. J., Makel, M. C., & Williams, W. W. (2005). The nature and nurture of talent: A bioecological perspective on the ontogeny of exceptional abilities. *Journal for the Education of the Gifted, 28*, 312–331.

Park, G., Lubinski, D., & Benbow, C. (2007). Contrasting intellectual patterns predict creativity in the arts and sciences. *Psychological Science, 18*, 948–952.

Park, G., Lubinski, D., & Benbow, C. (2008). Ability differences among people who have commensurate degrees matters for scientific creativity. *Psychological Science, 19*, 957–961.

Partnership for 21st Century Skills (2009). Framework for 21st century learning. Retrieved on July 28, 2009, from http://www.21stcenturyskills.org/index.php?option=com_content&task=view&id=254&Itemid=120.

Passingham, R. (2006). Brain development and IQ. *Nature, 440/30*, 619–620.

Passow, A. H. (1981). The nature of giftedness and talent. *Gifted Child Quarterly, 25*, 5–10.

Pepper, S. C. (1942). *World hypotheses.* Berkeley: University of California Press.

Perkins, D. N. (1995). *Outsmarting IQ: The emerging science of learnable intelligence.* New York: The Free Press.

Perkins, D. N., & Grotzer, T. A. (1997). Teaching intelligence. *American Psychologist, 52*, 1125–1133.

Perkins, D., & Ritchhart, R. (2004). When is good thinking? In D. Y. Dai & R. J. Sternberg (Eds.), *Motivation, emotion, and cognition: Integrative perspectives on intellectual functioning and development* (pp. 351–384). Mahwah, NJ: Lawrence Erlbaum.

Persson, R. S., Joswig, H., & Balogh, L. (2000). Gifted education in Europe: Programs, practices, and current research. In K. A. Heller, F. J. Monk, R. J. Sternberg, & R. F. Subotnik (Eds.), *International handbook of giftedness and talent* (2nd ed., pp. 703–734). Amsterdam: Elsevier Science.

Petrill, S. A., Ball, D., Eley, T., Hill, L., Plomin, R., McClearn, G. E., et al. (1997). Failure to replicate a QTL association between a DNA marker identified by EST00083 and IQ. *Intelligence, 25*, 179–184.

Phenix, P. H. (1964). *Realms of meaning.* New York: McGraw-Hill.

Phillips, D., & Burbules, N. (2000). *Postpositivism and educational research.* Lanham, MD: Rowman & Littlefield.

Piaget, J. (1950/2001). *The psychology of intelligence.* London: Routledge.

Piaget, J. (1972). *Psychology and epistemology: Toward a theory of knowledge.* Harmondsworth, UK: Penguin.

Piechowski, M. M. (2009). Peace pilgrim, exemplar of Level V. *Roeper Review, 31*, 103–112.

Piechowski, M. M., & Grant, B. A. (2001, November). *Talent development versus personal growth.* Paper presented at the annual convention of the National Association for Gifted Children, Cincinnati, OH.

Piirto, J. (1994). *Talented children and adults: Their development and education.* New York: Macmillan.

Pinker, S., & Spelke, E. S. (2005, April 22). A Pinker vs. Spelke debate on gender and science, organized by the Mind/Brain/Behavior Initiative (MBB). Cambridge, MA. Retrieved on July 27, 2008, from: http://www.edge.org/3rd_culture/debate05/debate05_index.html

Pintrich, P. R., & Schunk, D. H. (1996). *Motivation in education: Theory, research, and applications.* Englewood Cliff, NJ: Prentice Hall.

Piro, J. M. (1998). Handedness and intelligence: Patterns of hand preference in gifted and nongifted children. *Developmental Neuropsychology, 14*, 619–630.

Plomin, R. (1997). Identifying genes for cognitive abilities and disabilities. In R. J. Sternberg & E. L. Grigorenko (Eds.), *Intelligence, heredity, and environment* (pp. 89–104). New York: Cambridge University Press.

Plomin, R. (2001). The genetics of g in human and mouse. *Nature Reviews and Neuroscience, 2*, 136–141.

Plomin, R., DeFries, J. C., Craig, I. W., & McGuffin, P. (2003). *Behavioral genetics in the postgenomic era.* Washington, DC: American Psychological Association.

Plomin, R., Hill, L., Craig, I. W., McGuffin, P., Purcell, S., Sham, P., et al. (2001). A genome-wide scan of 1842 DNA markers for allelic associations with general cognitive ability: A five-stage design using DNA pooling and extreme selected groups. *Intelligence, 31*, 489–495.

Plomin, R., & Spinath, F. M. (2004). Intelligence, genetics, genes, and genomics. *Journal of Personality and Social Psychology, 86*, 112–129.

Plucker, J. A. (2000). Flip sides of the same coin or marching to the beat of different drummers? A response to Pyryt. *Gifted Child Quarterly, 44*, 193–195.

Plucker, J. A., & Barab, S. A. (2005). The importance of contexts in theories of giftedness: Learning to embrace the messy joys of subjectivity. In R. J. Sternberg & J. E. Davidson (Eds.), *Conceptions of giftedness* (2nd ed., pp. 201–216). Cambridge, UK: Cambridge University Press.

Plucker, J. A., Callahan, C. M., & Tomchin, E. M. (1996). Wherefore art thou, multiple intelligences? Alternative assessment for identifying talent in ethnically diverse and low income students. *Gifted Child Quarterly, 40*, 81–92.

Porath, M. (2006a). Introduction: A developmental view of giftedness. *High Ability Studies, 17*, 139–145.

Porath, M. (2006b). The conceptual underpinnings of giftedness: Developmental and educational implications. *High Ability Studies, 17*, 145–158.

Putnam, R. D., Leonard, R., & Nanetti, R. Y. (1994). *Making democracy work.* Princeton, NJ: Princeton University Press.

Pylyshyn, Z. W. (1984). *Computation and cognition: Toward a foundation for cognitive science.* Cambridge, MA: MIT Press.

Pyryt, M. C. (2000). Finding "*g*": Easy viewing through higher order factor analysis. *Gifted Child Quarterly, 44*, 190–192.

Rasmussen, J. (1993). Deciding and doing: Decision making in natural contexts. In G. A. Klein, K. J. Orasanu, R. Calderwood, & C. E. Zsambok (Eds.), *Decision making in action: Models and methods* (pp. 158–171). Norwood, NJ: Ablex.

Rawls, J. (1971). *A theory of justice.* Cambridge, MA: Harvard University Press.

Rea, D. W. (2000). Optimal motivation for talent development. *Journal for the Education of the Gifted, 23*, 187–216.

Reis, S. M., Kaplan, S. N., Tomlinson, C. A., Westberg, K. L., Callahan, C. M., & Coper, C. R. (1998). A response: Equal does not mean identical. *Educational Leadership, 56*(3), 74–77.

Reis, S. M., & Renzulli, R. S. (1982). A research report on the revolving door identification model: A case for the broadened conception of giftedness. *Phi Delta Kappan, 63*, 619–620.

Renzulli, J. S. (1977). *The enrichment triad model: A guide for developing defensive programs for the gifted and talented.* Mansfield Center, CT: Creative Learning Press.

Renzulli, J. S. (1978). What makes giftedness? Re-examining a definition. *Phi Delta Kappan, 60*, 180–184, 261.

Renzulli, J. S. (1986). The three-ring conception of giftedness: A developmental model for creative productivity. In R. J. Sternberg & J. E. Davidson (Eds.), *Conceptions of giftedness* (pp. 53–92). Cambridge, UK: Cambridge University Press.

Renzulli, J. S. (1994). *Schools for talent development: A practical plan for total school improvement.* Mansfield Center, CT: Creative Learning Press.

Renzulli, R. S. (1998, October). A rising tide lifts all ships. *Phi Delta Kappan, 80*, 105–111.

Renzulli, J. S. (1999). What is this thing called giftedness, and how do we develop it? A 25 year perspective. *Journal for the Education of the Gifted, 23*, 3–54.

Renzulli, J. S. (2002, September). Expanding the conception of giftedness to include co-cognitive traits and to promote social capital. *Phi Delta Kappan, 84*, 33–40, 57–58.

Renzulli, R. S. (2005). The three-ring conception of giftedness: A developmental model for promoting creative productivity. In R. J. Sternberg & J. E. Davidson (Eds.), *Conceptions of giftedness* (2nd ed., pp. 98–119). Cambridge, UK: Cambridge University Press.

Renzulli, J. S., & Dai, D. Y. (2003). Education of the gifted and talented. In J. W. Guthrie (Ed.), *Encyclopedia of education* (2nd ed., pp. 930–936). New York: Macmillan Reference.

Renzulli, J. S., & Reis, S. M. (1991). The reform movement and the quiet crisis in gifted education. *Gifted Child Quarterly, 35*, 26–35.

Renzulli, J. S., & Reis, S. M. (1997). *Schoolwide enrichment model: A how-to guide for educational excellence.* Mansfield Center, CT: Creative Learning Press.

Reuters (2007, October 20). DNA pioneer Dr James Watson dumped after Africa insult. *Herald Sun.*

Ritchhart, R. (2001). From IQ to IC: A dispositional view of intelligence. *Roeper Review, 23*, 143–150.

Roberts, B. W., & Pomerantz, E. M. (2004). On traits, situations, and their integration: A developmental perspective. *Personality and Social Psychology Review, 8*, 402–416.

Robinson, A. (1990). Cooperation or exploitation? The argument against cooperative learning. *Journal for the Education of the Gifted, 14*, 9–27.

Robinson, A. (2003). Cooperative learning and high ability students. In N. Colangelo & G. A. Davis (Eds.), *Handbook of gifted education* (3rd ed., pp. 282–292). Boston: Allyn and Bacon.

Robinson, A., & Clinkenbeard, P. R. (1998). Giftedness: An exceptionality examined. *Annual Review of Psychology, 49*, 117–139.

Robinson, A., Shore, B. M., & Enersen, D. L. (2007). *Best practices in gifted education.* Waco, TX: Prufrock Press.

Robinson, N. M. (2005). In defense of a psychometric approach to the definition of academic giftedness: A conservative view from a die-hard liberal. In R. J. Sternberg & J. E. Davidson (Eds.), *Conceptions of giftedness* (2nd ed., pp. 280–294). Cambridge, UK: Cambridge University Press.

Robinson, N. M. (2006). Report cards on the state of research in the field of gifted education. *Gifted Child Quarterly, 50*, 342–345.

Robinson, N. M., Zigler, E., & Gallagher, J. J. (2000). Two tails of the normal curve: Similarities and differences in the study of mental retardation and giftedness. *American Psychologist, 55*, 1413–1424.

Roeper, A. (2006). *The "I" of the beholder: A guide to an essence of a child.* Scottsdale, AZ: Great Potential Press.

Rogers, K. B. (1986). Do the gifted think and learn differently? A review of recent research and its implications for instruction. *Journal for the Education of the Gifted, 10*, 17–39.

Rogers, K. B. (2007). Lessons learned about educating the gifted and talented. *Gifted Child Quarterly, 51*, 382–396.

Rogoff, B. (2003). *The cultural nature of human development.* Oxford, UK: Oxford University Press.

Rogoff, R., & Lave, J. (1984). *Everyday cognition.* Cambridge, MA: Harvard University Press.

Rolfhus, E. L., & Ackerman, P. L. (1996). Self-report knowledge: At the crossroads of ability, interest, and personality. *Journal of Educational Psychology, 88,* 174–188.

Rolfhus, E. L., & Ackerman, P. L. (1999). Assessing individual differences in knowledge: Knowledge structures and traits. *Journal of Educational Psychology, 91,* 511–526.

Root-Bernstein, R. (2009). Multiple giftedness: The case of polymaths. In L. Shavinina (Ed.), *International handbook on giftedness* (pp. 853–870). New York: Springer.

Roring, R. W., & Charness, N. (2007). A multilevel model analysis of expertise in chess across the life span. *Psychology and Aging, 22,* 291–299.

Ross, P. O. (1993). *National excellence: A case for developing America's talent.* Washington, DC: U.S. Government Printing Office.

Rothenberg, A., & Wyshak, G. (2004). Family background and genius. *Canadian Journal of Psychiatry, 49,* 185–191.

Rothenberg, A., & Wyshak, G. (2005). Family background and genius II: Nobel laureates in science. *Canadian Journal of Psychiatry, 50,* 918–925.

Rousseau, J-J. (2003). *Emile, or on education.* (William H. Payne, Trans.). Amherst, New York: Prometheus Books. (Original work published 1762)

Runco, M. A. (1994). Creativity and its discontents. In M. P. Shaw & M. A. Runco (Eds.), *Creativity and affect* (pp. 102–123). Norwood, NJ: Ablex.

Sackett, P. R., Borneman, M. J., & Connelly, B. S. (2008). High-stakes testing in higher education and employment: Appraising the evidence for validity and fairness. *American Psychologist, 63,* 215–227.

Sapon-Shevin, M. (1994). *Playing favorites: Gifted education and the disruption of community.* Albany: State University of New York Press.

Sapon-Shevin, M. (1996). Beyond gifted education: Building a shared agenda for school reform. *Journal for the Education of the Gifted, 19,* 194–214.

Sapon-Shevin, M. (2003). Equity, excellence, and school reform: Why is finding common ground so hard? In J. H. Borland (Ed.), *Rethinking gifted education* (pp. 127–142). New York: Teachers College Press.

Sawyer, R. K. (1999). The emergence of creativity. *Philosophical Psychology, 12,* 447–469.

Sawyer, R. K. (2002). Emergence in psychology: Lessons from the history of non-reductionist science. *Human Development, 45,* 2–28.

Sawyer, R. K. (2003). Emergence in creativity and development. In R. K. Sawyer, V. John-Steiner, S. Moran, R. J. Sternberg, D. H. Feldman, J. Nakamura, & M. Csikszentmihalyi (Eds.), *Creativity and development* (pp. 12–60). Oxford: Oxford University Press.

Scarr, S. (1992). Developmental theories for the 1990s: Development and individual differences. *Child Development, 63,* 1–19.

Scarr, S. (1997). Behavior-genetic and socialization theories of intelligence: Truce and reconcilation. In R. J. Sternberg & E. L. Grigorenko (Eds.), *Intelligence, heredity, and environment* (pp. 3–41). New York: Cambridge University Press.

Schank, R. C., & Cleary, C. (1995). *Engines for education.* Hillsdale, NJ: Lawrence Erlbaum.

Scheffler, I. (1985). *Of human potential: An essay in the philosophy of education.* New York: Routledge & Kegan Paul.

Schlaug, G. (2001). The brain of musicians: A model for functional and structural adaptation. In R. J. Zatorre & I. Peretz (Eds.), *The biological foundations of music (annals of the New York Academy Sciences)* (Vol. 930, pp. 281–299). New York: New York Academy of Sciences.

Schlaug, G., Janke, L., Huang, Y., & Seinmetz, H. (1995). In vivo evidence of structural brain asymmetry in musicians. *Science, 267*(5198), 699–701.

Schlaug, G., Norton, A., Overy, K., & Winner, E. (2005). Effects of music training on the child's brain and cognitive development. *Annals of the New York Academy of Sciences, 1060,* 219–230.

Schmidt, F. L., & Hunter, J. E. (1998). The validity and utility of selection methods in personnel psychology: Practical and theoretical implications of 85 years of research findings. *Psychological Bulletin, 124,* 262–274.

Schneider, W. (2000). Giftedness, expertise, and (exceptional) performance: A developmental perspective. In K. A. Heller, F. J. Monk, R. J. Sternberg & R. F. Subotnik (Eds.), *International handbook of giftedness and talent* (2nd ed., pp. 165–177). Amsterdam: Elsevier Science.

Schoenfeld, A. H. (1992). Learning to think mathematically: Problem solving, metacognition, and sense-making in mathematics. In D. A. Grouws (Ed.), *Handbook of research on mathematics teaching and learning* (pp. 334–370). New York: Macmilam.

Schön, D. A. (1983). *Reflective practitioner.* New York: Basic Books.

Schuler, P. (2002). Perfectionism in gifted children and adolescents. In M. Neihart, S. M. Reis, N. M. Robinson, & S. M. Moon (Eds.), *The social and emotional development of gifted children* (pp. 71–79). Waco, TX: Prufrock Press.

Schulz, S. (2005). The gifted: Identity construction through the practice of gifted education. *International Education Journal, 5,* 117–128.

Searle, J., R. (2004). *Mind: A brief introduction.* New York: Oxford University Press.

Seok, B. (2006). Diversity and unity of modularity. *Cognitive Science, 30,* 347–380.

Sergiovanni, T. J., Kelleher, P., McCarthy, M. M., & Wirt, F. M. (2004). *Educational governance and administration* (5th ed.). Boston, MA: Allyn and Bacon.

Shavelson, R. J., & Towne, L. (2002). *Scientific research in education.* Washington, DC: National Academy Press.

Shavinina, L. (1999). The psychological essence of the child prodigy phenomenon: Sensitive periods and cognitive experience. *Gifted Child Quarterly, 43,* 25–38.

Shavinina, L. (2004). Explaining high abilities of Nobel laureates. *High Ability Studies, 15,* 243–254.

Shavinina, L. V., & Ferrari, M. (Eds.). (2004). *Beyond knowledge: Extracognitive aspects of developing high ability.* Mahwah, NJ: Lawrence Erlbaum.

Shavinina, L. V., & Kholodnaja, M. A. (1996). The cognitive experience as a psychological basis of intellectual giftedness. *Journal for the Education of the Gifted, 20,* 3–25.

Shavinina, L. V., & Seeratan, K. L. (2004). Extracognitive phenomena in the intellectual functioning of gifted, creative, and talented individuals. In L. V. Shavinina & M. Ferrari (Eds.), *Beyond knowledge: Extracognitive aspects of developing high ability* (pp. 73–102). Mahwah, NJ: Lawrence Erlbaum.

Shaw, P., Greenstein, D., Lerch, J., Clasen, L., Lenroot, R., Gogtay, N., et al. (2006, March 30). Intellectual ability and cortical development in children and adolescents [Letter to the editor]. *Nature, 440,* 676–679.

Shepard, L. A. (2000). The role of assessment in a learning culture. *Educational Researcher*, *29*(7), 4–14.

Shiffrin, R. M. (1996). Laboratory experimentation on the genesis of expertise. In K. A. Ericsson (Ed.), *The road to excellence* (pp. 337–345). Mahwah, NJ: Lawrence Erlbaum Associates.

Shore, B. M. (2000). Metacognition and flexibility: Qualitative differences in how gifted children think. In R. C. Friedman & B. M. Shore (Eds.), *Talents unfolding: Cognition and development* (pp. 167–187). Washington, DC: American Psychological Association.

Shore, B. M., & Delcourt, M. A. B. (1996). Effective curricular and program practices in gifted education and the interface with general education. *Journal for the Education of the Gifted*, *20*, 138–154.

Shore, B. M., & Kanevsky, L. S. (1993). Thinking processes: Being and becoming gifted. In K. A. Heller, F. J. Mönk, & A. H. Passow (Eds.), *International handbook of research and development of giftedness and talent* (pp. 133–147). Oxford: Pergamon.

Shore, B., & Lazar, L. (1996). IQ-related differences in time allocation during problem solving. *Psychological Reports*, *50*, 391–395.

Shulman, L. S. (1987). Knowledge and teaching: Foundations of the new reform. *Harvard Educational Review*, *57*(1), 1–22.

Siegle, D., & McCoach, D. B. (2009, April). *Gifted underachievement*. Paper presented at the annual meeting of American Educational Research Association, San Diego, CA.

Siegler, R. S. (1996). *Emerging minds: The process of change in children's thinking*. New York: Oxford University Press.

Siegler, R. S. (2002). Microgenetic studies of self-explanation. In N. Granott & J. Parziale (Eds.), *Microdevelopment: Transition processes in development and learning* (pp. 31–58). Cambridge, UK: Cambridge University Press.

Siegler, R. S., & Kotovsky, K. (1986). Two levels of giftedness: Shall even the twain meet. In R. J. Sternberg & J. E. Davidson (Eds.), *Conceptions of giftedness* (pp. 417–435). Cambridge, UK: Cambridge University Press.

Silverman, L. K. (1993). *Counseling the gifted and talented*. Denver, CO: Love.

Silverstein, A. (1988). An Aristotelian resolution of the idiographic versus nomothetic tension. *American Psychologist*, *43*, 425–430.

Simon, H. A. (1996). *The sciences of the artificial*. Cambridge, MA: MIT Press. (Original work published 1969)

Simonton, D. K. (1996). Creative expertise: A life-span developmental perspective. In K. A. Ericsson (Ed.), *The road to excellence* (pp. 227–253). Mahwah, NJ: Lawrence Erlbaum Associates.

Simonton, D. K. (1997). Creative productivity: A predictive and explanatory model of career trajectories and landmarks. *Psychological Review*, *104*, 66–89.

Simonton, D. K. (1999). Talent and its development: An emergenic and epigenetic model. *Psychological Review*, *3*, 435–457.

Simonton, D. S. (2002). *Great psychologists and their times: Scientific insights into psychology's history*. Washington, DC: American Psychological Association.

Simonton, D. K. (2003). Scientific creativity as constrained stochastic behavior: The integration of product, person, and process perspectives. *Psychological Bulletin*, *129*, 475–494.

Simonton, D. K. (2005). Giftedness and genetics: The emergenic-epigenetic model and its implications. *Journal for the Education of the Gifted*, *28*, 270–286.

Simonton, D. K. (2007). Talent and expertise: The empirical evidence for genetic endowment. *High Ability Studies*, *18*, 83–84.

Simonton, D. K. (2008). Scientific talent, training, and performance: Intellect, personality, and genetic endowment. *Review of General Psychology*, *12*, 28–46.

Singer, J. D., & Willett, J. B. (2003). *Applied longitudinal data analysis: Modeling change and event occurrence*. Oxford: Oxford University Press.

Slavin, R. E. (1990). Ability grouping, cooperative learning, and the gifted. *Journal for the Education of the Gifted*, *14*, 3–8.

Smith, L. D., & Thelen, E. (1993). *A dynamic systems approach to development: Applications*. Cambridge, MA: MIT Press.

Snow, C. E. (1999). Social perspectives on the emergence of language. In B. MacWhinney (Ed.), *The emergence of language* (pp. 257–276). Mahwah, NJ: Erlbaum.

Snow, C. P. (1967). *The two cultures and a second look*. London: Cambridge University Press.

Snow, R. E. (1992). Aptitude theory: Yesterday, today, and tomorrow. *Educational Psychologist*, *27*, 5–32.

Snow, R. E. (1994). Aptitude development and talent achievement. In N. Colangelo, S. C. Assouline, & D. L. Ambroson (Eds.), *Talent development* (Vol. 2, pp. 101–120). Dayton, OH: Ohio Psychology Press.

Snow, R. E. (1995). Foreword. In D. H. Saklofske & M. Zeidner (Eds.), *International handbook of personality and intelligence* (pp. xi–xv). New York: Plenum.

Snow, R. E., Corno, L., & Jackson, D. (1996). Individual differences in affective and conative functions. In D. C. Berliner & R. C. Calfee (Eds.), *Handbook of educational psychology* (pp. 243–310). New York: Simon & Schuster Macmillan.

Snow, R. E., Kyllonen, P. C., & Marshalek, B. (1983). The topography of ability and learning correlations. In R. J. Sternberg (Ed.), *Advances in the psychology of human intelligence* (Vol. 2, pp. 47–103). Hillsdale, NJ: Lawrence Erlbaum.

Snow, R. E., & Lohman, D. F. (1984). Toward a theory of cognitive aptitude for learning from instruction. *Journal of Educational Psychology*, *76*, 347–376.

Sosniak, L. A. (2006). Retrospective interviews in the study of expertise and expert performance. In K. A. Ericsson, N. Charness, P. J. Feltovich, & R. R. Hoffman (Eds.), *The Cambridge handbook of expertise and expert performance* (pp. 287–301). New York: Cambridge University Press.

Spearman, C. (1904). "General intelligence," objectively determined and measured. *American Journal of Psychology*, *15*, 201–292.

Spearman, C. (1927). *The abilities of man*. London: Macmillan.

Spelke, E. S. (2005). Sex differences in intrinsic aptitude for mathematics and science? A critical review. *American Psychologist*, *60*, 950–958.

Spelke, E. S., & Grace, A. D. (2006). Abilities, motives, and personal styles. *American Psychologist*, *61*, 725–726.

Stankov, L. (2003). Complexity in human intelligence. In R. J. Sternberg, J. Lautrey, & T. I. Lubert (Eds.), *Models of intelligence: International perspectives* (pp. 27–42). Washington, DC: American Psychological Association.

Stanley, J. C. (1996). In the beginning: The study of mathematically precocious youth. In C. P. Benbow & D. Lubinski (Eds.), *Intellectual talent* (pp. 225–235). Baltimore: Johns Hopkins University Press.

Stanley, J. (1997). Varieties of intellectual talent. *Journal of Creative Behavior, 31*, 93–119.

Stanovich, K. E. (1999). *Who is rational? Studies of individual differences in reasoning.* Mahwah, NJ: Lawrence Erlbaum.

Stanovich, K. E., & West, R. F. (1997). Reasoning independently of prior belief and individual differences in actively open-minded thinking. *Journal of Educational Psychology, 89*, 342–357.

Steele, C. M. (1997). A threat in the air: How stereotypes shape intellectual identity and performance. *American Psychologist, 52*, 613–629.

Steiner, H. H. (2006). A microgenetic analysis of strategic variability in gifted and average-ability children. *Gifted Child Quarterly, 50*, 62–74.

Steiner, H. H., & Carr, M. (2003). Cognitive development in gifted children: Toward a more precise understanding of emergent differences in intelligence. *Educational Psychology Review, 15*, 215–246.

Stelmack, R. K., & Houlihan, M. (1995). Event-related potential, personality, and intelligence. In D. H. Saklofske & M. Zeidner (Eds.), *International handbook of personality and intelligence* (pp. 349–365). New York: Plenum.

Sternberg, R. J. (1985). *Beyond IQ: A triarchic theory of human intelligence.* Cambridge, UK: Cambridge University Press.

Sternberg, R. J. (1986). GENECES: A framework for intellectual abilities and theories of them. *Intelligence, 10*, 239–250.

Sternberg, R. J. (1995). *A thriarchic approach to giftedness* (Research Monograph 95126). Storrs, CT: The National Research Center on the Gifted and Talented.

Sternberg, R. J. (1996a). Costs of expertise. In K. A. Ericsson (Ed.), *The road to excellence: The acquisition of expert performance in the arts and sciences, sports and games* (pp. 347–354). Mahwah, NJ: Lawrence Erlbaum.

Sternberg, R. J. (1996b). *Successful intelligence.* New York: Simon & Schuster.

Sternberg, R. J. (1997). *Thinking styles.* New York: Cambridge University Press.

Sternberg, R. J. (1999a). A propulsion model of types of creative contributions. *Review of General Psychology, 3*, 83–100.

Sternberg, R. J. (1999b). Intelligence as developing expertise. *Contemporary Educational Psychology, 24*, 359–375.

Sternberg, R. J. (2000). The concept of intelligence. In R. J. Sternberg (Ed.), *Handbook of intelligence* (pp. 3–15). Cambridge, UK: Cambridge University Press.

Sternberg, R. J. (2007a). Cultural concepts of giftedness. *Roeper Review, 29*, 160–165.

Sternberg, R. J. (2007b). Who are the bright children? The cultural context of being and acting intelligent. *Educational Researcher, 36*, 148–155.

Sternberg, R. J., & Davidson, J. E. (1986). Conceptions of giftedness: A map of the terrain. In R. J. Sternberg & J. E. Davidson (Eds.), *Conceptions of giftedness* (pp. 3–18). Cambridge, UK: Cambridge University Press.

Sternberg, R. J., & Grigorenko, E. L. (2002). *The general factor of intelligence.* Mahwah, NJ: Erlbaum.

Sternberg, R. J., Grigorenko, E. L., & Singer, J. L. (2004). *Creativity: From potential to realization.* Washington, DC: American Psychological Association.

Sternberg, R. J., & Kaufman, J. C. (1998). Human abilities. *Annual Review of Psychology, 49*, 479–502.

Stokes, D. E. (1997). *Pasteur's quadrant: Basic science and technological innovation.* Washington, DC: Brookings Institute Press.

Subotnik, R. F. (2003). A developmental view of giftedness: From being to doing. *Roeper Review, 26*, 14–15.

Subotnik, R. F. (2006). Longitudinal studies: Answering our most important questions of prediction and effectiveness. *Journal for the Education of the Gifted, 29*, 379–383.

Subotnik, R. F., & Coleman, L. J. (1996). Establishing the foundations for a talent development school: Applying principles to creating an ideal. *Journal for the Education of the Gifted, 20*, 175–189.

Subotnik, R. F., & Jarvin, L. (2005). Beyond expertise: Conceptions of giftedness as great performance. In R. J. Sternberg & J. E. Davidson (Eds.), *Conceptions of giftedness* (2nd ed., pp. 343–357). Cambridge, UK: Cambridge University Press.

Subotnik, R., Kassan, L., Summers, E., & Wasser, A. (1993). *Genius revisited: High IQ children grown up.* Norwood, NJ: Ablex.

Subotnik, R. F., & Olszewski-Kubilius, P. (1997). Restructuring special programs to reflect distinctions between children's and adults' experiences with giftedness. *Peabody Journal of Education, 72*, 101–116.

Subotnik, R., Orland, M., Rayhack, K., Schuck, J., Edmiston, A., Earle, J., et al. (2009). Identifying and developing talent in science, technology, engineering, and mathematics (STEM): An agenda for research, policy, and practice. In L. Shavinina (Ed.), *International handbook on giftedness* (pp. 1313–1326). New York: Springer.

Summers, L. H. (2005, January 14). *Remarks at NBER conference on diversifying the science and engineering workforce.* Retrieved on January 15, 2006, from http://www.president.harvard.edu/speeches/2005/nber.html.

Sweetland, J. D., Reina, J. M., & Tatti, A. F. (2006). WISC-III verbal/performance discrepancies among a sample of gifted children. *Gifted Child Quarterly, 50*, 7–10.

Swiatek, M. A. (2007). The Talent Search model: Past, present, and future. *Gifted Child Quarterly, 51*, 320–329.

Tannenbaum, A. J. (1983). *Gifted children: Psychological and educational perspectives.* New York: Macmillan.

Tannenbaum, A. J. (1997). The meaning and making of giftedness. In N. Colangelo & G. A. Davis (Eds.), *Handbook of gifted education* (2nd ed., pp. 27–42). Boston: Allyn and Bacon.

Tannenbaum, A. J. (1998). Programs for the gifted: To be or not to be. *Journal for the Education of the Gifted, 22*, 3–36.

Terman, L. M. (1925). *Genetic studies of genius, Vol. 1: Mental and physical traits of a thousand gifted children.* Stanford, CA: Stanford University Press.

Terman, L. M., & Oden, M. H. (1959). *Genetic studies of genius: The gifted group at mid-life.* Stanford, CA: Stanford University Press.

Tesch-Römer, C. (1998). Attributed talent is a powerful myth. *Behavioral and Brain Sciences, 21*, 427.

Thomson, G. H. (1916). A hierarchy without a general factor. *British Journal of Psychology, 8*, 271–281.

Threlfall, J., & Hargreaves, M. (2008). The problem-solving methods of mathematically gifted and older average-attaining students. *High Ability Studies, 19*, 83–98.

Tieso, C. L. (2007). Overexcitability: A new way to think about talent? *Roeper Review, 29*, 232–239.

Tomlinson, C. A. (1996). Good teaching for one and all: Does gifted education have an instructional identity? *Journal for the Education of the Gifted, 20,* 155–174.

Tomlinson, C. A., & Callahan, C. M. (1992). Contributions of gifted education to general education in a time of change. *Gifted Child Quarterly, 36,* 183–189.

Torrance, E. P. (1966). *Torrance tests of creative thinking: Norms-technical manual (Research ed.).* Princeton, NJ: Personnel Press.

Torrance, E. P. (1972a). Career patterns and peak creative achievements of creative high school students 12 years later. *Gifted Child Quarterly, 16,* 75–88.

Torrance, E. P. (1972b). Predictive validity of the Torrance Tests of Creative Thinking. *Journal of Creative Behavior, 6,* 236–252.

Toulmin, S. (1972). *Human understanding* (Vol. 1). Princeton, NJ: Princeton University Press.

Treffinger, D. S., & Feldhusen, J. F. (1996). Talent recognition and development: Successor to gifted education. *Journal for the education of the gifted, 19,* 181–193.

Triandis, H. C. (1989). The self and social behavior in differing cultural contexts. *Psychological Review, 96,* 506–520.

Turkheimer, E., Haley, A., Waldron, M., D'Onofrio, & Gottesman, I. I. (2003). Socioeconomic status modifies heritability of IQ in young children. *Psychological Science, 14,* 623–628.

van der Maas, H. L. J., Dolan, C. V., Grasman, R. P. P. P., Wicherts, J. M., Huizenga, H. M., & Rajimakers, M. E. (2006). A dynamic model of general intelligence: The positive manifold of intelligence by mutualism. *Psychological Review, 113,* 842–861.

van Geert, P. (2002). Developmental dynamics, intentional actions, and fuzzy sets. In N. Granott & J. Parziale (Eds.), *Microdevelopment: Transition processes in development and learning* (pp. 319–343). Cambridge, UK: Cambridge University Press.

van Gelder, T., & Port, R. F. (1995). It's about time: An overview of the dynamic approach to cognition. In R. F. Port & T. van Gelder (Eds.), *Mind as motion: Explorations in the dynamics of cognition* (pp. 1–43). Cambridge, MA: MIT Press.

Vandervert, L. R. (2003). How working memory and cognitive modeling functions of the cerebellum contribute to discoveries in mathematics. *New Ideas in Psychology, 21,* 159–175.

Vandervert, L. R. (2009). Working memory, the cognitive function of the cerebellum and the child prodigy. In L. Shavinina (Ed.), *International handbook on giftedness* (pp. 295–316). New York: Springer.

VanTassel-Baska, J. (2005). Domain-specific giftedness. In R. J. Sternberg & J. E. Davidson (Eds.), *Conceptions of giftedness* (2nd ed.). Cambridge, UK: Cambridge University.

VanTassel-Baska, J. (2006). NAGC symposium: A report card on the state of research in the field of gifted education. *Gifted Child Quarterly, 50,* 339–341.

VanTassel-Baska, J., Feng, A. X., & Evans, B. L. (2007). Patterns of identification and performance among gifted students identified through performance tasks: A three-year analysis. *Gifted Child Quarterly, 51,* 218–231.

VanTassel-Baska, J., Johnson, D. T., Hughes, C. E., & Boyce, L. N. (1996). A study of the language arts curriculum effectiveness with gifted learners. *Journal for the Education of the Gifted, 19,* 461–480.

VanTassel-Baska, J., Robinson, N. M., Coleman, L. J., Shore, B., & Subotnik, R. (2006).

Report cards on the state of research in the field of gifted education. *Gifted Child Quarterly, 50,* 339–355.

VanTassel-Baska, J., Zuo, L., Avery, L. D., & Little, C. A. (2002). A curriculum study of gifted students learning in the language arts. *Gifted Child Quarterly, 46,* 30–44.

Vellutino, F. R., Fletcher, J. M., Snowling, M. J., & Scanlon, D. M. (2004). Specific reading disability (dyslexia): What have we learned in the past 4 decades? *Journal of Child Psychology and Psychiatry, 45,* 2–40.

Vellutino, F. R., Scanlon, D. M., Small, S., & Fanuele, D. P. (2006). Response to intervention as a vehicle for distinguishing between children with and without reading disabilities: Evidence for the role of kindergarten and first-grade interventions. *Journal of Learning Disabilities, 39,* 157–169.

von Károlyi, C., & Winner, E. (2005). Extreme giftedness. In R. J. Sternberg & J. E. Davidson (Eds.), *Conceptions of giftedness* (2nd ed., pp. 377–394). Cambridge, UK: Cambridge University Press.

Vygotsky, L. S. (1978). *Mind in society: The development of higher psychological processes.* Cambridge, MA: Harvard University Press.

Wachs, T. D. (1992). *The nature of nurture.* Newbury Park, CA: Sage.

Wachs, T. D. (2000). *Necessary but not sufficient: The respective roles of single and multiple influences on individual development.* Washington, DC: American Psychological Association.

Walters, J., & Gardner, H. (1986). The crystallizing experience: Discovering an intellectual gift. In R. J. Sternberg & J. E. Davidson (Eds.), *Conceptions of giftedness* (pp. 306–331). Cambridge, UK: Cambridge University Press.

Watson, J. B. (1930). *Behaviorism* (Rev. ed.). Chicago: University of Chicago Press.

Webb, R. M., Lubinski, D., & Benbow, C. (2002). Mathematically facile adolescents with math-science aspirations: New perspectives on their educational and vocational development. *Journal of Educational Psychology, 94,* 785–794.

Webb, R. M., Lubinski, D., & Benbow, C. (2007). Spatial ability: A neglected dimension in talent searches for intellectually precocious youth. *Journal of Educational Psychology, 99,* 397–420.

Weisberg, R. W. (1999). Creativity and knowledge: A challenge to theories. In R. J. Sternberg (Ed.), *Handbook of creativity* (pp. 226–250). Cambridge, UK: Cambridge University Press.

Weisberg, R. W. (2006). Modes of expertise in creative thinking: Evidence from case studies. In K. A. Ericsson, N. Charness, P. J. Feltovich, & R. R. Hoffman (Eds.), *The Cambridge handbook of expertise and expert performance* (pp. 761–787). New York: Cambridge University Press.

West, T. G. (1991). *In the mind's eye: Visual thinkers, gifted people with learning difficulties, computer images, and the ironies of creativity.* Buffalo, NY: Prometheus Books.

Westberg, K. L., & Archambault, F. X. (2004). A multi-site case study of successful classroom practices for high ability students. In C. A. Tomlinson & S. M. Reis (Eds.), *Differentiation for gifted and talented students* (pp. 59–76). Thousand Oaks, CA: Corwin Press.

Whitehead, A. N. (1929). *The aims of education.* New York: The Free Press.

Wilkinson, S. C. (1993). WISC-R Profiles of children with superior intellectual ability. *Gifted Child Quarterly, 37,* 84–91.

Willett, J. B., & Sayer, A. G. (1994). Using covariance structure analysis to detect correlates and predictors of individual change over time. *Psychological Bulletin, 116*, 363–381.

Wineburg, S. S. (1991). Historical problem solving: A study of the cognitive process used in the evaluation of documentary and pictorial evidence. *Journal of Educational Psychology, 83*, 73–87.

Wineburg, S. S. (1998). Reading Abraham Lincoln: An expert-expert study in the interpretation of historical texts. *Cognitive Science, 22*, 319–346.

Winner, E. (1996). *Gifted children: Myths and realities*. New York: Basic Books.

Winner, E. (1997). Exceptionally high intelligence and schooling. *American Psychologist, 52*, 1070–1081.

Winner, E. (2000). The origins and ends of giftedness. *American Psychologist, 55*, 159–169.

Witty, P. A. (1958). Who are the gifted? In N. B. Henry (Ed.), *Education of the gifted. 57th yearbook of the National Society for the Study of Education, Part 2*. Chicago: University of Chicago.

Worrell, F. C. (2007). Ethnic identity, academic achievement, and global self-concept in four groups of academically talented adolescents. *Gifted Child Quarterly, 51*, 23–38.

Zhang, Q., Shi, J., Luo, Y., Zhao, D., & Yang, J. (2006). Intelligence and information processing during a visual search task in children: An event-related potential study. *NeuroReport: For Rapid Communication of Neuroscience Research, 17*, 747–752.

Ziegler, A. (2005). The actiotope model of giftedness. In R. J. Sternberg & J. E. Davidson (Eds.), *Conceptions of giftedness* (2nd ed., pp. 411–436). Cambridge, UK: Cambridge University Press.

Ziegler, A., & Heller, K. A. (2000). Conceptions of giftedness from a meta-theoretical perspective. In K. A. Heller, F. J. Monk, R. J. Sternberg, & R. F. Subotnik (Eds.), *International handbook of giftedness and talent* (2nd ed., pp. 3–21). Amsterdam: Elsevier Science.

Ziegler, A., & Raul, T. (2000). Myth and reality: A review of empirical studies on giftedness. *High Ability Studies, 11*, 113–136.

Zuckerman, H. (1983). The scientific elite: Nobel laureates' mutual influences. In R. S. Albert (Ed.), *Genius and eminence: The social psychology of creativity and exceptional achievement* (pp. 241–252). Oxford: Pergamon Press.

Zuckerman, M. (2004). The shaping of personality: Genes, environments, and chance encounters. *Journal of Personality Assessment, 82*, 11–22.

Author Index

Subject Index

About the Author

DAVID YUN DAI is an associate professor in the Department of Educational and Counseling Psychology, University at Albany, State University of New York. He received his PhD in psychology from Purdue University and worked as a post-doctoral fellow at the National Research Center on the Gifted and Talented at the University of Connecticut. He was a Fulbright scholar to China during 2008–2009 and the recipient of the Early Scholar Award in 2006 conferred by the National Association for Gifted Children. He serves on the editorial boards of *Gifted Child Quarterly*, *Journal for the Education of the Gifted*, and *Roeper Review*. He has published two books: *The Psychology of the Game of Go* and (with Robert Sternberg) *Motivation, Emotion, and Cognition: Integrative Perspectives on Intellectual Functioning and Development*. He has also published over 50 journal articles, book chapters, and reviews on general psychology, educational psychology, and gifted education. His current research interests include the psychology of talent development and foundational issues regarding gifted education.